THE VULNERABLE AGED

Zev Harel, Ph.D., is Professor and Chair of the Department of Social Work at Cleveland State University in Cleveland, Ohio. He received his M.S.W. from the University of Michigan and Ph.D. from Washington University in St. Louis, Missouri. He has conducted research and written extensively on mental health consequences of extreme stress, ethnicity and aging, and vulnerable populations. He has served in leadership roles with local, state, and national organizations in aging.

Phyllis Ehrlich, Ph.D., L.I.S.W., is Associate Director for Community Services at the Benjamin Rose Institute in Cleveland, Ohio. She received her doctorate in health education from Southern Illinois University at Carbondale (SIUC), and a master's degree from the Case Western Reserve University School of Applied Social Sciences in Cleveland, Ohio. She has developed and directed model community service projects for the elderly, for which she received national recognition for creative integration of theory and practice. Her academic experience has been in the areas of applied gerontology, community services, and mental health. Her research and publications have been in the social gerontological areas of housing, model community services, interdisciplinary education, informal caregivers, advocacy, alternative life-styles, and protective services.

Richard W. Hubbard, Ph.D., is Director of the Western Reserve Geriatric Education Center at the Case Western Reserve School of Medicine, where he also serves as Senior Clinical Instructor of Medicine and Senior Faculty Associate of the Center on Aging and Health. He received his doctorate in gerontological psychology from the University of Notre Dame, where he also served as Assistant Director of the Center for Gerontological Education, Research and Services from 1979 to 1986. His publications have been in the areas of educational gerontology and mental health and aging. His research interests include suicide and aging, alcoholism in the elderly, and models of interdisciplinary geriatric education.

THE VULNERABLE AGED:
People, Services, and Policies

Zev Harel
Phyllis Ehrlich
Richard Hubbard

Editors

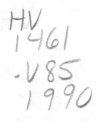

SPRINGER PUBLISHING COMPANY
New York

Springer Publishing Company, Inc.
536 Broadway
New York, NY 10012

90 91 92 93 94 / 5 4 3 2 1

Library of Congress Cataloging-in-Publication Data

The Vulnerable aged : people, services, and policies / [edited by] Zev
  Harel, Phyllis Enrlich, Richard Hubbard.
      p.   cm.
    Papers from a conference sponsored by the Benjamin Rose Institute,
  Cleveland State University, Center on Applied Gerontological
  Research, and Case Western Reserve Geriatric Education Center held
  at Cleveland State University, Apr. 1988.
    Includes bibliographical references.
    ISBN 0–8261–6860–4
    1. Aged—United States—Congresses.   I. Harel, Zev.   II. Ehrlich,
  Phyllis.   III. Hubbard, Richard.   IV. Benjamin Rose Institute.
  V. Cleveland State University. Center on Applied Gerontological
  Research.   VI. Case Western Reserve Geriatric Education Center.
HV1461.V85   1990
362.6'0973—dc20   90-9425
                                                                CIP

Printed in the United States of America

Contents

Preface   vii
Acknowledgments   ix
Contributors   xi

PART 1:   Vulnerability: Understanding Diversity and Service Needs

Introduction   3

1   Venerable and Perhaps Vulnerable: The Nature and
        Extent of Vulnerability Among the Aged   4
    Rosalie A. Kane

2   Defining the Vulnerable Older Population   18
    Robert C. Atchley

3   Health Vulnerability and Service Need Among the Aged   32
    Aloen Townsend and Zev Harel

4   Vulnerability and Sociodemographic Factors   53
    Wornie L. Reed

5   Coping Among Vulnerable Elders   64
    *Eva Kahana, Boaz Kahana,
    and Jennifer Kinney*

6   Vulnerability and Social Factors   86
    Linda K. George

7   Vulnerability and Socioenvironmental Factors   104
    M. Powell Lawton

8   The Impact of Neighborhoods and Ethnicity on Black and
        White Vulnerable Elderly   116
    David E. Biegel and Kathleen J. Farkas

PART 2:   Special Vulnerable Populations

Introduction   139

9   Abuse, Neglect, and Self-Neglect: Issues of Vulnerability   140
     Georgia J. Anetzberger

10 The Homeless Elderly: No Room at the End   149
     Marsha A. Martin

11 The Vulnerable Suicidal Elderly   167
     Nancy J. Osgood and John L. McIntosh

12 Family Caregivers: A Valuable but Vulnerable Resource   189
     Linda S. Noelker

PART 3:   Vulnerable Populations: Policies, Programs, and Services

Introduction   207

13 The Evolution of a Social Concern Base for Policy About
         Vulnerable Populations   208
     Robert Morris

14 Critical Policy Issues in Health and Long-Term Care   223
     Stanley J. Brody

15 National Policies and the Vulnerable Aged: Present,
         Emerging, and Proposed   235
     Robert H. Binstock

16 Federal Programs for the Vulnerable Aged   248
     John H. Skinner

17 Issues in Long-Term Care Services   261
     Sheldon S. Tobin

18 Benjamin Rose Institute: A Model Community Long-Term
         Care System   276
     Alice Kethley and Phyllis Ehrlich

19 Training Needs for Work with the Vulnerble Elderly   295
     John F. Santos and Richard W. Hubbard

Epilogue   307
Index   309

Preface

This book has developed out of a concern by the authors for the well-being and service needs of older members of our society, who are vulnerable because of personal, social, or societal reasons.

The book contains three sections: (1) Vulnerability: Understanding Diversity and Service Needs; (2) Special Vulnerable Populations; and (3) Vulnerable Elderly: Policies, Programs and Services.

The book is significant for three reasons. First, the manuscript breaks new ground by addressing a topic of great scientific, professional, and general importance. Vulnerability has been defined as being open, at risk, and possibly unprotected. Along these lines, every person may be vulnerable to a certain degree. However, some groups of people, including young children and the aged, are more likely to be at risk than others. Robert Atchley asserts in the second chapter of this book that "vulnerability is at the heart of aging, both as an individual concern and as an important social problem." Chapters in this book provide scientific and professional definitions of vulnerability in the aged and select examples of vulnerable populations. This book also offers conceptual discussions and empirical data on personal, social, societal, and environmental determinants, as well as consequences of vulnerability.

Second, these chapters draw attention to the growing number of vulnerable elderly Americans who, if they are to survive and live meaningful lives in our society, must be regarded as representing diverse characteristics and needs. They constitute groups whose needs for help must be recognized, understood, and addressed. A better understanding of vulnerability as well as the uniqueness and diversity of the more vulnerable aged should be of considerable importance in shaping public and professional concern for their well-being.

Third, this book crosses scientific and professional disciplines to shed light on the nature and service needs of those elderly members of our society who are in greatest need of organized benefits, assistance, and service. As such, it integrates the state of knowledge about vulnerability with the wisdom of practice as reflected in current policies, programs benefits, and services.

Chapters in this book offer a wide range of innovative theoretical formulations, rich current empirical data, and critical evaluations. They provide vistas for needed research for the refinement of knowledge and understanding concerning vulnerability and vulnerable populations and offer direction for policy and programmatic changes that are needed in interventive and preventive measures aimed to ensure the survival, safety, security, and well-being of all older Americans.

We hope that this book will further stimulate the refinement of knowledge, the development and refinement of policies, and more effective service planning to ensure a safe, secure, and dignified existence for all older Americans, including the vulnerable aged.

Acknowledgments

This book evolved from a conference on the topic, sponsored by three collaborating organizations and held at Cleveland State University in April 1988. One of the major purposes of the conference/forum was to foster a better understanding in the scientific and professional communities concerning the diversity and service needs of older vulnerable aged. This volume developed from presentations and exchanges that occurred at that conference and in its aftermath. The book represents a collaborative endeavor by representatives of three organizations: the Benjamin Rose Institute, an organization pioneering in the development and delivery of services for the aged for almost a century; the Cleveland State University Center on Applied Gerontological Research, which conducts research and prepares students to work in the field of aging; and the recently established Case Western Reserve Geriatric Education Center, engaged in the education and training of geriatric professionals.

We wish to thank each of these three primary sponsors of the conference for their institutional and financial support. First, the administration of Cleveland State University was both cooperative and generous in supporting the various activities of the conference. We are especially thankful to Dr. Georgia Lesh-Laurie, Dean of the College of Arts and Sciences, and Dr. Harry Andrist, Dean of the College of Graduate Studies. Special thanks are also due to Mr. Dan Meyer, Director of Conference Services, who was very diligent in overseeing all aspects of the planning and activities of the two-day event.

Second, thanks are due to the Benjamin Rose Institute Board of Trustees and administrative leadership for their generous support of the conference/forum. Special thanks are due to Mrs. Ruth Fiordalis, President; Dr. Alice Kethley, Executive Director; and Dr. Linda Noelker, Associate Director for Research.

Third, thanks are due to the Case Western Reserve Geriatric Education Center for financial support and administrative assistance for the conference/forum. Special thanks are due to Dr. Jerome Kowal, Director of the

WRGEC, to Ms. Nancy Wadsworth, Associate Director of WRGEC, and to the Bureau of Health Professions, which provides the funding for WRGEC.

During the planning and organization of this conference, students from the CSU Gerontological Studies Program and staff of the CWRU Western Reserve Geriatric Center volunteered to help with the various tasks that ensured a smooth running of the conference. Thanks are due to students of the Center on Applied Gerontological Research for assistance with the processing of various chapters in this book: Ms. Giacoma Farhat and Ms. Renee Wiltshire. A special acknowledgment extends to Ms. Lynn Hess, a student in gerontological studies, who assisted with the processing and editing of the chapters.

Finally, we thank all the authors who contributed the chapters in this book. Our goal, to prepare a thought-provoking and action-promoting state-of-the-art book on *Vulnerable Aged: People, Services, and Policies*, was achieved by the interest and dedication to the topic by the authors.

Zev Harel
Phyllis Ehrlich
Richard Hubbard

Contributors

Georgia J. Anetzberger, Ph.D., A.C.S.W., is Executive Director of the Western Reserve Area Agency on Aging in Cleveland, Ohio. She received her M.S.S.A. and Ph.D. from Case Western Reserve University School of Applied Social Sciences. She has extensive clinical, planning, and administrative experience in the field of aging. Her research and publications in applied gerontology include Abuse, Neglect and Exploitation and Protective Services for Older Adults. She has served in leadership roles in the State of Ohio in the promotion of advocacy and legislative enactments related to the protection of vulnerable aged.

Robert C. Atchley, Ph.D., is the Distinguished Professor of Gerontology and Director of the Scripps Gerontology Center at Miami University in Oxford, Ohio. He has conducted large-scale research projects and authored numerous books, chapters, and journal articles in gerontology. He is recognized as a pioneer and national leader in the field of gerontology and has received several prestigious awards. He has served as officer of various national organizations in the field of aging, including, as President of the American Society of Aging.

David E. Biegel, Ph.D., is the Henry L. Zucker Professor of Social Work Practice at the Mandel School of Applied Social Sciences and Director of the Practice Demonstration Program of Case Western Reserve University in Cleveland, Ohio. He has conducted research and written extensively on the effects of ethnicity, social support, and neighborhood in contemporary society; obstacles to the delivery of services to the hard-to-reach population groups; and caregiving and the relationship between informal and formal care.

Robert H. Binstock, Ph.D., is the Henry R. Luce Professor of Aging, Health and Society in the Department of Epidemiology and Biostatistics at the Case Western Reserve University School of Medicine in Cleveland,

Ohio. He has lectured extensively at select national and international forums; testified at local, state, and national hearings; and written extensively on national policies and aging. He has received several prestigious
awards and has served as a leader and officer of various national and state
organizations in aging, including as former President of the Gerontological
Society of America.

Stanley J. Brody, M.S.W., L.L.D., is a Professor Emeritus of Physical Medicine and Rehabilitation in Psychiatry in the Department of Physical Medicine and Rehabilitation at the University of Pennsylvania School of Medicine in Philadelphia. For several decades, he has been a pioneer and
national leader in the field of gerontology. He has conducted research and
demonstration projects and written extensively on national policies and
programs in health and long-term care. He has received several prestigious
awards and has served as officer of various national and state organizations in aging, including as Vice President of the Gerontological Society of
America.

Kathleen J. Farkas, Ph.D., is Assistant Professor at the Mandel School of
Applied Social Sciences of Case Western Reserve University, Cleveland,
Ohio. She holds a master's degree from the University of Chicago and
earned a doctorate from Case Western Reserve University. Her research
and practice interests include family caregiving issues, especially intergenerational support in caregiving. She is the Associate Director of the
Mandel School of Applied Social Sciences' Practice Demonstration Program and co-principal investigator of the Family Caregiving Project.

Linda K. George, Ph.D., is Professor of Sociology and Associate Director
of the Center on Aging and Human Development at Duke University in
Durham, North Carolina. She has been a leader in the field of gerontology,
including serving as former Editor of the Social and Behavioral Science
Section of the *Journal of Gerontology*. She has conducted national research projects and has authored numerous books, chapters, and articles
on basic and applied gerontological topics.

Boaz Kahana, Ph.D., is Professor of Psychology and Director of the Center
on Applied Gerontological Research at Cleveland State University in Cleveland, Ohio. He received his Ph.D. in human development and psychology
from the University of Chicago. He has conducted national research projects and has written extensively on basic and applied gerontology. His
research interests include relocation of the elderly to institutional settings,
interstate migration of the elderly, and stress and coping among older persons.

Eva Kahana, Ph.D., is Professor of Sociology and Director of the Elderly Care Research Center at Case Western Reserve University in Cleveland, Ohio. She has conducted national research projects and has written extensively on basic and applied gerontology. Her theoretical and research interests include person-environment fit among the aged, stress, coping and well-being, relocation among the aged, and health and vulnerability among older persons. She has received prestigious awards and served as Vice President of the Gerontological Society of America.

Rosalie A. Kane, D.S.W., is a Professor in the Schools of Public Health and Social Work at the University of Minnesota in Minneapolis. She has conducted several research projects and has written extensively on applied gerontological topics. She has been a leader in the field of aging, including serving as current Editor-in-Chief of *The Gerontologist.*

Alice Kethley, Ph.D., is the Executive Director of the Benjamin Rose Institute in Cleveland, Ohio. She received her Ph.D. in human development with an emphasis in gerontology from the University of Oregon. She has served in various leadership roles in policy, program development, and administration in the field of aging in academic and community settings. She has served on the editorial board of *Research on Aging,* on the Board of Directors of the American Society of Aging, on the Ohio State Governor's Task Force on Alzheimer's Disease, and on the State of Ohio Home and Community Care Council.

Jennifer Kinney, Ph.D., is an Assistant Professor of Psychology at Bowling Green State University, where she serves as Coordinator of the Graduate Certificate Program in Gerontology. After completing her Ph.D. in psychology at Kent State University, she was a postdoctoral research fellow at the Elderly Care Research Center at Case Western Reserve University. Her research interests include late life families and caregiving stress.

M. Powell Lawton, Ph.D., is the Director of Behavioral Research at the Philadelphia Geriatric Center. He has conducted national research and demonstration projects and has written extensively on environmental effects on aging and on psychological factors in aging. He has been a pioneer and national leader in the field of gerontology, for which he has received several prestigious awards. He has served as officer of various national organizations in aging, including as President of the Gerontological Society of America.

Marsha A. Martin, D.S.W., is Assistant Professor at Hunter College School of Social Work in New York, New York. Her research has been focused on coping and adaptation, homelessness and mental illness, and women's issues. She has served as consultant to the National Resource Center on Homelessness and Mental Illness and as Co-Chair of the Board of Directors of Women in Need Inc., a shelter serving homeless women and children.

John L. McIntosh, Ph.D., received his Ph.D. in psychology from Notre Dame University. He is an Associate Professor of Psychology at Indiana University-South Bend. He also serves as a Research Associate at the University of Notre Dame's Center for Gerontological Education, Research and Services. He is the coauthor of *Suicide and the Elderly: An Annotated Bibliography and Review*.

Robert Morris, D.S.W., is a Professor Emeritus of the Florence Heller School of Social Welfare at Brandeis University and is currently affiliated with the Gerontology Institute of the University of Massachusetts at Boston. He has written extensively on national social policies and social welfare. He has been a pioneer and national leader in the fields of social welfare and aging, for which he has received numerous awards. He has served as officer of various national and state organizations in aging, including as President of the Gerontological Society of America.

Linda S. Noelker, Ph.D., is the Director of the Margaret Blenkner Research Center at the Benjamin Rose Institute in Cleveland, Ohio. She received her master's and doctoral degrees from Case Western Reserve University, Cleveland, Ohio. Her recent research interests have focused on family caregiving, the elderly's service utilization patterns, and caregivers' respite. She has authored book chapters and journal articles on applied gerontological topics.

Nancy J. Osgood, Ph.D., is Associate Professor of Sociology and Gerontology at the Virginia Commonwealth University and Medical College of Virginia in Richmond. She received her master's degree in sociology at Drake University in Des Moines, Iowa, and her doctoral degree in sociology and a Certificate in Gerontology from Syracuse University in Syracuse, New York. She has written extensively on suicide and suicide prevention among the aged, mental health and aging, and leisure activity in later life.

Wornie L. Reed, Ph.D., is Chair of the Department of Black Studies and Director of the William Monroe Trother Institute of the University of Massachusetts at Boston. He is a medical sociologist with research and scholarly interests in factors affecting access to medical care and social factors in health and illness.

John F. Santos, Ph.D., is a Professor of Psychology and Director of the Center for Gerontological Education, Research and Services at the University of Notre Dame in Notre Dame, Indiana. He has written extensively about scientific and professional issues in gerontology and is the Editor of *Gerontology and Geriatrics Education.* He currently serves on the Board of Trustees of the Retirement Research Foundation and on the Advisory Council of the National Institute of Health.

John H. Skinner, Ed.D., is Assistant Professor for Health Policy and Management and Assistant Dean for Administration at the College of Public Health at the University of South Florida in Tampa. He received his doctoral degree from Columbia University. He has contributed to the development of gerontology through serving in leadership roles in policy, program development, and research organizations in the nonprofit, private, and public (government) sectors, as well as at universities. He has also served as former Vice President of the Gerontological Society of America. His research interests include resource allocation, service access and utilization, information management, quality of care, program evaluation, and minority aging.

Sheldon S. Tobin, Ph.D., is the Director of the Ringel Institute of Gerontology and Professor in the School of Social Welfare at the State University of New York at Albany. He is the past Editor-in-Chief of *The Gerontologist* and the author of numerous publications that have focused on psychosocial aspects of aging and on applied gerontological topics. Recent books include *Enabling the Elderly, The Experience of Aging,* and *Current Gerontology: Long-Term Care.*

Aloen Townsend, Ph.D., is Senior Research Associate with the Margaret Blenkner Research Center of the Benjamin Rose Institute in Cleveland, Ohio. She received her M.A. and Ph.D. in social psychology from the University of Michigan, Ann Arbor. Her most recent research project was a panel study of later life family caregiving and decision-making. Her research interests include adult development and family relationships, antecedents and consequences of changes in older persons' care arrangements, and social support.

PART 1
Vulnerability: Understanding Diversity and Service Needs

Introduction

The eight chapters in Part 1 of this book constitute an unprecedented effort to provide the conceptual approaches and empirical data needed to foster a better understanding of vulnerability, its determinants, and its consequences among the elderly. The chapters highlight the variability and diversity that characterize those aged who are vulnerable to such contingencies as death, suicide, morbidity, loss of control, involuntary relocation, and institutionalization.

The term *vulnerability*, as indicated by some of the authors, has had various scientific and popular uses; in gerontology, to date, it has had only a limited use. For these reasons, some authors readily accept the terms vulnerability and vulnerable populations, while others question the potential benefits and implications of their use.

The first two chapters address conceptual and applied issues in the definition of vulnerability and in the identification of vulnerable aged. The third and fourth chapters focus on health vulnerability, its determinants, and its implications for health and long-term service need. The fifth chapter reviews the role and importance of personal resources in the reduction or exacerbation of vulnerability among the aged. The last three chapters offer a review and discussion of the role and importance of social factors, such as social resources, social environments, and neighborhoods and ethnic communities in the production, exacerbation, amelioration, prevention, and moderation of vulnerability.

The eight chapters in Part 1 offer a critical overview of conceptual, philosophical, and practical issues related to the terms vulnerability and vulnerable aged. They also offer rich empirical data about defining elements of vulnerability and about factors that predispose to and/or moderate vulnerability. As such, these chapters offer a critical understanding of the living experiences of those who are vulnerable in our society, as well as clearly underscoring the need for organized arrangements in the form of benefits and the care and services that ensure their survival, security, and well-being in our contemporary society.

1

Venerable and Perhaps Vulnerable: The Nature and Extent of Vulnerability Among the Aged

Rosalie A. Kane

Yosarian also worried about Erwing's tumor and melanoma. Catastrophes were lurking everywhere, too numerous to count. When he contemplated the many diseases and potential accidents threatening him, he was positively astounded that he had managed to survive in good health for as long as he had. It was miraculous. Each day he faced was another dangerous mission against mortality. And he had been surviving them for twenty-eight years. (From *Catch 22* by Joseph Heller, 1955)

As the fictional hero of Joseph Heller's acclaimed novel *Catch 22* would readily attest, the world often seems like a dangerous place. Whereas some people give little thought to the ever-present possibility of natural and unnatural disasters, others go through life with an uncomfortable consciousness of their human vulnerability. In that sense, vulnerability, or at least the awareness of vulnerability, is unpleasant.

At the same time, popular psychological writing almost makes a virtue of vulnerability. Participants in group therapy are encouraged to "risk" themselves, to reveal weaknesses and fears to others, and to become, in the cliche, *vulnerable.* In view of these uses of the word, the growing tendency to refer to large groups of people as vulnerable is intriguing and somewhat worrisome. What, after all, does it *mean* to identify a whole category of people as vulnerable? Presumably, it means more than the ordinary vulnerability of human beings. Presumably too, when vulnerability is conferred as a label, it carries little of the positive valence that comes when it is self-proclaimed by earnest practitioners of popular psychology.

This chapter explores the concept of vulnerability. In teasing apart the idea, it raises questions. Is vulnerability remediable; that is, can people be rendered less vulnerable? To what extent is vulnerability preventable and, if it is preventable, does this require identifying people at risk of vulnerability? Or is vulnerability a condition, meaning that our challenge is to identify the vulnerable and then create the circumstances that protect them from harm?

EXEMPLARS OF VULNERABILITY

The five vignettes that follow describe people who might be considered vulnerable. Collectively, they illustrate the elusiveness of the concept.

Case A: Mr. Green, an elderly man with an unsteady gait, lives in a nursing home in a midsize town. He relishes his daily walk downtown, during which he browses in the retail stores, visits a local coffee shop, and sits in the town park. Nursing home staff observe him crossing the rather busy intersection at the corner where the facility is located, and worry that he sometimes begins crossing when the light is red. Moreover, he may not get across the street before the light turns red. Staff are afraid Mr. Green will be injured someday, but, so far, they have not interfered with his daily trips. Is Mr. Green vulnerable? Should something be done to protect him, and, if so, what?

Case B: Mrs. Brown is a somewhat confused woman who lives alone. Relatives urge her to enter a nursing home for her own safety, but she steadfastly refuses to consider the idea. Short of being physically coerced, she will not move out of her home to a more protected setting. However, without difficulty, Mrs. Brown is persuaded to enter a hospital for a thorough check of some troublesome symptoms she had experienced. After the hospitalization, she is discharged to a nursing home (which was the original intent of her doctor and her relatives). Is this woman a vulnerable person? When was she most vulnerable—in her home or in the hospital? Was she harmed by the discharge to a nursing home?

Case C: Mr. and Mrs. White, both in their late 70s, rotate between a sunbelt retirement community where they winter and an eastern seaboard city where they and their adult children live. He is legally blind, gregarious, and high-spirited. She is a shy, reserved woman, who began driving a car only ten years ago when her husband's failing eyesight transformed her into the chauffeur.

While in the winter location, she had a stroke, was admitted to the hospital, and was discharged with some home help. She is now ambulatory and, though she has no paralysis, she is somewhat aphasic and her hand movements, ambulation, and speech are very slow. Her husband has been doing much of the housekeeping, making strange mistakes because of his blindness. Their son and daughter-in-law visit about three weeks after the hospital discharge, and are shocked at the visible changes in their mother. They immediately make plans for both parents to return to the eastern city and move into a retirement community. They discuss these plans with the entire extended family, but not with their parents. Are the Whites vulnerable? To what and to whom? What is the greatest harm likely for the couple?

Case D: Miss Black, who lives alone in a three-bedroom house in a deteriorated neighborhood, was discharged from the hospital with recommendations for home health care and ongoing help from a homemaker. These services can be funded through a Medicaid waiver program because she is technically eligible for a nursing home placement. On the basis of her disability and financial limitation, the Medicaid waiver program can purchase services for her as long as these are less than 60% of the monthly Medicaid nursing home rate. Miss Black realizes that she is failing in health and stamina and that simple tasks are becoming burdensome. She understands that the program could offer her considerable service. Still, she does not like the idea of people coming into her home and judging her situation and skills. Therefore, she steadfastly refuses help and declines any service.

Case managers working in the waiver program are hesitant to leave people at home with less than the service packages they consider optimal. Recently, the case management staff had a vigorous debate over whether they should continue to purchase *any* services at all for a woman who, in their opinion, needs more care than the program is permitted to purchase. Some case managers believe that it was unethical for the program to sanction inadequate care plans and that it should force the issue by withdrawing all care. Others argued that if the client wanted to take an informed risk, the program should offer the maximum services it can legally allow. Miss Black, of course, was not privy to the debates of the service team. She simply has a sixth sense that it might be against her ultimate interests to accept help from the program. Is she a vulnerable person? Is she more or less vulnerable if she accepts formal services?

Case E: The final case is a true story of the tragic type described more and more frequently in the daily press. A man in a large, high-rise complex has been caring for his wife. She was in intractable pain because of osteoarthritis—she was also quite confused and very demanding. He perceived that she was suffering unconscionably, and that he himself was unable to meet her needs. He shot his wife and turned himself in to the police. In what ways were either or both husband and wife vulnerable? Could the death of the wife have been prevented?

WHAT IS VULNERABILITY?

Professional Usage

Vulnerability is a term frequently on the lips and pens of gerontologists, social workers, and other human-service professionals. The word is used rather loosely. Sometimes vulnerability is almost equated with *frailty*, and all those who are disabled, functionally impaired, cognitively impaired, or mentally ill are called vulnerable. In such instances, the word is often used as an adjective without further reference points. That is, the answer to the question "vulnerable to what?" may never be supplied.

Professionals, of course, may use the term much more precisely, as when vulnerability is measured. For example, Sherwood and her colleagues created a Scale of Vulnerability to use in their research (Sherwood et al., 1984). The ten-item HRCA (Hebrew Rehabilitation Center for Aged) Vulnerability Scale was developed as part of an evaluation of an emergency alarm system (Ruchlin & Morris, 1981). It includes items measuring activities of daily living (ADL), instrumental activities of daily living (IADL), mobility, orientation, and activity. When the scale was developed, the criterion for vulnerability was clinical judgment by a multidisciplinary team. This is perhaps the best known scale with the term "vulnerability" in its name.

When measuring an abstraction such as vulnerability, one is, at least for the moment, using the term with precision to mean the degree to which the person has the qualities measured by a particular scale. The question of the appropriateness of the name of the scale can then arise. Naming a scale is somewhat like naming a baby; the name can reflect a wish for what the child will be when he or she grows up and can actually influence his or her fate.

Vulnerability sometimes is inappropriately interchanged with *risk*, which is an epidemiological concept referring to characteristics associated with a greater likelihood of specific negative events. For example, compared to others, some people are more vulnerable to (that is, at higher risk of) developing diseases such as cancer, stroke, or heart disease; of having an accident; of being admitted to a nursing home; of being a victim of physical abuse; or of dying by a specific age. The insurance industry depends on being able to calculate risks or vulnerabilities with a fair degree of accuracy.

Among geriatricians and gerontologists, the term vulnerability most often seems connected with the topic of *abuse* or *neglect*. Adult protective services are designed to help the vulnerable. Sometimes the concept of vulnerability becomes entangled with the concept of *incompetence*, also used loosely in our field. In this usage, anyone cognitively incompetent would be judged vulnerable to abuse, neglect, and exploitation. Of course, we are all conscious that impaired decision-making capabilities and legally adjudicated incompetence are two distinct phenomena.

It is said that nothing is as practical as a good theory (though that, too, is a theory). Similarly, an abstraction like vulnerability can be practical and powerful. It can pinpoint populations possessing certain characteristics that render them in need of protection. As a powerful idea, it can also cut the other way. The concept of vulnerability can be used to abridge the freedom and rights of populations.

Dictionary Usage

Vulnerability is derived from the Latin *vulnus*, or wound. *Webster's Unabridged Dictionary* defines vulnerable as "capable of being wounded or physically injured" (as in, Achilles's heel was vulnerable); "open to attack or assault by armed forces" (as in, the Maginot Line proved vulnerable); and, by extension, "open to criticism or attack" (as in, his reputation as a scholar is vulnerable). Quite obviously, all human beings are capable of being wounded or physically injured; nobody is impervious. To make the definition sensible as a descriptor of a particular person or population, we must add a notion of degree; that is, a person vulnerable to injury or harm is one who is *more than ordinarily* capable of or likely to be injured. If we plan to use the concept to guide public policy, difficult operational decisions are needed about how much additional risk qualifies a person for the rights and restrictions associated with being labeled vulnerable. The dictionary definition also carries with it the idea of physical and, by implication, serious harm. We might wish to expand the concept of vulnerability to include openness to a wider array of harms or injury while retaining the idea of seriousness.

Minnesota Statutory Language

Minnesota has enacted a Vulnerable Adults Protection Act, which applies to adults of any age. It is instructive to examine who is included under the protections of this Act. The Minnesota statute recognizes two paths to vulnerability: categorical vulnerability and vulnerability due to frailty.

Categorical Vulnerability

Minnesota law considers that all patients in hospitals or residents in institutions are "categorically vulnerable." That is, the law views persons as at more than ordinary risk of injury or harm by dint of being in a nursing home or other institution. There seems to be an irony, in that people are encouraged to enter nursing homes for their well-being, safety, and protection; and yet, by taking that step, they have, at least in Minnesota's view, become automatically vulnerable. Why is this so? How would we characterize the vulnerability that attaches itself to being a resident of an institution?

Is the presumed vulnerability for institutional residents based on the lack of control that such residents have over their environment? Is it that nursing home residents are often cut off from ordinary channels of complaint and protest? Perhaps nursing home residents become less visible and, therefore, make staff feel more secure in imposing harms.

Mr. Green, the nursing home resident in Case A—the gentleman who took daily, probably unsafe walks downtown—would be categorically vulnerable by dint of being a nursing home resident. If the nursing home was in Minnesota, it would be required to have on record a "Vulnerable Adult's Abuse Protection Plan" for each resident, as well as a facility-wide plan to protect all residents. Whether such a plan would permit the daily trip downtown is unclear.

The law treats hospital patients as categorically vulnerable as well. One may ask whether vulnerability for hospital patients is of the same magnitude and type as for nursing home residents. Here we might consider Mrs. Brown, who was admitted to a hospital to facilitate later admission to a nursing home, despite her steadfast opposition to the latter. Once in the hospital, where she undoubtedly became somewhat more disoriented and where she found exercise of control more difficult, her doctors and family were able to ease her into a nursing home. The vulnerability of the hospital patient can be very similar to that of the nursing home resident. The busy, fast-paced, highly specialized, and technology-oriented world of the hospital is an environment where it is difficult for a sick, functionally impaired person to exert her will.

If we accept the principle of categorical vulnerability, perhaps the list of settings for such designation should be expanded. For example, an argument could also be advanced that all those who have guardians or conservators are, by definition, vulnerable to harm. This would be another paradox. Like the nursing home, the vehicles of conservatorship and guardianship are meant to protect the wards from harm. But, however valid the reasons, those under legal guardianships have lost their mechanisms to take action and are not easily heard. If we considered that those under guardianship are in positions that make them intrinsically vulnerable, we would be much more serious about developing processes for monitoring guardianship arrangements and, maybe, more hesitant to undertake them in the first place.

Vulnerability Due to Impairment

A second category of vulnerability under Minnesota law refers to persons who, because of their physical and/or mental limitations, are likely to have difficulty complaining or reporting that they have been abused or harmed. People with communication disorders that interfere with speech, hearing, and perception may particularly fall into this category, as well as people with cognitive impairments and mental illnesses. The operating principle here seems to be that people without the ability to resist abuse before the fact, or complain about it adequately after the fact, are also more likely to suffer abuse.

It is unclear how home care clientele fit into this scheme of vulnerability. A case could be made that some persons receiving home care are categorically vulnerable by dint of receiving the service, but this seems extreme. Perhaps a subgroup of home care clientele could be identified as categorically vulnerable; for example, people who are unable to ambulate or transfer and who live alone. Or, perhaps is it more appropriate to consider that many home care clients, but not all, are vulnerable by dint of their physical and/or mental infirmities, which make it difficult or impossible to protest abuse.

Authorities have recently stressed the potential for abusive, neglectful, or exploitative behaviors among providers of home care. The Miami area was shocked into attention to this issue when a 72-year-old woman recovering from hip surgery was "killed, her body cut up with a chain saw and dumped in a steamer trunk," and "the nursing aide . . . hired to help her recover was charged with murder" (*Miami Herald*, March 20, 1988). The newspaper clipping goes on to say that "beyond its obvious horror, the crime illuminates problems in the laws governing Florida's burgeoning home health care industry . . . By nature, those who need home care are *vulnerable*" (emphasis added).

One can argue persuasively that the vulnerability of the home care client results largely from the client's functional impairment; that is, the communication, mobility, and/or cognitive impairments that would render him or her vulnerable in any circumstances. An argument that the *category* of home care client automatically confers vulnerability does not seem nearly as strong as it would in the case of a nursing home resident. Conversely, one could also argue that a functionally impaired person who lives alone and who has severe communication, mobility, or perceptual difficulties is extraordinarily vulnerable to the paid strangers (and unpaid family members, for that matter) who enter his or her home to help.

VULNERABLE TO WHAT?

The original meaning of vulnerability relates to physical harm and injury. What other harms are lurking on the horizon for the elderly and other adults? Of course, it is easy to develop a litany of all the "ills flesh is heir to." These include subtypes of chronic illness (perhaps a form of physical harm); bereavement and loss, leading to loneliness, depression, and isolation; loss of personal meaning in life; extreme poverty and its associated problems; and, although not examined enough with the frail elderly, lack of personal freedom. Each of these phenomena is a negative event in itself and may also be a factor that places people at literal risk of physical harm.

To know who is vulnerable to each of these harms (say, extreme poverty, bereavement, loss of personal meaning), we would need more extensive, longitudinal research than is presently available. The preponderance of work in predicting negative outcomes for the elderly has been in the service of cost-effective public policies: the effort has been to predict the need for care; the likelihood of admission to a nursing home; and particularly, receipt of care at public expense.

ASSESSING VULNERABILITY

Assessing vulnerability will, of course, require reference points about what is meant by the term (i.e., vulnerable to what?). Otherwise, the word has little more specific meaning than the word *prone*. *Prone to* is sometimes used synonymously with *vulnerable to*, but the word *prone* never stands alone.

But, however defined, vulnerability is not an all-or-nothing concept. An assessment should be designed to determine the following: How much at risk of harm is the person? What types of harms are likely? How imminent is the harm? What strategies might be possible to reduce the risk? Assessment obviously must be multidimensional, touching all the salient domains or dimensions. These dimensions include the physical, the emotional, the cognitive, the social, and the environmental.

Physical factors include mobility, strength, communication abilities, and prognosis for health status in the future. *Emotional* factors include psychiatric status (that is, reality-testing abilities) and the presence of negative emotional states such as depression or anxiety (which lessen peoples' ability to protect themselves). In the case of the family caregiver who shot and killed his wife, it is quite possible that severe depression was affecting his reasoning power, rendering both him and his wife vulnerable. *Cognitive* assessment includes an analysis of decision-making capability. *Social* assessment includes social resources (without money, vulnerability to untoward events increases); social support and help being received; and quality of family relationships. *Environmental* assessment includes the safety of the immediate housing environment, as well as that of the community.

The relationship of family help to an older person's vulnerability is not clearly understood and seems ambiguous. It is easy to see how help from family can buffer the older person against harm and, indeed, this often happens. Family support can work paradoxically to create additional dependency and encourage older persons to place themselves in situations that make them categorically vulnerable. This is a complicated relationship, mediated by mutual concern much more than by hostility. The family may wish to protect the older person from harm, and the older person may fiercely desire not to be a burden to family. This is a relationship that we should try to understand better through research. And some programs are more likely to be used by people *without* families. For Mr. and Mrs. White, the vulnerability of the elderly couple to loss of autonomy following Mrs. White's stroke was increased by the presence and concern of a loving, protective family. Of course, family caregivers may themselves be elderly; functionally impaired; and vulnerable in the sense of being at-risk for various illnesses and conditions, including depression, anxiety, and isolation. We do not yet know enough about the repercussions of family caregiving to fully understand the financial vulnerabilities that are incurred.

The use of formal community services may also increase vulnerability. Older people seem to sense this when they resist formal services in their own homes, or when they resist moving to somewhat sheltered housing situations. There is a realistic fear that when helpers get their foot in the door, the older person's continued freedom will depend on satisfying an external judge that he or she is safe. The truth is in this contention can be seen when we consider that most case-managed, long-term care programs have clauses that require community care to cost no more than a specified percentage of nursing home care. Miss Black, the woman who rejected home care, had a hunch that allowing assistance from others might, in the long run, increase her vulnerability to a loss of control over her affairs.

Perhaps an assessment of vulnerability for those receiving formal care should also include examination of factors that make the client vulnerable to the will of the caregivers. For example, there may be strategies that can be developed to give the home care client more independent voice. It may be as simple as access to a telephone. It may involve technologies such as remote-controlled door openers and security systems. (A futuristic variety operated by the client that produces a record of who entered and exited the house, and when, might serve as a deterrent to theft and other exploitation.) Ideally, this facet of the assessment would also lead to strategies for trusted family members to use the device and thus partly ensure the safety of their vulnerable relative.

PREDICTING VULNERABILITY

Predicting Numbers of Frail Elderly

One cannot predict with certainty which people are vulnerable to becoming functionally impaired and, therefore, needing services. That is because the transition from independence to partial or complete dependence can be sudden. Typically, a health event (such as a fall, a fracture, or the advent of a disease) or a social event (such as bereavement, relocation of family members, loss of a dwelling place, or financial loss) sets in motion a chain of events that render a person quickly dependent.

Our inability to make individual predictions need not immobilize social planners. Although we cannot know whether a particular person will become functionally impaired, we do know quite well what proportion of the population over age 65 will become functionally impaired. This should be sufficient information for a community to begin planning services to meet the practical needs for long-term care.

The transition from relative independence, health, and security to functional incapacity and relative dependence, ill health, and insecurity can occur suddenly, with one triggering event having a domino effect. Predicting individual vulnerability, therefore, is less important than moderating the aura of crisis that is typically associated with a plunge into vulnerability. Systematic approaches are needed to identify points of pressure that may impede the ability of vulnerable older people and their families to make thoughtful, informed decisions. Arguably, the present service system in the United States and, in particular, the disjunctures at the boundaries between acute hospital care and other services, can lead unnecessarily to personal disaster for vulnerable elderly.

DISASTER CONTROL

One goal of health and human services should be to avert the disasters that render older people more vulnerable than necessary or that harm already vulnerable people. It is premature to present a tested strategy, but a multipronged strategy should be considered.

Information

Older people and their families need (and, indeed, crave) timely and accurate information to use in problem-solving. Although little research is available to back up this assertion, one can argue plausibly that information about how to handle a crisis has limited utility if it is offered in a general way and far in advance of the need to know. Although preretirement counseling has intuitive appeal, one cannot inoculate the prospective retiree with useful information that is presented along with the proverbial gold watch. First, information gets outdated quickly. Second, many people are uninterested and unreceptive until they confront a problem. Research does show us that middle-aged and young-old people rarely plan specifically for periods of vulnerability. Third, information needs to be marshaled in the specifics of a particular set of problems and circumstances rather than in the hypothetical and the general.

The information needs of many vulnerable elderly include specific details about the quality of services: for example, not just the characteristics of a good nursing home, but whether Nursing Home X meets those criteria. Unfortunately, the best packagers of information are those who advertise products. The gerontological community is unlikely to match the collective expenditures of those who try to influence the elderly for sales purposes. The main hope for influence resides in generating definitive sources. For some issues, such as health promotion, those sources can be national. But for information on the quality of human-service programs, gerontological authorities in each community will need to determine a way to generate, update, and distribute information that comes to be trusted as a definitive source.

Range of Services

Information alone will not suffice. A range of services, along with financing mechanisms, is necessary. In each community, a range of services for people in their own homes and a range of residentially based services are necessary. Moreover, these services must not merely be available, but also be *visible*. Gaining access to services when they are needed should be no more mysterious than gaining access to education for children.

Quality Control Mechanisms

Along with a range of services, mechanisms are needed for quality control. These strategies must include ways that older people and their families can complain with impunity and ways that prospective clientele can learn about the quality record of the various programs. Because we tread a delicate balance between the risks of abusive and neglectful caregiving and the risks of overregulating the lives of the very people whose lives we wish to enhance, quality must be defined to give prominence to (not merely to include) the autonomy of the person receiving care and the way that service influences his or her total well-being.

An underexamined but crucial issue in serving vulnerable populations is the labor force that does the work. When all is said and done, when each technologically sophisticated mechanical aid or prosthesis is in place, the residual care and surveillance necessary are labor-intensive activities that are typically performed by nurses' aides, homemakers, care attendants, and others with similar titles. Many in this labor force receive barely more than the minimum wage and lack benefits, job security, or hope of advancement. This situation is respectful neither of the vulnerable elderly nor of those we employ in their care, and it is unlikely to yield an adequate quality of service.

RISKS AND RISK-AVERSIVENESS

Consideration of vulnerable populations of any age entails consideration of how we will react as a society to the issue of personal risk. This requires twin decisions about how much effort and cost should be incurred to assist people at risk of being hurt or harmed, and whether our policies should permit people to choose risky behavior or life-styles as long as they are unlikely to harm others. It seems that no conscious public policy has been promulgated on this subject, but extrapolating attitudes from the effects of present social behavior and programs, one would conclude that there is a low toleration of risk-taking on the part of the frail elderly, combined with a considerable acceptance of risk-taking on the part of working-age persons and even teenagers. A more explicit consideration of the extent of tolerable risk might lead to a reversal of these public behaviors.

Risk taking, of course, is first an individual decision and only secondarily, and often indirectly, a collective one. It is a truism that people are amazingly varied, and it seems that they also differ from each other in the amount of risk they are willing to accept. Adults without functional impairment make conscious and unconscious personal decisions, weighing risks as they choose, for example, between a safer neighborhood and a less expensive neighborhood, or whether or not to undertake professions or avocations that involve predictable danger. But a frail older person faces more frequent risks to safety as a matter of daily life; for example, the simple acts of changing a light bulb, climbing a stair, or taking a bath may pose a degree of risk.

To develop a stance toward the vulnerable elderly, some of our research dollars might well be earmarked to study the personal preferences of older people, including their attitudes toward risks. We know that most older people, including those who begin to sense a failing of mental capacities, prefer to live in the community rather than to enter a nursing home. I am unaware of any body of research, however, that has queried cognitively intact older people who receive long-term care either at home or in nursing homes about their own attitude toward taking chances. Would they rather move about and risk the fall or accident? How protected would they wish to be? And although clinicians write of offspring who are exceedingly protective of their parents, systematic comparisons of risk-aversiveness among extended family members have not been undertaken.

Risk-aversiveness on the part of care providers is almost axiomatic in the current U. S. context. If we dissected this attitude, we would probably find that it derives both from a sense of responsibility that professionals assume, once becoming involved directly in a situation, and from a protective concern that they or their organizations have about ending up at the wrong end of a law suit if risk-taking leads to injury. Such attitudes have led community-based case managers to act conservatively, to purchase services only from licensed agencies, and to become alarmed if a person is living in the community with anything less than the minimum amount of care thought necessary. Risk-aversiveness has led to extremely cautious caregiving practices in hospitals and nursing homes that are, indeed, cemented by regulations. A woman may have used over-the-counter medications for 80 years, but once in a nursing home, her right to keep aspirin in her purse tends to vanish.

To address these issues, a new paradigm for considering risks will be necessary. We will need to determine which risks are at the discretion of the individual risk-taker, and which are not. We will need to determine who has a legitimate interest and voice in decision-making. For example, what is the appropriate role of family members and of professionals? How are the legitimate interests of caregivers in avoiding liability to be managed? It would seem helpful to reach these conclusions first with reference to cognitively intact frail elders, and then to tackle the more difficult case of the person with varying degrees of cognitive impairment. It will also be important for professionals and policymakers to recognize a range of risks; to recognize, for example, that loss of personal freedom is in itself a grave outcome.

In seeking this new paradigm in the care of the vulnerable, it is important to recognize that age alone does not render a person vulnerable; that many elderly are no more at risk of harm than are other humans; and that many younger persons are vulnerable, in the strict sense of the word.

Advocacy for the elderly might best be served by developing an age-free conceptualization of vulnerability, which includes concepts about how to guard against it, how to minimize it, how to protect those defined as vulnerable from unreasonable harm, and how to protect those already harmed from yet further harm. Above all, let us not treat venerable as synonymous with vulnerable, lest we create a self-fulfilling prophecy for old people in America.

REFERENCES

Kane, R. A., & Kane, R. L. (1987). *Long-term care: Principles, programs, and policies*. New York: Springer.

Morris, J. N., Sherwood, S., & Mor, V. (1984). An assessment tool for identifying functionally vulnerable persons in the community. *The Gerontologist, 24,* 373–379.

Ruchlin, H., & Morris, J. N. (1981). Cost-benefit analysis of an emergency alarm and response system: A case study of a long-term care program. *Health Services Research, 15,* 64–80.

2

Defining the Vulnerable Older Population

Robert C. Atchley

Vulnerability is at the heart of aging, both as an individual concern and as an important social problem. Because aging can increase vulnerability, individuals are afraid of aging and society turns away from its older members. This chapter begins with a discussion of both objective and subjective meanings of the concept *vulnerability*. It moves next to a brief discussion of individual and social causes of vulnerability and then details the extent of physical, financial, housing, and transportation vulnerability. The chapter concludes with a brief look at actions that could be taken to better meet the needs of those elders who are vulnerable.

CONCEPTS OF VULNERABILITY

The essence of vulnerability is risk, the prospect of loss or harm. Vulnerable people have a high potential for experiencing negative gradients in their lives. Everybody has some vulnerability. For example, we all have some risk of needing long-term care. But we define the vulnerable older population as having a more immediate potential need for long-term care. Older people who currently have a problem are often called *frail*. Other older people are at immediate risk; that is, a minor erosion in their capacity can cause them to enter into the frail population. These people are the *vulnerable* older population. Both catagories have a high potential need for assistance.

Vulnerability is not simply an objective characteristic. Vulnerability is also a subjective experience, and vulnerability can be experienced at any socioeconomic level. Obviously, objective definitions make it possible to target services, which means that objective concepts and measures must be developed. The cultural concept of vulnerability is rather general, but when we deliver services, we immediately must translate *vulnerability* into specific operational guidelines that allow us to act. At the same time, subjective vulnerability may be something to consider when there are equal situations with regard to objective characteristics. For example, if two people have the same degree of objective vulnerability and one of them is scared to death and the other sees little problem yet, we might want to consider serving the subjectively vulnerable person first.

There are also practical considerations that come out of the fact that vulnerability is a continuum that ranges all the way from people who consider themselves immortal/invulnerable—usually young people—to people who are currently experiencing extreme limits on what they can do—people we call frail. Our task is to find ways to break this continuum in sensible ways, with the understanding that whatever cutting points we use are going to be arbitrary. And those cutting points shift depending on the resources available. If there are more resources, we tend to be liberal with services. If resources are fewer, we are stricter. This probably is not fair, but the situation is unlikely to change as long as we are operating in a resource-poor environment.

Vulnerability is not evenly distributed throughout the population. For example, widowhood is an aspect of vulnerability because people who are widowed do not have a spouse to help them with personal care needs in the household and are substantially more likely to be poor than are married older people. Figure 2.1 shows the percentage of older people who are widowed. It shows very dramatically the effect of triple jeopardy—age, gender, and race. Black females have much higher rates of widowhood at all ages compared to the other groups. At age 85, 76% of black women are widowed. Notice also that 44% of black men are widowed by that age, compared to only 21% of white men. Thus, there is quite a bit of difference in the distribution of vulnerability in just this one area. In general, vulnerability is most prevalent in the oldest and most socially disadvantaged social categories.

CAUSES OF VULNERABILITY

Aging causes vulnerability to increase for two reasons. First, aging increases the likelihood of physical disability. Aging allows injuries to accumulate, and disabling chronic conditions such as arthritis and blindness increase with age in both incidence and severity. But an equally important

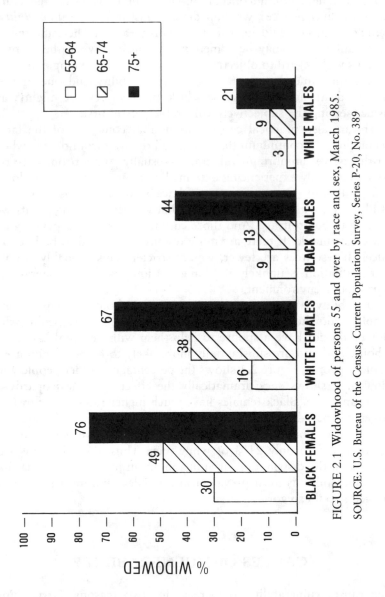

FIGURE 2.1 Widowhood of persons 55 and over by race and sex, March 1985.

SOURCE: U.S. Bureau of the Census, Current Population Survey, Series P-20, No. 389

cause of increased vulnerability with age is the structural inequality built into our society. Every person in American society does not have equal access to its institutions. We present very different opportunities to people depending on their age, gender, ethnicity, and religion.

Age discrimination in employment causes an increase in financial vulnerability. If older people experience an unusual drain on their income, they cannot generally adapt by increasing their earnings from employment, because jobs are hard to find for older people. Retirement substantially reduces income, which in turn reduces capacity to afford private market goods and services such as housing and personal care. As their real incomes drop, many older people find themselves in a lower social class category that is of little interest to businesses, which further increases vulnerability by reducing access to goods and services that might compensate for the effects of physical disability.

Much vulnerability in later life is created by inequality earlier in life. For example, many older women are vulnerable because of their low incomes. This stems mainly from gender inequalities in our economic and political systems. First, the Social Security system does not generate adequate retirement benefits for people unless they have worked 35 to 40 years at jobs covered by Social Security. Twenty years is not enough. Ten years makes a worker eligible, but it takes 35 to 40 years' service to generate an adequate Social Security retirement benefit. This situation is a structural artifact of the Social Security funding system, which is biased in favor of people who have lengthy work careers and against people who spent time out of the labor force to rear children or care for older parents. As a result, many older women have very inadequate Social Security benefits. Second, women are concentrated in occupations and sectors of employment in which private pensions are much less likely to be available compared to the occupations and organizations where men's employment is concentrated. As a result, women with low Social Security incomes are not likely to have private pensions that could reduce their economic vulnerability. These inequalities do not stem from individual factors, but from how women are treated as a class of workers.

SPECIFIC TYPES OF VULNERABILITY

This section deals with the extent of physical, financial, housing, and transportation vulnerability in the older population and the challenges that confront us in providing a more secure world for vulnerable older people.

Physical Vulnerability

To understand the extent of physical vulnerability, we will look at data on need for assistance and on activity limitation. Figure 2.2 shows the per-

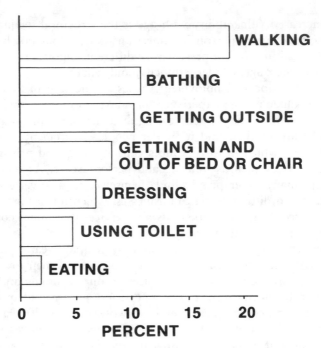

FIGURE 2.2 Percent of the noninstitutionalized population 65 years of age and over who have difficulty with instrumental activities of daily living, by type of activity, United States, 1984.

SOURCE: Division of Health Interview Statistics, National Center for Health Statistics: Data from the National Health Interview Survey 1984 Supplement on Aging.

centage of older people who have difficulty with activities of daily living (ADL). Walking is the only ADL that approaches 20% impairment in the noninstitutional population. Other ADLs show levels of impairment in 10% or less of the older population. Kunkel and Applebaum (1988) found that in 1986, about 7% of the older population was disabled on two or more ADLs.

Figure 2.3 shows data on instrumental activities of daily living (IADL). The percentage of older people having difficulty doing heavy housework is just over 20%. For other IADLs, the impairment figures are in the 10% range.

Kunkel and Applebaum (1988) found that both ADL and IADL impairment are much more prevalent among the oldest-old. For example, at age 75, about 7% of older people of both genders have two or more ADL impairments, but at age 85, the figure is 14% for men and 18% for women and at age 90, the figures are 18% and 27% respectively. Thus, the frail older population is concentrated in the oldest age categories.

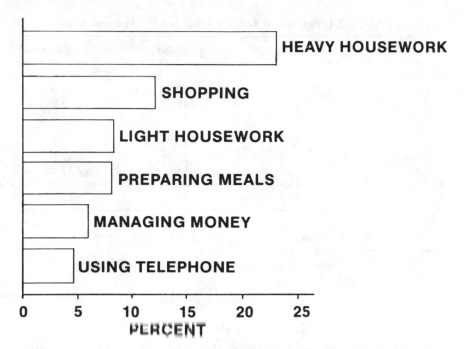

FIGURE 2.3 Percent of the noninstitutionalized population 65 years of age and over who have difficulty with activities of daily living, by type of activity, United States, 1984.

SOURCE: Division of Health Interview Statistics, National Center for Health Statistics: Data from the National Health Interview Survey 1984 Supplement on Aging.

Kunkel and Applebaum (1988) also combined data on ADLs and IADLs to estimate the extent of physical vulnerability. They found that from age 65 to 85, there were about 1.5 times more vulnerable older people than frail older people in each single-year age category. After age 85, the proportion vulnerable stabilized at around 12% to 15% while the proportion frail increased substantially for each successive age cohort.

Table 2.1 shows activity limitation data from the National Center for Health Statistics. If we take the severely disabled as the frail and the mildly disabled and the moderately disabled as the people who are vulnerable, then the percentage of people who are vulnerable goes up with age.

Taken together, these data on physical frailty and vulnerability show that vulnerability and frailty are common among community-dwelling older people. Vulnerability is more common than frailty among older people under age 85, and frailty is more common among those aged 85 and over.

There are many older people out in the community who would appear

TABLE 2.1 Percent of Elderly Disabled by Age and Sex

Age	Mildly disabled[a]	Disabled[b]	Severely disabled[c]
65 to 74			
Men	14.2	9.9	15.9
Women	14.8	14.4	8.2
Both sexes	14.5	12.4	11.6
75 and Over			
Men	20.2	10.7	9.8
Women	13.9	18.5	12.0
Both sexes	16.2	15.6	11.2
85 Plus	13.8	24.6	22.0
65 Plus	15.2	13.6	11.4

[a]Limited in outside activities only
[b]Kind or amount of activity
[c]Unable to perform usual activity
SOURCE: National Center for Health Statistics, National Health Interview Survey, Supplement on Aging, 1984.

by these objective criteria (IADL, ADL, and activity limitation data) to need formal long-term care services. Yet, if we look at the actual situations, some actually do not need formal services because adequate services are already being provided through some sort of informal system.

It has been asserted that there are a lot of older people in nursing homes who do not need to be there. This perception is about 10 years out of date. Medicaid regulations provide reimbursement only for older people with substantial illness and impairment. Most states are moving away from institutionalization for mildly impaired older people and toward services in-home. The family plays a big part in making this possible. For example, the PASSPORT system in Ohio delivers services in the community for Medicaid-eligible older people who need long-term care. These people would be eligible for institutional care under Medicaid. The cost of PASSPORT community-based services is about 30% of the cost of institutional care for those people (Applebaum, Atchley, & Austin, 1987). How can the needed services be provided at only 30% of the cost of institutional care? The answer is that families and informal caregivers do the largest share of the work of providing services. The PASSPORT service packages for individuals who do not have an effective informal support network are more than twice as expensive as packages for clients with effective informal supports.

Thus, the family is a very important part of our community-based long-term care system, which presents a problem in developing definitions of how one qualifies for service. If we were to decide eligibility for service based upon questions such as whether prospective clients have family and whether these family members are willing, then we would be in a very difficult decision-making situation indeed. It is not easy to make bureaucratic definitions that acknowledge informal caregiving situations, but lack of informal supports is an important dimension of physical vulnerability.

Our approach right now is to target a very impaired segment of the long-term care population. With both Medicaid institutional care and Medicaid home care, policymakers are not trying to meet the needs of the entire indigent older population in need of long-term care. They are trying to handle only the worst cases at this point, in part because bureaucrats, politicians, and the general public perceive that it is politically and economically impossible to provide services to all poor older people who need them.

Financial Vulnerability

Now let us look at financial vulnerability. Figure 2.4 shows the income distribution of the older population in comparison with the income distribution of households headed by someone under age 65. These data are biased toward the upper end of the income distribution because they reflect only multiperson households. The low incomes of single older people are not included in these figures. The vast majority of incomes of older couples are in the $10,000 to $20,000 range, whereas the distribution across the whole range of incomes is much bigger for the under-65 population. What does this mean? If couples in the older population need long-term care, they very quickly drop into an inadequate income category. Just having income above the poverty level isn't good enough. Having income just above the poverty level means high financial vulnerability.

In 1988, 150% of the poverty level was about $10,000 for a couple. What would it be like to be living on $10,000 and face the need to provide long-term care for one member of a couple when nursing home care costs $25,000 a year? This is financial vulnerability.

Figure 2.5 shows the relationship of age to assets. There is a steep increase with age in the amount of assets people have. But a vast majority of this is home equity, which means that older people usually have a very small cushion that can be used to offset any sort of catastrophic income need. Home equity is not a liquid asset, and it is very difficult to convert home equity into significant income unless the home is worth over $250,000 free and clear. Thus, assets seldom offset income vulnerability.

The 1984 poverty figures in Table 2.2 show that 14.7% of people under 65 were at the poverty level, compared to 12% of older people. Many people have said that this shows that the financial problems of older people have been solved. But if we look at 150% of the poverty level, 29% of

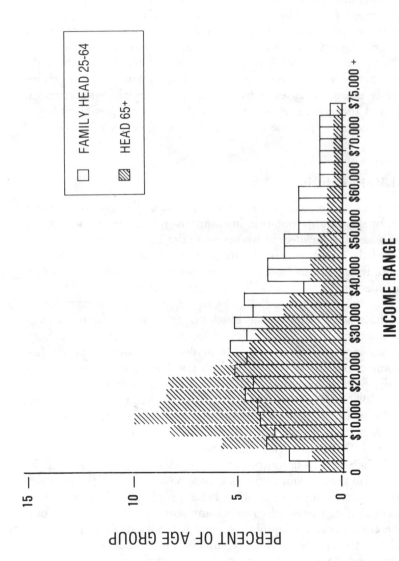

FIGURE 2.4 Distribution of money income of families, elderly and nonelderly, 1985.

SOURCE: U.S. Bureau of the Census, Current Population Reports, Series P-60, No. 154

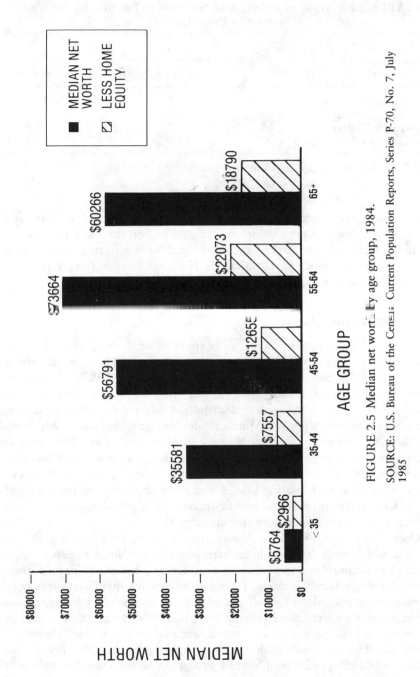

FIGURE 2.5 Median net worth by age group, 1984.

SOURCE: U.S. Bureau of the Census, Current Population Reports, Series P-70, No. 7, July 1985

TABLE 2.2 Percent of Elderly and Nonelderly Persons, by Ratio of
Income to Poverty: 1984

Ratio of income to poverty level	Age	
	Under 65	65 and over
Below poverty level	14.7	12.4
100–124% Poverty	4.5	8.8
125–150% Poverty	4.6	7.9
Total below 150% poverty	23.8	29.1

SOURCE: U.S. Senate Special Committee on Aging (1986:36).

older people are living at 150% of poverty level or below, compared to 24% of the under-65 population. As we saw earlier, the older population is much more concentrated at the lower end of the income distribution compared to the under-65 population. Thus, we have a very, very large financially vulnerable older population.

Housing Vulnerability

In 1985, 2.3 million older households spent more than 35% of their income on housing. For older women, the average was 50% of income spent on housing (U.S. Senate Special Committee on Aging, 1987). This translates into a high probability of housing loss. Obviously, housing vulnerability is related to the income distribution referred to earlier. Recently, there was a segment of "60 Minutes" devoted to people who had been middle class and who lost their housing in New York City. This story is being repeated in every major city. As rents go up, as low-rent housing is destroyed, and as housing programs from the federal government are cut back, the problem of housing loss is becoming an increasing issue among the older population, even the middle-income older population. We have a tremendous housing squeeze in this country.

Only about 650,000 older Americans live in shared housing. Many more could benefit from such an arrangement, but local housing codes often prohibit unrelated individuals from sharing a house in a part of town zoned for single-family housing. Living arrangements that have a true continuum of care availability—all the way from independent living, to assisted living, to intermediate nursing care, to skilled nursing care—tend to be relatively expensive, and as a result, are not very available. There is a severe shortage of small, middle-income housing units. This means that many middle-class older people are forced to cope with the demands of a dwelling that is much bigger than they can physically care for, but they have no choice because a smaller dwelling that has a comparable level of quality and the same level of affordability simply is not available.

Assisted living is expensive and seldom available. Government nursing home regulators talk about overbedding here and overbedding there, but the approach that says we have to limit the number of nursing home spaces because we want to control Medicaid costs means that someone has to live in the worst nursing home in town. The market cannot discriminate and weed out the poor providers, because there are not enough spaces. That is how a lot of substandard providers stay in business—the government requires older people to use them. Clandestine board and care homes are cropping up because of the lack of nursing home spaces. These facilities are not licensed. They lack adequate standards for admission, safety, sanitation, protection of civil rights, and a number of other issues.

Homelessness also involves the older population. Skyrocketing rents, particularly in inner-city areas; elimination of single-room occupancy dwellings; longer waiting lists for rent-subsidized housing; the lack of any kind of approach that would increase the availability of public housing—all of these issues increase the housing vulnerability for older people.

Transportation Vulnerability

Transportation vulnerability is increasing. Our suburban population of older people is increasing rapidly. In 1980, for the first time, we had more older people living in suburban areas than we had living in inner cities (Atchley, 1988). Transportation issues are much more difficult to deal with in a suburban environment than they are in an inner-city environment. Transportation is one of those problems that cannot be handled just by giving the older population a little more income. There must also be facilities, equipment, and services. About 15% or 5 million older people in America lack the transportation they need (U.S. Senate Special Committee on Aging, 1987). Targeting is taking place even within transportation services. In another 10 years, the general older population will probably not be able to use a lot of today's specialized transportation for older people because they will have been defined as a less needy category of older people. Notice that we are moving not in a direction of age-based eligibility in the area of transportation or housing or whatever, but in the direction of a needs-based system. And demand for specialized transportation is going to increase sharply because of the increase in our older population. Right now, the capacity of local taxes to support specialzed transportation is pushing its limits, and we have no initiatives being developed at the national or state levels to take needed action.

CONCLUSION

If we take all these dimensions of vulnerability together, about 7% of older people are in the frail category who have current disability and about 11% are immediately at risk. Nearly 30% of the older population is below the 150%-of-poverty level. Housing and transportation vulnerability are difficult to estimate, but both appear to be increasing. The frail and vulnerable populations increase as a percentage of the total as we move up the age categories within the older population.

Vulnerability is an organizing principle in the lives of the vulnerable. To not have the physical wherewithal to be self-sufficient, to lack the income necessary to buy essential goods and services, to be at risk of losing one's housing and having no means of replacing it, and to be unable to negotiate the environment for lack of transportation are possibilities that horrify most of us, and for a growing number of older Americans, these are the realities. To be vulnerable is to be insecure. Part of the role of social welfare programs is to reduce insecurity by promising to meet needs, should they arise. But when we promise security for everyone, but plan to deliver services only to the most needy, how can people feel secure? What can we do? What should we do? These questions will frame the debate, not only within this volume, but throughout our society as our population continues to age.

The needs both for personal assistance due to physical disability and for protection against loss of income are good candidates for federal social insurance. Even at relatively advanced ages, only a small minority would need benefits, which means that the cost of benefits could be spread over a much larger pool at relatively low cost. Private insurance is not a good way to meet either need, because private long-term care and income insurance are expensive and would therefore not be available to middle- and low-income people who are more likely to need insurance.

In 1987, Congress defeated a bill proposing national long-term care insurance. This defeat was not a clear rejection of the principle of social insurance for personal care needs. Rather, it was in large part a statement of our capacity to deliver services. Even if personal care benefits were available today, in many parts of the country there is no delivery system. There are no organizations and no trained staff to whom people could go for service. In other areas of the country, systems exist but are too small to meet an expanded demand. Thus, we must act to create not only funding but delivery systems as well.

We have the makings of a good social insurance program for income maintenance. The problem is that the floor of income protection is far too low. In many states, the floor of income protection for older people is the minimum Supplemental Security Income (SSI), which amounts to only about two-thirds of the poverty level. This is not very effective income security. We could improve on this substantially by raising minimum SSI to at least the poverty level. We could pay for the increase by reducing the number of older people forced to rely on SSI. This could be done by reducing from 40 to 20 the number of years used to determine average earnings upon which Social Security retirement benefits are computed. This would dramatically improve the Social Security retirement benefits and income security of many older women. To pay for this increased Social Security for the low-income population, a number of steps are possible. We could fully tax Social Security benefits for those with high incomes; we could tax private pension contributions in excess of those needed to replace pre-retirement earnings, which would affect mainly upper income workers; and we could sharply increase inheritance taxes on inheritances of over $500,000. None of these measures is likely to be popular with those who pay the taxes, but something needs to be done and somebody must pay for it.

Of course, if every adult in America had a good job that paid well and generated entitlement to adequate health care and income insurance, then patchwork proposals would not be necessary. But our track record on social justice is mostly of late, and we cannot expect fundamental restructuring of the economy.

The reality is that the vulnerable older population is much larger than the resources that are available or likely to be made available. The result we seem headed toward is a three-tiered system in which people of means will be able to purchase what they need, some small percentage of the poor will receive publicly funded services, and a large proportion of the middle class and the poor will simply be left out. If this comes to pass, the families of America can be expected to demand political action, but in the meantime, service providers can expect to see increasing distress among their vulnerable older clients.

REFERENCES

Applebaum, R. A., Atchley, R. C., & Austin, C. (1987). *PASSPORT: A program review.* Oxford, OH: Scripps Gerontology Center.

Atchley, R. C. *Social forces and aging.* (1988). Belmont, CA: Wadsworth Publishing Co.

Kunkel, S. R., & Applebaum, R. A. (1988). The future of long-term care: Projections and challenges. Paper presented at the annual meeting of the Gerontological Society of America, San Francisco, November 1988.

U.S. Senate Special Committee on Aging. (1987). Developments in aging, 1986: Volume 1. Washington, D.C.: U.S. Government Printing Office.

3

Health Vulnerability and Service Need Among the Aged

Aloen Townsend and Zev Harel

This chapter reviews conceptual perspectives and empirical findings on physical health, mental health, and functional competence to foster a better understanding of health vulnerability and the need for health and long-term care services among older persons. The first purpose is to define the physical, mental, and functional vulnerability of the aged. Second, the focus shifts to the interrelationship of these three aspects of health vulnerability. Third, factors that predispose or moderate the aged's health vulnerability are examined. Finally, this chapter reviews the implications of health vulnerability for health and long-term care service need among the aged.

Interest in the health status of the aged has increased because older people constitute a growing segment of the health and long-term care consumer market in the United States. The population aged 65 and over is expected to more than double between 1985 and 2020 (U.S. Senate, 1988). Higher relative growth has been occurring and will continue in the highest age groups. Thus, between 1990 and 2010, those 85 and older are projected to increase three to four times faster than the general older population (Doty et al., 1985). The elderly, especially those in the older age groups, consume a significant and disproportionately high fraction of health and long-term care services. Even though the aged constituted only slightly more than 10% of the total population, they accounted for over 30% of the health care expenditures during the 1970s and 1980s (National Council on Aging, 1978; Wolinsky et al., 1987). The projected population growth necessitates a better understanding of the nature of health vulnerability and its importance in determining the need for health and long-term care services among the aged.

DEFINING HEALTH VULNERABILITY

Vulnerability, by definition, entails being at risk. In later life, health becomes significantly more vulnerable because of increased morbidity from injury, illness, impairment, or disability. Physical and mental health problems are more likely to occur, along with declining functional competence, necessitating greater dependence on informal caregivers and/or service providers for gratification of basic needs. In addition, health vulnerability may lead to changes in living arrangements, including, for a significant fraction, the need for nursing home placement. Lastly, greater health vulnerability includes greater risk of mortality.

The health of older persons traditionally has been viewed from two perspectives: the medical perspective, emphasizing the presence or absence of disease; and the functional perspective, focusing on the ability of an aged individual to function effectively (Shanas & Maddox, 1985). In the following sections, four major approaches to defining older persons' health vulnerability are reviewed and discussed: physical health decline, mental and cognitive impairment, global health deterioration, and functional limitation.

This chapter discusses health vulnerability not only in terms of the prevalence of diseases, impairments, disabilities, and functional limitations, but also in terms of factors that determine the health status of the aged. Although health risks increase with age, they are neither inevitable nor universal. Thus, health vulnerability is a complicated and comparative concept (Longino & Soldo, 1987) that is multidimensional and dynamic, emphasizing degrees of vulnerability rather than clear-cut categories. Such a framework acknowledges that some older people's health is more vulnerable than that of others, that some aspects of health may be more susceptible to impairment than others, and that health vulnerability may fluctuate over time. Health status at any given time is a reflection of complex age-related and/or time-dependent processes (Soldo & Manton, 1985) that may indicate either normal changes or pathology (Brody, 1985). Furthermore, the need for health services as well as for institutional, community, and home-based long-term care services is determined in part by objective health vulnerability and in part by subjective perceptions of health by the aged and others.

PHYSICAL HEALTH VULNERABILITY

The two primary ways in which later-life physical health vulnerability has been defined are (1) the prevalence, incidence, and nature of physical diseases or illnesses, and (2) physical disabilities and sensory impairments related to age. In research on service need, these two domains have usually been operationalized by the presence or absence of a given disease, condition, or disability or by an index of the number of physical health conditions reported. Other dimensions of physical health vulnerability, such as energy levels, pain and discomfort, or disease severity, are rarely included (Fillenbaum, 1984; McDowell & Newell, 1987).

Physical Health Conditions and Illnesses

The incidence of physical health conditions and illness increases with age (Shanas & Maddox, 1985). Within this aggregate trend, however, there are considerable individual variations, with many among the oldest-old in good health (Kane & Kane, 1987; Longino & Soldo, 1987; Manton & Soldo, 1985). In addition to not being universal, many of the physical health problems associated with age are reversible.

Presently, the physical health ailments of older people are predominantly chronic rather than acute (Pegels, 1988; Shanas & Maddox, 1985), and multiple conditions are the norm (Longino & Soldo, 1987). Four-fifths (80%) of those 65 and older are estimated to have at least one chronic illness, the most prevalent being arthritis, hypertension, and heart disease (U.S. Senate, 1988). The leading causes of mortality among older Americans are heart disease, cancer, and stroke, accounting for 75% of deaths in those 65 and older (Havlik et al., 1987).

Physical health conditions affecting the elderly vary widely in how lethal and/or disabling they are (Ford et al., 1988; Soldo & Manton, 1985). They also vary in their onset (acute or chronic) and in whether the course of the disease is progressive, constant, or episodic. A combination of physical conditions among the elderly is often more significant than separate conditions (Longino & Soldo, 1987). Although some physical illnesses or diseases disproportionately affecting older people have their onset in later years, others are conditions that began earlier in life.

Physical Disabilities

The second approach to physical health vulnerability among the aged emphasizes impaired sensory status, anatomic structures, and/or physiological functions. These disabilities may arise from various illnesses, conditions, or injuries, as well as from normal age-related changes. Although these impairments are referred to as disabilities, older people may or may not consider themselves disabled.

Both sensory and motor impairments increase with age (Shanas & Maddox, 1985). Estimates of community-residing older Americans with some hearing impairment range from 28% to 50% (Havlik et al., 1987; Pegels, 1988). People aged 65 to 79 are four times more likely to have hearing impairment than those aged 45 to 64 (Shanas & Maddox, 1985). Orthopedic impairments afflict about 17% of those over 65 (Havlik et al., 1987). Between 10% and 15% of older people are estimated to have cataracts or other visual impairments (Havlik et al., 1987). Moderate to severe visual problems are twice as common among those aged 65 to 79 as among those aged 45 to 64 (Shanas & Maddox, 1985). Over half of older people have no natural teeth (Pegels, 1988), and almost 90% have some periodontal disease (Shanas & Maddox, 1985).

The rate of community-residing adults reported bedbound, most or all of the time, because of a chronic health problem, also rises with age. For every 1,000 people aged 18 to 44, 1.4 people are bedbound; for ages 65 to 74, the rate is 11.3; for ages 75 to 84, it is 25.6; and for ages 85 and over, 71.2 people per 1,000 are bedfast (Feller, 1983).

A common yet often treatable disability among the elderly is incontinence. Between 7% and 25% of older men and between 18% and 42% of older women in the community are estimated to experience some type of incontinence, and in nursing homes the rate of incontinence is estimated at 50% (Hooyman & Lustbader, 1986; Kane & Kane, 1987). Incontinence can have a significant negative impact on older people's life-styles, functioning, and self-esteem, and can increase their risk of institutionalization (Hooyman & Lustbader, 1986; Kane & Kane, 1987).

MENTAL/COGNITIVE VULNERABILITY

Less is known about the mental vulnerability of older Americans than about their physical vulnerability (Fillenbaum, 1984; Lurie, 1987). Sometimes, measures of mental/cognitive vulnerability are not even included in research on service need. Also, the methods used to assess mental or cognitive vulnerability are more diverse than those used for physical vulnerability, making comparison across studies difficult. Recent literature has emphasized the multidimensionality of mental or cognitive vulnerability of older people (Bliwise et al., 1987; Fry, 1986). This section discusses three major aspects of mental health vulnerability among older people: depression, mental illness, and cognitive impairment.

Depression

Depression is the most widely studied affective disorder among the aged. Estimates of the percentage of community-residing elders who experience symptoms of depression range from less than 10% to 30%, with rates being considerably higher among institutionalized aged (Brody, 1985; Fry, 1986; Schick, 1986). Approximately 4% to 5% of the depressed aged meet the criteria for major depressive illness (Bliwise et al., 1987). Although depressive symptoms increase with age, major clinical depression decreases in prevalence in later years. Estimated prevalence rates vary according to the nature of the sample, the assessment tool employed, and whether depressive symptomatology or clinical depression is the focus, among other factors. Although depression may be particularly difficult to diagnose in the elderly (Blazer, 1980; Fry, 1986), the need for proper diagnosis and treatment is underscored by increased risk of suicide among depressed elderly, especially older men (Blazer, 1980).

Mental Illness

Between 15% and 25% of community-residing older Americans are estimated to have significant symptoms of mental illness other than depression (Schick, 1986). Although research on mental illness in nursing homes is limited, the proportion of mentally ill nursing home residents is believed to be even higher. This is the case, in part, because of the transfer of patients from mental hospitals to long-term care facilities during recent decades (Lurie, 1987).

The three psychiatric disorders receiving the greatest attention in the gerontological literature are anxiety, schizophrenia, and paranoia. Anxiety disorders, which decrease in prevalence with age, nevertheless are believed to be more common among the elderly than is major clinical depression: 7% of those aged 65 and older have been reported to experience generalized anxiety, and an unknown percentage of elderly suffer from phobic and panic reactions (Bliwise et al., 1987). The fact that most long-term users of anti-anxiety medications are over 50 (Bliwise et al., 1987) suggests that anxiety disorders in older people may be of long-standing duration.

Schizophrenia and paranoia are believed to affect less than 2% of older people, although research on these disorders in late life is also limited (Bliwise et al., 1987). Using less stringent diagnostic criteria, Lowenthal and colleagues (1967) reported that 17% of community elders with significant psychological symptoms showed signs of suspiciousness and 13% had paranoid delusions. Because schizophrenia's onset typically occurs prior to age 35, its occurrence in later life usually reflects a chronic condition (Bliwise et al., 1987).

Cognitive Impairment

Although there is a lack of reliable, definitive data, between 4% and 18% of older people (65 +) are estimated to have some degree of cognitive impairment (Fry, 1986; Zarit & Zarit, 1983). Using a self-report measure, 15% of people aged 55 and over said they frequently had problems remembering things during the past year (Cutler & Grams, 1988). In approximately 5% of older people, severe dementia is present. Cognitive impairment is even more common among older people in long-term care facilities: 50% to 75% of institutional residents are estimated to be cognitively impaired (Bliwise et al., 1987; Zarit & Zarit, 1983).

Although some types of cognitive impairment are reversible, most are progressive and irreversible. Alzheimer's disease and related dementias account for the greatest proportion of cognitive impairment. Dementia is associated with a significantly reduced life expectancy. Although it is rarely recorded as the cause of death, it may rank as the fourth or fifth leading cause of death among older Americans (Bliwise et al., 1987). Although most cognitively impaired elders are cared for in the community, cognitive impairment is a significant predictor of older persons' institutionalization (Bliwise et al., 1987; Branch & Jette, 1982).

There is also a group of aged whose cognitive impairment is of longer duration, the mentally retarded. In 1970, it was estimated that older persons constituted 2.4% of the retarded population (DiGiovanni, 1978). The mentally retarded aged are likely to be living in family settings, in facilities for developmentally disabled adults, or in institutional settings.

GLOBAL HEALTH VULNERABILITY

In addition to specific measures of physical or mental health conditions and impairments, global assessments of elders' health are another way of defining health vulnerability. Although these assessments are generally obtained through older persons' self-evaluation of their overall health on a rating scale, other observers (e.g., a nurse, physician, or family member) sometimes provide such assessments. Other common variations include comparative health assessments, where health at present is compared with what it was in the past or with the health of others.

Most older people rate their health as good, very good, or excellent (Kovar, 1986; Schick, 1986). Researchers have been intrigued by the apparent lack of congruence between objective measures of health and older persons' subjective global assessments (McDowell & Newell, 1987; Shanas & Maddox, 1985). For example, people over 65 rate their health more positively than do younger people (Schick, 1986), despite also reporting more sick days, chronic health conditions, and sensory/motor impairments.

Various explanations for this discrepancy have been offered. One reason may be that older people are less likely than younger people to interpret symptoms such as weakness and aches as signs of illness (Prohaska et al., 1985). Many older people believe that symptoms they perceive as minor or chronic are simply normal, or at least inevitable, signs of aging, rather than illness or impairment (Brody, 1985). Another reason that older people may assess their health more positively is their perception that they are better off than other aged (Brody, 1985). At the same time, older adults worry more about their health than do middle-aged or younger adults (Veroff et al., 1981) and think of their health as more vulnerable (Prohaska et al., 1985).

FUNCTIONAL VULNERABILITY

An increasing number of gerontologists have suggested that functional impairments are the most relevant health dimensions for predicting older persons' need for long-term care services (Ford et al., 1988; Harel et al., 1985; Kane & Kane, 1987; Longino & Soldo, 1987). Functional impairments have been assessed in four major categories: (1) activities of daily living (ADL) or personal care activities such as eating, bathing, and dressing; (2) mobility; (3) instrumental activities of daily living (IADL), such as shopping, housework, and managing money; and (4) general questions about whether the older person's health limits or interferes with carrying out activities. Mobility is sometimes included with ADL or IADL items and is sometimes considered separately (Fillenbaum, 1984).

Tasks included for the assessment of personal care dependencies are fairly standard across studies (with the exception of measures of mobility); however, tasks used to measure instrumental difficulties vary widely in both content and number. Also, although ADL dependencies typically form a hierarchical pattern, little is known about the structure, if any, underlying IADL tasks (Fillenbaum, 1984). Instrumental activities indices were designed for noninstitutionalized populations, and performance on many of the instrumental tasks is affected by the person's physical and social environment.

Generally, measures of functional limitations are used as single items (e.g., difficulty walking) or as unweighted, additive scores summing all ADL or all IADL tasks. On many measures of functional impairment, older people who truly have no difficulty performing a task are not distinguished from those who have no difficulty because they have managed to compensate with mechanical or human assistance. The need to standardize functional impairment measures and to create better measures of functioning for institutional settings has been increasingly recognized (Kane & Kane, 1987; Longino & Soldo, 1987; McDowell & Newell, 1987).

Activities of Daily Living and Mobility

This category generally includes tasks pertaining to personal hygiene (e.g., bathing), personal appearance (e.g., grooming), basic self-maintenance (e.g., eating), and sometimes mobility. Approximately 23% of community-residing older people have difficulty performing one or more of these activities of daily living, the most prevalent being difficulty walking and the least common being difficulty eating (Dawson et al., 1987). Difficulties performing personal care activities increase dramatically with age: while about 15% of those aged 65 to 69 have one or more ADL dependencies, about 49% of those aged 85 and older do (Dawson et al., 1987). Limitation in performance of ADL activities is considerably higher among institutionalized aged and is one of the precursors to institutionalization (Branch & Jette, 1982). In a 1977 survey, 90% of nursing home residents were dependent in one or more ADL tasks (Soldo & Manton, 1985).

Fewer community-residing older people report receiving assistance from someone with activities of daily living than report having difficulty performing these tasks, indicating considerable unmet need. For example, only 42% of those aged 65 and older who reported difficulty with at least one ADL task said they received help with personal care (Dawson et al., 1987). The percentage of older people who report receiving ADL assistance increases with age (Dawson et al., 1987).

Instrumental Activities

At all ages, more difficulties are reported with IADL tasks than with personal care (ADL) tasks. Difficulty performing one or more instrumental activities is reported by 27% of Americans over 64. The most common difficulty is with heavy housework (24% of those aged 65+), and the least common (5%) is using the telephone. Limitations on IADL, like limitations on personal care tasks, increase sharply with age: only 18% of people aged 65 to 69 experienced difficulties with the performance of one or more instrumental activities, compared to 55% of those 85 and older (Dawson et al., 1987). Unlike personal care tasks, most of those who report difficulties with instrumental activities also report receiving help (Dawson et al., 1987).

General Activity Restriction

While indices of limitations in activities of daily living and instrumental activities are the methods most frequently employed to assess functional dependencies, some studies have used general questions to ascertain whether health problems interfere with respondents' "usual activities." To such a general question, 60% of people 65 and older said they had no limitations (Kovar, 1986). Global activity restriction increases with age: 62% of those aged 65 to 74 said they had no limitation in their usual activities, compared with 40% of those 85 and over (Kovar, 1986). The number of days on which one's usual activities reportedly have been restricted also increases with age (Koff, 1988). For most impaired elders, however, activity restrictions were not severe: only 12% of those 85 and older reported being completely unable to carry out their usual activities (Kovar, 1986).

THE RELATIONSHIPS AMONG PHYSICAL, MENTAL, AND FUNCTIONAL VULNERABILITY

With few exceptions (Liang, 1986; Wolinsky et al., 1984), gerontological research has paid little attention, to date, to relationships among indicators within each domain of health vulnerability (e.g., multiple measures of physical health vulnerability). Despite theoretical arguments that impairments often cluster together in older people (Bliwise et al., 1987; Ford et al., 1988), analyses are typically conducted without regard to any measurement model or much concern for multicollinearity among indicators.

There also has been limited research on relationships across vulnerability domains, beyond general agreement that physical and mental health are strongly correlated among older people (Fry, 1986; Lurie, 1987; Shanas & Maddox, 1985). Geriatric assessment literature routinely discusses the need to ascertain whether mental problems (e.g., depression or cognitive impairment) are due to medically reversible causes such as physical illness, polypharmacy, poor nutritional status, or sensory impairments (Blazer, 1980; Bliwise et al., 1987; Fry, 1986). To complicate the relationship between physical and mental health, many indices of depression include questions about energy levels and sleeping or eating patterns that may reflect acute or chronic illness or normal changes as a function of age (Bliwise et al., 1987; McDowell & Newell, 1987). Conversely, mental or cognitive problems may aggravate or exacerbate older persons' physical health vulnerability (Lurie, 1987), although this has received little empirical attention.

The limited research that does exist on the relationship between physical and mental or cognitive status in later life underscores the complexity of health vulnerability. While, generally, health vulnerability in one or more of these domains indicates a need for services, no adequate models have been developed to predict the amount or type of community-based or institution-based health and long-term care services needed (Soldo & Manton, 1985).

Research on the relationship between physical or mental impairments and functional limitations is particularly lacking. Longino and Soldo (1987), for example, suggest that functional dependence in IADL tasks is significantly influenced by the older person's cognitive functioning. With few exceptions, such as the Sickness Impact Profile (McDowell & Newell, 1987), functional limitations and specific diseases have not been linked together.

Research on need for services has rarely included interactive, nonlinear, or hierarchical models of health vulnerability. In addition, the paucity of longitudinal studies of older people's health means that causal and reciprocal connections both within and across domains remain unclear. Reliance on cross-sectional data also overemphasizes static conceptions of health vulnerability and neglects changes in health status. The limited panel data available suggest that, rather than universal decline changes in vulnerability can be bidirectional, reflecting short-term as well as long-term health problems (Branch & Stuart, 1985).

PREDISPOSING AND MODERATING FACTORS

One of the most important conclusions from recent geriatric and gerontological research on health vulnerability is that not all older people are at equal risk. This section reviews five major factors that predispose some older people to greater health vulnerability: genetics, family history, and life-style; sociodemographic characteristics; socioeconomic status; stressful life events; and social resources. At the same time, there is increasing evidence that many of these same factors moderate the impact of physical or mental impairment on functional vulnerability and the effects of health vulnerability on service need.

Genetic Factors, Family History and Life-Style

Genetics and family history have been found to increase the risks of developing many physical health conditions, such as coronary artery disease, and certain mental conditions, such as some forms of Alzheimer's disease. On the other hand, longevity and better health also may be related to genetic factors (Bliwise et al., 1987; Shanas & Maddox, 1985). In addition, a variety of life-style characteristics or behaviors—such as alcohol and drug use, cigarette smoking, and physical exercise—have been studied recently as factors affecting older people's health risks (Havlik et al., 1987; Manton et al., 1987; Shanas & Maddox, 1985). Included in this category are proactive or preventive health behaviors such as information seeking, medical and self-examination, and avoidance of risk (Rakowski et al., 1987), all of which may lead to better health.

Sociodemographic Factors

Age or cohort effects, race, and gender are the three major socio-demographic characteristics that have been studied as predisposing factors in research on health and long-term care services. The influence of age and/or cohort is evident from differences even among the elderly. In general, those over 85 are disproportionately prone to physical health problems, sensory/motor impairments, and functional limitations (Suzman & Riley, 1985). With respect to global health ratings, evidence is mixed: while some studies show a linear decline in health ratings with age (Schick, 1986), others show a curvilinear pattern, with people over 75 having more positive assessments than do the young-old (60 to 75) (Cockerham et al., 1983).

The relationship between age and mental vulnerability is less clear. While some research finds that depression increases in prevalence with age, other studies refute this (Feinson & Thoits, 1986). Evidence regarding increasing rates of psychopathology with age also is contradictory (Schick, 1986). For cognitive status, a clearer relationship exists: 20% of people aged 80 and older are estimated to have dementia, compared with approximately 4% of all those over age 64 (Zarit & Zarit, 1983).

Although it is difficult to disentangle age and cohort effects in most research, some authors have argued that more recent cohorts of older Americans are experiencing longer life expectancy but greater prevalence of chronic disease (Palmore, 1986). Changes in nutrition, life-style, occupations, and health care have been suggested as explanations for why recent cohorts ought to enjoy better health than prior generations (Longino & Soldo, 1987; Palmore, 1986; Suzman & Riley, 1985). These changes in health are likely to bring about higher rates of natural deaths and a "compression of disability and morbidity" in the older population (Fries, 1983). Manton and Soldo (1985) assert that while morbidity, disability, and death are interrelated, the age and cohort-related variations in these interrelationships are not sufficiently clear.

Significant differences in health vulnerability have also been found by race and ethnicity, although this research has focused primarily on differences between whites and blacks. The elderly are one of the fastest growing segments of the black population, with black elderly over 65 increasing by 32% in the 1970s and those over 85 increasing by 34% during the 1980s (O'Hare, 1987; Manton et al., 1987). Currently, blacks constitute 8% and Hispanics 3% of Americans aged 65 and over (Kovar, 1986; U.S. Senate, 1988). While the number of elderly whites is expected to increase 23% by the turn of the century, elderly blacks are projected to increase by 46% (Jackson, 1988). Elderly Hispanics are also increasing in numbers and in relative percentages (Markides & Mindel, 1987).

Death rates continue to decline more for whites than for blacks, and the health of older blacks is generally worse than that of older whites or older Hispanics (Markides & Mindel, 1987; U.S. Senate, 1988). Elderly black Americans suffer higher rates of heart disease and cancer, for example, than do elderly whites (Jackson, 1988). Among the oldest-old, though, a crossover "survivor effect" has been noted among blacks (Gibson & Jackson, 1987; Manton et al., 1987). Although less likely than whites to survive into their 80s, many black elderly who do are healthier than whites of the same age. This makes the oldest-old blacks a very heterogeneous and unique group (Gibson & Jackson, 1987).

Older blacks are more likely than older whites or older Hispanics to report activity restrictions due to chronic health problems (Manton et al., 1987; Markides & Mindel, 1987) and to rate their health as only fair or poor (Havlik et al., 1987; Markides & Mindel, 1987). Differences by race have also been found with respect to functional vulnerability. For example, although age and functional limitations are linearly related for whites, they are not for blacks, because older black Americans tend to be less functionally impaired (Gibson & Jackson, 1987). In addition, gender differences in functioning found among older whites are not found among older blacks (Gibson & Jackson, 1987).

Recent research has significantly revised earlier notions of greater mental health vulnerability among blacks and Hispanics. When socioeconomic differences are controlled, most differences in mental health by race or ethnicity disappear (Markides & Mindel, 1987; Neighbors, 1987). Also, differences between blacks and whites in prevalence rates of mental disorders decline after age 65 (Manton et al., 1987). In research on cognitive impairment in later life, race and ethnicity have rarely been considered (Baker, 1988).

Gender is the third predisposing sociodemographic factor that has received considerable attention. Women continue to have longer life expectancy than men; as a consequence, they constitute increasing proportions of the elderly (Suzman & Riley, 1985). Older women have higher rates of chronic physical health conditions than do older men, but chronic conditions are generally more disabling and serious in men (Verbrugge, 1983). Older women also have higher prevalence of vision impairment, restricted mobility, and bedfast days than do older men (Verbrugge, 1983). Global health assessments do not differ significantly by gender, however (Havlik et al., 1987).

In terms of functional vulnerability, older women report more functional limitations on most activities of daily living and instrumental activities of daily living (Dawson et al., 1987; Manton & Soldo, 1985). These gender differences in functioning are complicated by variations in life expectancy and in cultural expectations and training for the performance of various tasks. The fact that older men report fewer IADL limitations than do older women, for example, is partly due to women being more likely to perform housekeeping chores (Dawson et al., 1987).

With regard to mental vulnerability, no consistent gender differences have been found in rates of mental illness (Turner, 1987). On measures of depressive symptomatology or clinical depression, women usually evidence more depression (Feinson, 1987; Turner, 1987), but the reasons for this gender difference and its clinical significance have been subjects of considerable debate (Turner, 1987). Although gender differences in cognitive impairment have received little attention, older women do have a higher incidence of severe memory problems, including Alzheimer's disease, and they also report having more memory difficulties, even controlling for other factors such as age and health (Cutler & Grams, 1988).

Socioeconomic Status

Income and education also have an impact on the health status of older Americans. Findings indicate that higher socioeconomic status is associated with better physical and mental health (Larson, 1978). Approximately one-quarter of older Americans live at or near the poverty line (Koff, 1988). Elderly who are poor are twice as likely to report poor health and ADL restrictions as are elderly with moderate or high incomes (Commonwealth Fund, 1988). Despite government programs such as Medicaid and Medicare, older people pay for much of their health and long-term care services out-of-pocket (Koff, 1988; Shanas & Maddox, 1985).

The predisposing effects of income are difficult to untangle from income's moderating effects on health vulnerability. For example, the relationship of lower income to poorer self-rated health (Lurie, 1987; U.S. Senate, 1988) probably reflects both the fact that lower income impedes seeking medical care once health problems arise and the fact that limited economic resources lead to poorer nutritional status and, in turn, to poorer health.

Stress and Extreme Stress

The fourth factor predisposing some older people to poorer health than others is stressful life events. Foremost among these events is bereavement, the likelihood of which increases with age. Although results are somewhat equivocal, the death of a spouse has been associated with an increased likelihood of mortality, particularly among surviving husbands (Rees & Lutkins, 1967), and with increased somatic symptoms and depression (Gallagher et al., 1983). Recently bereaved older spouses report more new or worsened illnesses, greater use of medications, and poorer health ratings than do nonbereaved elders (Thompson et al., 1984). The duration of these negative physical and psychological effects is unknown, because of the paucity of longitudinal data over extended periods of time.

In addition, significant numbers of older persons have experienced extreme stress, including war-time stresses such as exposure to death and destruction, internment in POW camps, and the stresses experienced by Holocaust survivors. Clinical observations and research indicate that extreme stress may cause a wide range of physiological disorders, diseases, mental disorders, deviant behavior, and social pathology (Wilson et al., 1988). Although the specific mechanisms that cause these posttraumatic difficulties are not well understood, it is clear that when extreme stressors are severe and enduring, health and functional competence may be affected. Individuals who endured extreme stress continue to experience in later years some degree of physical and mental disabilities, and some may experience lasting physical and mental impairment (Wilson et al., 1988). It is not unusual for symptoms such as depression, startle responses, anxiety, hyperarousability, intrusive imagery, and sleep disturbance to persist for decades after the extremely stressful experience (Harel, 1988).

Stress research indicates, however, that there are substantial differences among individuals and groups in the way that they perceive and react to stressful situations and conditions (Lazarus & Folkman, 1984). The effects of stress vary because they are mediated through subjective psychological processes, which include both cognitive and emotional components, and because they are moderated by environmental, social, and personal resources. Exactly how these variables interact over one's life to determine different patterns of physical and mental health in an individual's later years is yet unknown.

Social Resources

Findings indicate that social support generally has a positive effect on the aged's functioning and physical and mental health. Conversely, social losses are associated with poorer health (George, 1990). Research shows that greater support received from family members, friends, acquaintances, coworkers, and the larger community decreases the likelihood of stress or illness; thus, the level of well-being increases (Dean & Lin, 1977). There is also evidence to indicate that greater social support is associated with better mental health among survivors of extreme stress (Wilson et al., 1988).

Concern about the relationship of social support to health vulnerability has directed attention to the nearly one-third of older Americans who live alone. Compared to those living with someone, older people living alone are less likely to have informal help and more likely to rely on paid help for personal care needs. Because older people living alone are more likely to be poor, and because health and poverty are related, older persons living alone are also in poorer health (Commonwealth Fund, 1988).

The conceptualization and measurement of social resources have been topics of consistent interest in the gerontological literature (Antonucci & Jackson, 1987; George, 1990). There is no clear evidence yet as to how and why social support and health vulnerability are related. Critical issues under consideration include the direct, indirect, and moderating effects of social resources on physical and mental health (George, 1990). Although most research has highlighted the positive effects of social resources, it is important to underscore that social networks also may create stress and increase health vulnerability, as evidenced by heavily burdened caregivers to impaired aged persons and by abused, neglected, and exploited older people.

Interrelationships Among Predisposing and Moderating Factors

Although most research has considered predisposing or moderating factors in isolation from each other, these variables are often interrelated. For example, older women tend to be poorer than older men; older blacks also tend to have lower socioeconomic status than do older whites (Manton et al., 1987). Recent cohorts of elders are presumed to benefit healthwise from improvements in nutrition, socioeconomic status, and changes in occupation, among other factors (Longino & Soldo, 1987; Suzman & Riley, 1985). Higher mortality rates among blacks mean that older black women are more likely to be widowed than are older white women (Manton et al., 1987). Older women are much more likely to live alone than are older men, and older white women are more likely to live alone than are older black women (Commonwealth Fund, 1988).

Many apparent gender differences in health are confounded with longer life expectancy among women (Verbrugge, 1983). Yet research rarely takes into account age as well as gender. When that is done in research on differences in symptom rates for psychoses or depression, gender differences either disappear after age 65 (Blazer, 1980) or reverse, with older men having higher rates than older women (Feinson, 1987).

There have been only limited studies in which predisposing or moderating effects on health vulnerability have been examined. Thus, it is imperative that future research employ multivariate and dynamic methods capable of examining these complex, interrelated factors, as well as sample sizes and sampling methods capable of adequately representing the most vulnerable elderly, such as the oldest-old and black females.

HEALTH VULNERABILITY AND SERVICE NEED

The need for health and long-term care services has drastically increased in recent years. Correspondingly, there has been a consistent rise in health care expenditures. Soldo and Manton (1985) note that, from 1977 to 1984, the total health care costs for persons aged 65 and over tripled. During that same period, total health care spending grew at an annual rate of 15.6%, far outpacing the growth of the older population (Waldo & Lazenby, 1984). As documented in this chapter, the number of older peo- ple needing health and long-term care services is likely to continue to rise because of increased disability and morbidity, especially among those in the higher age groups.

Based on the projected growth of the elderly population and current utilization rates of institutional and community-based long-term care services, drastic increases in the need for these services can be anticipated. However, it is evident from the reviewed literature on later-life health vulnerability that the implications for needed services are far from clear. Although older ages are associated with greater health vulnerability—in terms of likelihood of mortality, physical and mental morbidity, or functional impairment—within this general trend, there is considerable variability in older people's health. Some facets of health are more vulnerable to decline in later life than are others. Health deterioration follows many different trajectories, some health conditions or functional impairments have greater impact on older people's lives than do others, and some older people are more vulnerable than others.

Because of the paucity of multivariate and conceptual models of health vulnerability and need for services, the ways in which different facets of health interact or compound to increase older persons' need for services are poorly understood. In addition, further work is needed to explicate factors that predispose some older people to greater health risks than others, as well as those that moderate or mediate the relationships among physical health, mental health, and functional impairment and the link between health vulnerability and need for services. Current methods for characterizing and assessing later-life health vulnerability and need for services could benefit from theoretical and empirical refinement. One of the most pressing objectives for future research should be better delineation of the concept of need for health and long-term care services.

Furthermore, need for health and long-term care services is also affected by a number of other factors, which include health care policies, financing, and programs; the objectives and actions of elected and appointed public officials; the structural arrangements and barriers in service delivery; the attitudes and actions of human service professionals; and the needs, knowledge, attitudes, and actions of the aged service consumers themselves and members of their informal support networks. Yet such factors have rarely been incorporated into research on health vulnerability and need for services.

From a scientific point of view, there is a clear need for more complex and comprehensive conceptual and methodological approaches in research on the relationship of health vulnerability to health and long-term care service need. More refined approaches would yield data that would more adequately describe health vulnerability and its influences on need for services; the extent to which services have their intended impact on and benefits for the health of elderly users; and the ways in which health vulnerability may act as a barrier to effective service delivery or service use. Longitudinal research investigating changes in both health vulnerability and need for service would advance our understanding as well.

From a pragmatic point of view, a better understanding of health vulnerability and its relationship to need for health and long-term care services would provide a better basis for policy and program development. Concerns of public officials at all levels have been guided primarily by efforts to curtail the rising cost of health care and long-term care services. While such efforts are necessary, it is important to underscore the need for improvement in our national health and long-term care policies and programs. Future policies, programs, and services should more systematically and comprehensively address not only the costs of interventions related to acute and chronic diseases, but also the prevention of health vulnerability and the enhancement of life quality for all members of our society, including the aged.

REFERENCES

Antonucci, T., & Jackson, J. (1987). Social support, interpersonal efficacy, and health: A life course perspective. In L. Carstensen & B. Edelstein (Eds.), *Handbook of clinical gerontology*. New York: Pergamon.

Baker, F. M. (1988). Dementing illness and Black Americans. In J. S. Jackson (Ed.), *The Black American elderly: Research on physical and psychosocial health* (pp. 215–236). New York: Springer.

Blazer, D. (1980). The epidemiology of mental illness in late life. In E. Busse & D. Blazer (Eds.), *Handbook of geriatric psychiatry* (pp. 249–271). New York: Van Nostrand Reinhold.

Bliwise, N., McCall, M., & Swan, S. (1987). The epidemiology of mental illness in late life. In E. Lurie, J. Swan, & Associates (Eds.), *Serving the mentally ill elderly: Problems and perspectives* (pp. 1–38). Lexington, MA: Lexington Books.

Branch, L., & Jette, A. (1982). A prospective study of long-term care institutionalization among the aged. *American Journal of Public Health, 72,* 1373–1379.

Branch, L., & Stuart, N. (1985). Towards a dynamic understanding of the care needs of the noninstitutionalized elderly. *Home Health Care Services Quarterly, 6,* 25–37.

Brody, E. (1985). *Mental and physical health practices of older people.* New York: Springer.

Cockerham, W., Sharp, K., & Wilcox, J. (1983). Aging and perceived health status. *Journal of Gerontology, 38,* 349–355.

Commonwealth Fund Commission on Elderly People Living Alone. (1988). *Aging alone: Profiles and projections.* Baltimore, MD: Commonwealth Fund

Cutler, S., & Grams, A. (1988), Correlates of self-reported everyday memory problems. *Journal of Gerontology: Social Sciences, 43,* S82–S90.

Dawson, D., Hendershot, G., & Fulton, J. (1987). Aging in the eighties: Functional limitations of individuals age 65 years and over. *Advance data from vital and health statistics* (No. 133, DHHS Publication No. PHS 87-1250). Hyattsville, MD: U.S. Public Health Service.

Dean, A., & Lin, N. (1977). The stress-buffering role of social support. *Journal of Nervous and Mental Disease, 165,* 403–417.

DiGiovanni, L. (1978). The elderly retarded: A little known group. *The Gerontologist, 18,* 262–266.

Doty, P., Liu, K., & Weiner, Y. (1985). An overview of long term care. *Health Care Financing Review, 6,* 69–78.

Feinson, M. (1987). Mental health and aging: Are there gender differences? *The Gerontologist, 27,* 703–711.

Feinson, M., & Thoits, P. (1986). The distribution of distress among elders. *Journal of Gerontology, 41,* 225–233.

Feller, B. (1983). Americans needing help to function at home. *Advance data from vital and health statistics* (No. 92, DHHS Publication No. PHS 83-1250). Hyattsville, MD: U.S. Public Health Service.

Fillenbaum, G. (1984). Assessing the well-being of the elderly: Why and how functional assessment is being done in the United States and abroad. *Duke University Center for the Study of Aging Reports on Advances in Research, 8,* 1–9.

Ford, A., Folmar, S., Salmon, R., Medalie, J., Roy, A., & Galazka, S. (1988). Health and function in the old and very old. *Journal of the American Geriatrics Society, 36,* 187–197.

Fries, J. (1983). The compression of morbidity. *The Milbank Quarterly, 61,* 397–419.

Fry, P. (1986). *Depression, stress, and adaptation in the elderly: Psychological assessment and intervention.* Rockville, MD: Aspen.

Gallagher, D., Breckenridge, J., Thompson, L., & Peterson, J. (1983). Effect of bereavement on indicators of mental health in elderly widows and widowers. *Journal of Gerontology, 38,* 565–571.

George, L. (1990). Vulnerability and social factors. In Z. Harel, P. Ehrlich, & R. Hubbard (Eds.), *The vulnerable aged: People, services, and policies.* New York: Springer.

Gibson, R., & Jackson, J. S. (1987). The health, physical functioning, and informal supports of the Black elderly. *The Milbank Quarterly, 65* (Supplement 2), 421–454.

Harel, Z. (1988). Stress, aging and coping: Implications for social work practice. *Social Casework, 69,* 575–583.

Harel, Z., Noelker, L. & Blake, B. (1985). Comrehensive services for the aged: Theoretical and empirical perspectives. *The Gerontologist, 25,* 644–649.

Havlik, R., Liu, B., Kovar, M., Suzman, R., Feldman, J., Harris, T., & Van Nostrand, J. (1987). *Health statistics on older persons, United States, 1986.* (Analytical and Epidemiological Studies, Series 3, No. 25, DHHS Publication No. PHS 87-1409). Hyattsville, MD: U.S. Public Health Service.

Hooyman, N., & Lustbader, W. (1986). *Taking care: Supporting older people and their families.* New York: The Free Press.

Jackson, J. S. (1988). Growing old in Black America: Research on aging Black populations. In J. S. Jackson (Ed.), *The Black American elderly: Research on physical and psychosocial health* (pp. 3–16). New York: Springer.

Kane, R. A., & Kane, R. L. (1987). *Long-term care: Principles, programs, and policies.* New York: Springer.

Koff, T. (1988). *New approaches to health care for an aging population: Developing a continuum of chronic care services.* San Francisco: Jossey-Bass.

Kovar, M. (1986). Aging in the eighties: Preliminary data from the supplement on aging to the national health interview survey, United States, January–June 1984. *Advance data from vital and health statistics* (No. 115, DHHS Publication No. PHS 86-1250). Hyattsville, MD: U.S. Public Health Service.

Larson, R. (1978). Thirty years of research on the subjective well-being of older Americans. *Journal of Gerontology, 40,* 109–129.

Lazarus, R., & Folkman, S. (1984). *Stress, appraisal, and coping.* New York: Springer.

Liang, J. (1986). Self-reported physical health among aged adults. *Journal of Gerontology, 41,* 248–260.

Longino, C., & Soldo, B. (1987). The graying of America: Implications of life extension for quality of life. In R. Ward & S. Tobin (Eds.). *Health in aging: Sociological issues and policy directions* (pp. 58–85). New York: Springer.

Lowenthal, M., Berkman, P., Brissette, G., Buehler, J., Pierce, R., Robinson, B., & Trier, M. (1967). *Aging and mental disorder in San Francisco: A social psychiatric study.* San Francisco: Jossey-Bass.

Lurie, E. (1987). The interrelationship of physical and mental illness in the elderly. In E. Lurie, J. Swan, & Associates (Eds.), *Serving the mentally ill elderly: Problems and perspectives* (pp. 39–60). Lexington, MA: Lexington Books.

Manton, K., Patrick, C., & Johnson, K. (1987). Health differentials between Blacks and Whites: Recent trends in mortality and morbidity. *The Milbank Quarterly, 65* (Supplement 1), 129–199.

Manton, K., & Soldo, B. (1985). Dynamics of health changes in the oldest old: New perspectives and evidence. *The Milbank Quarterly, 63,* 206–285.

Markides, K., & Mindel, C. (1987). *Aging and ethnicity.* Newbury Park, CA: Sage.

McDowell, I., & Newell, C. (1987). *Measuring health: A guide to rating scales and questionnaires.* New York: Oxford University Press.

National Council on Aging. (1978). *Fact book on aging.* Washington, D.C.: National Council on Aging.

Neighbors, H. (1987). Improving the mental health of Black Americans: Lessons from the community mental health movement. *The Milbank Quarterly, 65* (Supplement 2), 348–380.

O'Hare, W. (1987). Black demographic trends in the 1980s. *The Milbank Quarterly, 65* (Supplement 1), 35–55.

Palmore, E. (1986). Trends in the health of the aged. *The Gerontologist, 26,* 298–302.

Pegels, C. (1988). *Health care and the older citizen: Economic, demographic, and financial aspects.* Rockville, MD: Aspen.

Prohaska, J., Leventhal, E., Leventhal, H., & Keller, M. (1985). Health practices and illness cognition in young, middle aged, and elderly adults. *Journal of Gerontology, 40,* 569–578.

Rakowski, W., Julius, M., Hickey, J., & Halter, J. (1987). Correlates of preventive health behavior in late life. *Research on Aging, 9,* 331–355.

Rees, W. D., & Lutkins, S. G. (1967). Mortality of bereavement. *British Medical Journal, 4,* 13–16.

Schick, F. (1986). *Statistical handbook on aging Americans.* Phoenix, AZ: Oryx Press.

Shanas, E., & Maddox, G. (1985). Health, health resources, and the utilization of care. In R. Binstock & E. Shanas (Eds.), *Handbook of aging and the social sciences* (Second edition, pp. 696–726). New York: Van Nostrand Reinhold.

Soldo, B., & Manton, K. (1985). Changes in the health status and service needs of the oldest old: Current patterns and future trends. *The Milbank Quarterly, 63,* 286–319.

Suzman, R., & Riley, M. (1985). Introducing the "oldest-old." *The Milbank Quarterly, 63,* 177–186.

Thompson, L., Breckenridge, J., Gallagher, D., & Peterson, J. (1984). Effects of bereavement on self-perceptions of physical health in elderly widows and widowers. *Journal of Gerontology, 39,* 309–314.

Turner, B. (1987). Mental health and the older woman. In G. Lesnoff-Caravaglia (Ed.), *Handbook of applied gerontology* (pp. 201–230). New York: Human Sciences Press.

U.S. Senate Special Committee on Aging. (1988). *Aging America: Trends and pro-jections* (1987–88 Edition). Washington, D.C.: U.S. Department of Health and Human Services.

Verbrugge, L. (1983). Women and men: Mortality and health of older people. In M. Riley, B. Hess, & K. Bond (Eds.), *Aging in society: Selected reviews of recent research* (pp. 139–174). Hillsdale, NJ: Lawrence Erlbaum.

Veroff, J., Douvan, E., & Kulka, R. (1981). *The inner American: A self-portrait from 1957 to 1976.* New York: Basic Books.

Waldo, D., & Lazenby, H. (1984). Demographic characteristics and health care use and expenditures in the United States. *Health Care Financing Review, 6,* 1–49.

Wilson, J., Harel, Z., & Kahana, B. (1988). *Human adaptation to extreme stress: From the holocaust to Vietnam.* New York: Plenum.

Wolinsky, F., Coe, R., Miller, D., & Prendergast, J. (1984). Measurement of the global and functional dimensions of health status in the elderly. *Journal of Gerontology, 39,* 88–92.

Wolinsky, F., Coe, R., & Mosely, R. (1987). The use of health services by elderly Americans: Implications from a regression-based cohort analysis. In R. Ward & S. Tobin (Eds.), *Health in aging: Sociological issues and policy directions* (pp. 106–132). New York: Springer.

Zarit, S., & Zarit, J. (1983). Cognitive impairment. In P. Lewinsohn & L. Teri (Eds.), *Clinical geropsychology: New directions in assessment and treatment* (pp. 38–80). New York: Pergamon.

4

Vulnerability and Sociodemographic Factors

Wornie L. Reed

This chapter reviews the distribution and status of the vulnerable elderly in the community. The vulnerable elderly are defined as persons over the age of 65 with functional deficits who need assistance with activities of daily living and with home management. National data are used to examine the extent of vulnerability in the noninstitutionalized population, and data from a survey of a major city are used to provide a sociodemographic profile of older persons described as vulnerable.

VULNERABILITY AND LONG-TERM CARE

The vast majority of older persons are able to perform most activities of daily living without any assistance. On the other hand, there are an increasing number of older persons with physical and mental disabilities who need the help of others to function in the community.

Long-term care has come to mean care for older persons in the community and in long-term care facilities. If care is provided in the community, long-term care in a residential facility may not be required. Home health care and adult day care provide support for older persons with activity-limiting conditions, and the successful provision of such services is directly related to alternatives to institutionalization. Consequently, just as we measure the distribution of medical problems in a community, it is important to assess the distribution of older persons in the community who need help to continue to live at home.

Estimates of the number of older persons in the community who need help and the type of help needed are important information for determining the extent and type of home care needs. To assist in providing such information, this chapter presents national as well as local data on the vulnerable elderly. There is no readily identifiable part of the population known as "the vulnerable elderly." The vulnerable elderly may be defined in several different ways. In some instances, they are considered to be older persons who are deemed to be potentially at risk for harmful effects of psychological, social, or environmental factors. Another definition considers the vulnerable elderly to be those older persons who depend most upon welfare services and who live in isolation without social suppports. Still another definition may view them in terms of deteriorating social, psychological, and physical functioning. Since the purpose of this chapter is to describe the distribution of vulnerable elderly in noninstitutional settings and to provide a general description of their needs, vulnerability is defined in terms of functional limitations. Thus, the vulnerable elderly are defined as persons over the age of 65 (1) who have functional deficits in physical activity (walking, going outside, bathing, dressing, using the toilet, getting in or out of a bed or chair, eating) and who need assistance in carrying out these daily functions; and (2) those needing help with home management (shopping, household chores, preparing meals, handling money).

Overall estimates, types of functional deficits, and sex and age distributions of these older persons are provided from data collected in the Home Care Supplement to the 1979 National Health Interview Survey. Other sociodemographic characteristics are provided from a sample survey of older persons in a large urban area (Reed, 1984).

VULNERABILITY BY AGE AND SEX

Based on measures of individuals needing help in one or more basic physical activities or needing help in selected home management activities, some 4.9 million adults living in the community were vulnerable (National Center for Health Statistics, 1983). Of these, the majority (2.8 million) were 65 years of age and older, constituting some 12% of persons over 65. Table 4.1 shows the age-related distribution of several measures of functional deficit among the elderly. The need for help is directly related to age. The greatest need among the aged is help with home management activities, followed closely by help with physical activity.

Table 4.2 identifies those older persons who need help in one or more basic physical activities by age and by type of help needed. Slightly more females than males needed help in each age group. Table 4.2 also shows the types of help needed by relative need: more older persons needed help

TABLE 4.1 Rate per 1,000 Adults Who Need Assistance, By Type of Need and Age: United States, 1979

Type of need	Age		
	65–74 years	75–84 years	85 years and over
	Rate for 1,000 persons		
Needs help in one or more basic physical activities	52.6	114.0	348.4
Needs help in one or more home management activities	57.3	141.8	399.0
Usually stays in bed	11.3	25.6	51.2
Has device to control bowel movements or urination	5.3	10.8	28.5
Needs help of another person in one or more of the above	69.9	160.3	436.5

SOURCE: National Center for Health Statistics, B. Fuller. Americans needing help to function at home. Advance Data from Vital Health Statistics, No. 92, DHHS Pub. No. (PHS) 83-1250, Hyattsville, Maryland: U.S. Public Health Service, September 1983.

in walking and going outside than in "getting in or out of a chair or bed" or "eating." For males and females and for each age group, the basic physical activities for which help is needed vary in severity, with the largest number of respondents needing help with walking around, followed by "going outside," "bathing," "dressing," "using the toilet," and "getting in and out of a chair." The fewest persons needed help with eating. The exception to these trends occurs among those 85 and older; slightly more of them need help with going outside than with walking around.

Home management activities covered in the Home Care Survey include shopping for personal items, doing routine household chores, preparing meals, and handling money. Table 4.3 shows that the distribution by age of older persons needing home management help is similar to that of persons needing help with basic activities. Less than 3% of all adults need home management help, but 6% of persons aged 65 to 74, 14% of persons aged 75 to 84, and 40% of persons aged 85 and older need help. Shopping and chores are the areas of greatest need. It is instructive to note, however, that needing help is associated with age and begins prior to age 65. Among those in the 45 to 64 age group, 2.5% also need help with home management.

Another indication of vulnerability is the necessity to stay in bed all or most of the time because of a chronic health problem. Table 4.4 shows distributions by sex and age of older persons who are usually restricted to

TABLE 4.2 Rate per 1,000 Adults Who Need Help in Basic Physical
Activities Because of a Chronic Health Problem, By Type of Activity,
Sex and Age: United States, 1979

| | Needs Help | | |
Sex and age	One or More basic activities	Walking	Going outside	Bathing
Both sexes				
65–74 years	52.6	39.2	34.2	20.4
75–84 years	114.0	83.6	73.5	50.7
85 years and over	348.4	259.7	268.8	172.9
Males				
65–74 years	49.4	37.7	28.0	22.8
75–84 years	101.7	73.5	52.6	45.6
85 years and over	301.7	204.8	225.3	149.0
Females				
65–74 years	55.0	40.2	38.8	18.6
75–84 years	121.4	89.7	86.2	53.7
85 years and over	372.0	289.7	292.7	185.5

Sex and age	Dressing	Using the toilet	Getting in/out of bed/chair	Eating
Both sexes				
65–74 years	14.4	11.6	9.0	3.9
75–84 years	32.9	28.4	25.8	8.4
85 years and over	116.6	104.9	72.5	37.6
Males				
65–74 years	14.3	12.0	8.0	5.2
75–84 years	31.3	22.0	20.1	7.3
85 years and over	111.7	72.6	63.3	33.5
Females				
65–74 years	14.5	11.3	9.8	2.8
75–84 years	34.1	32.0	29.2	9.1
85 years and over	118.1	120.0	78.4	39.7

SOURCE: National Center for Health, B. Fuller, 1983.

bed all or most of the time because of a chronic health condition. While
5.5 per 1,000 persons of all ages usually stay in bed, more than twice as
many persons 65 to 74 years of age are in this situation, and the rate
increases with age. Interestingly, among the old-old (85 and older), females
have a substantially lower rate of bed days than do males.

A summary measure of older persons with functional deficits is the rate
of persons needing the help of another person in essential activities due to

TABLE 4.3 Rate per 1,000 Persons who Need or Receive Help in Home Management Activities Because of a Chronic Health Problem, By Selected Combinations of Activities and Age: United States, 1979

	All adults	Age 65–74	75–84	85 and over
		Rate for 1,000 persons		
Persons needing help[a]	26.5	57.3	141.8	399.0
Persons needing help by type of activity[b]				
Any mention of				
Shopping	19.9	43.6	161.8	354.9
Chores	18.9	41.2	134.1	293.4
Handling money	8.9	15.2	73.9	175.5
Meals	12.3	25.3	94.6	224.7

[a]An unduplicated person count.
[b]A duplicative count in that a person is included in as many types of activities in which help is needed.
SOURCE: National Center for Health Statistics, B. Fuller. Americans needing help to function at home. Advance Data from Vital Health Statistics, No. 92, DHHS Pub. No. (PHS) 83-1250, Hyattsville, Maryland: U.S. Public Health Service, September 1983.

TABLE 4.4 Rate per 1,000 Adults Who Usually Stay in Bed All or Most of the Time Because of a Chronic Health Problem, by Sex and Age: United States, 1979

Sex and age	Adults who usually stay in bed
	Rate per 1,000 persons
Both sexes	
Total	5.5
65–74	11.3
75–84	25.6
85 years and over	51.2
Males	
Total	5.5
65–74	11.9
75–84	22.4
85 years and over	61.5
Females	
Total	5.6
65–74	10.9
75–84	27.6
85 years and over	45.6

SOURCE: National Center for Health Statistics, B. Fuller. Americans needing help to function at home. Advance Data from Vital Health Statistics, No. 92, DHHS Pub. No. (PHS) 83-1250, Hyattsville, Maryland: U.S. Public Health Service, September 1983.

a chronic health problem. A person is considered to need the help of another person if he or she has at least one of the following characteristics:

- Needs or receives the help of another person in performing one of the following activities: walking, going outside, bathing, dressing, eating, using the toilet, or getting in or out of bed or a chair
- Does not do one or more of the above activities
- Needs or receives the help of another person in one or more of the following activities: preparing own meals, shopping for personal items, doing routine chores, or handling own money
- Needs the help of another person in taking care of a device to control bowel movement or urination.

Table 4.5 shows the distributions of persons needing the help of another person with one or more such activities by age and sex. The need for help is associated with age, especially among the aged. Only 7% of those aged 65 to 74 need help, compared with 44% among those aged 85 and older. The rates for women are significantly higher than those for men. For example, 237.2 per 1,000 women 75 years of age and over needed help,

TABLE 4.5 Rate per 1,000 Adults Who Need the Help of Another Person in One or More Selected Activities, By Sex and Age: United States, 1979

Sex and age	Needs help of another
	Rate per 1,000 persons
Both sexes	
Total	31.7
65–74	69.9
75–84	160.3
85 years and over	436.5
Males	
Total	24.1
65–74	55.3
75–84	127.6
85 years and over	353.8
Females	
Total	38.4
65–74	81.1
75–84	180.0
85 years and over	479.2

SOURCE: National Center for Health Statistics, B. Fuller. Americans needing help to function at home. Advance Data from Vital Health Statistics, No. 92, DHHS Pub. No. (PHS) 83-1250, Hyattsville, Maryland: U.S. Public Health Service, September 1983.

compared with 166.6 per 1,000 men 75 years of age and over. In each age group, women were more likely to need help, compared with men.

SOCIODEMOGRAPHIC CHARACTERISTICS OF VULNERABLE ELDERLY

Data from a survey of elderly persons in the city of St. Louis in 1980 provide more detailed descriptions of the vulnerable elderly (Reed, 1984). Since the data from this survey are representative of older persons in the city of St. Louis, the ability to generalize these findings may be limited to other major urban areas. However, the data from this survey provide important information on the functioning of older persons.

The urban sample reviewed here had a slightly different definition of vulnerability (functional impairments) than did the national sample. Persons were considered functionally impaired if they (1) needed the help of another person in getting around inside or outside the house, (2) stayed in the house all or most of the time because of health, or (3) needed help in walking up or down stairs. Table 4.6 shows the age-, sex- and race-related association of functional impairment among persons over the age of 65. The urban sample displayed a pattern of age-associated functional impairment similar to that found in the national sample. In addition, females

TABLE 4.6 Rate per 1,000 Older Persons Who Are Functionally Impaired[a] By Age, Sex, and Race

Selected characteristic	Persons functionally impaired
	Rate per 1,000 persons
Age	
65–74	211
75–84	375
85 years and over	512
Sex	
Male	222
Female	317
Race	
White	275
Black	306

[a]A person is considered functionally impaired if he or she (1) needs the help of another person in getting around inside or outside the house, (2) stays in the house all or most of the time because of health, or (3) needs help in walking up or down stairs.

were found to be more functionally impaired than males, and blacks more than whites.

Table 4.7 provides data on socioeconomic status (SES) and social resources related to functional impairment. Findings presented in this table indicate that older persons with less education, less income, and lower occupational status are more vulnerable than are their counterparts—they have higher rates of functional impairments. The greatest difference is seen in income categories: older persons with less than $4,000 yearly income were found to have four times higher rates of functional impairment than did those older persons with a yearly income over $7,000. Also, older persons who live alone and without a spouse are more vulnerable than those who have a spouse or do not live alone. These data lend converging evidence to the data from the national study, indicating that vulnerability is a function of age (higher) and sex (women). In addition, these data offer evidence for the importance of economic and social resources in the prediction of functional vulnerability.

TABLE 4.7 Rate per 1,000 Older Persons Who Are Functionally Impaired, By Selected Sociodemographic Characteristics

Selected characteristic	Persons functionally impaired
	Rate per 1,000 persons
Education	
8 years of less	356
Some high school or more	181
Occupation	
White collar	140
Blue collar	324
Housewife	385
Income	
Less than $4,000	425
$4,000–6,999	297
$7,000 or more	98
Live alone	
Yes	306
No	267
Live with spouse	
Yes	190
No	325
Being alone is	
No problem	267
Somewhat of a problem	262
Very important problem	756

Vulnerability by Race

There are no meaningful differences between older blacks and whites in age-, sex- or education-related vulnerability (see Table 4.8). Blacks are more vulnerable than whites, and the excess of disability rates among older blacks is maintained across these variables. There are some differences, however, by other SES measures and "aloneness"-related vulnerability. White-collar workers among black elderly are less likely to be functionally impaired than are their white counterparts, and black housewives are more likely to be functionally impaired than are white housewives. Also, income level is more of a factor among blacks. Low-income

TABLE 4.8 Rate per 1,000 Older Persons Who Are Functionally Impaired, By Selected Sociodemographic Characteristics and Race

	Race	
Selected characteristic	White	Black
	Rate per 1,000 persons	
Age		
65–74	194	236
75–84	363	406
85 years and over	521	615
Sex		
Male	207	244
Female	302	348
Education		
8 years or less	352	264
Some high school or more	175	195
Occupation		
White collar	148	77
Blue collar	351	372
Housewife	328	535
Income		
Less than $4,000	397	456
$4,000–6,999	281	294
$7,000 or more	92	74
Live alone		
Yes	315	295
No	225	309
Live with spouse		
Yes	152	250
No	325	328
Being alone is		
No problem	257	292
Somewhat of a problem	216	414
Very important problem	962	473

blacks have more functional impairment than do whites. Higher income blacks have less functional impairment than their white counterparts. Living situation is not as much a factor among blacks as among whites. There is no great difference among blacks, whether they live alone or with someone. And, among those with spouses, blacks are more likely to be functionally impaired than are whites.

SUMMARY AND DISCUSSION

Vulnerability has been defined here as functional impairment. Persons who are limited in carrying out their personal care needs are potentially at risk. They have definite needs, that if unmet in the community, will require them to be placed into some type of residential care facility to receive the needed care.

Vulnerability is significantly a function of age (as would be expected); however, the rate of vulnerability is related to other sociodemographic characteristics as well. Females are more vulnerable than males and blacks are more vulnerable than whites. In addition, vulnerability is a function of socioeconomic status and living situation. The more disadvantaged persons, in terms of socioeconomic status, are those with lower income, followed by those with lower educational and occupational status. Also, living alone contributes significantly to the functional vulnerability of older persons. These data add to our understanding of vulnerability: functional impairment is maldistributed in the elderly, and those persons who tend to be more functionally impaired tend to have fewer resources to deal with their situations. They tend to have less income and education, and they are more likely to live alone. When viewed in this manner, distinctions can readily be seen among persons who live alone—it can be a serious problem for some persons and not a problem for others, depending upon their resources.

There is an interaction between race and the two vulnerability-related factors, socioeconomic status and aloneness. Low income and occupational status make more difference in the vulnerability of blacks, while living alone or without a spouse is more problematic for whites.

This chapter reviewed the extent and distribution of functional impairment of older persons in the community. It did not address the issue of whether the required assistance was readily available. The review of vulnerability reminds us of the negative aspects of growing older. With older age comes increasing personal vulnerability and functional deficits. The challenge to policymakers is to ensure that mechanisms are in place to effectively match helpers and persons with an impaired level of functioning.

In American society, adults are expected to take care of themselves and to be self-supporting. This implies that older persons need to have the physical mobility and social and economic resources to care for themselves. The data presented and discussed in this chapter demonstrate very clearly that there are some older persons in the community who have more difficulty caring for themselves and managing their households than do others. If society is to move in the direction of taking care of such persons, then the concept of vulnerability may serve as a means of aiding such an effort.

REFERENCES

National Center for Health Statistics, B. Fuller. (1983). *Americans needing help to function at home. Advance data from vital and health statistics*, No. 92 Pub. No. (PHS) 83-1250 Hyattsville, MD: U.S. Public Health Service.

Reed, W. L. (1984). *Access to services by the urban elderly.* MTIS Publication No. PB84-245364. Final Report and Executive Summary.

5

Coping Among Vulnerable Elders

Eva Kahana, Boaz Kahana, and Jennifer Kinney

It has been argued by gerontologists that the elderly are a population at risk because they experience stressful life situations at a time when their adaptive capacities are diminished (Rosow, 1967). While notions of diminished adaptive capacities and vulnerability have been associated with late life, a careful review of empirical and theoretical work does not provide conclusive evidence that age inevitably leads to diminished coping skills or to adverse psychosocial outcomes (McCrae, 1984). Accordingly, the majority of aged persons live independently and exhibit relatively few signs of vulnerability until very late in life. To allow for a useful review and analysis of research relevant to coping and vulnerability, it is important to place these terms into a meaningful and cohesive conceptual framework. We aim to provide such a framework in the first portion of this chapter. Subsequently, we will explore the psychological resources of vulnerable elders by considering data from our own research with frail and vulnerable as well as healthy older populations. We will also review findings of other researchers that shed light on the nature and value of psychological coping resources and strategies among vulnerable elders.

As a first step in developing this discussion, we will identify parameters of vulnerability. Later in the chapter, we distinguish between personal coping resources and strategies. The conceptual linkages between vulnerability and personal coping resources may be best understood when considered in the framework of a broader paradigm of stress research. A large volume of research and conceptual contributions has elucidated the dynamic relationships among potential *stressors* (generally conceptualized as events external to the person), *social and personal resources*, and *outcomes of health and psychological well-being* (Kahana & Kahana, 1984; Lazarus & Folkman, 1984). It has been amply documented that diverse stresses result in diminished health and well-being and that the adverse effects of stress may be mediated or buffered by social as well as personal resources (Menaghan, 1983). Accordingly, the ill effects of stress are likely to be reduced in the presence of social supports and personal coping resources or skills. These relationships initially were documented with younger age groups, and more recent studies have confirmed similar sequelae and mediators of stress among older adults (Lazarus & DeLongis, 1983; Simons & West, 1984). The basic paradigm of stress research is outlined in Figure 5.1.

How then does the concept of vulnerability relate to this stress paradigm? Who, in fact, are the vulnerable aged? A closer examination of our clinical and intuitive understanding of vulnerability appears to be in order here. Such an approach will permit us to realize that vulnerability could be applied to basic elements of the stress paradigm. Understanding the diverse sources of vulnerability also provides a useful background for intervention efforts. The term *vulnerability* is loosely applied in the gerontological literature to describe elderly persons suffering from a multiplicity of problems. Although the stress paradigm is seldom explicitly referred to in discussing vulnerability, the "vulnerable" designation is used to refer to groups afflicted with diverse stresses ranging from familial abuse (Hooyman et al., 1982) to ravages of chronic debilitating illnesses such as Alzheimer's disease (Kiyak & Montgomery, 1988). In addition, vulnerability has also been defined as an absence of social or environmental resources (Morris & Sherwood, 1983).

If we seek an operationally meaningful definition of vulnerability, it is useful to note that vulnerability is generally related to some definition of increased risk. In the following discussion, we will consider vulnerability as the increased probability of adverse health and psychosocial outcomes. Such a definition represents a simple and readily operational criterion for vulnerability, which allows for organizing those factors that contribute to late life vulnerability. We will now turn to a consideration of gerontological research relevant to vulnerability along different components of the stress paradigm. Figure 5.2 depicts some of the major sources of late-life vulnerability in the framework of a stress paradigm.

FIGURE 5.1 Basic Paradigm of Stress Effects on Well-Being Outcomes.

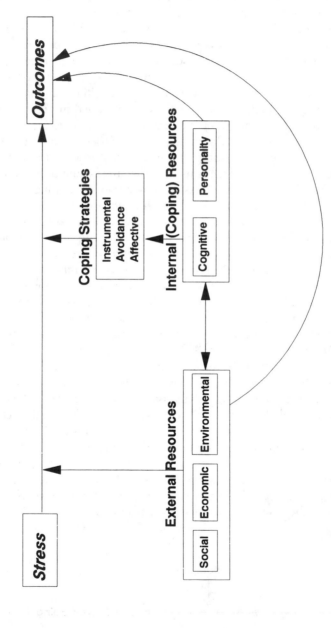

FIGURE 5.2 Examples of Late Life Vulnerability in the Framework of a Stress Paradigm.

STRESS

Older persons may be defined as vulnerable if they have experienced stressful or negative life events such as *widowhood, relocation, financial reverses, or illness of a family member.* Although the elderly have been shown to experience relatively few stressful life events (Kahana & Kahana, 1984), they are more likely than younger persons to experience negative life events that pose threats to them (Folkman et al., 1987). By the very definition of the stress paradigm, these stresses essentially render them more vulnerable (i.e., at higher risk) to adverse physical health and mental health outcomes. The exact mechanisms of such vulnerability are not well understood at present, but both biochemical and psychosocial mechanisms have been proposed (Cohen & Wills, 1985).

Stress is still a relatively little understood and multidimensional construct. Greater specification of the full spectrum of stresses that contribute to negative outcomes for the elderly is needed if we are to understand demands made on the older individual for adaptation and resources that could diminish adverse stress effects. The voluminous literature on stress in late life generally focuses on recent life events that bring about life changes for the elderly (Kahana & Kahana, 1984). However, it is increasingly recognized that more enduring and chronic environmental stimuli and life frustrations also are important components of stress that impinge on the elderly (Kahana et al., 1987b). While stresses are generally considered as distinct from resources (such as social supports), it is useful to recognize that many major stressors in fact comprise changes (generally loss) of specific resources. Thus, bereavement may also involve a major loss of social support. Retirement is likely to involve loss of economic resources. Residential moves may result in diminished environmental resources. Furthermore, extreme examples of the absence of social resources, such as social isolation and homelessness, may be viewed as stressors in their own right. They may then contribute to vulnerability by creating disequilibrium for the person or by rendering him or her defenseless in dealing with other stressors.

The experience of one set of stressors may also impact on the perception of other stressors and on the interpretation of potential sources of stress involving threat or harm for a given individual. Applying this notion to the elderly, we might anticipate that a recently widowed older person may perceive a residential move as more stressful and threatening than would a married older person who will be undertaking a similar residential move along with (and supported by) his or her spouse. Similarly, elderly persons who had endured a great deal of cumulative stress throughout their lives (Antonovsky, 1979) or who had been victims of extreme stress (Kahana et al., 1988) may be more vulnerable to recent life events experienced later in life.

HEALTH AND WELL-BEING OUTCOMES

An alternative definition of vulnerability may be proposed by considering health and psychological well-being outcomes of stress (see Figure 5.2). We have thus far focused on health or mental health outcomes as results of stressful life situations. We may alternatively postulate that poor health or mental health will serve as an important source of further stress that places the elderly at greater risk of developing additional health or mental health problems. It is a well-documented fact that a prior history of adverse psychosocial states increases the risk of adverse outcomes when new stresses arise. Based on Lawton and Nahemow's (1973) environmental docility hypothesis, such persons are also more strongly affected by environmental problems than are their less frail counterparts. For example, an older person suffering from anxiety and depression after the loss of a sibling has an increased risk of health and mental health problems should he or she encounter yet another stressful life situation. In fact, typical longitudinal research designs in stress research generally evaluate the impact of stress on well-being outcomes at Time 2 while controlling for well-being outcomes at Time 1 (Kessler, 1987). Consequently, we expect that a history of health and mental health problems will result in greater vulnerability to future stress or diminished resources that may be encountered by an older person.

RESOURCES

Both external (social) resources and internal (psychological) resources have been identified in the stress literature as factors that buffer the adverse effects of stress. The proposed role of these coping resources in diminishing vulnerability through enhancement of positive outcomes is depicted in Figure 5.3. Studies have documented the protective roles of social, economic, environmental, and psychological resources as playing important roles in diminishing adverse stress effects (Norris & Murrell, 1984). Resources may counteract negative stress effects, or their absence may render the older individual more defenseless in the face of stressful life situations. Resource deficits will thus constitute important determinants of late-life vulnerability. Resources may be viewed as having a direct and/or indirect effect on outcomes. Persons who are devoid of resources have an increased probability of adverse outcomes, either because loss or absence of resources constitutes stress or because resources are not available to counteract adverse stress effects. Resources may thus be considered as shields of varying strengths, while resource losses may be seen as direct insults placing the older person at high risk of adverse outcomes.

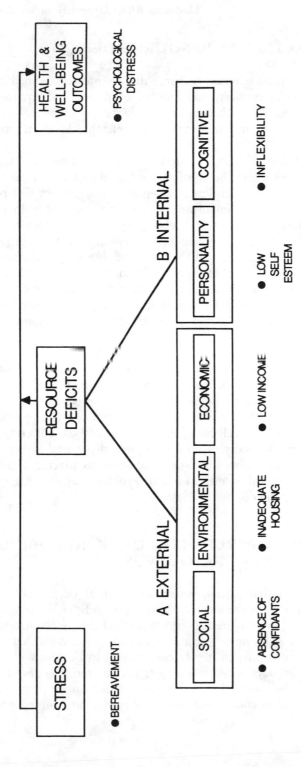

FIGURE 5.3 The role of Coping Strategies and Resources in Reducing Adverse Stress Effects

EXTERNAL RESOURCE DEFICITS

Vulnerability based on external resource deficits may be defined in terms of absence of social supports and lack of economic and environmental resources (see Figure 5.2). Absence of confidants and social isolation have also been identified as important factors that put the elderly at risk (Lowenthal & Robinson, 1976).

Environmental resources may be defined in terms of physical and social features that contribute to the comfort level of the older person (Golant, 1984). Incongruence between environmental characteristics and personal needs may be seen as an important source of vulnerability in late life, particularly in institutional settings where degrees of freedom are limited in regard to either altering or leaving the environment (Kahana et al., 1980). Homelessness may exemplify an extreme but very real state of vulnerability that is based on absence of social and environmental resources. Lack of *economic resources* also renders the elderly vulnerable to adverse stress effects. Recent research by Simons and West (1984) found income to be the single most powerful buffer of life change among community-living elderly.

The proposed model of vulnerability thus considers absence of external resources as placing the older individual at risk of adverse outcomes. While such risk is greatest in the presence of stress, absence of resources may be viewed as having an independent negative effect as well as a mediating negative effect. Thus, it is acknowledged that social supports have a direct positive effect on well-being in addition to their buffering role in stressful situations. Similarly, it may be argued that social isolation has a direct adverse effect on well-being, in addition to placing a person at greater risk for physical or mental health problems when other losses or problems occur (Cohen & Wills, 1985).

INTERNAL PSYCHOLOGICAL AND COPING RESOURCES

In addition to external (social) resources, internal or psychological resources have also been demonstrated to buffer adverse effects of stress (Dean et al., 1981) (see Figure 5.2). Psychological coping resources may be best described as enduring self-attitudes and cognitive skills that facilitate the use of specific coping strategies called upon in dealing with stressful life situations. Although some researchers use the terms *coping resources* and *coping strategies* interchangeably, differentiation of these two constructs helps to clarify conceptualizations of coping and vulnerability.

While coping strategies have often been considered synonymously with coping resources, the present model considers coping resources and strategies as distinct concepts. In contrast to coping resources, coping strategies are defined here as specific responses to stressors or problem situations. The use of specific strategies is not expected to have a direct effect on outcomes in the absence of stress and, hence, the definition of vulnerability is not based on an elderly person's use of specific coping strategies (see Figure 5.2).

Before turning to a review of research on psychological resources among vulnerable elders, it is useful to consider the array of relevant psychological resources. Some researchers (Elwell & Maltbie-Crannell, 1981) include all forms of potential resources, including age, income, and health, under the term coping resources. A personal resources scale developed for use with the aged (Clark, 1982) includes dimensions of age, health, and occupation along with self-confidence as indicators of resources. A more meaningful definition, however, limits consideration of coping resources to those psychological resource domains that enhance the effectiveness of coping responses by the individual. Variables most frequently included in this category are cognitive and personality resources such as competence, mastery, self esteem, and locus of control. Psychological buffers have been broadly classified as (1) coping resources (self-esteem, coherence, mastery, locus of control), and (2) coping strategies. Stress researchers have alternatively focused on coping resources or coping strategies, but few researchers have specified the interrelationships of these two types of psychological resources.

Psychological coping resources, akin to social resources, are generally described as traitlike constructs that may be linked to psychosocial outcomes even in the absence of stress. Accordingly, high self-esteem and internal locus of control are generally associated with high levels of psychosocial well-being (Menaghan, 1983). While research has focused primarily on *personality* characteristics that comprise coping resources, the importance of cognitive skills and resources in facilitating the application of appropriate coping strategies has been acknowledged recently (Antonovsky, 1979) (see Figure 5.3). Absence of these coping resources has been viewed as placing the elderly at a higher risk of adverse outcomes and thus constitutes a source of vulnerability. Lack of coping resources may also render the individual less able to deal with stress and thereby exacerbate adverse stress effects.

The most frequently studied coping resources refer to personality dispositions such as self-esteem and internal locus of control, self-efficacy, or mastery. Consideration of these concepts in relation to late-life vulnerability reveals that they, too, are very distinct constructs.

Self-Esteem

Research by Pearlin and Schooler (1978) and Antonovsky (1979) supports the view that positive self-attitudes in the form of self-esteem serve as useful buffers in stressful life situations. To the extent that self-esteem is a relatively enduring dimension of self-attitudes, it should serve as a continuing resource throughout late life. However, recent stress research has also acknowledged the likelihood of synchronous effects, suggesting that stress can impact on self-esteem even as self-esteem serves as a coping resource in confronting stressful life situations (Johnson et al., 1986). Research by these authors used a longitudinal design to examine the stability of self-esteem among bereaved elderly and the buffering role of self-esteem. Data support a dynamic view of the stress process. They suggest that, in spite of general stability in self-esteem and in coping responses, persistent stress exerts a significant deleterious effect on coping resources such as self-esteem.

Locus of Control, Self-Efficacy, and Mastery

Internal locus of control (LOC) has been generally defined as a coping resource and demonstrated to result in better psychosocial outcomes among community residents (Lefcourt, 1982). Yet, there are indications that for elderly nursing home residents (Felton & Kahana, 1974), as well as for chronically ill hospitalized elderly (Baltes & Reizensein, 1986), external rather than internal locus of control may provide a better psychological coping resource.

Similarly, empirical research focusing on the elderly has not found support for the expectations based on research with younger age groups that feelings of self-efficacy would serve as significant buffers against stresses produced by life changes (Simons & West, 1985). When older individuals encounter high levels of life change, strong perceptions of self-efficacy are associated with increased probability of ill health (Simons & West, 1985). This finding confirms an accumulating body of findings in institutional settings (Felton & Kahana, 1974) that suggests that elderly persons with internal LOC and strong expectations for environmental controllability do more poorly in total institutional settings than do those who acknowledge the reality of external control.

To the extent that expectations of external control fit in with the reality of the life situations of the elderly, they fulfill the criteria suggested by Antonovsky (1979) that maturity of coping is reflected in the accuracy and objectivity with which the individual appraises his or her life situation. Accordingly, in recent research, Simons and West (1985) consider circumstances where self-efficacy could serve either as a coping inhibitor (rather than a resource) or as a stress exacerbator (rather than a buffer). These research findings and conceptual considerations lead us to question the generally accepted inclusion of locus of control, self-efficacy, and mastery as a useful coping resource during late life. It is possible that this construct is more profitably viewed as a personality disposition whose utility is life stage or situation-specific. Based on a perusal of the literature as well as our own research, we wish to argue for expanding consideration of concepts subsumed under the rubric of late-life coping resources.

Data from our research on elderly survivors of the Holocaust (Kahana et al., 1988) points to the value of psychological resources that have a positive impact on psychosocial well-being in the aftermath of traumatic life situations. Accordingly, *self-disclosure, altruism*, and *finding meaning in adversity* emerged as constructs of important heuristic value among elderly victims of psychic trauma. These coping resources proved to be better predictors of psychosocial well-being in late life than did specific types of stress experiences. These brief examples illustrate the heuristic value of considering the roles of hitherto neglected coping resources in contributing to well-being and diminishing vulnerability of elders.

COPING STRATEGIES

Coping strategies may be distinguished from coping resources and may be defined as specific responses or behaviors used by the elderly when stressful or problem situations arise. They may be aimed at diminishing the stress (problem-focused coping) or at minimizing emotional distress (emotion-focused coping) (Folkman & Lazarus, 1980). Menaghan (1983) proposes further distinctions between enduring predispositions to dealing with problem situations and more variable specific coping responses. While such additional distinctions may ultimately prove useful, the gerontological literature does not, at present, warrant such separate discussions.

There have been several prevalent and sometimes overlapping definitions of coping strategies presented in the literature. Billings and Moos (1982) distinguished active behavioral, active cognitive, and avoidance-oriented strategies as critical components, while Pearlin and Schooler (1978) differentiated coping strategies that alter the situation, modify the meaning of the situation, or control the stress of the situation. Lazarus and Folkman (1984) proposed a bidimensional formulation of coping based on problem- versus emotion-focused dimensions. Work by Kahana et al. (1987a) on institutionalized elderly supported a tripartite view of coping, including instrumental, affective, and avoidance strategies.

Regardless of their classification, coping strategies are widely recognized as important buffers between stressful life events and adverse mental or physical health sequelae. Interest in the construct is justified by documented associations between modes of coping with problem situations and a range of outcomes. Previous research has documented the usefulness of coping strategies in enhancing psychosocial well-being, subsequent to institutional placement of the elderly (Kahana et al., 1987a); among caregivers to frail elderly (Stephens et al., 1988); and in response to chronic strain with finances, parenting, and occupations (Pearlin & Schooler, 1978; Pearlin et al., 1981).

Individual differences in coping strategy use are based on long-term, enduring personality characteristics (McCrae & Costa, 1986). Supporting this view, Kahana et al., (1987a) found that the coping strategies of elderly persons did not change after institutionalization. Yet, coping strategies are increasingly conceptualized as having situation-specific as well as traitlike components (Kahana & Kahana, 1984). Coping strategies are activated only in the presence of stressful or problem situations, and their utility is likely to depend on the particular problem confronted. Both environmental constraints and opportunities may thus be expected to impact on modes of coping with stress. It is for these reasons that we do not define absence or presence of given coping strategies as reflections of personal vulnerability in our conceptual model (see Figure 5.3).

To better understand the effectiveness of specific coping processes, we must specify the adaptive tasks older persons are dealing with as well as situational constraints on the coping options that are available to them. Thus, for example, an elderly person confronting stress created by loss of income due to retirement may not readily find new employment; hence, there are limits on specific instrumental actions he or she can take to increase his or her income. Similarly, opportunities to ask for assistance may be limited for elderly persons whose children have relocated at a distance from them. Thus, the very losses in resources that are so apt to characterize old age also serve to limit the coping options available to the older person. Consequently, coping resources are likely to influence the use of specific coping strategies. Our model for understanding the interrelationships of coping resources and coping strategies in the framework of the stress paradigm is presented in Figure 5.3.

It has been argued that environmental constraints or opportunities change the appropriateness, the value, and the consequences of diverse coping strategies (Appley & Trumbull, 1986). One of the most interesting examples of the special meaning of certain psychological or behavioral responses for the vulnerable aged is the case of dependent responses among institutionalized elderly. Dependent behaviors have been generally assumed by gerontologists to reflect helplessness and diminished environmental mastery (Kalish, 1969). Yet, Baltes and Reizensein (1986) demonstrated that residents of nursing homes get contingent reinforcements only when they exhibit dependent modes of behaving. This research suggests, therefore, that exhibiting dependent modes of behavior represents a useful and important form of secondary control for the institutionalized aged.

Recent work in the area of coping (Kahana et al., 1984) has underscored that processes of coping must be distinguished from both coping resources and the outcomes of coping and that different types of coping strategies may be useful in different problem situations (Kahana & Kahana, 1984). Accordingly, instrumental coping may be useful in dealing with stresses of relocation, whereas avoidance coping may play a useful buffering role in illness situations. To the extent that an older person is not facing stressful situations, our model does not propose that coping strategies should have a causal relationship with outcomes. It is for this reason that the use of any given coping strategy should not be viewed as an indication of vulnerability per se. However, the ability to use a broad spectrum of coping strategies and to use coping strategies that are appropriate to the stress confronted may be seen as providing useful buffers in dealing with stressful life situations.

RELATIONSHIP OF COPING RESOURCES AND COPING STRATEGIES

Research based on the elderly has not generally sought to explore linkages between coping resources and coping strategies. There is relevant data from younger populations suggesting that such linkages exist. Research by Pearlin et al. (1981) found significant positive relationships between high self-esteem and instrumental coping efforts in dealing with marital and occupational problems. In a small-scale study of elderly persons anticipating relocation, Dougherty et al. (1982) also found coping strategies to be highly correlated with self-esteem. Personal and social resources were also found to be significant predictors of coping behavior in a study of a large national sample of elderly Britons (Clark, 1982). Similarly persons with internal mastery or locus of control have been found by these authors to use more instrumental and less avoidant coping styles. Although the roles of cognitive resources such as intelligence and cognitive styles such as flexibility have been recognized (Antonovsky, 1987), these have not been linked to the use of specific coping efforts. Their presence may be critical, however, in the older person's ability to use a range of coping strategies and to select strategies that are most appropriate to dealing with specific problem situations. Development of such skills has, in fact, served as an important aspect of intervention efforts in enhancing coping skills of the aged (Kahana & Kahana, 1983).

To the extent that we seek to go beyond the general recognition of the buffering roles of coping resources and coping strategies in diminishing adverse stress effects, consideration of the interrelationships of diverse social and coping resources and of coping strategies may be particularly useful. Accordingly, it is useful to consider the complex interplay between coping strategies, locus of control and social supports. While internal locus of control is likely to promote instrumental coping strategies, such strategies may also activate social support which, in turn, may either diminish or enhance the level of internal locus of control (Thoits, 1983; Turner, 1983; Turner et al., 1983). Receipt of instrumental support may thus reinforce beliefs in the role of powerful others. On the other hand, affective support may reinforce the older person's sense of competence and enhance internal locus-of-control beliefs.

Despite the promise and potential usefulness of the concept of coping in studies of late-life stress, findings about components, predictors and sequelae often have been inconsistent, and the methodology for assessing coping also has been criticized. Assessment of coping has been based on measures with questionable validity which ask respondents to judge how likely they would be to use a series of alternative coping strategies in dealing with hypothetical or actual problem situations.

ANTECEDENTS OF COPING

To the extent that stress may define vulnerability in late life, predictions about the general impact of stress on adaptation represent a central concern. There are two conflicting views in the literature regarding the impact of stress on coping and psychological resources. According to some theorists (Eysenck, 1982), prior exposure to stress facilitates adaptation to later stressors. This view has been termed the *inoculation hypothesis*. This position contrasts with Selye's (1956) view that extended exposure to stress results in a general adaptation syndrome (GAS) culminating in the breakdown of the organism. Since older adults have had a greater opportunity than younger persons to be exposed to stresses throughout their lives, one may expect them to portray better or poorer adaptive skills than younger persons depending on which of the above views is being endorsed.

Types of coping and adaptation may also depend on personal characteristics such as demographic and social-psychosocial factors or type of illness, or they may depend on environmental factors. Coe's (1965) research offers evidence that modes of adjustment in institutional settings are related to the characteristics of the institution. Thus, characteristics of the institution often precluded certain forms of coping; for example, integration into patient subculture. Thus, institutions may often reinforce potentially maladaptive forms of coping, such as withdrawal and acquiescence, while they censure more active coping styles such as complaining or attempts to change the environment. Structural characteristics of the institutional environment, such as ownership and location, as well as the social psychological milieu, have been found to contribute to the different coping styles of residents (Kahana et al., 1984).

The differential use of coping strategies based on age also poses a relevant consideration. In addition, recent research indicates that cognitive problems and stress brought on by developing illness also impact on the coping strategies of the elderly. Accordingly, research by Kiyak and Montgomery (1988) demonstrates significantly greater use of wish-fulfilling coping strategies among persons affected by Alzheimer's disease than among members of a normal comparison group.

DEVELOPMENTAL CHANGES IN COPING

The issue of changes in coping as a function of age has not been resolved. In terms of specific coping responses, as measured by self-report, there seem to be no age-related changes in coping. Instead, the source of stress seems to play a much greater role in coping responses than does age per se (McCrae, 1984). On the other hand, research based on projective tests portrays consistent and cross-culturally confirmed shifts from active to passive mastery. Such changes have been supported by Neugarten and Gutmann's (1968) findings on Thematic Apperception Test (TAT) data and by data based on the Sentence Completion Test (Kahana, 1978). Although these shifts appear in both men and women, additional TAT studies paradoxically depict older women as being more assertive and aggressive than younger women, while older men portray greater nurturance and less dominance than do younger men (Lowenthal, 1977). Recent cross-sectional data (Aldwin & Revenson, 1988) suggest cohort differences in coping strategies. Older respondents have been found to be less likely to use problem-focused coping or to seek information and help from others. Interestingly, the elderly also felt that they were not responsible for the occurrence or management of their problems.

RESEARCH ON THE ROLE OF PSYCHOSOCIAL RESOURCES FOR VULNERABLE ELDERS

We will now turn to a review of some research evidence relevant to personal and psychological resources in response to stressful life situations commonly associated with vulnerability in late life. We will review and compare data that we collected in two research projects dealing with stress and coping. Our first data set explored the role of coping strategies in facilitating well-being after institutionalization. Institutionalization has been demonstrated to be a life change that reflects a major stressor because of the involuntary nature of the relocation as well as the major life changes posed by the altered life circumstances faced by elders (Kahana et al., 1987a). Elderly persons entering institutions may be defined as vulnerable, both because of their prior history of health and/or mental health problems and because of the major stresses that they confront. Two hundred fifty-three older adults were interviewed in a longitudinal study prior to entering institutions. A second study explored diverse stressors impinging on 400 community-living elderly and the role of social and personal resources in ameliorating adverse stress effects (Kahana et al., 1987b). Respondents in this community survey were randomly selected from subscribers (age 65 +) of a Detroit-area health maintenance organization (HMO).

In an effort to consider the relationship between vulnerability and coping strategies, we compared coping strategies reported by the institutionalized (vulnerable) elderly in the first project to those reported by the community-dwelling elderly in the second project. In both studies, coping was measured by the Elderly Care Research Center (ECRC) Coping Scale (Kahana et al., 1982). This is a 27-item scale designed to measure a range of coping strategies among the elderly. For each item, respondents rate on a four-point scale (ranging from "not at all likely" to "very likely") how apt they are to use each strategy in dealing with an unspecified stressful problem situation.

When we compared institutionalized and community-living respondents' reports of how they typically cope with a difficult situation, several interesting findings emerged. The most frequently endorsed coping strategies for both noninstitutionalized and institutionalized (vulnerable) respondents involved instrumental strategies (e.g., get more information about the situation; do something definite about the situation). For both groups of respondents, affective strategies were endorsed with the least frequency (e.g., expect the worse; become angry/irritable; blame others). There were very few differences in endorsement of specific coping strategies between community-living and institutionalized elders.

Focusing on the institutionalized sample, we also addressed the issue of changes in coping as persons undergo the stress of institutionalization and face the increased likelihood of adverse psychosocial outcomes. Findings with respect to stability or change in coping over the preinstitutional to eight-month postinstitutional period indicated substantial continuity of coping behavior. Thus, our initial comparison of vulnerable and nonvulnerable elderly failed to reveal striking differences in the types of coping strategies used. Nevertheless, some evidence of change in coping behaviors subsequent to institutionalization was portrayed when individual items making up the ECRC Coping Scale were considered. For example, there was a significant decrease after institutionalization in endorsement of "going out to forget problems" and "trying to see the humor in the situation." Coping by crying was found to increase significantly after institutionalization. Nevertheless, more than 85% of the individual coping behaviors remained stable during the course of the initial period of institutional life.

Despite the finding that coping strategies are similar for community-dwelling and institutionalized elderly, living arrangement is only one way to differentiate between vulnerable and nonvulnerable aged. To explore differences in coping strategies between more and less vulnerable elders, we turned to our data on 400 community-dwelling elderly (age 65 +) residents of the Detroit area. Again, we looked for differences in coping between more and less vulnerable adults, differentiating respondents in terms of age (i.e., young-old vs. old-old), perceived income (i.e., adequate vs. inadequate), and marital status (i.e., married vs. widowed) Here we assumed that older respondents, with fewer economic resources and without a spouse, are especially vulnerable due to their diminished resources.

To identify age related differences in the endorsement of coping items, respondents were categorized as young old (under 75) or old-old (75 +). Only one significant difference emerged in the area of affective/emotional coping. While there was little difference between the two groups in the area of affective/emotional coping, there were numerous significant differences in both instrumental/behavioral and cognitive/escape coping. Young-old persons were significantly more likely to endorse both instrumental and cognitive/escape strategies. For example, four times as many young-old as old-old were likely to reduce tension by eating, drinking, or smoking.

Respondents differing in economic resources demonstrated similar use of affective/emotional and cognitive/escape coping. However, several differences emerged between the two groups with respect to instrumental/behavioral coping strategies. Respondents reporting adequate or better incomes were more likely to make alternative plans for dealing with a troublesome situation than were those with less than adequate incomes. Those with fewer economic resources tended to accept the situation as it was presented, without alternative planning.

Widows were significantly and substantially more likely than married respondents to cry, turn to religion, or attempt to go on as if nothing had happened. These coping responses, which span the range of the different coping types, also reflect strategies appropriate to stressful life situations. In contrast, married respondents were more likely than widowed to become angry and irritable toward others and to avoid being with people.

These responses may reflect both the interpersonal opportunities and the potential conflicts inherent in being part of a marital dyad.

Our data suggest that, compared to young-old, the old-old show a generalized reduction in the use of varying coping strategies. These data support Neugarten and Guttmann's (1968) classic study on the increasingly passive mastery characterizing late-life adaption. Findings also raise some important questions and challenges for the conceptualization and measurement of coping. What does it mean if old-old persons are less likely to endorse most forms of coping? Is there a meaningful overall coping construct wherein some people are more likely to engage in general coping effort?

Chronic illness may also be viewed as a major type of vulnerability in late life (Felton & Revenson, 1987). Differences in coping strategies between well and health-impaired elders living in the community have been explored in one of our recent papers (Borawski et al., 1987). Elderly respondents were subdivided into three health categories, based on the combined scores of three health indices (activites of daily living, sick days, and number of illnesses). Comparisons were made between the coping responses of persons in the three health groups reflecting those in excellent (N = 88), those in fair (N = 245), and those in poor (N = 63) health. Responses to the coping scale were categorized, based on factor analysis, as (1) instrumental or problem-focused coping, (2) emotion-focused coping aimed at stress reduction, or (3) cognitive coping aimed at changing the meaning of the situation.

Significant differences were observed only in emotion-focused coping, with those in poor health exhibiting significantly more emotion-focused responses than those in excellent health or fair health. It is interesting to note, however, that emotion-focused coping was not associated with adverse outcomes (psychological distress) in this group. These data are at variance with findings based on institutionalized elderly (Kahana et al., 1987a), where emotion-focused coping was found to result in negative mental health outcomes.

These data regarding differences in coping strategies of more vulnerable and less vulnerable elders provide greater evidence of commonalities than of differences in modes of coping between differentially vulnerable older populations. We must also exercise caution in interpreting differences in coping as being attributable to changes within more vulnerable older individuals. Such differences may also reflect differential environmental opportunities or constraints on specific coping styles for persons devoid of social or economic resources. It may also be expected that different sources of vulnerability (stress, lowered social resources, or adverse psychosocial outcomes) would differentially impact on different aspects of coping. The data we reviewed provided some useful suggestions relevant to the coping strategies of differentially vulnerable elders. However, research is needed that is specifically designed to explore the relationship between different sources of vulnerability and different coping responses. Such research might also use a more expanded definition of coping to include life-styles and other macro definitions of coping, along with more traditional micro-level indicators.

Systematic empirical data regarding coping resources and coping responses are available mostly for specific coping strategies. These data provide intriguing suggestions that certain modes of responding are more common among the frail or vulnerable elderly. Yet, it is important to note that coping responses may be considered using different conceptual and operational definitions. Accordingly, dependency, mastery, locus of control, and self-esteem reflect potentially useful indices of coping that may have special adaptive value for vulnerable elders.

The conceptualization that we have presented favors the integration of dispositional and situation-specific views of coping efforts. The utility of specific coping efforts must be judged and empirically assessed, however, based on their efficacy in buffering adverse effects of specific problems or stressful life situations. It should be noted, however, that some scholars have suggested categorizing coping efforts to reflect higher level versus lower level coping modes (Nailliait, 1976). The literature does not provide much empirical support for this view. Furthermore, there may be an ageist bias in any formulation that considers certain modes of coping as superior, based on their increased prevalence during certain phases of the life cycle (young and middle adulthood). In fact, such differential prevalence of certain coping modes may reflect the choice of appropriate strategies on a life-stage-related basis.

CONCLUSIONS

Diverse attempts at theoretical integration converge in acknowledging the dynamic, and interactive, relationships among components of the stress and coping paradigm and point to increasingly complex models of stress. Interrelationships are also "layered" to encompass the physiological, psychological, social, and cultural levels. Assumptions about the long-term effectiveness of certain "desirable" coping behaviors also merit examination. What appear to be effective short-term problem resolutions may not necessarily be functional for long-term solutions. Thus, the energy expenditure involved in actively coping in the face of a hostile environment may prove to be too much for an older person, and decline may set in after an apparently successful initial adjustment to a given stressor.

Research, however, lags far behind in its ability to deal operationally with the complexities suggested by theoretical analyses of coping. Meanwhile, gerontological practitioners and policymakers await research-based guidelines for practice and are called upon to work with vulnerable elderly even before such guidelines become available.

As we reflect on this chapter, we believe that our discussion of coping among vulnerable elderly has raised more questions than it has answered. We do see one common theme throughout our discussion—that of complexity. First, there is the complexity of placing vulnerability in the larger context of a stress paradigm. The model of stress, resources, and outcomes presented here incorporates vulnerability in each component, rather than relegating it to a single specific component of the model. This complexity is of a conceptual nature, and we are not sure that vulnerability can ever be conceptualized more simply.

Consideration of the coping resources and strategies of vulnerable elders within a delineated and cohesive conceptual framework of stress research holds both important challenges and promise for integration of gerontological research and theory in practice relevant directions. It is one area where gerontological researchers can benefit from input from clinicians and service providers, as well as from elderly consumers, in defining and operationalizing their constructs. Hopefully, it is also an area where practice-relevant data may be obtained based on consideration of the coping skills and adaptive responses of elders, even as they confront vulnerability. This is very important on a philosophical as well as on a research and practice level, since it invites us to refrain from patronizing even the most vulnerable elders through acknowledging and expressing respect for their personal and psychological resources. It also holds hope for building on coping resources and working for therapeutic change through intervention aimed at reinforcing coping skills and enhancing coping resources.

REFERENCES

Aldwin, C. M., & Revenson, T. A. (1987). Does coping help? A reexamination of the relation between coping and mental health. *Journal of Personality and Social Psychology, 53*, 237–348.

Antonovsky, A. (1979). *Health, stress, and coping.* San Francisco: Jossey-Bass.

Antonovsky, A. (1987). *Unrevealing the mystery of health: How people manage stress and stay well.* San Francisco: Jossey-Bass.

Appley, M. H., & Trumbull, R. (1986). Development of the stress concept. In M. N. Appley & R. Trumbull (Eds.), *Dynamics of stress.* New York: Plenum.

Baltes, M. M., & Reizensein, R. (1986). The social world in long-term care institutions: Pyschological control toward dependency? In M. M. Baltes and P. B. Baltes (Eds.), *The psychology of control and aging.* Hillsdale, NJ: Lawrence Erlbaum Associates.

Billings, A. G., & Moos, R. H. (1982). Stressful life events and symptoms: A longitudinal model. *Health Psychology, 1,* 99–117.

Borawski, E., Kahana, E. & Kercher, K. (1987, November). Coping strategies as predictors of psychological distress among health impaired elders. Paper presented at the 40th annual Meeting at the Gerontological Society of America, Washington, D.C.

Clark, A. W. (1982). Personal and social resources as correlates of coping behavior among the aged. *Psychological Reports, 31,* 577–578.

Coe, R. M. (1965). Self-conception and institutionalization. In A. M. Rose & W. A. Peterson (Eds.), *Older people and their social world.* (pp. 225–243). Philadelphia: Davis.

Cohen, S., & Wills, T. A. (1985). Stress, social support, and the buffering hypothesis. *Psychological Bulletin, 98,* 310–357.

Dean, A., Lin, N., & Ensel, W. M. (1981). The epidemiological significance of social support systems in depression. *Research in Community and Mental Health, 2,* 77–109.

Dougherty, L. M., Krauss, I. K. & Finello, K. M. (1982). *Coping with anticipated relocation by the elderly.* Andrus Gerontology Center. Los Angeles: University of Southern California.

Elwell, F. & Crannell-Maltbie, A. D. (1981). The impact of role loss upon coping resources and life satisfaction of the elderly. *Journal of Gerontology, 10*(1), 223–232.

Eysenck, H. J. (1982). Stress, disease and personality: The innoculation effect. In C. L. Cooper (Ed.), *Stress research: Issues for the 1980s.* New York: Wiley & Sons.

Felton, B., & Kahana, E. (1974). Adjustment and situationally bound locus of control among institutionalized aged. *Journal of Gerontology, 29,* 295–301.

Felton, B. J. & Revenson, T. A. (1987). Age differences in coping with chronic illness. *Psychology and aging, 2,* 164–170.

Folkman, S., & Lazarus, R. S. (1980). An analysis of coping in a middle-aged community sample. *Journal of Health and Social Behavior, 21,* 219–239.

Folkman, S., Lazarus, R.S., Pimley, S., & Novacek, J. (1987). Age differences in stress and coping processes. *Psychology and Aging, 2,* 171–184.

Hooyman, N. R., Rathbone E., & Klingbel, K. (1982). Serving the vulnerable elderly: The detection, intervention, and prevention of familial abuse. *Urban and Social Change Review, 15*(2), 9–13.

Johnson, R. J., Lund, D. A., & Dimond, M. F. (1986). Stress, self-esteem and coping during bereavement among the elderly. *Social Pyschology Quarterly, 49*(3), 273–279.

Kahana, B. (1978). Projective testing with the aged. In M. Storandt, I. Siegler, & M. Elias (Eds.), *Clinical psychology and aging.* New York: Plenum.

Kahana, B., & Kahana, E. (1984). Stress reactions. In P. Lewinsohn & L. Teri (Eds), *Clinical geropsychology.* New York: Pergamon Press.

Kahana, B., Harel, Z., & Kahana, E. (1988). Predictors of psychological well-being among survivors of the Holocaust. In J. Wilson, Z. Harel, & B. Kahana (Eds.), *Human adaptation to extreme stress: From the Holocaust to Vietnam.* New York: Plenum Press.

Kahana, E., & Kahana. B. (1983). Environmental continuity, discontinuity, futurity and adaptation of the aged. In G. Rowles & R. Ohta (Eds.), *Aging and milieu: Environmental perspectives on growing old.* New York: Academic Press.

Kahana, E., Fairchild, T., & Kahana, B. (1982). Adaptation. In D. J. Mangen & W. A. Peterson (Eds.), *Research instruments in social gerontology, 1.* Minneapolis: University of Minnesota Press.

Kahana, E., Kahana, B., & Young, R. (1984). Social factors in institutional living. In W. Peterson & J. Quadragno (Eds.), *Social bonds in later life: Aging and independence.* Beverly Hills: Sage.

Kahana, E., Kahana, B., & Young, R. (1987a). Strategies of coping and postinstitutional outcomes. *Research on Aging, 9,* 182–199.

Kahana, E., Kahana, B., & Young, R. (1987b). Influences of diverse stressors on health and well-being of community aged. In A. M. Fowler (Ed.), *Posttraumatic stress: The healing journey.* Washington, D.C.: Veterans Administration.

Kahana, E., Liang, J., & Felton, B. (1980). Alternative models of person-environment fit: Prediction of morale in three homes for the aged. *Journal of Gerontology, 35* (4), 584–595.

Kalish, R. A. (1969). Introduction. In R. A. Kalish (Ed.), *Dependencies of old people.* Ann Arbor: University of Michigan Institute of Gerontology.

Kessler, R. C. (1987). The interplay of research design strategies and data analysis procedures in evaluating the effects of stress on health. In S. V. Kasl and C. L. Cooper (Eds.), *Stress and health: Issues in research methodology.* Great Britain: Wiley & Sons Ltd.

Kiyak, H., & Montgomery, R. (1985). Coping patterns among older persons with Alzheimer's disease and their families. *Social Gerontologist, 25,* 171–172.

Lawton, M. P., & Nahemow, L. (1973). Ecology and the aging process. In C. Eisdorfer & M. P. Lawton (Eds.), *Psychology of adult development and aging.* Washington, D.C.: American Psychological Association.

Lazarus, R. S. (1966). *Psychological stress and the coping process.* New York: McGraw Hill.

Lazarus, R. S., & Delongis, A. (1983). Psychological stress and coping in aging. *American Psychologist, 38*(3), 245–254.

Lazarus, R. S., & Folkman, S. (1984). *Stress, appraisal, and coping.* New York: Springer.

Lefcourt, H. M. (1982). (Ed.). *Locus of control: Current trends in theory and research.* Hillsdale, NJ: Lawrence Erlbaum Associates.

Lowenthal, M. F. (1977). Toward a sociopsychological theory of change in adulthood and old age. In J. E. Birren & K. Warner Schaie (Eds.), *Handbook of the psychology of aging.* New York: Van Nostrand Reinhold.

Lowenthal M. F., & Robinson, B. (1976). Social networks and isolation. In R. Binstock & E. Shanas (Eds.), *Handbook of aging and the social sciences.* New York: Van Nostrand Reinhold.

McCrae, R. R. (1982). Age differences in the use of coping mechanisms. *Journal of Gerontology, 37,* 454–460.

McCrae, R. R. (1984). Situational determinants of coping responses: Loss, threat, and challenge. *Journal of Personality and Social Psychology, 46,* 919–928.

McCrae, R. R. & Costa, P. T. (1986). Personality, coping, and coping effectiveness in an adult sample. *Journal of Personality, 54*, 385–405.

Menaghan, E. (1983). Individual coping efforts and family studies: Conceptual and methodological issues. *Marriage and Family Review, 6*(1 & 2), 113–135.

Morris, J. & Sherwood, S. (1983). Informal support resources for vulnerable elderly persons: Can they be counted on, why do they work? *International Journal on Aging and Human Development, 18*(2), 1983–1984.

Neugarten, B., & Guttman, D. (1968). Age-sex roles and personality in middle age: A thematic apperception study. In B. Neugarten (Ed.), *Middle age and aging*. Chicago: University of Chicago Press.

Norris F., & Murrell F. (1984). Protective function of resources related to life events, global stress and depression in older adults. *Journal of Health and Social Behavior, 25*, 424–437.

Pearlin, L. I., & Schooler, C. (1978). The structure of coping. *Journal of Health and Social Behavior, 19*, 2–21.

Pearlin, L. I., Lieberman, M., Menaghan, E., & Mullan, J. (1981). The stress process. *Journal of Health and Social Behavior, 22*, 337–356.

Rosow, I. (1967). *Social integration of the aged*. New York: Free Press.

Selye, H. (1956). *The stress of life*. New York: McGraw Hill.

Simons, R. L., & West, G. E. (1985). Life changes, coping resources and health among the elderly. *International Journal on Aging and Human Development, 20* (3), 1984–1985.

Stephens, M. A. P., Norris, V. K., Kinney, J. M., Ritchie, S. W. & Grotz, R. C. (1988). Stressful situations in caregiving: Relations between caregiver coping and well-being. *Psychology and Aging, 3*, 208–209.

Thoits, P. A. (1983). Multiple identities and psychological well-being: A reformulation and test of the social isolation hypothesis. *American Sociological Review, 48*, 174–187.

Turner, R. J. (1983). Direct and indirect and moderating effects of social supports on psychological distress and associated conditions. In H. Kaplan (Ed.), *Psychological distress trends in theory and research*. New York: Academic Press.

Turner, R. J., Frankel, B. G., & Levin, D. M. (1983). Social support: Conceptualization, measurement and implications for mental health. *Research in Community and Mental Health, 3*, 67–111.

6

Vulnerability and Social Factors

Linda K. George

The major theme of this chapter is that social factors can produce, protect against, and correlate with vulnerability in later life. Social factors are not unique in that regard—biological, psychological, and environmental factors play similar roles. But the focus here will be on selected social factors and the ways in which they are related to particular forms of vulnerability that are prevalent in later life.

The chapter is organized into three major sections. First, the concept of vulnerability is examined: what it means conceptually; the diverse forms of vulnerabililty affecting the older population; and identification of the kinds of vulnerability that will be discussed in this context. Second, the literature documenting the relationships between social factors and well-being will be briefly reviewed. This research base was developed without reference to the concept of vulnerability. Consequently, the first two sections are independent. In the third section, I will attempt to link the concept of vulnerability to what we know about the relationships between social factors and well-being in later life. This section also includes recommendations for future research.

Before turning to the concept of vulnerability, a brief comment is needed about the basic theoretical orientation underlying this discussion. I will rely on a conceptual foundation based on the stress and adaptation paradigm. More specifically, I will focus on three generic concepts: (1) stressors, which are conceptualized as conditions that pose adaptive challenges for individuals; (2) resources that operate as protective factors for individuals, either because they counteract the potentially negative effects of stress or because they reduce the likelihood of experiencing stress; and

(3) well-being, as measured in multiple dimensions, which is conceptualized as a relevant outcome against which the effects of stress and resources can be observed. My choice of the stress perspective rests on two factors. First, because most of my research is based explicitly or implicitly on a stress perspective, I have a proclivity for framing scientific problems using the terminology, models, and assumptions of that paradigm. Second, I believe that the stress perspective serves as a useful framework for exploring the links between social factors and vulnerability. Nonetheless, I believe and hope that the conclusions made in this chapter can be related to other theoretical paradigms. Thus, one need not be a devotee of the stress perspective to understand or give credence to the issues addressed in this chapter.

VULNERABILITY: DEFINITION AND IMPLICATIONS

Webster (1961) defines *vulnerable* as "capable of being wounded" and "open to attack or damage." Thus, in everyday usage, vulnerability connotes a sense of being at risk for negative or harmful outcomes. The source of risk is definitionally unimportant, as is the nature of the negative outcomes. There are many kinds of attacks that humans can suffer and multiple kinds of damage that can result from those attacks.

The term vulnerability also has become popular in gerontological circles—as evidenced, in part, by the theme of this volume. Interestingly, however, specific conceptual and/or operational definitions of vulnerability are virtually absent in the gerontological literature. Instead, the term vulnerability typically is used in a shorthand way and in a manner very similar to the usage recommended by Webster—that is, as a method of connoting high risk for negative outcomes. Though this shorthand mode of communication may be adequate for some gerontological purposes (sensitizing an audience to age-related risks), it is not adequate for the two most important issues addressed by the gerontological community: research and policy. Research requires concepts that can be defined in specific conceptual and operational terms. Given the absence of a scientifically adequate definition, it is not surprising that virtually no current research is based directly on the concept of vulnerability. The development, targeting, and implementation of public policies also requires specificity. It would be impossible, in the absence of at least an implied definition, to design or implement policies for the vulnerable elderly.

As one begins to grapple with the concept of vulnerability in relation to later life, it becomes immediately obvious that there are multiple forms of vulnerability. As noted previously, humans are vulnerable to many kinds of attack and are at risk of multiple types of damage. It has been argued that older adults are at increased risk of mortality, physical disability, mental illness and intellectual decline, poverty, and social isolation—to name but a few illustrations—compared to their middle-aged and younger peers. More important perhaps than the recognition that negative outcomes take multiple forms in later life is the awareness that different conditions—different sources of vulnerability, if you will—generate these varying outcomes. There is no such phenomenon as *the* vulnerable elderly. Rather, there are distinct, albeit potentially overlapping, subgroups of the elderly who are at increased risk for different negative outcomes.

Thus far, I have made the points that (1) the terms *vulnerable* and *vulnerability* are definitionally vague; (2) multiple forms of vulnerability are experienced by humans in general and older adults in particular; and (3) precisely because of its multiple forms, it is probably impossible to forge a precise and scientifically adequate definition of vulnerability. Given these conclusions, perhaps the term vulnerability should be purged from the vocabulary of the gerontological community. Given its inherently ambiguous nature, perhaps use of the term causes problems rather than helps in the development of solutions. After all, the epidemiologists already have developed a useful vocabulary for scientific discussions of being "open to attack or damage." Epidemiologists have contributed the concept of risk factors for disease and other negative outcomes and the notion of at-risk populations as a method of identifying those persons most likely to experience disease or other negative outcomes.

In terms of addressing specific research questions or developing specific policy options, I believe that the term *vulnerability*, as it is conventionally defined, should be deleted from the gerontological vocabulary. Use of the term simply does not strengthen our ability to generate knowledge about later life or to develop effective policies for older adults. Before striking this term from our lexicon, however, it may be worth examining its emergence and use from another perspective. Perhaps we should ask ourselves *why* this term has become popular among gerontologists and attempt to identify the assumptions and goals underlying its use. I do not pretend to have special insights into those issues. In thinking about the emergence of the term vulnerability in the gerontological community, however, I was struck by two facets of its use that may help to explain its attraction and/ or illuminate the underlying goals and concerns of those who use it. Though this is purely speculation, I will briefly share those two ideas with you.

The first aspect of the term vulnerability that engaged my attention is the fact that it focuses attention on persons who are "capable of being wounded," not on those who have already been wounded. Thus, although the term may not always have been used this way, it appears that the vulnerable elderly are those who are at risk of negative outcomes, rather than those who already exhibit damage in whatever area of well-being is under consideration. Hence, if I am interested in the negative outcome of disability, the vulnerable elderly are those who are not yet disabled but are at risk of becoming so. Given this focus on being at risk rather than having experienced negative outcomes, the term *vulnerability* appears to share some assumptions with the term *prevention*, which also has become popular in the health and social science literature in general and the gerontology literature in particular. In terms of the intellectual history of science, it is perhaps more than coincidental that the terms vulnerability and prevention emerged and became popular at approximately the same time.

The second facet of the term vulnerability that engaged my interest also is related to the notion that vulnerable people are persons who have not yet been wounded, but are at risk of damage. If those conditions define the vulnerable, then who are the nonvulnerable? It appears that there must be at least two groups of the nonvulnerable. One group consists of those persons who have already experienced attack and suffered resulting damage. The second group might be described as the *invulnerable*—as those who are not at risk of being wounded. It is this latter group that interests me the most and leads me to question the nature of the implicit goals being sought by those scientists and policymakers who wish to focus our attention on the vulnerable elderly. To make any progress in understanding what vulnerability is and why it is important, we also need to know what invulnerability is.

It is my assumption that those who are concerned with the vulnerable elderly somehow hope to move them to the invulnerable category. But what does it mean to be invulnerable? More specifically, and more important for our purposes, who are the invulnerable elderly? One possibility is a definition based on absolutes—that is, the invulnerable are those who are incapable, in an absolute and permanent sense, of being wounded. Given the kinds of outcomes with which most gerontologists are concerned—outcomes such as chronic illness and disability; social isolation; mental health and intellectual vigor; and, of course, mortality—an absolute definition of invulnerability is not realistic. Regardless of age, no one is absolutely invulnerable to negative outcomes in these life domains. (An interesting exception to this rejection of the notion of absolute invulnerability might be minimal economic security. Many gerontologists—and I am one of them—believe that policies can be developed that would ensure that all older adults are invulnerable to poverty.)

If, however, we can agree that the notion of absolute invulnerability is generally unrealistic, then some more relativistic definition must be sought. And here, frankly, is where I become confused—a state that, I believe, is shared more generally by those in the gerontological field. What is a realistic definition of invulnerability in general, and for older adults in particular? What do we need to know to make the vulnerable elderly invulnerable? How can we know whether public policies effectively serve the vulnerable elderly? There are numerous ways that we could define invulnerability in relativistic terms. One possibility is simply that of lessened risk. The vulnerable elderly are at high risk of some kind of negative outcome; therefore, our task is to lessen their risk. Fine, but how much is enough? Should we be satisfied with a 10% risk reduction, should we hold out for a 25% risk reduction, or what? If we are going to think in terms of vulnerability versus invulnerability, there will always be pressures to identify a cutoff point that distinguishes one category from the other. Moreover, in the absence of a consensual cutoff point, there will be serious disagreements about how effectively the vulnerable elderly have been served.

Another possibility, also based on relativistic criteria, is to conceptualize invulnerability in more dynamic terms. From this perspective, our efforts are successful when we prevent vulnerability from leading to negative outcomes for longer and longer periods of time. After all, although being vulnerable is not as pleasant as being invulnerable, it is the attack and resulting damage that one most wants to avoid—and the longer one can avoid it, the better. But again, we are haunted with questions about how much is enough. How do we rate the success of a medical treatment for a terminal illness that prolongs life a year longer than previous treatments, but nonetheless does not cure the disease? Will the gerontological community be satisfied with programs that delay rather than preclude negative outcomes? Can we be satisfied with time-limited invulnerability rather than permanent invulnerability?

A final method of assessing invulnerability is to choose an objective, but nonabsolute, reference as a basis of comparison. Though its use may be implicit, I am convinced that this is the typical way that scientists, policymakers, and practitioners measure progress toward reduced vulnerability. There are numerous examples of this mode of thinking. We have become a society that is willing to live with an unemployment rate of 5% to 6%. Areas with unemployment rates lower than 5% are viewed as unusually prosperous; those with unemployment rates in excess of 6% are viewed as economically troubled communities in need of special efforts. This definition of an acceptable level of unemployment clearly is relative. In such a society, the population is not invulnerable to unemployment in an absolute sense. Given that unemployment does not rise above the reference point of 5% to 6%, however, economic conditions will be viewed as "good enough"—and special efforts to further reduce vulnerability to unemployment are unlikely.

I believe that gerontologists concerned about the vulnerable elderly also have an implied reference point in their minds, a reference point that will allow them to know when conditions are "good enough." My hypothesis is that, for many gerontologists, that reference point is the conditions of younger and middle-aged adults. That is, I believe that gerontologists typically compare the conditions of older adults to those of middle-aged and younger adults—and when older adults appear to be on the short end of the stick, we view them as vulnerable. Thus, the areas we worry about most are those where age itself is a risk for negative outcomes. For many gerontologists, the vulnerable elderly are those older persons who are at greater risk of negative outcomes than are their younger or middle-aged peers. If my interpretation is correct, any of us can accept the fact that life is imperfect, but we do not want to believe that life is inherently and systematically less perfect for older adults.

Perhaps the best illustration of this approach to defining vulnerability and invulnerability is the literature on the economic status of the elderly as it has evolved over the past 20 to 25 years. During the 1960s, the majority of literature on the economic status of the elderly focused on differences between the elderly and the nonelderly in terms of poverty rates—and, at that time, older persons were at substantially greater risk of poverty than were middle-aged and younger adults (Orshansky, 1965). During the 1970s, a number of policy changes and cohort differences began to generate an older population that was characterized by much lower rates of poverty than had been true in earlier periods for earlier cohorts. Consequently, by the late 1970s and consistently during the 1980s, older adults generally have been at no greater risk of poverty than their younger peers (Duncan et al., 1987; Radner, 1986). Scientists and policymakers have come to see this situation as "good enough." As a consequence, there now are fewer studies of age differences in economic status, those studies that are performed lead to less heated discussion, and many gerontologists are now willing to seriously debate the need to redistribute some of the economic resources of the wealthy elderly to other segments of the population (Chen, 1985; Crystal, 1986).

Obviously, this notion that vulnerability in later life constitutes greater risk than that experienced by middle-aged and younger adults is not the only way that vulnerability is implicitly conceptualized by gerontologists. Moreover, there are clearly areas to which this kind of definition does not apply. To choose the most obvious, gerontologists do not expect equality in mortality rates across age groups. Nonetheless, many of us would like to believe in Fries's (1980) notion of the rectangularized life expectancy curve, in which all of us would live healthy, disability-free lives until our life span is realized. Under this scenario, proximity to death would continue to distinguish the elderly from the nonelderly, but many other sources of age-based vulnerability would be eliminated.

In summary, I believe that the term vulnerability, as it is conventionally used, offers little to the gerontological enterprise in terms of setting the stage for important research or effective policy. Nonetheless, if I have analyzed some of its implied meanings correctly, it sensitizes us to two implicit and important concerns of gerontologists: (1) concerns that efforts be focused on at-risk older adults to reduce, delay, or prevent the damage for which they are at risk; and (2) concerns that, to the extent possible, old age itself be reduced or eliminated as a source of risk for negative outcomes.

SOCIAL FACTORS AND WELL-BEING IN LATER LIFE

There is vast literature on the relationships between social factors and multiple dimensions of well-being in later life. I obviously cannot do justice to this literature in this chapter. To restrict this review to a manageable scope, discussion will be focused in two major ways. First, this review will focus on four *generic models* of the relationships between social factors and well-being in later life. Extant research suggests that these models represent the primary methods by which social factors are hypothesized to produce, modify, and protect against vulnerability in later life. Examples of research illustrating these four generic models will be cited, but the range of research based on these models will not be comprehensively reviewed. In line with my previous comments, special attention will be paid to age differences in both the distribution of social factors and their associations with well-being.

Second, I will focus on those social factors that can be conceptualized as social resources—as factors that protect against and/or minimize the effects of potentially harmful events or circumstances (George, 1980; Pearlin et al., 1981; Wheaton, 1983). Examples of social factors generally viewed as social resources include social support, social integration, economic resources, and relevant socialization experiences. Although all these social resources may be broadly beneficial, extant research suggests that they are especially important during times of stress or other forms of attack.

Restricting my review to social resources obviously neglects some of the social factors that previous research suggests are closely related to well-being during later life, especially demographic factors. This decision rests in part on simple expedience; only so much material can be covered in a single chapter. But the decision also rests in part on the theoretical ambiguity of most demographic variables. Demographic variables are commonly assumed to serve as proxies for underlying, typically unmeasured, mechanisms and processes. Unfortunately, it is seldom clear whether or not the underlying mechanisms are social. Sociologists typically assume that race and gender differences, for example, represent the effects of different socialization experiences or differential access to society's opportunity structures. Biologists are likely to interpret those same relationships as indicators of genetic or physiological mechanisms. Though this kind of ambiguity applies to other factors commonly examined by social scientists, demographic factors appear to be particularly problematic in this regard.

Loss of Social Resources as Causes of Declines in Well-Being

Perhaps the simplest model of the relationships between social resources and well-being posits that loss of social resources can lead directly to decrements in well-being (Dohrenwend, 1973; Lin et al., 1979). This model explicitly recognizes that social resources constitute a double-edge sword: the presence or gain of social resources promotes well-being; the absence or, especially, the loss of social resources not only decreases the availability of protective agents, but also is a form of stress that can directly decrease well-being. Thus, the loss of social resources is a kind of "double-whammy" because it represents both a source of attack or stress and a loss of resources that makes coping with other stressors more difficult.

Loss of social resources can have different outcomes, depending on the magnitude of the loss. If the loss is sizable in terms of either objective parameters or psychological significance, immediate decrements in well-being may result. If the loss of social resources is not very severe, well-being may be sustained at the preloss level, although the individual is left with fewer resources for confronting future stressors.

A large research base supports the hypothesis that loss of social resources can lead to negative outcomes in multiple domains, including physical health, mental health, and subjective well-being (DeLongis et al., 1982; Dohrenwend, 1973; Lin et al., 1979; Pearlin et al., 1981; Williams et al., 1981). Most of this research is based on a stress and coping paradigm. Three qualitatively different kinds of stressors have been examined—chronic stressors, stressful life events, and daily hassles—and all three types have been related to increased risk of declines in well-being (Burks & Martin, 1985; DeLongis et al., 1982; Holahan et al., 1984; Kanner et al., 1981; Monroe, 1983). Though not all stressors represent losses of social resources, many can be viewed that way. Examples of stressors that represent losses of social resources include the termination of relationships with significant others (via death, disability, or disagreement), disruptions in relationships with significant others, financial setbacks, and loss of valued roles.

A more theoretically elegant variant of this basic model is to posit that social resources mediate or intervene between stressors and well-being. The purpose of mediating variable models is to explicate the process by which an antecedent variable impacts upon an outcome of interest—to hypothesize and test a causal model. If social resources are examined as mediators of the effects of stress on well-being, the hypothesis tested is that stress has negative effects on well-being *because* experience of the stressor leads to the loss of important social resources. Thus, this model is simply an elaboration of the hypothesis that loss of social resources can lead to decrements in well-being.

Mediating models have received limited attention in the gerontological literature. Available evidence, however, suggests that such models may advance our understanding of the processes by which social factors affect well-being. For example, several studies suggest that marital dissolution can have negative consequences for well-being in part because loss of spouse represents loss of a significant other, loss of income, and loss of access to other valued roles—all of which are losses of social resources (Chiriboga, 1982; Glick et al., 1974). Similarly, although the vast majority of retirees are pleased to leave the labor force, those persons who find the retirement transition stressful typically miss one or more resources previously provided by the job (e.g., relationships with work peers, income) (Palmore et al., 1984; Atchley, 1976). Mediating variable models hold considerable promise for informing us as to why particular transitions are experienced as stressful and merit increased attention in future research.

In this society, access to social resources tends to be age-related, with older adults generally concentrated at the lower end of the distribution. Some age differences in social resources reflect cohort effects. For example, because of cohort differences in education and occupation, as well as in macro-level economic conditions, older cohorts average lower levels of economic resources than do younger cohorts (Duncan et al., 1987). Similarly, older cohorts have had different socialization experiences than their younger peers—socialization experiences that, because of rapid social change, are sometimes less useful than those obtained by younger cohorts (George, 1983). Distributions of social resources also reflect age effects. Retirement is a nearly universal social institution and, though it is typically voluntary, leads to an average 50% decline in annual income (Palmore et al., 1985).

Role loss is generally greater during later life than earlier in life, resulting in lower levels of social integration during old age (Rosow, 1985). Age-related patterns of mortality and morbidity result in shrinking support networks for many older adults. Thus, there is substantial evidence that older adults are, on average, more disadvantaged in social resources than are their younger peers. Consequently, loss of social resources might be expected to be a more prevalent cause of declines in well-being among older than younger adults. Unfortunately, evidence supporting this hypothesis is lacking.

Social Resources as Compensatory Factors

Another popular model of the role of social factors in promoting well-being during later life posits that social resources can compensate for losses experienced in other domains. That is, provided that resources are sufficient, it is possible to experience significant stress without resulting declines in well-being. Again, the degree to which the outcome is favorable is expected to be a function of the magnitude of the resources available, as compared to the severity of the demands generated by the stressor. If the ratio is very high, social resources may totally compensate for the stressor, precluding declines in well-being. If relevant social resources are absent or severely limited, a decline in well-being is expected.

Tests of the compensatory hypothesis require analyses in which persons who experience the same stressor(s), but who differ in the availability of social resources, are compared in terms of well-being outcomes. The social science literature in general and the gerontological literature in particular include numerous studies based on this general model (Billings & Moos, 1984; Norris & Murrell, 1984; Krause, 1986). In general, results suggest that social resources can compensate for losses experienced in other domains and can either sustain or minimize declines in well-being. The presence of adequate social support has been demonstrated to reduce the probability that stressors will lead to physical or mental health problems (Billings & Moos, 1984; Krause, 1987). Similarly, the risk of institutionalization can be minimized if significant others are willing to provide sufficient instrumental assistance (Colerick & George, 1986). Financial resources often play a significant compensatory role in coping with stress (Norris & Murrell, 1984). Given sufficient financial resources, one often can simply purchase solutions, or at least partial solutions, to problems. Social integration and relevant socialization experiences also can help individuals to effectively confront stress and minimize its potential negative consequences (George, 1983).

Age differences in social resources again bode poorly for older individuals, as compared to their younger peers. Precisely because social resources typically shrink during later life, older individuals might be expected to have fewer ways to compensate for the losses that they experience. Again, however, empirical evidence supporting this hypothesis is lacking.

Social Resources as Moderating Variables

A somewhat more complex model posits that social resources moderate or condition the effects of stress on well-being (Cronkite & Moos, 1984; Wheaton, 1983, 1985). Whereas the two previous models are, in statistical terms, main-effects models, the moderating hypothesis is an interaction model. In general, moderating variables operate in more complex and specific ways on outcomes than do main-effect variables. According to the moderating hypothesis, the effects of stress on well-being differ at varying levels of social resources. Note that moderating-variable models are compatible with the compensatory perspective described earlier, in that social resources are viewed as potentially counteracting the effects of stress, so that negative outcomes are precluded or minimized. But the moderating-variable model is more complex than the main-effects model based on compensatory mechanisms, in that, in the former, social resources are expected to have nonlinear effects on risk of negative outcomes.

Because of their complexity and limitations on generalizability, social scientists, including gerontologists, have paid only limited attention to the moderating effects of social resources in previous research. Perhaps the most widely investigated model of social resources as moderating variables is the stress-buffering hypothesis. According to this hypothesis, stress increases the likelihood of depression (and perhaps other physical and mental health outcomes) only under conditions of low social support. Conversely, in the presence of adequate emotional and instrumental assistance from significant others, stress should not result in depression. This hypothesis has received mixed, but predominantly positive, support in extant research (Cohen & Wills, 1985; Kessler & McLeod, 1985). And some of this research has been based on samples of older adults.

Again, multiple outcomes are expected, depending on the level of social resources available relative to the demands posed by the stressor. If the resources available are adequate, declines in well-being may be precluded. If relevant social resources are unavailable, declines in well-being are expected. If moderate levels of social resources are available, declines in well-being may be demonstrable, but minimized. As is true for all four models, the relative deprivation of social resources among older people as compared to younger cohorts suggests that older people may suffer more stress-related decrements in well-being than do their younger peers.

An important and frequently ignored issue concerns the degree to which age moderates both the effects of stress on well-being and the effects of social resources in the stress process. My colleagues and I have explored this "age as moderator" hypothesis in several contexts, and we typically find substantial evidence that age moderates a number of relevant relationships. A few examples will illustrate this point, as well as highlighting the nature of conditional relationships more generally. One interaction of possible interest is the degree to which age affects the strength of or adaptational challenges posed by particular kinds of stressors. In line with several other researchers, we find that age significantly moderates the impact of widowhood on mental health outcomes. More specifically, widowhood has more negative consequences for the mental health of young and middle-aged widows than it does for older widows (George et al., 1985). This pattern is typically interpreted as reflecting the degree to which widowhood is experienced as "on-time" versus "off-time."

We also have found that age moderates the effects of social resources on a variety of well-being measures. With regard to life satisfaction, for example, we have reported that income is a less potent predictor for older than for middle-aged adults (George et al., 1985). We also have found that demographic variables are significant predictors of depression and anxiety symptoms for young and middle-aged adults, but are unrelated to symptom levels among older adults (George et al., 1987). Finally, and perhaps most interestingly, in a recent study of recovery from clinical depression, we found that social support facilitated recovery for middle-aged psychiatric patients, but not for older psychiatric patients (George et al., 1989). Thus, the research available suggests that the moderating effects of social resources on well-being merit further investigation, both within the older population and across age groups.

Social Factors as Inoculators Against Stress

A final model of the role of social resources in promoting well-being during later life is what might be called the inoculation model. This model rests on the assumption that social resources have the potential to prevent stresses that would occur in the absence of appropriate social resources (Mitchell & Moos, 1984; Norris & Murrell, 1984). Because this model is preventive in orientation, it is potentially very important. Demonstrating that social resources preclude stressors that place individuals at high risk of negative outcomes would constitute perhaps the strongest possible evidence that social resources merit serious scientific and public policy attention.

Unfortunately, it is very difficult to assemble convincing evidence bearing on the inoculation hypothesis. It is difficult to meet the criteria for causal inference when one is attempting to demonstrate that X causes Y— it is almost impossible to demonstrate that had it not been for X, Y would not have occurred. Although data are always less plentiful than is desirable, there are longitudinal data bases available that permit us to identify subgroups of respondents with high and low levels of social resources and to monitor their subsequent stress experiences. Thus far, however, investigators have examined the effects of social resources on subsequent levels of well-being rather than the effects of social resources on subsequent stress. The good news is that these studies consistently demonstrate that social resources promote well-being. The bad news, from the perspective of the inoculation hypothesis, is that it remains unclear whether social resources directly facilitate well-being, whether resources operate indirectly on well-being by inoculating individuals against stress, or both. To the degree that the inoculation hypothesis has merit, concerns might again be raised about the relative status of older adults. Because they are somewhat disadvantaged in social resources compared to younger and middle-aged adults, older adults may have less access to stress inoculation.

The inoculation hypothesis has tremendous appeal. At a common sense level, many of us seem to subscribe to it. That is, many of us think that there are people who are so resource-rich that they are virtually immune to trouble. At a scientific level, evidence supporting the inoculation hypothesis would inform us about the antecedents of stress—a topic that has received surprisingly little attention thus far. Clearly, this is one area in need of effort in the future.

In what ways has research based on these four models of the relationships among social factors and well-being contributed to gerontologic policy and practice? My guess is that they have had very little impact beyond sensitizing the gerontological community to the concept of social resources. Most of this research has been performed to further our understanding of the ways in which social factors affect well-being in the older population—thus focusing on social resources as they operate in the absence of intervention. Very little of this research has examined either the levels of social resources needed to generate specific levels of well-being or the degree to which interventions designed to alter the distribution of social resources have the same salubrious effects that are observed in nature. In the absence of more specific information, it is not clear that this research base can have a major impact on gerontological policy or practice.

SOCIAL FACTORS, VULNERABILITY, AND WELL-BEING

Our review of the relationships between social resources and well-being indicated that (1) social resources are robustly related to well-being, and (2) social resources function in several ways to affect well-being (i.e., loss of social resources can lead to decrements in well-being; social factors can operate as compensatory mechanisms, diffusing the consequences of stress; social factors can moderate the effects of stress on well-being; and social resources may inoculate individuals against stress). The question to be addressed now is what this has to do with vulnerability during later life. And, of course, an answer to that question depends on what vulnerability is. Thus, we return full circle to the definition of vulnerability.

As noted previously, one definition of vulnerability is increased risk of negative outcomes. Using that definition, previous research on the relationship between social resources and well-being clearly is relevant—and that research strongly suggests that lack of social resources constitutes increased vulnerability for negative outcomes in several domains, including physical health, mental health, subjective well-being, and risk of institutionalization. Moreover, because older adults tend to be disadvantaged in social resources compared to middle-aged and younger adults, it is possible that lack of social resources may make older adults more vulnerable than their younger peers. The problem with this scenario is that, as noted earlier, this definition of vulnerability has no unique meaning and contributes nothing new to our understanding of well-being during later life. The body of research reviewed above documents the relationships between social resources and well-being without any explicit reference to the concept of vulnerability.

In an effort to identify some ways that the term might be usefully included in the gerontological vocabulary, I previously described two issues raised in my mind by the term vulnerability: (1) the notion that vulnerable individuals are persons at risk of negative outcomes rather than those who already have experienced negative outcomes, and (2) the need to develop a meaningful and realistic definition of invulnerability (or nonvulnerability). If those are relevant issues—and I think that they are—then we might ask whether available research concerning the relationships between social resources and well-being informs us about those two issues. Unfortunately, my conclusion is that extant research tells us very little about them.

Though we know that lack of social resources increases the risk of negative outcomes, we know very little, in specific terms, about who is and is not at risk of decrements in well-being. It is helpful, in this regard, to consider the three groups mentioned in our earlier discussion of vulnerability: (1) those who have already experienced declines in well-being; (2) those who are, in at least relative terms, invulnerable and not at risk of negative outcomes; and (3) those who have not yet experienced negative outcomes, but are at risk of them. My review of the literature suggests that we have almost no information to distinguish between the last two groups. That is, we may know, especially after the fact, who does and does not experience declines in well-being, but we are not at all astute in distinguishing amount of risk among those who are currently exhibiting adequate well-being. Similarly, we know very little about how much of a particular resource is needed to substantially reduce the risk of negative outcomes. Thus, there is no accepted definition of relative invulnerability and no evidence indicating the conditions under which individuals are and are not relatively invulnerable to decrements in well-being.

How can we profitably focus our efforts on gaining a better understanding of being at risk and being relatively invulnerable to decrements in well-being? There are no easy answers to this question, but I have three recommendations for beginning efforts. The first two suggestions focus specifically on the role of social factors in reducing the risk of declines in well-being. The third recommendation is the more generic and methodological.

First, more attention needs to be focused on the *specific* relationships among social resources, stressors, and well-being outcomes. There is a general assumption in the social science literature that social resources are broadly beneficial—for example, that social integration assists in coping with all stressors or that all dimensions of social support are equally salient for all well-being outcomes. This is probably an untenable assumption. It is more likely that specific social resources are differentially important for specific stressors and/or specific outcomes. For example, emotional support is probably the most important dimension of social support for preventing depression in the face of stress, whereas instrumental support is probably the most salient dimension of social support for preventing or delaying institutionalization of the impaired elderly. Greater attention to the specificity of the relationships among stress, social resources, and well-being would advance our understanding of who is at risk of what negative outcomes under what conditions.

Second, virtually all current research focuses on *amount* or *quantity* of social resources as predictors of well-being (regardless of which generic model is being tested). Examination of the *quality* of social resources is long overdue. In addition to quantifying social resources, guidelines are needed for assessing their quality, and empirical evidence is needed concerning how quantity and quality combine to affect well-being outcomes. Fortunately, this issue is receiving increased attention in some research on social factors and well-being. In the social support arena, for example, investigators are beginning to develop measures of the quality as well as the quantity of support. Information about the quality of social resources also would advance our ability to specify who is at risk of negative outcomes.

Third, and finally, new analytic methods are needed to examine the concepts of being at risk for, versus being relatively invulnerable to, specific types of negative outcomes. Extant research is based largely on correlational techniques that estimate the linear relationships among stressors, social resources, and well-being outcomes. Such models are useful. Nonetheless, there are limitations inherent in such models. In addition to knowing how individuals rank in order with regard to social resources and well-being, which is the basis of correlational studies, we also need to know about the absolute values of variables under consideration. We need to know not only that more social resources are better, but also how much is enough. In addition, the world does not operate in a fully linear fashion, and statistical techniques that estimate linear relationships are of little help in determining cutoff points for categorizing degrees of risk or levels of well-being. We need to be looking for possible thresholds and determining the minimum levels of resources needed to substantially reduce the risk of negative outcomes. Thus, exploration of being at-risk and of being relatively invulnerable will require creative attention to methodological issues.

Conceptual and empirical efforts directed toward distinguishing between the vulnerable and invulnerable also will be required, I believe, before research concerning the relationships between social factors and well-being will be useful for purposes of policy and practice. As noted previously, it is very difficult to translate research findings into policy- or practice-relevant terms in the absence of information about which older adults are at risk of which negative outcomes. Similarly, policymakers and practitioners find it difficult to think about the redistribution of social resources in the absence of concrete information about the levels of social resources that are needed to substantially reduce the risk of negative outcomes among at-risk older adults. Extant research has been highly useful for painting a picture, in broad brush, of the types of social factors that predict well-being during later life and the multiple ways in which those resources affect well-being. The development of policies and practice guidelines, however, requires information of a more specific nature that is of documented validity in predicting outcomes for individuals and subgroups as well as populations.

In conclusion, the term vulnerability can be used in one of two ways: as a general mode of connoting risk for negative outcomes or as a way of focusing attention on the meaning of being at-risk versus being relatively invulnerable. In my opinion, the term will play a more useful role in the gerontological enterprise if we focus on the latter usage. The development of knowledge about the meaning of being at-risk versus being relatively invulnerable would be a major contribution to social science as a whole, as well as to gerontological research and policy in particular.

REFERENCES

Atchley, R. C. (1976). *The sociology of retirement.* Cambridge, MA: Screnkman.

Billings, A. G., & Moos, R. H. (1984). Coping, stress, and social resources among adults and unipolar depression. *Journal of Personality and Social Psychology, 46,* 877–891.

Burks, N., & Martin, B. (1985). Everyday problems and life change events: Ongoing versus acute sources of stress. *Journal of Human Stress, 11,* 27–35.

Chen, Y. (1985). Economic status of the aging. In R.H. Binstock & E. Shanas (Eds.), *Handbook of aging and the social sciences* (2nd ed.). New York: Van Nostrand Reinhold.

Chiriboga, D. A. (1982). Adaptation to marital separation in later and earlier life. *Journal of Gerontology, 37,* 109–114.

Cohen, S., & Wills, T.A. (1987). Stress, social support, and the buffering hypothesis. *Psychological Bulletin, 98,* 310–357.

Colerick, E.J., & George, L.K. (1986). Predictors of institutionalization among caregivers of Alzheimer's patients. *Journal of the American Geriatrics Association, 34,* 493–498.

Cronkite, R. C., & Moos, R. H. (1984). The role of predisposing and moderating factors in the stress-illness relationship. *Journal of Health and Social Behavior, 25,* 372–393.

Crystal, S. (1986). Measuring income and inequality among the elderly. *The Gerontologist, 26,* 56–59.

DeLongis, A., Coyne, J., Dakof, G., Folkman, S., & Lazarus, R.S. (1982). Relationship of daily hassles, uplifts, and major life events to health status. *Health Psychology, 1,* 119–136.

Dohrenwend, B. S. (1973). Life events as stressors: A methodological inquiry. *Journal of Health and Social Behavior, 14,* 167–175.

Duncan, G. J., Hill, M. S., & Rodgers, W. (1987). The changing economic status of the young and old. In National Research Council (Ed.), *Demographic change and the well-being of children and the elderly.* Washington, D.C.: National Academy Press.

Fries, J. F. (1980). Aging, natural death, and the compression of morbidity. *New England Journal of Medicine, 303,* 130–135.

George, L. K. (1980). *Role transitions in later life: A social stress perspective.* Monterey, CA: Brooks/Cole.

George, L. K. (1983). Socialization, roles and identity in later life. In A.C. Kerckhoff (Ed.), *Research in the sociology of education and socialization, volume IV: Personal change over the life course.* Greenwich, CT: JAI Press.

George, L. K., Hughes, D. C., Blazer, D. G., & Fowler, N. (1989). Social support and the outcome of major depression. *British Journal of Psychiatry, 154,* 478–485.

George, L. K., Landerman, R., & Blazer, D. G. (1987). Age differences in the antecedents of depression and anxiety: Evidence from the Edpidemiologic Catchment Area Program. Paper presented at the annual meetings of the American Association for the Advancement of Science, Chicago.

George, L. K., Okun, M. A., & Landerman, R. (1985). Age as a moderator of the determinants of life satisfaction. *Research on Aging, 7,* 209–233.

Glick, I. O., Weiss, R. D., & Parkes, C. M. (1974). *The first year of bereavement.* New York: Wiley.

Holohan, C. K., Holahan, C. J., & Belk, S. S. (1984). Adjustment to aging: The role of life stress, hassles, and self-efficacy. *Health Psychology, 3,* 315–328.

Kanner, A. D., Coyne, J. C., Schaefer, C., & Lazarus, R. S. (1981). Comparisons of two modes of stress measurement: Daily hassles and uplifts versus life events. *Journal of Behavioral Medicine, 4,* 1–39.

Kessler, R. C., & McLeod, J. D. (1985). Social support and mental health in community samples. In S. Cohen & S. L. Syme (Eds.), *Social support and health.* New York: Academic Press.

Krause, N. (1986). Social support, stress and well-being among older adults. *Journal of Gerontology, 41,* 512–519.

Krause, N. (1987). Chronic financial strain, social support, and depressive symptoms among older adults. *Psychology and Aging, 2,* 185–192.

Lin, N., Simeone, R. S., Ensel, W. M., & Kuo, W. (1979). Social support, stressful life events, and illness: A model and an empirical test. *Journal of Health and Social Behavior, 20,* 108–119.

Mitchell, R. E., & Moos, R. H. (1984). Deficiencies in social support among depressed patients: Antecedents or consequences of stress? *Journal of Health and Social Behavior, 25,* 438–452.

Monroe, S. M. (1983). Major and minor life events as predictors of psychological distress: Further issues and findings. *Journal of Behavioral Medicine, 6,* 189–205.

Norris, F. H., & Murrell, S. A. (1984). Protective function of resources related to life events, global stress, and depression in older adults. *Journal of Health and Social Behavior, 25,* 424–437.

Orshansky, M. (1965). Counting the poor: Another look at the poverty profile. *Social Security Bulletin, 28,* 3–29.

Palmore, E., Burchett, B., Fillenbaum, G. G., George, L. K., & Wallman, L. (1985). *Retirement: Causes and consequences.* New York: Springer.

Palmore, E. B., Fillenbaum, G. G., & George, L. K., (1984). Consequences of retirement. *Journal of Gerontology, 39,* 109–116.

Pearlin, L. I., Lieberman, M. A., Menaghan, E. G., & Mullan, J. T. (1981). The stress process. *Journal of Health and Social Behavior, 19,* 2–21.

Radner, D. B. (1986). *Change in the money income of the aged and nonaged, 1967–1983.* Social Security Administration Studies in Income Distribution No. 14. Washington, D.C.: U.S. Department of Health and Human Services.

Rosow, I. (1985). Status and role change through the life cycle. In R. H. Binstock & E. Shanas (Eds.), *Handbook of aging and the social sciences* (2nd ed.). New York: Van Nostrand Reinhold.

Webster's Third New Interntional Dictionary. (1961). Springfield, MA: G. & C. Merriam Company.

Wheaton, B. (1983). Stress, personal coping resources, and psychiatric symptoms: An investigation of interactive models. *Journal of Health and Social Behavior, 24,* 208–229.

Wheaton, B. (1985). Models for the stress-buffering functions of coping resources. *Journal of Health and Social Behavior, 26,* 352–364.

Williams, A. W., Ware, J. E., & Donald, C. A. (1981). A model of mental health, life events, and social supports applicable to general populations. *Journal of Health and Social Behavior, 22,* 324–336.

7
Vulnerability and Socioenvironmental Factors

M. Powell Lawton

Understanding the vulnerable aged certainly demands that we understand the forces that act upon them to compound or mitigate their vulnerability. It is to this facet of our concern that a great deal of my career has been devoted; giving attention to the improvement of housing, neighborhood, and institutional environments. This chapter outlines some issues in relation to the kinds of effects that environments have on vulnerable elders; specifically, ordinary unplanned housing, planned housing, and institutions. However, these topics will be preceded by an equally important issue: the effects that vulnerable elders have on our social environment. In other words, as Neugarten (1982) has reiterated so many times, gerontologists must constantly remind ourselves that the aged are part of our society and that although we sometimes view them as object and society as subject, this represents a very limited view. "An aging society" is characterized by the sweeping demographic changes of which we are all aware. Therefore, the chapter will begin with some thoughts about the social environment to which all of us are exposed. How do vulnerable elders help determine the character of the social environment and what are the consequences of these characteristics for the ultimate well-being of the aged and its vulnerable subgroups? I shall suggest that the presence of a growing number of older people in the daily life of our society will have an impact upon the socialization of people to old age. Their situation will be contrasted with the situation of the subgroup that is vulnerable. I shall suggest further that such changes in the socialization process will affect value changes in a direction leading from a separate generational perspective to that of a life-span perspective. In the section on the vulnerable person, dealing with the more traditional causal direction, the effects of three representative environments on the older person will follow. In overview, however, the systemic nature of the interaction between person and environment will be made obvious, where causality is reciprocal rather than unidirectional.

THE SUPRAPERSONAL ENVIRONMENT

In my earlier work on the interactions between the person and the environment, I proposed that one facet of all that can be called "environment" is the "suprapersonal environment" (Lawton, 1970). The suprapersonal environment refers to the aggregate characteristics of the people within physical proximity to the target person, exclusive of the qualities associated with one-on-one interpersonal relationships. A very salient suprapersonal characteristic is the age mix of the people in one's vicinity. This characteristic has been much studied by gerontologists in relation to questions regarding age-segregated versus age-integrated housing.

Much less attention has been paid to the age-related suprapersonal environment as it impinges on society at large. Think first in terms of the statistical probability that one might see in the course of an average day a person who "looks old," if one lived in 1900. That probability has increased almost threefold since that time. The increase in the probability of seeing a vulnerable person is not so easily calculated, but it has undoubtedly increased by some equally astounding factor.

Why is the frequency of seeing an old face significant to society? It is, of course, what we experience that establishes an anchoring point for defining expectations, norms, and the boundaries of deviance. An old face is not nearly so notable today as it was in 1900. Thus, old age is very likely in the process of being defined as increasingly older in a chronological sense as our society ages, as we incorporate a wider range of young-old in our concept of the ordinary, and as we differentiate more finely among the gradations of "old." I am talking here about an across-all-ages effect, over and above the familiar effect due to the distance between a particular perceiver's age and the perceived person's age.

Getting used to the sight of chronologically old people in the environment is significant because such people begin to be included in one's definition of a normal society mix. Not only has the *sight* of older people become a part of everyday life, but with an increase in their number, behavioral interaction skills with older people have become learned more easily by younger people. What to expect of the generalized older person becomes familiar, but so also does the individuality within the class of "old." Increased knowledge of older people means that the desirable features of a mutual process of social integration become recognized and practiced.

One's standards for the expected proportion of older people in daily life are probably very sensitive to deviations from the expected proportions, however. The statistical nature of people's unconscious perceptions is very impressive. Some old research in the study of decision-making presented an experimental subject sitting in front of two lights with the task of predicting whether a light on the left or on the right would light next. The "formula" did not have a "key"; in fact, the sequencing of lights was random within a series of different experimenter-determined proportions of lefts and rights. Yet the distribution of people's predictions for this insoluble problem typically approximated very closely the appropriate actual proportion of lefts and rights. With such a good capacity for probabilistic thinking, people are apt to notice and sometimes react to concentrations or overrepresentative proportions of people with any particular shared characteristic. Thus, where older people appear in an environmental context in the proportion generally expected in that context, people's perceptions of them will be mainstreamed. Where they appear in higher than expected concentrations, social perceptions of them will be refocused on the characteristics of the people that differentiate them from people in general, with possible stigmatization. For example, some have argued that the sight of disabled older people sitting outside an institution contributes to negative social stereotypes about aging in general. The proportion of people over 65 who appear in such stigmatizable concentrations is relatively small. Across all experiences of older people in public view, the normalizing trend should overcome the stigmatizing trend.

Will it be different as the proportion of vulnerable older people among all older people, as in the old-old, increases? As background for considering this question, let us consider what we know about where they are to be found, since visibility is a major facet of the suprapersonal environment. Although only 5% of all people aged 65+ are in institutions, almost one-quarter of those aged 85+ were in institutions as of 1980 (National Center for Health Statistics, 1987a). Another large group is generally homebound. About 10% of all people aged 65+ in the community require help with one or more activities of daily living (ADL), but this figure rises to almost one-third among people 85 and over (National Center for Health Statistics, 1987b). These institutionalized and homebound old-old people, who are thus removed from the suprapersonal environments inhabited by most of us, represent more than half of this age group. This banished population is the most physically stigmatized, in terms of the high probability that some external sign of physical or mental disability exists among the majority of these people. The half of the oldest-old that is left for exposure to the public will tend to be the the more vigorous. Thus, the difference between the well and the sick old-old is emphasized by their differential visibility.

THE SUPRAPERSONAL ENVIRONMENT AND SOCIAL VALUES REGARDING AGING

The presence of more people 65 and over and the public visibility of those who are least impaired will, I predict, lead to some far-reaching changes in personal and social values. The invisibility of the most vulnerable, in turn, may have a very different kind of effect. On the positive side, as I have suggested, the sight of older people engaging in everyday affairs should reduce their perceived deviance. Furthermore, the likely continued improvement in their financial condition, their increasing participation in middle-class leisure pursuits, and the statistical preponderance of older people in good physical health should lead to a decrease in the negative stereotypes about the latter third of life. The mixing of the healthy oldest-old in this pool of increasingly socially integrated people should have the effect of moving upward the age range of what is considered normal. Among other effects of such perceived normality may be a relaxation of the mechanism of denying one's own age. Gerontologists have always been fond of castigating the common folk (that is, the nongerontologists!) for their inability to take a life-span perspective. Persons with a healthy, non-denying life-span perspective are able to relate themselves at present to a trajectory in time whereby they will continue to contribute to and share in society's resources, albeit in different ways as they grow older. At present, we see a personal denial of the life-span perspective running rampant in the form of the panic evidenced among political conservatives over the issue of "generational equity" (Kingson et al., 1986). I see evidence already of a slower, but impressively effective, reaction against this naive type of living in the present. People are at least partly rational beings. Their perception of the widening range of normal aging cannot help but be accompanied by an ability to construe some decisions that they make in the present as having relevance for their well-being in the future, as long as that future is anchored in terms of a good life in old age. In short, we may be able to plan with better ability to project ourselves in future time. The net result should enhance the perception of generational interdependence and acceptance of the idea that to assist the present cohort of older people is to build a basis for helping oneself in later years.

While the dominant attitude and the direction of value changes will be positive in enhancing the status of the class of people aged 65 +, on the negative side, there is the issue of how the vulnerable fit into the picture. The invisibility of a noticeable proportion of the old, and especially the oldest-old, is a feature that emphasizes the difference between them and the rest of us. Their segregation in such large numbers (either in institutions or as homebound people) may fuel unrealistic fantasies regarding their characteristics. One of the major conclusions of age-attitude research is that negative age stereotypes are easy to apply to older people if they are portrayed in the aggregate, while social judgments of specific older people are much more positive (Weinberger & Milham, 1975). If half of the oldest-old are never seen, the stage is set to think of them in pejorative stereotypic terms. Thus, people's unwillingness to think of themselves as future participants in that oldest-old state of life could be amplified by removing the most vulnerable from everyday scrutiny. Such a distancing of self from an entire class of people is the raw material for scapegoating. We thus are faced with conflicting directions of social attitudes, the embracing of the healthy half of the oldest-old and the rejection of the banished impaired.

Robert Binstock (1983) has depicted persuasively the dangers posed by our scientific focus on the oldest-old as a class in creating a new ageism based on the perception that it is those aged 85+ who are not only the lame and the halt, but also the disproportionate consumers of society's resources. I suggest that the new stereotyping is likely to be based particularly on the perceived nonpersonhood of a subgroup that is both sick and banished. If we are lucky, attitudes toward aging will undergo a net improvement based on both the objectively increased well-being of many of the oldest-old and the upper extension of the age range considered normal. By countering this trend, attitudes toward the combination of age and disability will intensify in the negative direction.

Binstock (1983) discusses several directions in which an informed policy and philosophy of social planning might take us to counteract the new old-oldism. We clearly need such concern on a macrosocial level to combat a society-wide problem. On a different level, I shall suggest that there is also an intraindividual and an attitude-based complement to social policy that can assist in tipping the balance toward positive views of the vulnerable and, further, that research can lead us toward this goal. The social purpose of this research into the psychological interior of the most vulnerable aged lies broadly in reducing the perceived nonpersonhood of the most impaired segment and in reducing the psychological, if not the physical, segregation of them as well.

THE VULNERABLE PERSON

Most of what has been termed "environment and aging" has included concerns with the effects of environments on older people, including vulnerable older people. This section will discuss vulnerable people and the environments they inhabit.

In the geropsychological literature, there is a striking absence of scientific study of individuals as they cope with vulnerability and impairment. We do have statistical descriptions of vulnerable people in the aggregate. Such descriptions are static, however, usually describing outcomes and not processes. The most important principles for guiding our thinking about vulnerable people as individuals are, first, that there are many routes to the same outcomes; and second, that the outcomes themselves must be interpreted in terms of how well they fit into the person's overall goals and mix of capabilities and disabilities. It is desirable to be able to characterize the proportion who are cognitively intact, whose psychological well-being is high, or whose engagement with friends is maintained, but this information does not get us beyond the level of the statistical stereotype. What we need is enough knowledge of how the "fourth-age" person, if you will, copes with and uses the complex mix of personal and environmental resources available in pursuing a dynamic life plan (Ryff, 1985). Although the content of people's life plans varies widely, my assertion is that all people create over a lifetime a preferred mix of challenge and support, stimulation and retreat, that they regulate across time, according to the situation, and in response to their internal biology and psychology. Continuity is part of most people's goals because continuity really means the ability to maintain the active role in such self-regulation. The regulatory techniques learned in earlier periods of life will, other things being equal, continue to serve one in very old age and, thus, stability is actively sought.

The perturbations to continuity that have been well studied in aging generally are more marked in the most vulnerable. Poor health, psychological risk, interpersonal losses, and environmental discontinuities are examples. If we are to fortify the ability of our science to tell society about the persistence of individuality and the fallacy of the stereotype of nonpersonhood, we shall have to answer much better than we now can a number of important questions:

- What are the determinants of the ability of some people to continue as vital, engaged, creative, and generative people at the far end of the lifespan?
- What are the factors that lead some vulnerable people to maintain a sense of overall well-being despite the incursion of physical illness or major loss?
- How do people adjust the levels of challenge and stimulation, as resources diminish, to maintain their sense of well-being?

If we are to understand these highly individualized ways of dealing with stressors, we shall also need to consider how environmental stressors interact with different people's needs. This section will examine several environmental types and consider ways in which each might be improved in a way that could counteract vulnerability.

As we look at the individual needs and capabilities of vulnerable people, we see immense variety in the amount of challenge accepted, the amount of challenge actively created by the person, the amount of security provided, and the amount of security deliberately designed by the person into his or her everyday world.

The task of stating what is best for the vulnerable elderly is thus a hopeless one, stated in such categorical terms. When we design a physical environment or make rules and establish practices that dictate suprapersonal environments, we are, in a sense, no longer designing for the individual but for the aggregate. Accounting for the individualized needs of the person is perhaps the key to environmental solutions to the problems of vulnerability and impairment. How to accommodate individual needs and how to encourage the person to perform his or her own accommodation is the theme of this section.

It has become clear over the past two decades that the residential environment must be considered an important part of the long-term care system. The continuum of support may range from the low supportive level of the unplanned housing and service-rich housing to the institution. The supportive quality of any form of residence may be enhanced by the assistance of other people (a nearby child, a healthy spouse, or formal service delivery). Vulnerability may be counteracted in any residential environment not only by informal and formal supports, but also by the older person's own effort, a mode that is easy to neglect in our zeal to provide external support. In this section, some ways of maintaining function in unplanned community housing, planned housing, and institutions will be discussed.

Unplanned Community Housing

The number of vulnerable people living in unplanned housing is in the neighborhood of 2.5 million (the 9.6% ADL-dependent people among the 25 million 65 and over who are neither in institutions nor in planned housing) (National Center for Health Statistics, 1987b). This is an important segment of the banished aged, in that their mobility is limited. In recent years, considerable attention has been devoted to this group. Much growth in the range of in-home services has occurred, and we have in progress a number of demonstrations of creative ways to extend the tenure of mobility-impaired persons in the community (Capitman, 1986; Kemper et al., 1987).

Once again, however, our knowledge is much better in the aggregate than it is regarding the individuals who form the aggregate. What is in the interior of a person struggling to maintain himself or herself in his or her familiar home environment? How can we obtain clues about personal preferences and foster the maintenance of personal choice and autonomy among the severely impaired?

Some observations that we made while studying the households of a group of very old recipients of in-home services illustrate qualitatively this dynamic process of maintaining continuity and autonomy in the face of change and enfeeblement (Lawton, 1985; Saperstein et al., 1985). Our research was concerned with enhancing the ability of the housing unit to contribute to the well-being of very impaired homeowners living alone. It was clearly the availability of the in-home services that allowed these people to remain outside an institution.

As we visited these people and toured their homes, it gradually dawned on us that many of them had managed to maintain their proactivity despite their impairments by actively constructing a home environment that maximized their well-being. We identified the "control center" as a frequent aspect of this microenvironment. A control center consists, first, of a chair, well-chosen for both its comfort and its ability to make getting up easy. That chair is oriented to afford maximum information about the near environment. From it, the person has a clear view of the front door and the front window and the optimal visual angle for seeing the outside entrance, sidewalk, and street. The control center extends the microenvironment by having a television set and a radio within arm's reach. The right and left arms' reach areas have tables or other surfaces where important paraphernalia are kept: food, water, medicine, reading material, pictures, and so on. For a few people, it was necessary to reserve space for a commode that could be accessed without walking far.

Note first that the size of the effective environment is grossly reduced—impairment does reduce the size of one's behavioral world. Second, function is not maintained at its premorbid level. Third, the *best* is made of the reduced ability to function, by environmental knowledge, access, self-care ability, environmental stimulation, and other functions that are fortified by the control center. Finally, the impaired person shapes this environment, despite the heavy effect of other constraining forces. Does such environmental proactivity enhance the sense of well-being and protect the person from mental pathology or from daily institutional dependency? These certainly are questions worthy of research, but we need no research to tell us that such striving to maximize autonomy must be a very powerful motive for a large number of the oldest-old.

I suggest that intensive study is necessary of how the delicate balance between security-maintaining and autonomy-maintaining mechanisms is maintained among the very impaired, not only to increase our ability to serve their individual needs, but also to enable us to counteract the image of nonpersonhood that feeds scapegoating.

Our service interventions for homebound people would benefit considerably from training workers in ways to support proactive behavior, including learning how to encourage vulnerable people to redesign their home environments. If such redesign must be performed by professionals, there is a great deal that can be done by the in-home service worker, given some basic sensitization and training in recognizing home maintenance and livability needs.

We have not fully exploited the possibilities of using neighborhood networks to keep people informed about the individual needs and personalities of local shut-ins. A number of models of neighborhood-level interventions are at hand (Ruffini & Todd, 1981; Spitler & Newcomer, 1986), all, to be sure, designed to bring in support to the vulnerable. But every such program, in turn, has its effects on the neighbor-helpers, such as reminding them that extremely vulnerable people can nonetheless define and act effectively to maintain their own sectors of autonomy and proactivity.

Planned Housing

Another location for vulnerable people is housing planned for older people. Our federal housing programs have produced about one million housing units designed especially for older people (Lawton, 1987). The private sector's effort is impossible to count with the same accuracy, but is by now at least the equal of that number. Think of the original goal of the authors of these programs: a shelter for the vigorous and independent where life could be enriched by the presence of other people like oneself and a program of activity in keeping with these people's motivation.

Most planned housing begins this way, but we now have housing environments that are 25 years old or more and hundreds of thousands of older tenants who have "aged in place." My colleagues and I have studied and written about how some of these environments accommodated to the growing vulnerability of the tenants (Lawton et al., 1980; Lawton et al., 1985).

Service very often must be added as tenants become more vulnerable. This may be accomplished by building new space or converting old space into a congregate kitchen and dining room and adding staff to assist with personal and medical care. More frequently, the functional equivalent of congregate services may be provided on a smaller and more individually targeted scale by local service agencies that come into the housing site with supportive services.

We have never fully reported some of the most disturbing data from our 12-year follow-up of five sites that we studied at the time of their first occupancy (Lawton et al., 1985). Our data show very clearly a decline in both social activity and more indicators of subjective well-being, beyond what might be ascribable to overall changes in the average health of tenants over that time period. We estimated that about 17% of people in the older housing environments had substantial vulnerabilities, which might amount to over 300,000 people in federal and private planned housing. Thus, serving the vulnerable in planned housing means not only attention and care for physical decline, but also increased concern for the personal and social aspects of aging in place.

It seems to me that we have failed to adjust some aspects of the social environment to the individual changes that must occur over the life-span of housing environments. What is laudable self-determination among tenants early in the environment's history may well be best matched by a managerial style that allows challenges to develop and be dealt with by tenants in their own fashion. The realities of chronic illness, however, will inevitably change somewhat the balance between acceptable challenge and necessary security. It is essential that managerial styles accommodate to such changes.

Whether even the best managerial style can support individual needs is not known, but there is clearly a need to pay much more attention to this very salient aspect of the social environment. In particular, a technology for discerning *how* vulnerable is each tenant and for applying managerial effort that assists the person to accept reasonable challenges while recognizing where security and reassurance are required is a tremendous need.

Institutions for the Aged

The 5% of the aged population that lives in institutions may all be classed as vulnerable. They are also unlikely to improve; the great majority of the institutional population at any given time is likely to spend most of the rest of their lives there. Given such permanency, is there any relevance to the idea of maintaining function among these most vulnerable people?

I have argued elsewhere that the competent performance of tasks constitutes a goal of high social value and that both therapeutic and prosthetic steps toward competence are therefore legitimate, no matter how impaired the person (Lawton, 1968). My colleague, Elaine Brody (Brody et al., 1971), has also performed research demonstrating the utility of diagnosing functional areas where the nursing home resident is performing less well than might be expected from physical impairment alone. Targeting treatment on such "excess disabilities" proved to be an effective route toward increasing competent behavior among deeply impaired Alzheimer's patients.

Two other measures may be suggested as potentially useful. One is institutional treatment based on enhancing the degree to which the person feels in control of his or her environment. Classic experiments that taught methods of exerting personal influence on the course of their everyday life to nursing home residents showed favorable effects of such control on both physical and psychological health (Langer & Rodin, 1976; Schulz, 1976).

A second possibility would be for administration in nursing homes to pursue the goal of continued visibility more permeable to outsiders. The more extended family, neighbors, and prospective client families (prospective in the sense of 10 or more years of anticipatory learning) that can be induced to participate in visiting and other institutional activities, the more personalized will be more people's conceptions of the vulnerable elder.

CONCLUSIONS

The number of vulnerable elders whose relative invisibility contributes to the negative social stereotype of aging consists of 1.3 million in institutions, 2.5 million relatively homebound people in ordinary communities, and 0.3 million in planned housing; a total of 4.1 million or about 14% of all older people. Our aging-services network has become aware of their needs for support. This chapter has called attention to the danger that the combination of their impairment and their removal from social visibility will lead to increased ageism. One route toward mitigating such negative stereotyping is to generate new knowledge about vulnerable people as individuals, on the theory that scapegoating is facilitated by aggregation but diffused by personalization. We must know particularly how vulnerable people living in ordinary communities, in planned housing, and in institutions continue to direct their own lives. A focus on how our physical environments, our approaches to managements, our facilitation of contact with normal communities, and our training of direct-care staff can enhance, rather than undermine, personal proactivity is likely to aid in this effort.

REFERENCES

Binstock, R. H. (1983). The aged as scapegoat. *The Gerontologist, 23,* 136–143.

Brody, E. M., Kleban, M. H., Lawton, M. P., & Silverman, H. (1971). Excess disabilities of mentally impaired aged: Impact of individualized treatment. *The Gerontologist, 11,* 124–132.

Capitman, J. A. (1986). Community-based long-term care models, target groups, and impacts on service use. *The Gerontologist, 20,* 389–397.

Kemper, P., Applebaum, R., & Harrigan, M. (1987). Community care demonstrations: What have we learned? *Health Care Financing Review, 8,* 87–100.

Kingson, E. R., Hirshorn, B. A., & Cornman, J. M. (1986). *Ties that bind: Interdependence of generations.* Washington D.C.: Seven Locks Press.

Langer, E., & Rodin, J. (1976). The effects of choice and enhanced personal responsibility for the aged. *Journal of Personality and Social Psychology, 34,* 191–198.

Lawton, M. P. (1968). Social rehabilitation of the aged: Some neglected aspects. *Journal of the American Geriatrics Society, 16,* 1346–1363.

Lawton, M. P. (1970). Ecology and aging. In L.A. Pastalan & D.H. Carson Eds.). *The spatial behavior of older people.* Ann Arbor: Institute of Gerontology, University of Michigan.

Lawton, M. P. (1985). The elderly in context: Perspectives from environmental psychology and gerontology. *Environment and Behavior, 17,* 501–519.

Lawton, M. P. (1987). Housing for the elderly in the mid-1980s. In G. Lesnoff-Caravaglia (Ed.), *Handbook of social gerontology.* New York: Human Sciences Press.

Lawton, M. P., Greenbaum, M., & Liebowitz, B. (1980). The lifespan of housing environments for the aging. *The Gerontologist, 20,* 56–64.

Lawton, M. P., Moss, M., & Grimes, M. (1985). The changing service needs of older tenants in planned housing. *The Gerontologist, 25,* 258–264.

National Center for Health Statistics. Dawson, D., Hendershot, G., & Fulton, J. (1987a). Functional limitations of individuals age 65 years and over. *Advance Data, Vital* and *Health Statistics,* No. 133. Hyattsville, MD: Public Health Service.

National Center for Health Statistics (1987b). Use of nursing homes by the elderly: Preliminary data from the 1985 national nursing home survey. *Advance Data,* No. 135. Hyattsville, MD: U.S. Public Health Service.

Neugarten, B. L. (Ed.). (1982). *Age or need?* Beverly Hills, CA: Sage.

Ruffini, J. L., & Todd, H. F. (1981). "Passing it on": The Senior Block Information Service of San Francisco. In M. P. Lawton & S. L. Hoover (Eds.), *Community housing choices for older Americans* (pp. 135–145). New York: Springer.

Ryff, C. D. (1985). The subjective experience of lifespan transitions. In A. S. Rossi (Ed.), *Gender and the life course* (pp. 97–113). New York: Aldine.

Saperstein, A., Moleski, W. H., & Lawton, M. P. (1985). Determining housing quality: A guide for home-health care. *Pride Institute Journal, 4,* 41–51.

Schulz, R. (1976). Effects of control and predictability on the physical and psychological well-being of the institutionalized aged. *Journal of Personality and Social Psychology, 33,* 563–573.

Spitler, B.J.C., & Newcomer, R. J. (1986). Neighborhoods and self-help programs among the elderly. In R. J. Newcomer, M. P. Lawton, & T. O. Byerts (Eds.), *Housing an aging society* (pp. 161–167). New York: Van Nostrand Reinhold.

Weinberger, L. E., & Milhan, J. (1975). A multidimensional multimethod analysis of attitudes toward the elderly. *Journal of Gerontology, 30,* 343–348.

8

The Impact of Neighborhoods and Ethnicity on Black and White Vulnerable Elderly

David E. Biegel and Kathleen J. Farkas

The interaction of person and environment has long intrigued human ecologists and students of human behavior. Scholars have argued the issues of separateness and interrelatedness between people and the places they live. Practitioners have concerned themselves with how best to understand the impact between person and place and how to use each to their optimum potential. Both have looked at how the person, the environment, and their interaction changes with different types of settings, personalities, and problems.

Environment has been defined as the place that "possesses a structure interrelating physical, social and cultural properties to encourage certain behavior patterns" (LaGory et al., 1985). Aspects of the environment, therefore, are important for all people, but are of special importance to those who experience problems and deficiencies. Lawton et al., (1980) explain that the three strongest factors in determining the link between the person, the environment, and behavior are socioeconomic status, place in the life cycle, and ethnicity. The elderly, in general, and the urban ethnic elderly, in particular, are especially sensitive to environmental characteristics and the impact these characteristics have upon their needs, problems, and behaviors.

The elderly have been described as especially vulnerable to environmental pressures because of age-related changes in physical health and social function (Golant, 1979; Lawton, 1980; Rawles, 1978). The relationship between physical and cognitive competence and environmental needs among the elderly has been conceptually clarified by the writings of Lawton and Nahemow (1973). These authors proposed the ideas of *environmental docility* and *environmental press*.

As people grow older, they often experience health and social problems that limit their ability to function in the community without assistance. Elderly people with these problems become, according to Lawton and Nahemow, "environmentally docile"; they become more passive in manipulating their environments to meet their needs. As the individual becomes less active, the "press" of the environment takes on more significance and becomes a stronger force in determining behavior, satisfaction, and well-being. In other words, the more vulnerable one becomes, both physically and cognitively, the more dependent one is upon the various physical, social, and cultural properties of the environment.

Urban ethnic elderly individuals have become a special concern of gerontologists interested in the impact of environment upon behavior and well-being. The inner city is most often where poverty, ill health, and other social problems are most severe. The inner city is also where a large proportion of elderly, particularly minority and ethnic elderly, reside. As these people grow older and experience the social and physical changes that are concomitants of aging, they become more sensitive to, and dependent upon, their environment for support.

The 1960s and 1970s witnessed a revival of interest in the concept of ethnicity and its extension from a previous focus on minority racial groups to include examinations of ethnicity among white immigrant populations. During this period, traditional theories of America as a melting pot changed to a recognition of cultural pluralism. For the purposes of this chapter, ethnicity is defined as group membership based on integration of values, feelings, practices, and behaviors that arise through historical roots in the family of origin and through common cultural, religious, national, and/or linguistic background and that culminate in a shared symbol system and sense of shared identity (Kalish, 1986a).

Minority elderly constitute almost three million individuals. They are twice as likely to be poor as are white elderly, to have more chronic health problems, and to have a shorter life expectancy. Of the white elderly, almost seven million persons can be defined as ethnic—Italian, Polish, Greek, Jewish, Hungarian, Estonian, Latvian, Ukrainian, Irish, German, French, Swedish, and so on. Many white ethnic elderly, over two million individuals, do not speak English in their daily communications. This represents a significant problem in interactions with the wider community (Guttman, 1982). Because minority and ethnic white elderly often live in inner city areas where crime and poverty are commonplace and because minority and some ethnic elderly have lived their lives under shadows of discrimination and poverty, these groups of elderly are seen as vulnerable. That is, urban minority and white ethnic elderly are both at greater risk of experiencing negative social, emotional, and/or physical events than are other groups of elderly individuals. Thus, by definition, they can be seen to be more vulnerable than the elderly population in general.

People solve their problems and meet their needs in varying ways. Human service and health delivery systems have not always been aware of, or responsive to, the role that ethnicity plays in problem definition and help-seeking. If formal and informal services are to be successful, planners and practitioners must take issues of cultural distinctiveness and identity into account. While the press-competence model is widely used to understand and explain the interaction of the elderly and their environments, it is not necessarily predictive of the behaviors of subgroups of elderly or of elderly individuals. People with different life-styles and different cultural beliefs have different environmental needs (LaGory et al., 1985). Not only must we understand the special needs of the elderly and their environments, but also we must incorporate information about the impact of ethnicity upon the aging process and upon the elderly's perceptions of and interactions with their environments. The unique views of ethnic and minority persons as they age need to be considered to understand the interpretive role of the individual in interaction with his or her environment.

This chapter focuses on the role of a particular small-scale environment, the urban neighborhood, and its interplay with ethnicity, for white and black elderly. It reviews the literature on black and white ethnic elderly to better understand their perceptions of the strengths and limitations of their neighborhood support systems. Neighborhood roles, as locus for psychological attachment and social interaction and as an access point in help-seeking and receiving, are examined with particular attention given to exploring similarities and differences in these roles, if any, by ethnicity and their impact on vulnerability. In recognition of the fact that informal support networks of the aged are largely, but not exclusively, neighborhood-based, differences in support systems, both within and without the neighborhood, are examined to see if ethnicity makes a difference in help-seeking and receiving by the aged. Aspects of neighborhood change are introduced, and the possible implications for role and function for these groups are discussed. Suggestions for future research, policy, and practice are presented. We begin first with a discussion of the neighborhood.

URBAN NEIGHBORHOODS

There is no consensus among scholars and professionals about how to define *neighborhood*. Most recent definitions reflect both the physical and social elements of neighborhoods (Downs, 1981; Hallman, 1984; Keller, 1968; Morris & Hess, 1975; Warren & Warren, 1977). Neighborhoods are both objective realities and subjective entities differently perceived and valued by their residents.

From an objective viewpoint, neighborhoods may be seen as a geographic place where social interaction takes place. However, the specification of place varies widely. Similarly, the social interaction component of neighborhood is also seen to differ widely, depending in part on such variables as the age, social class, ethnicity, income, race, life-styles, and customs of a neighborhoods' residents. An additional complicating factor is that social relationships may be limited to those within the neighborhood's boundaries, or they may encompass extraterritoriality bonds; "not only social bonds between members of the designated population, but all bonds that group has to non-neighbors as well" (Warren & Warren, 1977, p. 28).

Neighborhoods have also been defined from a subjective viewpoint, focusing on the psychological identification of neighborhood residents. Morris and Hess (1975) note when people "say 'my neighborhood' it usually means they have found a place to live where they feel some human sense of belonging, some sense of being *part* of a society, no matter how small, rather just being *in* a society, no matter how large" (p. 1).

Neighborhoods serve as a locus for a number of important social functions ranging from friendship and sociability, interpersonal influence and socialization to mutual aid and informal helping (Warren & Warren, 1977; Naparstek et al., 1982). There has been some debate on the degree to which an individual's interpersonal ties are neighborhood-based. For most individuals, interpersonal ties are not exclusively neighborhood-based, although for particular population groups, such as ethnic elderly, neighborhood-based ties are extremely important (Ahlbrandt, 1984; Wellman, 1979).

The neighborhood also serves an organizational function, a place where a large variety of institutional units and small local organizations exist. Neighborhood institutions such as schools, human service agencies, and government agencies serve broad purposes. For example, they may provide jobs for neighborhood residents; they can enhance psychological identification with, and commitment to, the neighborhood by its residents; they help to integrate neighborhood residents to the norms and values of society; they provide opportunities for participation in voluntary activities ranging from educational or religious to self-improvement; and they provide a wide range of direct services, including education, individual counseling, economic assistance, and assistance in obtaining governmental services.

NEIGHBORHOODS AND THE ETHNIC ELDERLY

Although service delivery problems have been noted for both minority and white ethnic populations (Biegel & Naparstek, 1982; Hooyman, 1983; President's Commission on Mental Health, 1978), some elderly white ethnics in particular have been reticent to demand services. This underutilization of services is attributable to a number of factors, including the intimidation caused by the assimilation and melting-pot theories; the strong value on help as a family or ethnic community responsibility; pride and self-reliance; and the fear of stigmatization in accepting welfare services (Biegel & Sherman, 1979; Guttmann, 1982; Kolm, 1980).

Neighborhood–Based Support Systems

Biegel (1985) has identified the strengths as well as the limitations of support systems of the elderly. Family members provide extensive support and represent the elderly's most significant social resource. Most basic and extended needs of the elderly are provided within the family network. Children of the elderly provide significant amounts of support, and children of frail elderly assume an even larger proportion of care needs. The great majority of older persons live near at least one child and see their children frequently. Cantor (1979) reports that these family interactions involve the giving as well as the receiving of assistance by the elderly. Friends and neighbors are also significant providers of social support for the elderly. In fact, because of their physical proximity, neighbors may be the most valuable resource to the elderly in times of emergency.

Support systems, however, have limitations. A small but disturbing number of elderly have no significant others they can turn to for help and assistance. Cantor (1979) reports this to be 8% of her overall sample, while Guttmann's (1982) research with Euro-American elderly indicates that although 90% of the respondents stated that they had a confidante, when asked who they would turn to for help outside of the family, almost one-fifth (18%) said no one and 19% said that they had no one to turn to in a crisis. Other support system limitations may include lessened availability of family supports in the future, increasing geographic distances between the elderly and their children, and burdens experienced by caregivers that may lessen assistance to the elderly.

Roger Ahlbrandt's (1984) survey of 5,777 urban residents in Pittsburgh neighborhoods comes the closest of any single study to focusing on neighborhoods and the ways that the elderly use them. Using Fischer's (Fischer et al., 1977) choice-constraint model, Ahlbrandt (1984) found the neighborhood to be a more important resource for older than for younger respondents because the elderly are more geographically restricted and thus more place-bound. Older respondents had more friends living in the neighborhood than did younger respondents of no difference by race or social class (5.6 compared to 3.4 for the population aged 18 to 34). When asked to name their primary social contact—the individual with whom they visit or socialize most often—almost two-thirds (62%) of the elderly reported this contact as living in the neighborhood, as compared with less than half (49%) of the 18 to 34 age group. There were little differences by race, with 58% of the primary social contact for blacks living in the neighborhood as compared to 54% for white elderly.

Elderly respondents also were more likely to rely upon neighborhood residents for emotional and social support. However, even within their own neighborhoods, they tend to be more isolated than younger populations. Ahlbrandt found that the elderly have fewer interactions with their neighbors than do young populations, reflecting a lesser frequency of social interactions on the part of the elderly. He also found that the elderly turn less to others for emotional support. A reanalysis of the Ahlbrandt (1984) data, for this chapter, revealed that elderly respondents were significantly less likely than younger respondents to engage with neighbors in borrowing, visiting, receiving assistance with small tasks, and contacts for assistance in an emergency. Elderly respondents were also less likely to turn to others to discuss personal matters; one-third (33%) of the elderly seldom or never discussed this, as compared to 11% of those 18 to 44 who never discuss. However, the elderly are more likely than younger respondents to rely on kin. Over half (59%) of the elderly turn to kin for support, compared to 41% of the 18 to 34 age group, indicating that the elderly, when they do turn to others for help, seldom turn to someone outside the family, as compared to younger people. More of the elderly's providers of social support lived in the neighborhood than was the case with younger respondents; 36% for the elderly compared to 28% for those aged 18 to 34. This can be linked to the elderly's narrower social/environmental base, brought on by physical and economic limitations.

Concerning neighborhood attachment, residents of all ages report positive attitudes about their neighborhood. Almost two-thirds (63%) of the entire sample are strongly attached to their neighborhood, and an identical proportion report greater loyalty to their neighborhood than to the city as a whole. An even higher proportion of the total sample (72%) rate their neighborhood as an excellent or good place to live. Older respondents report greater attachment and higher levels of satisfaction with the neighborhood as an excellent or good place to live. When differences by age were examined, older respondents reported greater attachment to the neighborhood. Almost three-quarters (74%) of the elderly are very strongly attached to their neighborhood, as compared with 60% of the nonelderly respondents. There were no significant differences by age, however, in the rating of the neighborhood as a place to live.

The following sections review and discuss neighborhood attachment, the neighborhood as a locus for social interaction, and the neighborhood as a locus for help-seeking and receiving behaviors in black and white ethnic elderly.

Black Elderly

Locus of Neighborhood Attachment

Data from the Ahlbrandt (1984) study showed that elderly respondents reported greater attachment and loyalty to their neighborhood than did younger respondents. However, when this finding was reexamined by ethnicity, there were no differences between black and white ethnic elderly. Almost three-quarters of both black and white ethnic elderly reported being strongly or very strongly attached to their neighborhood, and over two-thirds of black and white ethnic elderly reported feeling more loyalty to their neighborhood than to the city as a whole. However, only slightly over half (51%) of the black elderly rated their neighborhood as a good or excellent place to live, compared with almost three-quarters (74%) of the white ethnic elderly. This latter difference is probably a reflection of the objective differences in the quality and availability of facilities and resources in predominantly black versus predominantly white neighborhoods. The reanalysis of the Ahlbrandt (1984) data indicates that blacks reported significantly fewer grocery stores, small item stores, churches, and health and recreation facilities in the neighborhood, compared with white ethnic respondents.

Locus of Social Interaction

For urban black elderly, the neighborhood plays a salient role as the locus of social interaction. For many years, poverty and discrimination kept blacks in particular neighborhoods and communities. These neighborhoods, therefore, became the locus of social and emotional life for black people of all ages. For the elderly blacks who remain in the inner city, the neighborhood still holds the role of providing day-to-day social interaction, even though there are factors that limit the degree to which elderly blacks can make use of their social contacts.

How often and for how long black elderly have contact with family and friends is strongly affected by distance. In fact, the farther a friend or family member lives from an older person's home, the less often the older person is likely to see him or her, regardless of race (Shanas et al., 1968).

In a study of urban black elderly (Wolf et al. 1983), it was found that respondents had social contact with family and friends in the neighborhood at least twice as often as with family and friends who lived in the city, but out of the neighborhood. The frequency of neighborhood contacts varied by the types of relationship. Elderly parents who had children living in the neighborhood saw those children almost daily, compared with seeing other children who lived in the same city about 11 times a month. This pattern of more frequent social contacts held for other relatives and friends who lived in the neighborhood. On the basis of these data, the neighborhood clearly plays an important role as the locus of social interaction with family and friends.

Reanalysis of Albrandt's data by the authors revealed that black elderly were significantly less likely than white ethnic elderly to engage in borrowing and visiting with neighbors. There were no differences by ethnicity in reported availability of help from neighbors and in the number of neighbors who could be counted on in an emergency. This finding is supported by Warren (1975); he found that blacks engaged in less social visiting but relied more on their neighbors as helpers. Warren believes that the black ghetto, which restricts blacks to more limited and generally lower income areas, leads to greater reliance on the neighborhood level of help, even though the neighborhood is not suited to meet all the additional needs of the elderly black population caused by economic and social discrimination.

Other studies have shown that characteristics of urban neighborhoods have hindered the black elderly's ability to interact with their friends, family, and neighbors. Urban problems such as crime, poor lighting, bad sidewalks, and inaccessible stairs, for example, have an impact on how often and how successfully elderly people are able to meet and socialize with people who live close by. Morse (1976) analyzed themes in oral history data from 100 older black Americans and found that the most uniformly addressed topic was that of personal security in the neighborhood. Many of the participants felt that they were, in a sense, imprisoned in their own homes and apartments by the threat of robbery or violence on the street. While this study is dated, there is little to argue that crime or the perceptions of crime among inner city elderly have diminished significantly over the past decade. Other issues that inner city residents discussed included the problems of adequate shopping facilities and transportation. While these services might be located in the neighborhood, they often were out of the reach, financially, of the people who would *most* need to use them.

One neighborhood institution, the black church, has been cited as a frame of reference, a mediating institution, and a catalyst for economic, social, and political change in the black community (Eng et al., 1985). The church also promotes social activities and interaction among black elderly. The black neighborhood church is also seen as an important source of social support for elderly blacks. Specifically, the writings of Taylor and Chatters (1986a; 1986b) point to the black church as a cornerstone of support that is accessible and that develops and changes over time and in response to life events. Black elderly who attended church frequently were most likely to talk about the importance of being a church member and said they received assistance from other church members more often than did nonattendees (Taylor & Chatters, 1986a). This relationship appears to be especially salient for old-old people who have adult children to facilitate the linkages to church support networks. In fact, very old church members with several generations who belong to the church tend to receive more supports than any other group. Age rather than membership is at issue here, because the very old nonmembers were also found to receive more support from the church than did younger nonmembers.

Access Point for Help-Seeking and Receiving

The types of help available from the black church as reported by Taylor and Chatters (1986a) are also of interest in understanding neighborhood-based help-seeking and receiving. The most frequent type of help that elderly blacks said they received from the church was help when ill. The others, listed by frequency of mention, were prayer, companionship, and advice and encouragement. Less frequently discussed, but still available, were the help of goods and services and financial assistance. These findings fall into line with other research underscoring the strengths of neighbors in dealing with time-urgent tasks and daily social interaction, as well as the inability of neighbors to perform tasks that require long-term commitments of time and resources (Chatters et al., 1986; Litwak, 1979).

A number of scholars have underscored the importance of the extended family in providing social supports and social interaction for elderly blacks. It has been hypothesized that black families have strong intergenerational systems of mutual interdependence to a greater degree than do white families and that blacks are more likely to include in their households relatives besides their own children (Hays & Mindel, 1973; Martin & Martin, 1978; Woehrer, 1978).

Research by Mitchell and Register (1984) provides only partial support for the thesis that black families have stronger extended family networks than do whites. Using data collected by Louis Harris and Associates, they found that while blacks were more likely to receive help from children and grandchildren and to provide shelter for grandchildren, white elderly see their children and grandchildren more frequently than do blacks. The authors note that the slight differences between blacks and whites may be accounted for by socioeconomic status, which may play a larger role than race in explaining help provided by the elderly to their children and grandchildren.

Several additional studies provide only limited support for the thesis that blacks have a stronger and more extended family network (Baum et al., 1986; Cantor, 1979; Mayor's Office for Senior Citizens, 1976). Cantor's (1979) study of New York elderly compares black, Hispanic, and white elderly's connection with significant others. Her study focused on "functional networks," which emphasized the availability of, and interaction with, informal supports rather than just the presence of ties per se. Her findings did not support the thesis that black elderly have more supportive family networks than do white elderly. A study of black and white low-income elderly, 75 years and older, in Pittsburgh, found no differences in levels of social support or size of social networks between black and white elderly; nor were there any differences in the number of network members living in the same neighborhood as the elderly respondent (Baum et al., 1986).

Neighbors have the advantage of being available as helpers, but are not necessarily the first choice of elderly blacks when they need assistance. Data from the National Survey of Black Americans show that all the respondents over 55 years of age indicated that they had a neighbor, but only older blacks who were separated or never married selected neighbors as their first choice for whom they would choose as their informal helper network (Chatters et al., 1986). Donald Warren's research in Detroit, conducted in 1974, is one of the few studies that offer data comparing helping networks by race among the urban elderly. Survey respondents were asked to identify helpers approached in coping with a recent concern. Among all age groups, blacks, regardless of sex or income levels, sought help from neighbors to a greater degree than did whites. These findings also hold true for the elderly, although the differences in use of neighbors by race is smaller for the elderly than it is for younger population groups. Among retired persons, over one third (37%) of black women reported using a neighbor for a recent concern, as compared to 30% for white women. For males, the racial differences were larger. Almost four out of ten black males (38%) reported using a neighbor, as compared to 26% for white males (Warren, 1976).

White Ethnic Elderly

Locus of Neighborhood Attachment

Kalish (1986b), in describing the importance of neighborhood for white ethnic elderly, notes that many ethnic elderly have continuously lived in the same neighborhood to which they went immediately upon coming to the United States. He notes, as does Fischer above, that the strong sense of identification with place is based in large part upon social relations. For the ethnic elderly, the neighborhood is the place where they have most of their friends and many family members and where they engage in a significant amount of their social activities. Many ethnic elderly belong to neighborhood churches; participate in neighborhood ethnic, fraternal, or social organizations; and socialize in neighborhood bars.

Empirical evidence on neighborhood attachment of white ethnic elderly in a predominately Polish section of Milwaukee, Wisconsin, is provided by Biegel and Sherman (1979). They report high levels of attachment and satisfaction with the neighborhood among the study population, with few differences by age except for perceptions concerning size of the neighborhood. Almost all (97%) of the ethnic elderly reported living in the community for at least 10 years, indicating high residential stability. Guttmann (1982) also found high levels of residential stability in a study of eight white ethnic populations, with almost three-quarters (73.9%) of the sample having lived in the same neighborhood for the past 6–20 years.

Residents of all ages in the Biegel and Sherman study expressed satisfaction with the neighborhood. Over three-quarters (76.6%) were satisfied or very satisfied, over one-third (35%) being very satisfied. There were no differences reported by age or ethnicity. These satisfaction levels were even higher than those reported by Ahlbrandt (1984) for residents of Pittsburgh. Over half (58%) of the interviewees stated that they saw their neighborhood as the place where they belonged. Again, there were no significant differences by age or ethnicity.

Respondents reported that their neighborhood consisted of 10 blocks or less; the elderly viewed their neighborhood as smaller than did nonelderly. Almost half (45%) of elderly respondents reported their neighborhood as a place where they really belonged, with no differences by age or ethnicity. In a companion survey of community leaders and helpers, Biegel and Sherman (1979) found that natural helpers, neighborhood leaders, and clergy felt very positive about the neighborhood, with human services agency staff feeling considerably less positive. Attitudes toward the neighborhood were directly related to who lived in the neighborhood. Helpers and leaders who lived in the neighborhood felt much more positve than did helpers and leaders who did not live in the neighborhood. In a follow-up study, Biegel et al., (1982) found that among the elderly, there was a significant correlation between two aspects of neighborhood attachment (satisfaction with neighborhood and neighborhood loyalty) and mental health status.

Guttmann (1982) found similar high levels of neighborhood attachment, with almost all respondents (97%) indicating that they liked their neighborhood and felt safe in it. Few respondents (13%) reported wanting to live in another neighborhood. Whereas Biegel and Sherman's respondents lived in a predominantly single ethnic group neighborhood, most of Guttmann's respondents lived in mixed ethnic communities. Yet, few of

Guttmann's respondents (one out of six) indicated a desire to live in an ethnically homogeneous environment. This is important to note, since ethnically mixed neighborhoods occur more frequently as compared to single ethnic enclaves. In the future, we can expect ethnic communities to become more mixed as the ethnic population becomes more geographically dispersed and as social class differences between elderly ethnics and their children increase.

Locus of Social Interaction

It has been noted that the elderly participate in organizations less than do nonelderly persons, due largely to factors of health, transportation, and safety. However, Biegel and Sherman (1979) reported greater participation in organizations (largely neighborhood-based) by elderly than by younger respondents. Almost half (48%) of community respondents of all ages stated that they belonged to one or more organizations, as compared with slightly more than half (52%) of those respondents aged 65 and over. However, the greatest differences by age were in the number of organizations. Almost one-third (31%) of those aged 65 and older belonged to more than one organization, as compared with 13% of those under age 65. This finding was not supported by a reanalysis of the Ahlbrandt (1948) data, in which there were no age-related differences found in the number of organizations to which the white ethnic respondents belonged.

Guttmann (1982) found significant differences among white ethnic groups in the numbers of elderly respondents who belong to neighborhood-based ethnic organizations, ranging from a high of about 90% for Estonian and Polish elderly to a low of 35% among Italian elderly. However, all groups felt a very strong sense of ethnic identity and exhibited strong neighborhood-based ties. Respondents were heavily involved in the religious life of their neighborhoods, ranging from 97% of the Polish respondents who were members of a religious congregation to 55% of Jewish respondents.

Access Point for Help–Seeking and Receiving

For many white ethnic elderly, the neighborhood is the location where they have most of their friends and many family members. These neighborhood-based support systems can decrease vulnerability and isolation and increase an overall sense of belongingness. There is tremendous variation among white ethnic elderly, however, in attitudes toward help-seeking outside the family and in the proximity and availability of family members. Guttmann (1982) found that over one-quarter (28%) of Jewish elderly reported that they would not go outside the family for help, while only 11% of the Polish elderly would not do so. There were even greater differences among ethnic groups in whether they would use friends for assistance.

Concerning proximity and avilability of family, Gelfand's (1986) review of the literature notes that while one study of Polish and Italian middle-aged men and women in Baltimore found that 70% of the sample had parents who lived in the same community, another study of Polish, Italian, and Irish groups found that the Irish family members were more dispersed than the other two population groups. Guttmann and his colleagues (1979) reported significant differences in findings from a study of eight Euro-American ethnic groups in the proportions of elderly who live with their children. Not surprisingly, in a later study Guttman (1982) notes that ethnic elderly prefer ethnic friends by a two-to-one margin over nonethnic friends.

Hayes et al. (1986) note that in 1980, over one-third of the elderly lived in the suburbs and that between 1960 and 1980, the growth of the suburban elderly population was twice the growth of the urban elderly population. The suburban elderly population includes significant numbers of Euro-American ethnic groups. Kalish (1986a) notes that they tend to live in less affluent suburbs and that often these areas lack good public transportation systems. This may make it more difficult for elderly persons who do not drive for health or financial reasons to maintain contact with family members and friends who have remained in their old neighborhood.

The underutilization of professional services by the white ethnic elderly has been well noted. Guttmann (1982) asked elderly respondents from eight white ethnic groups if they had recently used any of ten different formal services. Only the church was used by more than 10% of the total sample. Of the total sample, over half (58%) made no use of any services.

Among the white ethnic elderly, there is a strong preference for meeting a variety of needs within the family. Fandetti and Gelfand (1978), in a study of Polish and Italian neighborhoods in Baltimore, noted that the extended family was seen as the principal resource for advice on emotional problems. The preference for families taking care of their own and not using services was, in part, related to social class. Respondents were asked to indicate preferred living arrangements for an elderly relative without a spouse. Second and third generations were more willing to support independent, as opposed to within-family, living arrangements. Further support for this finding was reported by Gelfand and Fandetti (1980) in another study of working-class and suburban Italians. Suburban middle-class Italians expressed greater willingness to use nursing homes for their parents rather than have their parents live with them. These findings suggest that human service and health agencies need to address issues of ethnicity among subethnic groups, as well as issues of social class within ethnic subgroups.

IMPLICATIONS

Research during the past several decades has increased the level of knowledge about black and white ethnic elderly. While the importance of ethnicity is now widely recognized, the impact of aging and ethnicity is not clear. As Bengtson (1979) indicates, there are two contradictory views about ethnicity and aging: the double-jeopardy hypothesis and the age-leveling hypothesis.

The double-jeopardy hypothesis suggests two possible avenues of thought about the interaction of the aging process and minority status (Dowd & Bengtson, 1979; Ward, 1983). On the one hand, it focuses on blacks as the major and perhaps most disadvantaged minority in the United States and suggests that minority aged are at a disadvantage as compared to white elderly. Elderly blacks are very much more likely than elderly whites to fall below the poverty level for income, and median incomes for elderly blacks are substantially less than for elderly whites (U.S. Bureau of the Census, 1984). The black elderly also show a distinct disadvantage in health status, as indicated at this stage in the life cycle by a lower life expectancy of approximately five years compared to whites (National Center for Health Statistics, 1984). Markides and Mindel (1987) also argue that mental-health-related statistics support the double-jeopardy hypothesis.

On the other hand, the double-jeopardy hypothesis suggests that there is a compensatory factor for minority persons reaching old age. Minority aged belong to subcultures that represent shared responses to a history of discrimination and that generate protective social environments for their members. There is some continuing controversy about the structure of the black family, but little remaining doubt that this kinship system was grounded in its own cultural heritage and is not simply an inadequate copy of the white family (Staples, 1981). Stack (1974) and Shimkin et al. (1978) found the larger black extended family system to be highly integrated and to be an important resource for self-help and survival. A potentially very stressful old age may be offset by means of a caring family system.

A second view of the role of ethnicity and aging suggests that age is in effect a leveler of inequities between groups that existed in midlife. According to this viewpoint, there will be less relative disadvantages between ethnic groups among the elderly than among younger population cohorts.

For the ethnic elderly, as Harel (1986) indicates, ethnicity can impact upon well-being and/or vulnerability in a positive or negative fashion. From the positive perspective, ethnic identity can enhance participation in ethnic organizations; can enhance identification with, and participation in, the local community; and can promote the use of self-help and mutual help activities. On the other hand, ethnicity or informal support networks in general, as Gottlieb (1982) notes, can inhibit or prevent participation in the wider community and can block access to needed professional and community-wide services. A key issue, as Biegel and Naparstek (1982) have noted, is the necessity of building upon the positive strengths of ethnicity and ethnic solidarity to develop partnerships and relationships with organizations and institutions in the wider community.

The studies reviewed for this chapter lend support to both avenues of thought concerning the impact of aging minority and white ethnic persons. Research indicates many similarities as well as differences across ethnic groups. In addition, it has been noted that there are tremendous variations within individual ethnic groups themselves. Although ethnicity may represent a common and unifying characteristic, there are in-group differences based upon age, education, income, and socialization.

The neighborhood serves as a focus of social interaction and attachment for all elderly, but is of particular importance for blacks and ethnic whites. Both these groups have developed a reliance on specific neighborhoods, but for different reasons. Blacks have been subject to racial discrimination and were limited to particular neighborhoods. White ethnics, many of whom moved to this country for political reasons, stayed in neighborhoods because they felt comfortable around people who practiced the same customs and spoke the same language. Both groups have evidenced a larger number of social contacts in the neighborhoods than have younger people.

The greater reliance on neighborhood can put the well-being of these people into a precarious balance as they grow older and as neighborhoods change. As people experience the social and physical losses of age, their need for support increases. For those elderly who have depended upon neighborhood-based supports throughout their lives, neighborhood change is especially significant. The trends in most inner city neighborhoods have included growth in poverty, continued decline of property, decreased public and commercial services, and increased crime. In neighborhoods where these problems are severe, those who are able to move usually do so. The people who are left behind are more vulnerable and consist of those who have neither the social nor the financial resources to allow them to leave. A different, but related, problem for vulnerable elderly occurs in neighborhoods that are enjoying a revitalization or gentrification. These neighborhoods usually meet the needs of minorities and white ethnics except for one: they are too expensive. The elderly, some of whom have long tenure in the area, cannot afford the inflated costs of housing (increases in either property taxes or rent) and services that accompany a surge in a neighborhood's popularity and renovation. Often, the only housing within financial reach is in neighborhoods that are on the decline.

Since distance is a factor for the social relations of all elderly and since ties to place are often a reflection of the strength of social networks, implications of neighborhood change for social interactions are important for vulnerable elderly. As younger generations of family move away from the old neighborhood and as friends die, the neighborhood base of social interaction can become weaker, not stronger, as elderly become more frail. For both blacks and white ethnics, one key to shoring up the neighborhood support system is the church. The church is an institution that is at once accessible, flexible enough to meet changing needs, and a natural locus of social interaction and activity. The church can also provide a way for younger people who have moved to the suburbs to maintain a relationship and a weekly presence in the old neighborhood. Since the church is accepted by both black and white ethnic elderly as a normative institution to meet human needs, church-sponsored programs may have a greater impact on the most vulnerable than the efforts of human service agencies alone. City planners and social agencies involved in neighborhood development and service would do well to acknowledge the organizing and outreach potential of the black and the ethnic church in urban neighborhoods. Roles for churches in helping to address the needs of the vulnerable elderly include the direct delivery of services, cosponsorship of agency services to help address issues of underutilization due to stigma, and serving as a site for human service programs.

Neighbors are another possible resource for strengthening the neighborhood base of supports. While research indicates that neighbors are seldom the first choice for help among either blacks or white ethnics, neighbors are available and usually accessible to most people. Black elderly tend to rely upon neighbors for help more often than do white ethnics. Neighbors tend to lend the most help for short-term, concrete tasks. For some frail elderly, however, the presence or absence of a caring neighbor who can run occasional errands and stop by or call daily can make a difference in the elderly person's ability to live safely in the neighborhood. A well-organized neighboring network in an apartment building or a small section of the neighborhood can bolster the number of social contacts and strengthen the neighborhood as a place of social interaction for all ages. Strategies to strengthen ties to neighbors for vulnerable elderly include the development of a telephone reassurance program, a friendly visiting program, or the identification of neighbors who are "natural helpers" and intervention with these helpers to expand their assistance network to vulnerable elderly individuals (Collins & Pancoast, 1976). Further practice-based research on these service strategies is needed.

Clearly, neighbors and church members have not taken over the roles of family and close friends for most elderly blacks and white ethnics. Family ties remain strong for the majority of blacks and white ethnics. However, as families continue to move away from the inner cities and sometimes out of the general area, and as the social and physical needs of the elderly increase, how can the strengths of the church and the neighborhood social structure be maximized? Certainly, the past research on similarities and differences among different groups and subgroups is helpful and should lead to more neighborhood-based service strategies. Further research on the possible expanded roles of the church and ethnic organizations in meeting the needs of urban elderly is warranted. Also important is a focus on the possible roles for professional practitioners in these informal systems. While research has offered role sets for practitioners building informal networks with the elderly (Biegel et al., 1984), there remain questions about the nature of interactions between churches and human service professionals and how the two can most effectively serve minority and ethnic elderly within the boundaries of their organizations' missions. The role of churches and human service professionals in prevention of further neighborhood problems rather than continued efforts in remediation is another avenue of potential research and demonstration.

We have also noted that the ethnic elderly, especially the white ethnic elderly, are becoming geographically dispersed through movement into suburban communities. They represent a particularly vulnerable population group that needs more study. These groups of elderly are often more disadvantaged than their neighbors and are generally located in less affluent suburban areas. They are particularly at risk of becoming isolated due to the increased distance from their friends and relatives in their old neighborhood and due to the lack of transportation to the more dispersed community resources in their new communities.

We believe that the concept of neighborhood will be of continued importance in addressing the vulnerability of minority and white ethnic elderly in the future. However, the notion of the traditional homogeneous, urban, ethnic neighborhood in the city will give way to more heterogeneous urban and suburban neighborhoods where future cohorts of minority and white ethnic elderly will live. The effects of these changes upon the well-being of the elderly deserve careful study. Unfortunately, most of the research concerning the importance of neighborhood to the ethnic elderly was conducted a decade ago. There is a need for renewed attention to this topic by researchers, practitioners, and policymakers.

REFERENCES

Ahlbrandt, R., Jr. (1984). *Neighborhoods, people and community*. New York: Plenum.
Baum, M., Biegel, D., & Magaziner, J. (1986). *The relationship between social*

support and the use of helping systems by the high risk elderly: An exploratory study. Pittsburgh: University of Pittsburgh.

Bengtson, V. (1979). Ethnicity and aging: Problems and issues in current and social
science inquiry. In D. Gelfand & A. Kutzik (Eds.), *Ethnicity and aging: Theory, research and policy*. New York: Springer.

Biegel, D. (1985). The application of network theory and research to the field of
aging. In W. J. Sauer & R. T. Cloward (Eds.), *Social support networks and the
care of the elderly: Theory, research, practice*. New York: Springer.

Biegel, D., & Naparstek, A. (1982). The neighborhood and family services project:
An empowerment model linking clergy and agency professionals. In A. Jeger
& R. Slotnik (Eds.) *Community mental health and behavioral ecology: A
handbook of theory, research and practice*. New York: Plenum.

Biegel, D., Naparstek, A., & Khan, M. (1982). Social support and mental health in
urban ethnic neighborhoods. In D. Biegel & A. Naparstek (Eds.), *Community
support systems and mental health: Practice, policy and research*. New York:
Springer.

Biegel, D., & Sherman, W. (1979). Neighborhood capacity building and the ethnic
aged. In D. Gelfand & A. Kutzik (Eds.), *Ethnicity and aging*. New York:
Springer.

Biegel, D., Shore, B., & Gordon, E. (1984). *Building support networks for the
elderly: Theory and applications*. Beverly Hills, CA: Sage Publications.

Canton, M. (1979). The formal support system of New York's inner city elderly. In
D. Gelfand & A. Kutzik (Eds.), *Ethnicity and aging*. New York: Springer.

Chatters, L., Taylor, R., & Jackson, J. (1986). Aged Blacks' choices for an informal helper network. *Journal of Gerontology, 41*(1), 94–100.

Collins, A., & Pancoast, D. (1976). *Natural helping networks*. Washington, D.C.:
National Association of Social Workers.

Dowd, J. J., & Bengtson, V. L. (1978). Aging in minority populations: An examination of the double jeopardy hypothesis. *Journal of Gerontology, 33*, 427–
436.

Downs, A. (1981). *Neighborhoods and urban development*. Washington, D.C.:
The Brookings Institution.

Eng, E., Hatch, J., & Callan, A. (1985). Institutionalizing social support through
the church and into the community. *Health Education Quarterly, 12*(1), 81–
92.

Fandetti, D., & Gelfand, D. (1976). Care of the aged: Attitudes of white ethnic
families. *The Gerontologist, 16*, 544–549.

Fischer, C. S., Jackson, R. M., Stueve, C. A., Gerson, K., Jones, L. McC., & Bald-
assare, M. (1977). *Networks and places*. New York: The Free Press.

Gelfand, D. (1986). Families, assistance, and the Euro-American elderly. In C. L.
Hays, R. A. Kalish, & D. Guttmann (Eds.), *European-American elderly: A
guide for practice*. New York: Springer.

Gelfand, D., & Fandetti, D. (1980). Urban and suburban white ethnics: Attitudes
toward care of the aged. *The Gerontologist, 20*, 588–594.

Golant, S. (1979). *Location and Environment of Elderly Population*. New York:
H. V. Winston.

Gottlieb, B. (1982). Social support in the workplace. In D. Biegel & A. Naparstek (Eds.), *Community support systems and mental health: Practice, research and policy.* New York: Springer.

Guttmann, D. (1982). Neighborhood as a support system for Euro-American elderly. In D. Biegel & A. Naparstek (Eds.), *Community support systems and mental health: Practice, policy and research.* New York: Springer.

Guttmann, D., Kolm, R., Mostwin, D., Kestenbaum, S., Harrington, D., Mullaney, J. W., Adams, K., Suziedelis, G., & Varga, L. (1979). Informal and formal support systems and their effect on the lives of the elderly in selected ethnic groups. Final Report, Administration on Aging Grant No. 90-A-1007. Washington, D.C.: National Catholic School of Social Service, Catholic University of America.

Hallman, H. W. (1984). *Neighborhoods: Their place in urban life.* Beverly Hills, CA: Sage.

Harel, Z. (1986). Ethnicity and aging: Implications for service organizations. In C. L. Hays, R. A. Kalish, & D. Guttmann (Eds.), *European-American elderly: A guide for practice.* New York: Springer.

Hayes, C. L., Kalish, R. A., & Guttman, D. (Eds.). (1986). *European-American elderly: A guide for practice.* New York: Springer.

Hays, W. C., & Mindel, C. H. (1973). Extended kin relationship in black and white families. *Journal of Marriage and the Family, 35,* 51–57.

Hooyman, N. (1983). Social support networks in services to the elderly. In J. K. Whittaker & J. Garbarino (Eds.), *Social support networks: Informal helping in the human services.* Hawthorne, NY: Aldine.

Kalish, R. A. (1986a). The meanings of ethnicity. In C. L. Hays, R. A. Kalish, & D. Guttman (Eds.), *European-American elderly: A guide for practice.* New York: Springer.

Kalish, R. A. (1986b). The significance of neighborhoods in the lives of the Euro-American elderly. In C. L. Hays, R. A. Kalish, & D. Guttman (Eds.), *European-American elderly: A guide for practice.* New York: Springer.

Keller, S. (1968). *The urban neighborhood: A sociological perspective.* New York: Random House.

Kolm, R. (1980). Issues of Euro-American elderly in the 1980s. Paper presented at the National Center on Urban Ethnic Affairs, Washington, D.C.

La Gory, M., Ward, R., & Sherman, S. (1985). The ecology of aging: Neighborhood satisfaction in an older population. *The Sociological Quarterly, 26*(3), 405–418.

Lawton, M. P. (1980). *Environment and aging.* Belmont, CA: Wadsworth.

Lawton, M. P., Moss, M., & Moles, E. (1984). The suprapersonal neighborhood context of older people. *Environment and Behavior, 16*(1), 89–109.

Lawton, M. P., & Nahemow, L. (1973). Ecology and the aging process. In C. Eisdorfer & M. P. Lawton (Eds.), *The psychology of adult development and aging.* Washington, D.C.: American Psychological Association.

Litwak, E. (1979). Support networks and the disabled: The transition from the community to the institutional setting. Paper presented at the annual meeting of the Gerontological Society, Washington, D.C.

Markides, K. S., & Mindel, C. H. (1987). *Aging and ethnicity*. Beverly Hills, CA: Sage.

Martin, E., & Martin, J. (1978). *The black extended family*. Chicago: University of Chicago.

Mayor's Office for Senior Citizens (1976). Senior citizens in great cities: The case of Chicago. *The Gerontologist, 16*(1, Part 2), 3–88.

Mitchell, J., & Register, J. C. (1984). An exploration of family interaction with the elderly by race, socioeconomic status and residence. *Gerontologist, 24*(1), 48–54.

Morris, D., & Hess, K. (1975). *Neighborhood power: The new localism*. Boston: Beacon Press.

Morse, D. W. (1976). Aging in the ghetto: Themes expressed by older Black men and women living in a northern industrial city. *Industrial-Gerontology, 3*(1), 1–10.

Naparstek, A., Biegel, D., & Spiro, H. (1982). *Neighborhood networks for humane mental health care*. New York: Plenum.

National Center for Health Statistics. (1984). *Health indicators for Hispanic, Black and White Americans*. Vital and Health Statistics, Series 10, No. 148. Washington, D.C.: U.S. Government Printing Office.

President's Commission on Mental Health. (1978). *Report to the President from the President's Commission on Mental Health* Washington, D.C. U.S. Government Printing Office.

Rowles, G. (1978). *Prisoners of Space? Exploring the geographical experience of older people*. Boulder, CO: Westview Press.

Shanas, E., Townsend, P., Wedderburn, D., Friis, H., Milhoj, P., & Stehouwer, J. (1968). *Old people in three industrial societies*. New York: Atherton Press.

Shimkin, D. B., Shimkin, E. M., & Frate, D. A. (1978). *The extended family in black societies*. The Hague, Netherlands: Mouton.

Staples, R. (1981). The Black American family. In C. H. Mindel & R. W. Habenstein (Eds.), *Ethnic families in America*. New York: Elsevier.

Stack, C. B. (1974). *All our kin*. New York: Harper & Row.

Taylor, R., & Chatters, L. (1986a). Patterns of informal support to elderly Black adults: Family, friends, and church members. *Social Work, 31*(6), 432–438.

Taylor, R., & Chatters, L. (1986b). Church-based informal supports. *The Gerontologist, 26*(6), 637–642.

U.S. Bureau of the Census (1984). Demographic and socioeconomic aspects of the aging in the United States. *Current population reports*. Special Studies, Series P-23, No. 138. Washington, D.C.: U.S. Government Printing Office.

Ward, R. A. (1983). The stability of racial differences across age strata. *Sociology and Social Research, 67*, 312–323.

Warren, D. (1975). *Black neighborhoods: An assessment of community power*. Ann Arbor: University of Michigan Press.

Warren, D. (1976). *Helping network study data report*. Ann Arbor: Program in Community Effectiveness, University of Michigan.

Warren, R. B., & Warren, D. (1977). *The neighborhood organizer's handbook*. Notre Dame, IN: University of Notre Dame Press.

Wellman, B. (1979). The community question: The intimate networks of East Yorkers. *American Journal of Sociology, 84*(3), 1201–1231.

Woehrer, C. E. (1978). Cultural pluralism in American families: The influence of ethnicity on social aspects of aging. *The Family Coordinator, 15,* 329–339.

Wolf, J. H., Breslau, N., Ford, A., Zeigler, H. D., & Ward, A. (1983). Distance and contacts: Interactions of black urban elderly adults with family and friends. *The Journal of Gerontology, 38*(4), 465–471.

PART 2
Special Vulnerable Populations

Introduction

Part 2 moves from the conceptual, empirical approach to vulnerability to an examination of selected vulnerable populations. The data and case examples outlined in Part 1 suggest that vulnerable populations can be found among elders who are institutionalized, who are homebound, and/or who have special, categorical problems, as well as among caregivers who are the providers of resources to meet the dependent needs of elders.

Though many elderly populations could have been chosen for inclusion in this section, the three highlighted—abused and neglected, suicidal, and homeless—most dramatically represent vulnerability at the high end of need. The identification of informal caregivers as members of a vulnerable group reinforces their significance to any system's response to vulnerability.

The four chapters in Part 2 of this book challenge public officials, professionals, scholars, and the general public to recognize and address the needs of vulnerable older adults. At any point in time, it is estimated that approximately one of every five older Americans cannot, on their own, care for themselves. One-fourth of this vulnerable older population (5% of the aged) are likely to be found in long-term care facilities. Over one-half of them (11% of the aged) are homebound in their own residences or in the homes of their relatives, and another one-fifth of them (4% of the aged) include those aged who are homeless; those aged who are neglected, abused, and exploited; and those aged in various unprotected or semi-protected living situations. In addition, there are those who live in unsafe and/or deteriorated housing and those with severe limitations on economic and social resources. It is apparent that those who are among the vulnerable aged of today, and those who are likely to join their ranks in the future, require that elected and appointed officials in our society address their needs, as well as the needs of those who provide informal care and support for them.

9

Abuse, Neglect, and Self-Neglect: Issues of Vulnerability

Georgia J. Anetzberger

Vulnerability to elder abuse or neglect can assume two forms. The first relates to characteristics of the individual. Older people are more likely to suffer maltreatment or self-neglect if they have certain features or live under certain conditions. Individual characteristics associated with elder abuse or neglect can be personal, situational, environmental, or cultural in nature.

The second form that vulnerability to elder abuse or neglect can assume relates to characteristics of systems. Laws and services designed to protect abuse or neglect victims in fact may offer little security and may erode their personal freedom. When this happens, it is usually because these interventions are inadequate, inappropriate, or restrictive. This chapter explores vulnerability and elder abuse or neglect in both forms.

CHARACTERISTICS OF THE INDIVIDUAL

Every year, over one million older Americans are believed to suffer abuse or neglect (Block & Sinnott, 1979; Pillemer & Finkelhor, 1988; Tatara, 1990; U.S. House Select Committee on Aging, 1981, 1990). Some of them are beaten, others are conjured out of life savings. Some are belittled or called names, others are denied proper medical care or sufficient food. Some live in deteriorated and infested housing that threatens their health and safety, others are denied the right to decide where to live or with whom to spend time. Some decay in waste and want, unable to meet personal needs and having no one around to help.

Elder abuse takes many forms, and it can threaten any older American. However, some older people are more vulnerable to maltreatment and self-neglect than are others. Personal, situational, environmental, or cultural characteristics increase their vulnerability, making abuse or neglect more likely to happen, especially repeated or chronic abuse and neglect.

Personal Characteristics

Personal characteristics that contribute to abuse occurrence include impairment and isolation (Block & Sinnott, 1979; Chen et al., 1981; Lau & Kosberg, 1979; Phillips, 1983; Pillemer & Finkelhor, 1988; Steinmetz, 1988; Wolf et al., 1984). Physical or mental impairment can make older people more dependent on others for care, care that may prove inadequate or improper. Impairment can reduce decision-making capacity, resulting in choices that place the individual at risk of endangerment. Impairment also decreases the ability to escape from or retaliate against abuse.

Isolation can happen through estrangement, living alone, or out-living family and friends. If others are not around to help at a time when help is essential to preservation, it can result in self-neglect. Isolation can foster repeated abuse by reducing the number of people in and around the home who can "keep an eye on things," thereby offering surveillance and protection. Isolation can also minimize understanding of laws and knowledge of community services that could alleviate conditions of abuse and neglect.

> Clarence was both impaired and isolated. He had a heart condition and was, in general, frail. His wife had died recently. At first, Clarence felt fortunate that a neighbor came forth and agreed to give him a home and provide care in exchange for his monthly Social Security check. He later changed his mind, when this same neighbor proceeded to lock him in the basement and physically abuse him into signing over all of his income and savings.

Situational Characteristics

Situational characteristics can contribute to abuse occurrence (Anetzberger, 1987; Hwalek et al., 1984; Pillemer, 1985, 1986). For example, caregivers may be mentally ill or alcoholic. Unable to tolerate frustration, they may become abusive toward the older people in their lives. Or, poverty can force family members who never got along to live together, leading to resentment and abuse.

> Sarah lived with her aged mother in subsidized housing. Since she had no income of her own, she depended on her mother's pension for food and other

things. Sarah spent most of her time sitting at the kitchen table, depressed. Divorced eight years ago, she had never managed to find a satisfactory life-style as a single person. Now she lived with the mother who had always "driven her crazy," who had always found fault. But it was worse now than it had been growing up. As a result, Sarah's anger was an ever-present part of the household. In fact, sometimes her shouting was so loud and her threats so frighening that the police were called.

Environmental Factors

Environmental factors that can foster maltreatment and self-neglect include deteriorated housing and crime-ridden neighborhoods (Finley, 1983; Gray Panthers of Austin, 1983; Liang & Sengstock, 1983). Substandard housing may include inadequate heating, poor ventilation, inadequate insulation, and improper plumbing, all of which can promote ill health. The perceived or actual prevalence of crime in any locale can "imprison" older people, making them less likely to leave home even for life essentials.

> Antonia had lived in Germantown her entire life, and in her present home for nearly 50 years. She was not about to leave. Not only was there nowhere else to go that she could afford, but this was Antonia's home and the neighborhood was all she had ever known. However, the neighborhood had changed and so had her home. Instead of civic centers, there were bars. Instead of neighbors watching out for one another, drug users watched the remaining houses for a "quick take." The house itself needed painting and repairs too numerous to list. There was neither running water nor electricity. Broken windows were as many as the rats that raced across Antonia's yard. But who could Antonia trust to do the repairs, and how could she pay for the repairs, even if she found someone to trust?

Cultural Factors

Finally, cultural factors can contribute to elder abuse. Because certain heritages have greater tolerance for violance, group members may find abuse of the old more acceptable (Carroll, 1975; Hennan & Photiades, 1979; Anetzberger, 1987). In addition, partly because women often are socialized toward dependence and helplessness, they are more frequently victims of abuse and neglect than are men (Block & Sinnott, 1979; Gioglio & Blakemore, 1983; Lau & Kosberg, 1979; O'Malley et al., 1979; Sengstock & Liang, 1982; Steinmetz, 1983; Tatara, 1990, Wolf et al., 1984).

> Although Mildred was born and raised in Appalachia, she had lived the last 30 years in Cleveland. Most of that time was spent raising her children.

Lately, however, she had taken to bed, where she remained night and day. Mildred had stopped trying to do things on her own. She had come to accept her daughter, Connie, as her caregiver, now and forever. When Mildred wanted something, she yelled to Connie to bring it. If Connie didn't want to bring it, she yelled back. And, if the yelling back and forth bothered Connie too much, she spanked Mildred. In line with their cultural proclivity, both Mildred and Connie accepted the yelling and spanking. Neither seemed contrary to what you might expect from family.

CHARACTERISTICS OF THE SYSTEM

Characteristics of older people and their caregivers can render them vulnerable to abuse or neglect, but so too can the characteristics of laws and services established to protect them. Particularly significant in this regard are laws and services that offer promises of protection that cannot be realized or that inappropriately erode the individual freedom of abuse victims.

For instance, 45 states have elder abuse reporting laws (Tatara, 1990). These laws require health and social service professionals to report any known or suspected incidents of elder abuse to authorities, or to face potential penalty. Unfortunately, enacting such laws provides no guarantee that services are in place to effectively address reported maltreatment or self-neglect. Effective services may not be in place for two reasons: first, inadequate funding; and second, inappropriate services.

Inadequate Funding

Only 11 states enacted elder abuse reporting or adult protective service laws with any discrete appropriations for services (American Public Welfare Association, 1987). All the rest relied on already scarce resources. This scarcity worsened, however, during the 1980s, through federal funding cuts, competition with more popular abused populations (usually children), and growth in the target aged population overall. Consequently, we have seen the accumulation of elder abuse reports throughout the country that often receive only cursory investigation and few protective services by overworked, underpaid public servants. This situation of scarce dollars and growing need raises the ethical question, "Is it reasonable to enact reporting laws or to make abuse reports when there aren't enough resources to deal with the problem?"

Inappropriate Services

An ineffective system of protection can also result from inappropriate services. More specifically, we have developed interventions for addressing elder abuse before adequately understanding the causes of the problem. Elder abuse was studied first during the late 1970s. Yet, it was not until the mid-1980s that its origins were explored through systematic investiagion. Since most laws and services for addressing maltreatment and self-neglect developed prior to that time, they were based on an incomplete understanding of the problem or a potentially inappropriate analogy with other abused populations.

Early explanations of elder abuse emphasized the dependence of older people, much as with children (Douglass et al., 1980; Lau & Kosberg, 1979; Rathbone-McCuan, 1978). We now realize that the dependency of older people, when it does occur, is not simply the dependency of children with gray hair and wrinkles (Schene & Ward, 1988). It is categorically different in certain important respects. First, older people, as adults, have rights and responsibilities that are denied children in our society. The most important right in this regard is the right to make life choices, even unpopular or self-endangering ones. Second, older people with chronic illnesses that render them care-dependent are unlikely to become completely independent again. This differs from the dependency of children, which is seen as temporary, decreasing through latency and adolescence and then eroding altogether with adulthood. Third, the dependency of children is never challenged. Childhood is considered a life stage wherein protection and care is expected. In contrast, the dependency of older people is always subject to question. On this basis, assessments are considered good practice in health and social services to determine the changing functional status of impaired older people and the extent to which they can resume the tasks associated with adulthood.

Early explanations of elder abuse also underscored the importance of severe stress associated with caregiving (O'Malley et al., 1979; U.S. Select Committee on Aging, 1981). Probably because elder abuse is more taboo in our society than is abuse against other populations, we have difficulty imagining abuse occurring in any context other than that of caregiver stress. However, recent research has suggested that at least physical abuse does not stem from caregiver stress. Rather, it is associated with such conditions as pathology and perceived social isolation on the part of the perpetrator (Anetzberger, 1987; Pillemer, 1986).

Premature Policy and Practice

In general, we were premature in developing policy and practice related to elder abuse. There have been three unfortunate consequences of this action. First, we frequently fashioned adult protective laws and services after child protective laws and services (Salend et al., 1984). Lacking an alternative model, we adopted the one closest at hand, and by so doing, furthered the stereotypic and ageist thinking of elderly people as childlike and dependent (Faulkner, 1982; Krauskopf & Burnett, 1983). Some other thinking on the subject suggests that domestic violence and advocacy may offer more viable intervention models (Crouse et al., 1981; Gioglio & Blakemore, 1983). At least they target adult populations and give them responsibility for initiating services. They also usually span both the civil and criminal justice systems in a way that recognizes the abuse perpetrator potentially as both victim and culprit.

Second, we focused interventions on individuals and victims at the expense of the family system and perpetrator. Consequently, we have failed to protect victims, because we have not recognized their relationship with their perpetrators or generated meaningful models for dealing with these individuals.

Most abuse perpetrators are family members, either adult children or spouses (Pillemer & Finkelhor, 1988). Many provide considerable care to their victims (Anetzberger, 1987; Steinmetz, 1988). Therefore, victims often refuse to discuss elder abuse out of shame, a desire to protect the perpetrator, or a fear that the alternative to family care (no matter how abusive) is placement in a nursing home. Furthermore, as previously discussed, perpetrators often commit elder abuse out of individual pathology, caregiver incompetence, greed, or financial dependence. This suggests that some interventions must be developed in addition to those at departments of human services or aging, if they are to be effective. Minimally, interface with mental health, mental retardation, alcoholism, and criminal justice systems is required, and generally has not occurred.

The third, and last, consequence of premature policies and practices has been the overuse of familiar and restrictive interventions. Too often, repeated abuse or chronic self-neglect results in the victims being placed under guardianship or in a nursing home (McLaughlin, 1988; Quinn & Tomita, 1986). This is the "quick and dirty" approach. It robs abuse victims of personal freedom and social connection. It requires the least imagination and resourcefulness. It reflects an underdeveloped protective service system and undertrained protective service workers. It bespeaks the early evolutionary stage of elder abuse treatment as it exists today.

Clarence, Sarah, Antonia, Mildred, and Connie are all real victims or perpetrators. Each has suffered abuse or neglect, or caused someone else to suffer them. Yet, every one of these individuals also has suffered from current protective laws and services designed to prevent and treat elder abuse. Clarence's perpetrator could never be charged with theft, despite Clarence's loss of thousands upon thousands of dollars. Sarah had no alternative living arrangement except coresidence with her mother, because no local training program existed to equip her for employment. The existence of criminal codes did not make Antonia safe in her home, and municipal codes did nothing to upgrade her neighborhood. Finally, hospital social workers angered Connie so much that she refused to allow Mildred further contact with psychiatric specialists who might have decreased her hypochondria and dependency.

POLICY IMPLICATIONS

Clearly, issues of vulnerability in elder abuse and neglect do not begin and end with the characteristics of victims. Likewise, resolving the problem of elder abuse will not come from changing victims and their circumstances alone. Resolution will emerge only from a multifaceted approach that considers victims in the context of family and those established policies and practices to prevent and treat elder abuse that reflect a sound understanding of the problem's etiology and dynamics.

The system of protection that would emerge from a multifaceted approach has certain minimal features. First, it needs to be adequately funded. Implementation cannot rely on existing resources alone. There must be a recognition that new imperatives require new sources of support.

Second, periodic assessment of the appropriateness, effectiveness, and efficiency of prevailing policies, programs, and services is essential. It is also important to ensure that research and practice evaluations be conducted to gain new insights on the problem and needed changes.

Third, restrictive interventions need to be inhibited. These may include statutory provisions requiring the use of less restrictive legal alternatives, such as those indicated in the adult protective service law, before the appointment of guardianship can be made.

Fourth, although elderly victims of maltreatment continue to be the focus of intervention, an evolved system of protection needs to include the approach that, when elder abuse is a family problem, intervention should involve all affected members.

Finally, a system of protection is necessary to invoke changes at the societal level, in an attempt to eradicate the underlying causes of elder abuse. Change of this nature may promote the empowerment of women, improvement of housing, development of neighborhoods, and creation of informal networks of support. All these changes may reduce the vulnerability of individuals and, in turn, decrease the likelihood of abuse occurence.

REFERENCES

American Public Welfare Association and National Association of State Units on Aging. (1987). *A comprehensive analysis of state policy and practice related to elder abuse.* Washington, D.C.

Anetzberger, G. J. (1987). *The etiology of elder abuse by adult offspring.* Springfield, IL: Charles C. Thomas.

Block, M. R., & Sinnott, J. D. (Eds.), (1979). *The battered elder syndrome: An exploratory study.* College Park, MD: University of Maryland, Center on Aging.

Carroll, J. C. (1975). *A cultural consistency theory of family violence in Mexican-American and Jewish subcultures.* Paper presented at the Annual Meeting of the National Council on Family Relations.

Chen, P. N., Bell, S. L., Dolinsky, D. L., Doyle, J., & Dunn, M. (1981). Elderly abuse in domestic settings: A pilot study. *Journal of Gerontological Social Work, 4*(1), 3–17.

Crouse, J. S., Cobb, D. C., Harris, B. B. et al. (1981). *Abuse and neglect of the elderly in Illinois: Incidence and characteristics, legislation, and policy recommendations.* Springfield, IL: Sangamon State University and Illinois Department on Aging.

Douglass, R. L., Hickey, T., & Noel, C. (1980). *A study of maltreatment of the elderly and other vulnerable adults.* Ann Arbor, MI: University of Michigan, Institute of Gerontology.

Faulkner, L. R. (1982). Mandating the reporting of suspected cases of elder abuse—An inappropriate, ineffective and ageist response to the abuse of older adults. *Family Law Quarterly, 16*(1), 69–91.

Finley, G. E. (1983). Fear of crime in the elderly. In J. I. Kosberg (Ed.), *Abuse and maltreatment of the elderly: Causes and interventions* (pp. 21–39). Boston: John Wright.

Gioglio, G. R., & Blakemore, P. (1983). *Elder abuse in New Jersey: The knowledge and experience of abuse among older New Jerseyans.* Trenton, NJ: New Jersey Department of Human Resources.

Gray Panthers of Austin. (1983). *A survey of abuse in the elderly in Texas.* Unpublished manuscript. Austin, TX.

Hennan, C. B., & Photiades, J. (1979). The rural Appalachian low-income male: Changing role in a changing family. *The Family Coordinator, 28,* 608–615.

Hwalek, M., Sengstock, M. C., & Lawrence, R. (1984). Assessing the probability of abuse of the elderly. Paper presented at the Annual Meeting of the Gerontological Society of America.

Krauskopf, J. M., & Burnett, M. E. (1983). The elderly person: When protection becomes abuse. *Trial, 19* (December), 60–67, 97–98.

Lau, E. E., & Kosberg, J. I. (1979, October). Abuse of the elderly by informal care providers. *Aging,* 10–15.

Liang, J., & Sengstock, M. C. (1983). Personal crimes against the elderly. In J. I. Kosberg (Ed.), *Abuse and maltreatment of the elderly: Causes and interventions* (pp. 40–67). Boston: John Wright.

McLaughlin, C. (1988). "Doing good": A worker's perspective. *Public Welfare,* 46(2), 29–32.

O'Malley, H., Segars, H., Perez, R., Mitchell, V., & Kneupfel, G. M. (1979). *Elder abuse in Massachusetts: A survey of professionals and para-professionals.* Boston: Legal Research and Services for the Elderly.

Phillips, L. R. (1983). Abuse and neglect of the frail elderly at home: An exploration of theoretical relationships. *Journal of Advanced Nursing, 8,* 379–392.

Pillemer, K. A. (1985, Fall). Social isolation and elder abuse. *Response,* 2–4.

Pillemer, K. A. (1986). Risk factors in elder abuse: Results from a case-control study. In K. A. Pillemer & R. S. Wolf (Eds.), *Elder abuse: Conflict in the family* (pp. 239–263). Dover, MA: Auburn House.

Pillemer, K. A., & Findelhor, D. (1988). The prevalence of elder abuse: Findings from a random-sample survey. *The Gerontologist, 28,* 51–57.

Quinn, M. J., & Tomita, S. K. (1986). *Elder abuse and neglect: Causes, diagnosis, and intervention strategies.* New York: Springer.

Rathbone-McCuan, E. (1978). Intergenerational family violence and neglect: The aged as victims of reactivated and reverse neglect. Paper presented at the XIth International Congress of Gerontology.

Salend, E., Kane, R. Satz, M., & Pynoos, J. (1984). Elder abuse reporting: Limitations of statutes. *The Gerontologist, 24(1),* 61–69.

Schene, P., & Ward, S. F. (1988). The relevance of child protection experience. *Public Welfare, 46(2),* 14–21.

Sengstock, M. C., & Liang, J. (1982). *Identifying and characterizing elder abuse.* Detroit: Wayne State University, Institute of Gerontology.

Steinmetz, S. K. (1983). Dependency, stress, and violence between middle-aged caregivers and their elderly parents. In J. I. Kosberg (Ed.), *Abuse and maltreatment of the elderly: Causes and interventions* (pp. 134–149). Boston: John Wright.

Steinmetz, S. K. (1988). *Duty bound: Elderly abuse and family care.* Newbury Park, CA: Sage.

Tatara, T. (1990). *Summaries of national elder abuse data: An exploratory study of state statistics based on a survey of state adult protective service and aging agencies.* Washington, D.C.: National Aging Resource Center on Elder Abuse.

U.S. House Select Committee on Aging. (1981). *Elder abuse (An examination of a hidden problem)* (Committee Publication No. 97-277). Washington, D.C.: U.S. Government Printing Office.

U.S. House Select Committee on Aging (1990). *Elder abuse: A decade of shame and inaction* (Committee Publication No. 101-752). Washington, D.C.: U.S. Government Printing Office.

Wolf, R. S., Godkin, M. A., & Pillemer, K. A. (1984). *Elder abuse and neglect: Final report from three model projects.* Worcester, MA: University of Massachusetts Medical Center, University Center on Aging.

10
The Homeless Elderly: No Room at the End

Marsha A. Martin

There is a growing awareness in the United States that homelessness is a problem of immense proportions. In every major city in the United States, and in smaller ones, there is an identifiable group of individuals who are homeless. In large metropolitan centers, such as Los Angeles, Chicago, Houston, and New York, the number of homeless individuals (including family members) ranges from 25,000 to more than 70,000 (Cuomo, 1983). The exact number of homeless individuals is unknown; however, estimates range from 250,000 to more than 2.5 million men, women, and children nationwide (Hombs and Snyder, 1982; U.S. HUD, 1984). Regardless of the absolute number of homeless persons nationwide and the degree of disability within the homeless population, the problem of homelessness is a very serious one (Martin & Long, 1987). For men and women who are older adults, homelessness is a problem not often discussed. Although it has been estimated that as many as 27% of the homeless are 60 years of age and older, little attention has be paid to their needs (Cohen et al., 1988).

This chapter on homelessness will present an overview of the current problem of homelessness in the United States; describe the phenomenon among older adults through the presentation of vignettes that focus on the magnitude of the experience of being homeless; examine some of the underlying causes among older adults; discuss the process of adaptation to homelessness; and suggest an approach to working with homeless older adults that acknowledges, understands, and addresses various life-cycle needs.

OVERVIEW OF HOMELESSNESS

At no time since the Depression has the homeless population represented so wide a cross section of American society as it does today (CSS, 1982). Prior to the 1980s, the "skid-row alcoholic," typically a white male in his late 50s or early 60s and the "shopping bag lady," bundled up in a corner wrapped in layers of mix-matched clothing, represented "the homeless." Today, however, the homeless are truly a cross section of American society, as the following descriptions reveal:

> They are men, women and children of all ages and all ethnic and religious backgrounds. They are single persons, couples, and families. They represent all educational levels, occupations and professions. (Arce & Vergare, 1983)
>
> The homeless of today are extremely heterogenous. No longer do they fit the traditional stereotype—a single, middle-aged white alcoholic male. They are men, women, runaway youths, and families. Some have chronic disabilities—mental illness, alcoholism and other forms of substance abuse. (Connell, 1987)
>
> The homeless are a much more heterogenous group consisting of women (including "battered women") as well as men, people of all age groups (including runaway youth), Blacks, Hispanics, Asian-Pacific Islanders as well as whites, those with alcohol, drug abuse and mental-health related problems, families as well as single persons, those who have never been employed (or have been unemployed for a very long time) and those recently unemployed . . . they are people with chronic disabilities; people who have suffered adverse economic conditions. (HUD, 1984)
>
> The homeless are a heterogenous population comprised of many subgroups including runaway children, immigrants, migrants, so-called bag ladies, displaced families, a certain number of the unemployed, battered women, minorities, the elderly, and an overrepresentation of persons with serious alcohol, drug abuse and mental health disorders. (Levine, 1983)
>
> More recently, the "new homeless" include persons who have lost their jobs or public assistance, lost their residences, and were subsequently unable to find affordable housing. (GAO, 1985)
>
> The homeless are the poorest of the poor. Not only do they lack material resources, they lack human resources as well—family who will take them in. (Piliavin & Sosin, 1987)

These descriptions reveal the nature of homelessness in the United States; that is, the diversity of individuals, family structures, economic bases, ethnic and racial composition, health and employment status, demographic characteristics, and sociocultural and political influences. While history may provide some understanding of the social, cultural, political, and economic forces that occurred during the years preceding the Depression, understanding what forces have come together during the last 20 years of U.S. prosperity to once again create massive numbers of homeless is not only difficult, but the complexity of the interactive dynamics of the forces also makes addressing the problem of homelessness extremely difficult, with attention turning toward structural solutions.

During the past decade, research studies using sample populations, consisting of individuals and families who have become homeless, have increased our knowledge and understanding about homelessness. The causes have been identified and delineated: absence and inadequacy of affordable housing, hospitalization policies, unemployment, fragmentation of human services, changing family structure, inflation, increases in alcohol and substance use and abuse, and poverty. Service needs have been identified and assessed: shelter, food, clothing, alcohol and substance abuse rehabilitation, mental health treatment, medical care, socialization, vocational training and employment, safety, permanent housing, case management services, and someone who cares (Martin, 1986).

While much has been learned from these research efforts, very little is known about the characteristics of subgroups that exist among the homeless nationwide. As the preceding descriptions illustrate, the homeless population includes men, women, and children of all ages. Yet very little attention has been directed toward those individuals who are 65 years of age and older. In fact, research on the homeless has guided the discussion about the homeless in the opposite direction. Increasingly, the focus has been on the phenomenon of youthfulness; that is, the fact that the homeless are getting younger. "The homeless population is . . . changing and includes . . . a younger population in their mid-30's" (GAO, 1985). Statements such as this one appear with frequency in the media. A review of the Health Care for the Homeless projects confirms and offers an explanation for this trend:

> The fact is, homeless people are surprisingly young. The median age of HCH adults is thirty-four years; all recent studies of homeless populations have remarked on the low average age, perhaps because the stereotype is that the homeless tend to be old. Today, the average homeless adult male is somewhere in his early to middle thirties.
>
> The low average age of the homeless sustains an important and often overlooked conclusion, namely, that the rise of the "new homeless" is in some sense a result of the so-called baby boom, the immensely large generations born in the United States between 1947 and 1964. As a cohort, the average age of the baby boom is now in the early thirties, almost identical to the average of homeless people. (Wright, 1988)

Unfortunately, this new trend has resulted in less attention being given to the needs of the homeless older adult. Consequently, efforts to ameliorate homelessness have tended to focus on opportunities for younger individuals and families. The homeless who are older adults (usually considered to be those individuals 55 years of age and older) are overlooked. Although earlier research studies on homelessness contained sample populations of middle-age and older men, it was their "Bowery," "skid row" life-style and their alcoholism that appeared to be of greater interest to the researchers and social scientists than their age stage or life-cycle issues. Ironically, now that age is finding its place among the demographic characteristics to consider when researching and discussing homelessness and related issues, the homeless elderly are again overlooked and left out of the definition of those in need. This general lack of attention to the importance of age differences among the homeless has resulted in limited useful information for planning, program development, and service delivery.

THE HOMELESS ELDERLY

It is very difficult to fully understand and accept the circumstances that result in homelessness for older adults. The following vignettes identify and highlight the varied routes to homelessness and some of the characteristics of the older adult homeless population.

Mr. Jones, 80 years of age, with no family in New York City, had no one to turn to when the landlord stopped performing general maintenance services, and so he abandoned the apartment building where he had been living.

> Mr. Winston Jones was an independent eighty-year-old black man, who lived on social security. Mr. Jones had an extensive work history and had been retired since he turned sixty-five. He had lived for twelve years in his last apartment. His landlord failed to provide essential services—heat, hot water, repairs, etc. and New York City housing department eventually took possession of the building. The building, although managed by the city, continued to deteriorate, tenants left and scavengers began to rob and burglarize tenants. Mr. Jones, having been burglarized and unable to function without essential services, was forced to leave the building.
>
> Mr. Jones had no family left in NYC to turn to for assistance. Instead, he turned to the Port Authority Bus Terminal, located in Times Square, where he found lockers to store his personal belongings, and chairs in waiting rooms to rest on. He passed time in all night movie theaters in the area and rode subways at night. Occasionally, he would catch some sleep in a terminal waiting room. He looked for another place to live, but could not find decent, affordable housing. Mr. Jones, accustomed to an independent lifestyle, was not ready to consider an adult home, a nursing home or the sofa at his 65-year-old sister's house in Philadelphia.
>
> Because of failing physical conditions, Mr. Jones accepted shelter at one of

the "flophouses" on the Bowery. Although it provided Mr. Jones with a bed and limited supports, it was necessary to negotiate four flights of stairs in order to "go and come" as he felt was necessary to maintain his lifestyle. Additionally, Mr. Jones had to contend with a younger population of men, who typically took advantage of the older men on the Bowery. Increasingly fearful for his life, Mr. Jones accepted an offer from his sister in Philadelphia to move in with her and her family.

Following a month of "trying to adjust," Mr. Jones returned to New York City, where he returned to living on the street, dependent on transportation centers to meet his needs. Mr. Jones was eventually hospitalized for pneumonia, and died in Bellevue Hospital. (MBC, 1985)

Ms. Ethel Baker, a woman in her 60s, could no longer afford the rent at the welfare hotel on her meager Social Security check. She could stay at the shelter, but only three nights of the week. There were so many other "homeless ladies" that the shelter staff had to rotate the women in and out of the 12 beds and the 24 "sit-up" slots.

Ms. Ethel Baker was an energetic sixty-six year old white woman who had been living on the street for four years . . . Originally from Brooklyn, she called Manhattan her home. She had one brother who was homeless, who she reported seeing "every once in a while." She had been an "electronics" factory worker most of her life, learning her trade during the "Rosie the Riveter" days during the war. Ms. Baker retired at age sixty-two and began receiving Social Security benefits shortly thereafter. Ms. Baker had been living in a single room occupancy hotel (SRO) until her meager monthly income could no longer "cover the rent." She lost her room "due to the prevailing circumstances" and began to make a life for herself "doing the best" she could with what she had.

Like many of the other older homeless women in the Times Square area of New York City, Ms. Baker spent most of her days in and around the Port Authority Bus Terminal. A small shelter for homeless women which offered meals and a bed on a limited basis had opened near the transportation center and it provided Ms. Baker and other homeless women with opportunity to address some of their pressing needs.

Because the shelter program was small, the women who were able to stay there had to do so on a rotating basis. Each could spend three nights at the shelter, on the other four nights, they would have to seek shelter elsewhere. On those nights, Ms. Baker would leave the shelter carrying her few possessions in a small shopping bag and a black hand bag. Ms. Baker hated the nights when she had to find alternate shelter, living on the street was "damn hard."

On one of her "nights out" on rotation, Ms. Baker was brutally murdered. The press called it an act of human vandalism. (Martin, 1982)

Kathryn Boston, 57 years of age, lost her job due to a worsening health condition. In the absence of disability coverage, she was not able to keep up with her monthly expenses, including rent, and finally was forced to seek refuge in a 24-hour transportation facility.

> Kathryn Boston, a fifty-seven year old white woman spent her days (and nights) in Pennsylvania station, like many other homeless women. Divorced, with no children, no close family ties and no close friends, Kathryn went to Penn Station because the neighborhood was familiar to her.
>
> Kathryn had worked at clerical and waitress jobs for the last fifteen years, supporting herself and residing in midtown SRO hotels. A worsening sinus condition, coupled with her age, made it difficult for her to find and hold a steady job. When her last temporary job ended, she could not find employment and was forced to leave her hotel room as she could no longer afford the weekly rent. She tried to find employment through the state employment service, but was without the proper identification and documentation: birth certificate and social security card. In attempting to secure a new social security card, Kathryn was told she would need a birth certificate and proper identification in order to receive a replacement card. With the support of an outreach program, which operated in the midtown area, Kathryn was able to secure the necessary documents, apply for government entitlement funds and secure permanent housing. (MBC, 1985)

Mary Jones, a woman who looked much older than she was, had been hospitalized on several occasions by the neighborhood police department. As a result of her mental disorder, schizophrenia of the paranoid type, she was not able to live in the community unassisted or unsupervised.

> Mary Jones, a middle-aged white women diagnosed with paranoid schizophrenia, had been living off and on the street between two and four years. She had a history of several psychiatric hospitalizations characterized by bizarre delusions: people who were putting parts of animals into her body and spirits that were controlling her mind. She had been removed from the street by police on several occasions, hospitalized in a municipal hospital, and released to the street. On several occasions, through the support of an outreach team, she had been able to secure shelter and at least once, find a hotel room. However, she eventually lost that room as a result of her poor hygiene, her habit of rummaging through garbage receptacles in the hotel lobby, and letting her shower overrun to cause numerous floods. Refusing to accept any further help from the outreach teams, she returned to the street.
>
> Ms. Jones was approached on several occasions on the street corner where she had set up "house." She had specific areas for sleeping, washing-up, bathing, eating and so forth . . . She remained suspicious and disturbed and continued to have bizarre paranoid and somatic delusions. She was hospitalized involuntarily at a municipal hospital and later transferred to a state psychiatric facility, where she remains. (Martin, 1987)

As evidenced by these vignettes, to be homeless or to be shelterless is to be without the most basic of resources. To be homeless is to be without a structure, a foundation, a base of operations, a resting place. Home is the place for emotional nourishment, a place to close out the world, a place to regroup, to realign, a place to center oneself. It is from the home that we travel into the world, and it is the home to which we return. It is our first and primary place and space.

To not have a home is to have and be no place. Homelessness is a devastating experience to the body, mind, and spirit. And as public officials and private organizations have found, being homeless means more than being without a home. It means being without those bonds that link settled persons to a network of interconnected social structures. Being homeless involves being without the resources, internal as well as external, necessary for meeting basic human needs.

CAUSES OF HOMELESSNESS FOR OLDER ADULTS

In 1985, the total number of people residing in the United States was 238,631,000. Of these, 11.8% (or 29,319,000) were 65 years of age and older. By 1990, the projected total population for the United States is expected to reach 249,657,000; for those over 65, it is expected to reach more than 32 million (12.6%). Unfortunately, of all persons living in poverty, more than 10% will be within this age cohort (65 and over) (Rosen et al., 1987). Of the 23 million individuals in the United States living in substandard housing, the elderly are overrepresented (Birch, 1985). This age cohort will also represent 35% of all householders living in subsidized housing with median household incomes of less than $4,087 (Rosen et al., 1987). Although poverty among the elderly has been well documented, its impact has not lessened in relation to the increase in knowledge about the nature of it. Poor elderly adults are constantly forced to choose options that offer little more than the choice "between a rock and a hard place." As Dr. Sanjek writes,

> The elderly poor pay most of their income for rent; then they cover telephone and medical expences. What is left, they spend on food. Most report they run out of money before the end of the month . . . The poor elderly tend to be older and more isolated, and to include more women than the elderly population in general . . . The elderly poor are more socially isolated than the elderly population. Half of the elderly have no living children, and those who do are less likely to see or visit their children than are the elderly in general . . . One-third of the elderly poor have no friend or friends in their neighborhood. (Sanjek, 1984)

More specifically, the homeless elderly are those individuals who can no longer afford to pay rent and eat. They are individuals with low incomes, those persons who have been forced out of the labor pool. They are those with disabling health and mental health problems, and they are simply individuals with few resources and no place to go—the poorest of the poor.

"For the . . . elderly, those characterized as having few resources . . . survival is a struggle of immense proportions. Obtaining food, shelter, safety, medical attention, conviviality, money, and clothing are daily preoccupations. When conventional means are closed or out of reach . . . the only alternative" (Frankfather, 1977) for some is life on the street.

ADAPTATION TO HOMELESSNESS

For homeless older adults, living on the street represents a survival strategy, "not just a temporary solution to a situational problem . . . Personalized methods for acquiring such necessities as food, clothing, showers, shelter and financial support" are created (Martin, 1982). These created strategies for meeting basic needs and acquiring essential resources are enhanced by strategies that lessen the impact of the stress of living outdoors as well as assist the older homeless individual in maintaining some sense of self-worth. These maintenance strategies include such defense mechanisms as denial, rationalization, fantasy play, and self-entertainment, as well as basic survival skills such as the ability to eat anything, to select discarded food carefully, to sleep sitting up, to locate sheltering materials with insulation qualities, to bathe in a sink, to secure a safe place to rest, to stand in line for hours on end, and to live life in the public view. These strategies and skills enable the older homeless adult to live outdoors, on the streets, in parks, and in transportation centers with some modicum of success.

For homeless older adults who live in shelters and drop-in centers, the above-mentioned strategies and skills remain in effect with minor adjustments in their intensity. Some shelter programs provide sleeping accommodations in a dormitory style, which may necessitate a certain degree of denial in order to experience some privacy; however, securing insulation materials is not necessary. Some shelter and drop-in center programs provide meals, yet the older homeless adult rarely has a choice in what is served. And finally, many drop-in center programs do not provide beds, but very often provide chairs for individuals to sleep in overnight, necessitating the continuance of the ability to sleep sitting up.

Health status and health care are very important components in the adaptation process: "Physical health is a key variable in determining ability to fulfill needs" (Cohen et al., 1988). If an older homeless adult is physi-

cally ill and/or physically debilitated, the successful acquisition of resources to meet needs will be hampered. Additionally, constant exposure
to changing and inclement weather, resulting in a lower resistance and
defense against infection and disease, can effectively reduce the life span of
an older adult.

What Does Homelessness Mean to an Older Adult?

> I can stretch out but I can't relax my body, lay down and sleep. It's no joke
> sitting up in a hard bench sleepin'. Everytime somebody passes I'm woke. My
> nerves is on edge 'cause I've seen people attacked in the park. (Cohen et al.,
> 1988)
> I get mugged nearly every month. This month I lost my entire check right
> after I cashed it. (Cohen et al., 1988)
> I'm really tired, I'm worn out. You walk back and forth from 23rd street
> Madison Square Park to 42nd Street to the Bowery. I must walk 30 miles a
> day. (Cohen et al., 1988)
> Sometimes I don't eat for a day or two, until someone gives me some
> money or food. (Martin, 1982)
> I hate pants, but that's all they have. I'm used to wearing a dress or a skirt.
> But they don't have any in my size. (Martin, 1982)
> Be careful over there at the Port. It's dangerous. They hit you with sticks
> and tell you to get out. At Penn Station, they're always fighting, the ladies in
> the bathroom. It's not safe. (Martin, 1982)
> I used to sleep on Fifth Avenue in a box until people started bothering me.
> (Martin, 1982)
> It's dangerous out there, we ain't supposed to sleep out there, they have to
> give us shelter. (Martin, 1982)

Homelessness and older adulthood together present an array of demands and challenges. Not only is it necessary to be concerned with over-
coming tremendous obstacles to meet basic human needs, such as food,
clothing, safety, shelter, and so on, it is also necessary to respond to the
demands of the concluding task of the life cycle, the crisis of aging: integrity versus despair (Erikson, 1963, 1986). During this crisis stage, the experience of social, physical, emotional, and material loss, coupled with the
struggle to conserve one's identity, creates an extraordinary challenge. This
is especially difficult and further compounded for individuals who have
become homeless, where loss and change of roles and functions are so
keen and acute. For homeless adults, whose primary activities appear to
involve securing resources to meet basic needs and not to result in the
conservation of identity and/or the process of consolidation, homelessness
itself is an challenge that must be mastered for the ego to complete an
emotional integration process.

The research of Cohen and Douglass (Cohen et al., 1988; Douglass et al., 1988) provide some interesting data to support this process. Cohen and associates studied older adult males on the Bowery and found that various survival strategies emerged that are primary in the lives of the older adult male population. In fact, these survival techniques allow the men on the Bowery to live on very little, to barely survive. As one of the respondents said, "I won't say I 'live' on the Bowery, I'd say 'survive'" (Douglass, et al., 1988). This statement suggests that the concrete elements of survival take precedence over quality of life issues and concerns.

Douglass and associates studied older homeless men and women in Detroit (women represented approximately 10% of the sample) and found them to be an extremely vulnerable group, subject to victimization and, consequently, isolation resulting from the need for safety and protection (Douglass et al., 1988) Fear among the homeless elderly is a common experience, especially when physiological and psychological changes hamper the ability to protect and take care of oneself in an unsheltered, outdoor setting.

According to Erikson (1986), the emotional integration process involves not only the ability to look back with satisfaction and ahead with serenity at one's whole life through the life review process, but also the ability to experience a sense of personal integrity and completeness. During this time, when the experience and reality of physical loss are more acute, the focus returns to the self, one's achievements and the integrity of one's whole life. During this age stage, the individual attempts to accept his or her life history, to be able to see the effect he or she has had on the world through his or her relationships and accomplishments. It is the time for order and meaning, the time for emotional integration of a lifetime of activity. Is is possible to be homeless and resolve this task? The answer to the question is yet to be fully researched. What is known is that the special needs of homeless older adults for basic resources, coupled with the aging process, the increased vulnerability, and the absence of affiliation and safety, demand a very different type of interventive response than currently exists.

INTERVENTIVE RESPONSES AND STRATEGIES

Problems that result from homelessness present startling challenges to the social welfare system on both the federal and local levels. As has been illustrated elsewhere in this chapter, the men and women who are homeless or who are at risk of homelessness have a multiplicity of problems and possess a complex array of needs. Most social service systems are not organized to respond to this level of need. These men and women need a complex and well-coordinated system of care: outreach, assistance in meeting basic needs, mental health care, 24-hour crisis assistance, housing, primary medical care, education, family support and counseling, employment and vocational services, case management services, and the development of natural support networks (NIMH, 1980; Stroul, 1986). In 1987, with the passage of the Stewart B. McKinney Homeless Assistance Act (PL 100-77), federal dollars were made available to states and municipalities for emergency and some long-term relief (NMHA, 1988). The act created a variety of categorical funding streams for such programs as community mental health, primary health care, housing, emergency food and shelter, job training, and education. The act also authorized expansion of some existing programs: veterans job training, community service block grants, food stamps, and so on, to ensure eligibility for homeless persons.

With the additional support from the McKinney Act, states and localities have been able to expand existing services and develop new ones. Almost every major city in the United States has a program designed to bring relief to the homeless (U.S. Conference of Mayors Report, 1988). However, there is no perfect community-based system of care for individuals and families who are at risk of becoming homeless. What exists is a hodge podge of outreach, drop-in center, health care, emergency, and transitional services. Most of these services provide little more than a bed or a chair to sleep on, a hot meal, health assessment and screening, and a refuge from inclement weather. Additionally, very little attention is given to the special needs of the individuals for whom the services are designed. With the exception of families, very little assessment and coordinated services are available. Very often, persons with mental disabilities are sheltered along with those with primary health needs and substance use problems. Young men and women are often sheltered with older adults. In an ideal setting, this type of integration might be beneficial; however, in the absence of purposeful planning and programming, special needs are neglected, and so are special people.

If the responses to the needs of the homeless older adult are to be effective, they must take into consideration the multiple needs of the homeless older adult. Services for homeless older adults must reflect a holistic approach to the elderly individual's health, mental health, social welfare, and familial/affiliative needs. In defining services, the whole person must be taken into consideration, as well as the accompanying life-style. All services essential for an older adult's well-being are essential when he or she is homeless.

In addition to the problems inherent to homelessness, the homeless older adult experiences a variety of health, mental health, and social welfare problems. Common health problems include diabetes, hypertension, cardiovascular problems, upper respiratory problems, dermatological problems, malnutrition, and exposure. Mental health problems include schizo-phrenia, depression, character disorders, organic brain syndrome, and alcohol and drug abuse. The social welfare problems include lack of access to public and/or private agencies and service systems, ineligibility due to no address, client-resistant service programs, fragmentation of services, lack of coordination of services, and limited income. Although the elderly are entitled to receive a variety of government benefits, such as Food Stamps, Medicare, Social Security, and Supplemental Security Income, these programs are not sufficient to meet the multiple needs of the home-less older adult. What is needed are programs that base their approach on an "age-stage" life-cycle developmental model (Erikson, 1963); that is, programs that attempt to integrate the life-cycle, developmental needs of the older adult with resources typically designed to respond to the needs of the "generic" homeless.

Thus far, services for the homeless have clustered around three program models: outreach services, drop-in centers, and transitional shelters. Taken together, these program models comprise the essential components of a good emergency relief system of care for the homeless. What follows is a discussion of these models highlighting various aspects adapted for their use with older homeless adults.

Outreach Services

> It took two years of persistent, aggressive reaching out—knocking on her door, offering coffee and services with entitlements, friendly conversation— to get a 73-year-old frightened, fifteen-year resident of the Amsterdam Hotel to open her door. After many more follow-up non-threatening visits she fi-nally agreed to come to a drop-in center for a sandwich. Since that time ten years ago, she continues to attend the center regularly. (Sanjek, 1984)

A variety of outreach services and programs have been designed to work with the homeless. Some outreach programs provide access to community-based services designed to meet basic needs; others represent satellite of-fices, a kind of outposting of essential services in areas where homeless men and women congregate. Regardless of the approach, outreach pro-grams are very often the first step back toward indoor living for most homeless individuals. Consequently, great care must go into developing an appropriately sensitive program. What might such a program look like for the older adult homeless population?

While the intent of outreach is to link homeless men and women to community-based services, very often it is necessary to provide concrete services and ongoing case management to facilitate movement from the street and/or transportation centers. Recognizing the importance of familiarity and continuity to homeless older adults, outreach programs that develop consistency in two areas—program design and team composition—can provide the first step back toward rehabilitation and indoor living. Outreach teams/programs may be the first professional assistance offered to many homeless men and women and, therefore, have the opportunity to represent structure in the form of consistency. While they may not offer physical spaces, outreach programs can offer a psychological place for grounding. They become, in essence, the testing ground for the reestablishment of relationships. Fear of loss may keep a homeless older adult at a distance initially: refusing assistance, insisting that everything is all right. Fear of death may serve to motivate an older homeless individual to remain on the street where safety and care may be perceived to be more accessible from random passersby and police officers on patrol than in an isolated hotel/board and care home room or with family members. Loss and death are real issues for all older adults; for older homeless adults, they may fuel a retreat from connectedness and perceived isolation and entrapment. The story of 67-year-old Rebecca Smith illustrates this phenomenon:

> During the week of January 24, 1987, Rebecca Smith was found frozen to death in a makeshift cardboard box dwelling. Attempts had been made repeatedly to "coax" her into a hospital or a city shelter, "but she refused." She was described by her daugher as a woman who "basically wanted her freedom" . . . She didn't want to be penned in. She was very determined . . . to be independent. (Martin, 1982)

Outreach programs serving older homeless adults can be effective if the approach to outreach incorporates knowledge of the dynamics of aging with respect for the elder. This approach helps to reactivate self-esteem. Most older homeless adults see themselves as "bums" (this is also true for women) and sense that the world feels the same. Approaching homeless men and women over time, with the recognition that they have wants, needs, and a sense of self based on a life of varied and valuable experiences, will result in a desire to reconnect and move from the street and/or transportation center existence toward an indoor one.

Drop-in Center Services

"The use of the generic term *drop-in centers* seems to convey a philosophy or an attitude rather than a specific physical structure or type of program. Drop-in centers are often distinguished from more formal programs by their zealous commitment to helping meet the survival needs of their guests, while respecting the dignity and worth of the individual. As implied by their title, they require no commitment or formal affiliation for a night's respite from the streets. Their appeal is their accessibility and acceptability" (Levine, 1983). For older homeless adults, drop-in centers not only provide basic services (including food, clothing, respite, showers, delousing, psychiatric and medical attention, socialization, and safety), but do so in an atmosphere that respects the individual's desire and need for anonymity, autonomy, and competence.

After a period of time has elapsed (usually defined by the homeless individual in consultation with staff), allowing the older homeless man or woman to adapt to the drop-in center ambience and routine, some drop-in centers provide opportunities for work and rehabilitation through the development of groups and various day programming and vocational rehabilitation-type activities. These programs can be designed around the age-stage needs of older homeless adults. For example, the guests could participate in life review groups. They could also contribute to the operation of the drop-in center by volunteer work in their articulated areas of expertise. Both of these structured activities provide the opportunity to reflect on life's past accomplishments and help to reinforce a positive sense of self through the accomplishment of certain necessary tasks. Many older adults participate in volunteer programs that provide the much needed extra help to both public and private agencies. Understanding the importance of similar opportunities for older homeless adults can result in drop-in center programs that are enhancing levels of functioning, not just maintaining them.

Transitional Shelter

Outreach and drop-in center services provide the much needed first invitation to return to "indoor living" (Martin, 1982). These two basic services, by design, permit the older homeless adult to reaffiliate through a slowly developing process. It may be months, and sometimes years, before older homeless adults are able to regain a sense of self, self-sufficiency, and trust necessary for changing the adaptation from life outdoors to life indoors. However, once the shift begins, transitional housing can provide the structure in which to complete the adaptation back to indoor living.

Transitional shelter provides the physical space necessary for trust to develop. Unfortunately, many older homeless adults will have experienced a variety of emotional and physical assaults, resulting in a lack of trust as well as in a well-defended exterior. Understanding this, transitional shelter services must include age-linked, sensitive, and creative programming. An example of this might be in response to personal hygiene needs.

In some shelter programs, showers and daily hygienic services are a priority. Yet limited attention has been paid to the needs of the older homeless adult for privacy and the reduction in the feeling of vulnerability. Asking a homeless person to shower is asking him or her to become completely vulnerable. It is important to keep in mind that the clothes on his or her back represent the only protection/shelter from the elements that he or she may have. To remove this protective layer is assuming, expecting, and literally asking too much; and for what—to take a shower? However, if bathrooms, which afford a small amount of privacy, were considered a priority in transitional shelter programs, perhaps, after a few days, a few weeks, or a few months, older homeless adults might start to concern themselves with their hygienic needs.

Additionally, smaller residences, with private rooms and common living spaces, approximating a home environment, help to reduce the scope of the homeless older adults' environment and enhance their ability to know and trust their own perceptions and the support of others. Although most outreach and drop-in center programs provide access to medical care, transitional shelter programs are better suited to provide health and mental health care services. When and if bed rest is prescribed, it is possible within a transitional shelter. When management of diet is required, smaller transitional shelters are more equipped to respond.

CONCLUSION

The above-mentioned components of a service program for older homeless adults are essential in creating the first step out of homelessness. These components will assist in the provision of immediate and short-term relief. However, they will not provide the necessary ongoing structural support that is needed to curb homelessness. Services are often fragmented, poorly oganized, and limited in scope. Sound planning and distribution of funds must be the next steps to ensure a continuum of services.

A continuum of services can be created based on the development and implementation of community-wide plans that would include the identification of needs, the existing network of services, and coordination of service delivery. A sound implementation plan would encompass a coordinated system of care for older homeless adults, including mandated linkages between outreach and drop-in center services; between drop-in centers and housing programs; between housing programs and leisure time activities and vocational programs; between daytime programs and medical and mental health programs.

Homelessness and those affected by it have become a major social concern during the past 10 years. Although governmental programs and entitlements have expanded the size of the safety net, older men and women continue to fall through the cracks. Medicare, Food Stamps, Supplemental

Security Income, Social Security, and other employment-related income streams do not adequately protect older adults from the risk of losing housing and becoming homeless. The following vignette highlights this reality.

> Celia Wong, 79, Astoria, Queens, a former librarian, came to a 1981 conference sponsored by the National Social Security. Her husband died recently, and she lives entirely on Social Security.
>
> "I can't live on it," she said. "I've been trying to find a job, but no one will hire someone my age. I don't qualify for food stamps, so I wind up buying tired vegetables, food in dented cans and outdated cold cuts. I'm one step away from picking garbage cans . . . In the past the life experience of the elderly was considered valuable," she said, "but today it's considered worthless." (Sanjek, 1984)

The services that have been developed, organized, and institutionalized during the more recent wave of homelessness are equally inadequate. Fabricant and Burghardt (1987), in their recent examination of the safety net, suggest that the value of the programs designed to fill the cracks are, at best symbolic in their effectiveness. They write:

> The few and scattered services that have recently been organized to meet the needs of citizens falling below the safety net often have more symbolic than real value. Shelters are temporary residences that do not address permanent housing needs; soup lines and food pantries are stop-gap measures that usually offer a couple of meals a week but cannot meet the basic dietary needs of citizens; workfare programs do not lead to permanent jobs for A.F.D.C. beneficiaries and the few job programs available to recently unemployed do not allow them to duplicate their former earning power or compete in regional labor markets. Relatedly, such programs are scarce commodities and, consequently, can only address a fraction of the need of the homeless, hungry, or recently unemployed. (Fabricant & Burghardt, 1987)

Changes in the sociocultural, political, and economic arenas, coupled with the changes in physical, social, and psychological abilities of older homeless adults, warrant the development of specialized services beyond those that currently exist. Additionally, once homeless, older adults are required to fend for themselves. This experience of disaffiliation and isolation is the opposite of what is necessary to complete the life-cycle tasks satisfactorily. Services, interventive approaches, and program models must provide a variety of options in response to individual differences and changing physical, personal, and social needs, as well as recognize and support the adulthood, individual capacities, and dignity of all homeless persons.

Erik Erikson, now approaching 90, suggests that "the sense of trust that begins to develop from the infant's experience of a loving and supportive environment becomes, in old age, an appreciation of human interdependence . . . Life doesn't make any sense without interdependence . . . We need each other and the sooner we learn that the better for us all" (Goleman, 1988). Older homeless men and women must relearn to trust that interdependence. Programs that seek to respond to the needs of the older homeless adult must also reflect the ideology of interdependence. Only then will the problem of homelessness be appropriately addressed.

REFERENCES

A Report to the Secretary on the Homeless and Emergency Shelters. (1984). Washington, D.C.: U.S. Dept. of Housing and Urban Development.

Arce, A. & Verfare, M. (1983). A psychiatric profile of street people admitted to an emergency shelter. *Hospital and Community Psychiatry, 34*, 812–817.

Birch, E. (1985). *The unsheltered women: Women and housing in the 1980s.* New York: Transaction Publications.

Cohan, C., Terent, J., Holmes, D., & Rich, E. (1988). Survival strategies of older homeless men. *The Gerontologist, 28*, 58–65.

Community Service Society (1982). *One year later: The homeless poor in New York City.* New York: Community Service Society.

Connell, S. (1987). Homelessness. In *Encyclopedia of social work, 18th edition.* Silver Spring, MD: NASW.

Cuomo, M. (1983). 1933/1983—Never Again: A Report to the National Governor's Association. New York: NY State Executive Chamber.

Douglass, R. et al. (1988). *Aging, adrift and alone: The urban homeless elderly.* Ypsilanti, Michigan: Eastern Michigan University.

Erikson, E. (1963). *Children and society, second edition.* New York: W.W. Norton.

Erikson, E. (1986). *Vital involvement in old age: The experience of old age in our time.* New York: W.W. Norton.

Fabricant, M., & Burghardt, S. (1987). *Working under the safety net: Policy and practice with the new American poor.* Beverly Hills, CA: Sage Publications.

Frankfather, D. (1977). *The aged in the community.* New York: Praeger.

Goleman, D. (1988). In his own old age, Expands his view of life. *The New York Times,* June 14, 1988.

Government Accounting Office. (1985). *Homelessness: A complex problem and the federal response.* Washington, D.C.

Hombs M., & Snyder, M. (1982). *Homeless in America: A forced march to nowhere.* Washington, D.C. Community for Creative Non-Violence.

Levine, I. (1983). Homelessness: Its implications for mental health policy and practice. Presented at the annual meeting of the American Psychological Association. Anaheim, CA.

Manhattan Bowery Corporation Case record. (1985). New York, New York.

Martin, M. (1982). *Strategies of adaptation: Coping patterns of urban transient females.* Unpublished dissertation. New York: Columbia University.

Martin, M. (1986). *The implications of NIMH-supported research for homeless mentally ill racial and ethnic minority persons.* Rockville, MD: NIMH.

Martin, M. (1987). Homelessness among chronically mentally ill women. In C. Nadelson & L. Bachrach (Eds.), *Treating chronically mentally ill women.* American Psychiatric Association.

Martin, M., & Long. L. (1987). Homelessness: A challenge to social work education. Presented at the annual program meeting of the Council on Social Work Education, St. Louis, MO.

National Institute of Mental Health (1980, September). Essential CSS functions. In Announcement—Community Support Systems Strategy Development and Implementation Grant. Rockville, MD: NIMH.

National Mental Health Association. (1988). *Urgent relief for homeless: A summary of the Stewart B. McKinney Homeless Assistance Act of 1987 (PL 100–77).* Alexandria, VA.

Piliavin, I., & Sosin, M. (1988). Tracking the homeless. *Focus, 10*(4), 20–24.

Rosen, S., Fanshel, D., & Lutz, M. (1987). Face of the nation. Statistical supplement to the 18th edition of the *Encyclopedia of social work.* Silver Spring, MD: NASW.

Sanjek, R. (1984). *Crowded out: Homelessness and the elderly poor in New York City.* New York: Coalition for the Homeless.

Stroul, B. 1986. Models of community support services: Approaches to helping persons with long-term mental illness. *Community Support Program.* Rockville, MD: NIMH.

U.S. Conference of Mayors. (1988). *A Status report on the Stewart B. McKinney Homeless Assistance Act of 1987.* Washington, D.C.

Wright, J. (1988). The worthy and unworthy homeless. *Society, 25*(5), 64–69.

11

The Vulnerable
Suicidal Elderly

Nancy J. Osgood and John L. McIntosh

Vulnerability to suicide is indicated by rates of suicide among the elderly that are considerably higher than for the nation as a whole. The multiple sources of change and loss associated with aging frequently place older adults in circumstances associated with stress and heightened suicide risk. As will be seen below, many life situations and characteristics associated with increased risk of suicide are also correlated with age. The result of these associations places the elderly among groups particularly vulnerable to the act of suicide. Indeed, at all ages, suicide is a multidetermined act, but the old are most likely to be experiencing this multiplicity of factors in their lives. Barter (1969) suggested that suicides of older adults seem to be a response "to a total life situation more than to a single event" (p. 9). Farberow and Moriwaki (1975) observed the same thing in elderly Veterans Administration patients who committed suicide. They concluded that the "accumulation of losses becomes so distressing that they prefer to end their lives" (p. 334). Suicidal older adults experience hopelessness and helplessness about their lives and feel there are few coping options available to them. Coupled with the many changes, losses, and stresses in their lives, suicide, therefore, is more probable and is seen by the elderly individual as a reasonable choice.

This chapter will focus on the multiple factors that increase the vulnerability of particular subgroups in the older population to suicide. Vulnerability resulting from demographic group membership as well as the presence of psychosocial factors such as depression and alcoholism, loneliness and social isolation, bereavement and widowhood, and the impact of terminal illness will be examined. Additionally, the chapter will highlight strategies and services for preventing suicide in this vulnerable population.

VULNERABILITY TO SUICIDE: DEMOGRAPHIC FACTORS

Not all older individuals are equally vulnerable to suicide. Demographic characteristics associated with vulnerability to suicide in old age include the age of the older adult, gender, race/ethnicity, and marital status.

Age

Suicide rates in general increase with advancing age, such that the peak occurs in older adulthood (Table 11.1). Despite highly publicized long-term increases in suicide by the young, the vulnerability of older adults to suicide remains higher than any other age group and more than 50% greater than that of the young or the nation as a whole. For example, in 1986, U.S. suicide rates were 12.8 per 100,000 population for the nation, 13.1 for those 15 to 24 years of age, and 21.5 for those 65 and over (National Center for Health Statistics, 1988). Making this considerably higher vulnerability of older adults even more remarkable is that long-term trends in elder suicide have shown decreases of approximately 50% (McIntosh, 1985). Recent figures have shown a slowing in this decline and, annually from 1981 to 1986, rates for the elderly have actually increased (while rates for the young have been stable or even declined slightly since 1979).

Not only do suicide rates increase with age and peak past age 65, but within the older adult population there is also differential vulnerability and higher rates with increasing age. As McIntosh (1984) noted, rates are greater among the old-old (75+ years of age) compared to the high rates

TABLE 11.1 United States Suicide Rates by Age, Sex, and Race, 1985

| Age groups | Number of Suicides per 100,000 population | | | | |
	Total	Male	Female	White	Nonwhite
Total	12.3	19.9	5.1	13.4	6.6
15–24	12.9	21.4	4.4	13.8	8.9
25–34	15.2	24.5	5.9	15.9	11.0
35–44	14.6	22.3	7.1	15.6	8.3
45–54	15.6	23.5	8.3	16.9	7.5
55–64	16.7	26.8	7.7	17.9	7.0
65+	20.3	40.4	6.6	21.6	8.4
65–74	18.5	33.3	6.9	19.6	8.6
75–84	24.1	53.1	6.8	25.6	8.7
75+	22.9	53.6	6.2	24.4	8.1
85+	19.1	55.4	4.6	20.3	5.9

SOURCE: NCHS, 1985, volume of Vital Statistics of the United States.

of the young-old (65 to 74 years of age; see Table 11.1). If the old-old age group is considered in more detail, suicide rates usually are highest for the 75 to 84 age group and slightly lower for the oldest-old (85 + years of age), although in the latter case, rates generally remain at levels higher than for any group younger than 65 +

Gender

Males kill themselves at all ages at much higher rates and numbers than do women, and gender differences are greatest in old age. For 1985, male rates of suicide for all ages combined were 3.9 times those for females, while this ratio was 6.1 at age 65 and above and 12.0 for 85 years of age and above (NCHS, 1985).

Race/Ethnicity

Suicide rate differences between whites and nonwhites in the United States are great at all ages above 35 (similar rates but higher for whites below 35) and largest above age 65 (Table 11.1). Even more pronounced are racial differences in old age by gender. White males are clearly the group most vulnerable to suicide (1985 rate: 43.2 per 100,000 population), while non-white males, white females, and nonwhite females are at considerably lower risk (1985 rates: 14.9, 6.9, and 3.9 per 100,000 population, respectively). These observations are generally true for blacks, native Americans, and Hispanics (whose rates peak in young adulthood) when specific ethnic rates are calculated. However Asian-Americans (Chinese-, Japanese-, and Filipino-Americans) display peak rates in old age, but at levels lower than for whites (McIntosh, 1987a).

Marital Status

Recent data (McIntosh, 1987b) indicate that suicide rates are highest for the divorced and widowed, with lower rates for single individuals and lowest vulnerability for the married. For the elderly, however, vulnerability to suicide is greatly affected by sex of the individual. The order above is true in old age also, divorced older adults being the group most vulnerable to suicide. Among elderly males, the differences between divorced and widowed are slight, with the single suicide rate only somewhat lower and the married less than half as vulnerable as are the divorced and widowed. For example, McIntosh (1987b) found that among males aged 65 to 74 for 1979–1981, the suicide rates were 66.4, 63.6, 44.0, and 23.4 per 100,000 population for the divorced, widowed, single, and married, respectively. Among females of the same ages, the rates were much lower in all cases and less disparate (9.9, 8.4, 5.6, and 5.5 per 100,000 population, respectively).

Other Demographic Factors

As observed in the United States as a whole (NCHS, 1988) and for the young (Seiden, 1984), suicide by the elderly occurs most often in the Western (West Coast and Rocky Mountain states) region of the country, with lower rates (in descending order) in the South, Midwest, and Northeast regions (McIntosh, 1988). Firearm use is the most common method of suicide in the United States (59.0% in 1985) and the old (65 and above years of age) use firearms (65.9% of 1985 suicides) and other lethal methods in even higher proportions than do other age groups (McIntosh & Santos, 1985–86). This is particularly true for older males who died by firearms (73.9% of their 1985 suicides).

Several factors and their interactions, which are associated with aging, increase the risk of death from suicide for older people (Osgood & McIntosh, 1986), including significant loss (physical, social, cognitive, emotional, financial); increased stress and decreased resistance to stress; lack of sociocultural norms related to the aged role; negative stereotypes that devalue aging and the aged; mental and physical health problems and especially depression; social isolation and loneliness; and heightened perception of life circumstances as hopeless (i.e., without solutions) and feeling personally helpless to effect changes (Shneidman, 1985). In addition, compared to younger individuals, the old openly communicate their suicidal intent less frequently, have poorer recuperative powers to recover from physical damage sustained in a suicide attempt, are more intent to die, and less often attempt suicide as a means of gaining attention or to cry for help. All these factors increase the risk of death from suicide for older people.

Clearly, the elderly are the most at-risk age group for completed suicide. Certain demographic factors increase the risk of suicide. In particular, elderly white males are most at risk, and the unmarried are at higher risk than the married.

VULNERABLE GROUPS OF ELDERLY

In addition to the demographic factors just discussed, certain other characteristics distinguish those elderly who are most vulnerable to suicide. The depressed, alcoholic, widowed, socially isolated, and lonely, as well as those with physical health problems, survivors of suicide, and the institutionalized, are groups vulnerable to suicide in late life. These subgroups of elderly possess life circumstances or characteristics that significantly increase susceptibility to suicide as reflected by high rates.

Depressed Elderly

The strong relationship between major affective disorder (depression) and suicide is widely recognized. Extremely high suicide rates are observed among depressed individuals, with rates many times that for the nation as a whole. Follow-up studies of depressed individuals have consistently shown that approximately one-sixth (15% to 17%) of depressives will eventually commit suicide. This represents an extremely serious situation because depression is the most common mental health problem, affecting millions of Americans annually (Miles, 1977)

Depression is also the most common mental health problem in old age, and rates of depression increase with advancing age, as do incidence rates of mental health problems generally (Blazer, 1982). More than any other age group, depression seems to be a factor in completed suicides for the elderly. Batchelor (1957) suggests that depression is a major factor in at least 80% of all elderly suicides and states that "all suicidal old people are depressed" (p. 291).

Depression may be produced by a number of factors associated with aging and discussed in this chapter, including stresses, losses, changes, illness, and feelings of hopelessness and helplessness. These factors may contribute to depression and heighten the risk of suicide or may themselves directly lead to suicide ideation and behavior. Among the symptoms of depression associated with suicidal behavior, none have been implicated as clearly or consistently as hopelessness. Indeed, hopelessness has been frequently observed as a more important predictor of suicide than depression per se (Beck et al., 1975).

Older Adults with Organic Brain Syndromes (OBS)

The relationship of OBS and suicide in old age is not clear. Lecso (1989) notes a possible link between aggressive/violent behavior including suicide among Alzheimer's disease (AD) patients, but notes that "suicide is not commonly reported" (p. 167) among AD patients. Pierce's (1987) study of patients seen at a general hospital after suicide attempts revealed that "only 3% had an established dementia" (p. 105). On the other hand, two studies of extremely serious attempters suggest an association between OBS and nonlethal suicide attempts in old age. Sendbuehler and Goldstein (1977) found that one-half of their aged attempters had OBS. They concluded that the OBS impaired the fatal completion of suicide by interfering with coordination, planning, determination, and awareness of reality.

Kiorboe (1951) observed that there were no symptoms of dementia in any of the 14 institutionalized elderly completers studied, but there were in 11 of the 21 attempters. Kiorboe suggested that "a debilitated constitution may aggravate an existing dementia and provoke an attempt at suicide, which is seldom successful because of mental and physical weakness" (p. 235).

Although OBS's relation to elder suicide may be uncertain, it is possible that fear of OBS, institutionalization, and especially AD with its slow and certain loss of independence, memory, and self may be a motivation to suicide in old age. With increasing life expectancy and the accompanying increase in older adults and the number of AD cases, the possiblity of suicide ideation in OBS cases should be assessed.

Alcoholic Elders

Alcohol abuse is the most common form of substance abuse among the elderly. Estimates of alcohol abuse or alcoholism among the elderly range from 2% to 10% (Williams, 1984). Elderly alcoholics are particularly vulnerable to death from suicide. Alcoholism also increases the risk of mortality from a variety of other causes.

Given the unique health status of the elderly, both alcohol use and abuse are very important issues. Blazer (1982) and many others have identified the following physical health problems related to alcoholism in the aged: decreased ability to perform motor tasks; profound changes in sleep patterns, such as decreased rapid eye movement (REM) sleep; a number of diseases such as inflamed intestinal tract, pancreatitis, ketoacidosis, hyperlitemia, fatty liver, gout, alcoholic hepatitis, and cirrhosis; decreased resistance to infections such as pneumonia; negative effects on the cardiovascular system resulting in hypertension and cardiomyopathy with heart failure; and insensitivity to pain.

Drug interactions are a serious problem for the elderly. Of those persons 65 and older, 75% take at least one prescribed medication (Kasper, 1982). Even those who drink alcohol only occasionally are at risk of drug/alcohol interactions, and heavy drinking can cause serious problems or even result in death.

The physiological impact of alcohol is significantly greater in older individuals. For a given dose of alcohol, a 60-year-old individual will have a 20% higher blood alcohol concentration than an individual under 60. This decreased ability to metabolize alcohol may further impair the fragile state of cognitive and motor skills in older individuals and increase the risk of death from drug/alcohol interactions.

The connection between alcohol abuse and suicide is well documented (Roy & Linnoila, 1986). As many as one-half of all suicides in the United

States are associated with alcohol use (Frances et al. 1987). Palola et al. (1982) suggest that alcoholism is a substitute for suicide. Others who have studied alcoholism and suicide claim that both problems are effects of the same cause (i.e., depression, hopelessness, stress).

Alcohol and suicide are serious, related problems among the elderly. Although the association between alcohol and suicide is high in every age group, it is greatly increased in those 60 and over (Blazer, 1982). Bienenfeld (1987) reported that elderly alcoholics' risk of suicide is five times greater than that of nonalcoholic elderly. The high rate of suicide in elderly alcoholics is a product of what Dunlop (1986) calls the double negative, alcoholism plus old age.

To relieve depression and loneliness and to escape from the multiple problems and stresses of growing old, many elderly people turn to alcohol. Instead of relieving depression, ingesting large quantities of alcohol actually increases depression and anxiety. Alcohol acts as a depressant on the central nervous system and may also alter moods and decrease critical life-evaluating functions of the ego, allowing unconscious self-destructive impulses to gain control. Several studies have confirmed that alcoholics experience increasing anxiety and depression with continued heavy drinking (Blazer, 1982). Continuous heavy drinking may produce what Mayfield and Montgomery (1972) have called "a depressive syndrome of chronic intoxication." As Blazer (1982) notes: "Withdrawal from alcohol may precipitate a state of discomfort and agitation associated with depressive symptoms that likewise may increase the risk of suicide" (p. 37).

The depressant effects of alcohol may reduce inhibitions and self-control and contribute to the courage that some feel is a factor in suicide. As Blazer (1982) points out: "The intake of alcohol frequently blunts inhibitions about suicide and may blunt the potential pain secondary to a suicide attempt" (p. 37).

Continued regular use of alcohol often results in the deterioration of important social relationships, primarily in the family and among friends, leading to social alienation and isolation. Anger, hostility, and belligerence associated with frequent drinking alienate family members and close friends at the time when the depressed elderly drinker most needs social and emotional support. Coupled with increased social isolation and alienation are intense feelings of shame, guilt, denial, pessimism, and lower self-concept, all factors in suicidal behavior.

Widowed Older Adults

Widowhood places older adults at increased risk of suicide. The eminent French sociologist, Emile Durkheim (1897/1951), first emphasized the association between widowhood and suicide over 90 years ago in his classic work in which he characterized the vulnerability of the widowed as an indicator of "domestic anomie"; that is, a deregulation of behavior associated with the loss of a spouse. Durkheim recognized that participation in the family represented one of the most important ties among society's members. He suggested that the state of marriage and membership in a family integrate societal members by exerting a regulative force on them and by acting as a stimulant to intensive interpersonal relations that draw the members into firm and meaningful union, thus providing some degree of immunity, the "coefficient of preservation," against suicide. He viewed the loss of the spouse as weakening the familial integration of the individual. Thus, the suicide of widows and widowers may be referred to as both "anomic" and "egoistic." Durkheim's classic explanation for the greater proportion of suicides among widowers as compared to widows—namely, that men derive more from marriage than do women—reflects this important gender difference among those growing older.

Numerous empirical studies conducted in more recent years have confirmed the increased risk of suicide among the widowed, particularly widowed males. In their early study, MacMahon and Pugh (1963) studied 320 widows and widowers who committed suicide in Massachusetts between 1948 and 1952. They found that the suicide rate among the widowed population was 2.5 times higher in the first six months after bereavement and 1.5 times higher in the first, second, and third years after bereavement than in subsequent years. This finding suggests that the event of losing a spouse is a powerful etiological factor in death by suicide. Paykel et al. (1975) similarly found that 21% of persons who committed suicide had reported bereavement within six months prior to the suicide, as compared with 4% of a matched control group. In a recent study, Kaprio et al. (1987) found higher than expected mortality from violent causes to be especially common in the first year following the death of a spouse, and there was some degree of increased mortality during the entire duration of the study.

Several explanations have been offered for the increased vulnerability to suicide experienced by the widowed. Following the lead of Durkheim, several recent writers have focused on the loss of social support and social relationships as a key factor in suicide of the widowed. Berardo (1968, 1970) describes the situation of widows and widowers as vague and unstructured, lacking clear guidelines for behavior, and lacking supportive interactions with friends, kin, and coworkers. Two other of Durkheim's followers, Henry and Short (1954), have explained suicide in terms of the weakening of the relational system constituted by marriage; and Bock (1972) points out that "marriage not only integrates the individual into a close and meaningful association but also regulates him by requiring him to take the other person into account in activities and decisions" (p. 72).

The elderly widower is particularly vulnerable to suicide. Several explanations for the increased vulnerability of widowers have been offered. After some pioneering studies, Berardo (1970) suggested more than 15 years ago that the elderly widower suffers doubly because he loses not only his role in the family system, but, through retirement, his role in the occupational sphere as well. He also pointed out that in our society, the woman has assumed the responsibility for integrating the kinship group and maintaining contacts with friends and relatives over the years. As a result, she has the support of the kinship group when her husband dies, but the elderly widower is left totally alone. Miller (1979) has further noted that the loss of family role combined with the loss of occupational role and the resultant downward social mobility places the elderly widower in a particularly vulnerable position.

Bock and Webber (1972), who also found elderly widowers to be at considerably greater risk of suicide than their female counterparts, described the elderly male widower as much more isolated, socially and emotionally, than the elderly widow. Widowers were less likely than widows to have relatives living nearby in the community or to belong to social organizations. Their greatly weakened social relational system places elderly widowers at very high risk for suicide. Widowers also experience greater role discontinuity when they lose their spouses. As Berardo (1970) points out, the lack of clear-cut role expectations is felt more acutely by the widower who, unlike the widow, is unfamiliar with domestic and other roles not associated with a formal occupation.

Psychological explanations for the increased vulnerability of the widowed to suicide have focused on the negative psychological consequences of loss and bereavement. Winokur (1974) has called bereavement the "paradigm of reactional depression." Kastenbaum (1969) has described a phenomenon called "bereavement overload," in which an individual is psychologically overwhelmed by the loss of a significant love object. In a recent study, Bromberg and Cassel (1983) found that depression occurs in about 20% of widows and widowers during the first year after the spouse's death. Recognizing the significance of the loss of a spouse, Holmes and Rahe's (1967) research on their Social Readjustment Rating Scale gave widowhood a much heavier rating than any of the other life events likely to occur in a lifetime.

Isolated and Lonely Elderly

Older adults lose others in a number of ways, particularly through death and the loss of contact due to the mobility of family and others and the tendency on the part of older adults to remain where they reside. The loss itself may be a motivation to suicide, as seen above, but the social isolation leaves fewer social supports and resources in circumstances of suicidal ideation and risk. The old are the group most likely to be socially isolated, social isolation has been found to have a strong association with increased suicidal vulnerability (Gove & Hughes, 1980), and living alone is frequently found among elderly suicides (Cattell, 1988). Loneliness is a common cognitive attribute of the suicidal (Shneidman, 1985) and obviously may accompany the social isolation and multiple losses experienced by older adults (Sainsbury, 1962).

Older Adults with Physical Health Problems or Terminal Illness

Physical health problems have been one of the most consistent and replicated findings associated with vulnerability to suicide in old age. Physical decline and health problems (both chronic and acute) are prominent in old age and in elderly suicides. Most older adults have at least one chronic condition, and such health circumstances may be motivations or contributors to suicide. Sainsbury (1962), for example, observed in London suicides that although physical illness was not a factor in young suicides, it was the major factor in late life suicides. Dorpat, et al. (1968) found that for those suicides in persons 60 and above that they studied, physical illness was the most common precipitating factor and 84.8% had active illnesses at the time of their suicides, compared to 68.8% of suicides in persons aged 40 to 59 and 40% for those under 40. The pain, loss of independence, debility, social changes, and fears of physical illness, particularly in the circumstances of multiple changes and loss of old age, may precipitate or contribute to elderly suicidal behavior.

Although terminal illness is perhaps the most often cited example among those who advocate a right to suicide, self-determination, or death with dignity (Osgood & McIntosh, 1986), it is unknown how frequently the terminally ill commit suicide or contemplate it (Saunders & Valente, 1988). Siegal and Tucker's (1984–85) contention that cancer patients seem to have no elevated suicide risk compared to the general population has been observed in some, but not all, studies.

Factors associated with vulnerability to suicide among cancer patients were reported to be

> prognosis or advanced stages of illness, with a prior psychiatric history . . . a history of previous attempts or a family history of suicide. In addition, the recent death of friends of spouse, few social supports, depression, particularly when hopelessness is a key feature, poorly controlled pain, delirium, and recently having been given information about a grave prognosis are significant risk factors. (Massie & Holland, 1988, p. 6)

Saunders and Valente (1988) suggest that cancer patients may view suicide as an escape from their pain and circumstances. They further suggest that knowledge of cancer or terminal illness, as well as present or anticipated pain, may lead to depression and possibly suicide. Treatment of the resulting depression may therefore lessen vulnerability to suicide.

Survivors of Elderly Suicides

The family and friends of those who commit suicide (called *suicide survivors*) must grieve the loss of a loved one as occurs with a death by any cause, but there may be additional aspects of their bereavement process with which to deal (Calhoun et al., 1982). Although many similarities have been found for survivors of suicide and other causes of death, among the differences in grief and bereavement that have been implicated for suicide survivors are greater feelings of guilt and a need to understand the death, as well as less social support from others following the death. Few studies of survivors of elderly suicide per se have been conducted, although McIntosh (1987d) reviewed the literature on survivors of spouse suicides, many of whom were elderly. Issues of stigma and social discomfort seemed to be different and more intense among many widows who survived a spouse's suicide. Anger toward the dead spouse is often felt and this, too, may produce feelings of guilt by the survivor. Therefore, although many widows received support and compassion from family, neighbors, and friends, others felt blamed and ostracized to such an extent that the survivor moved from the community. Blame and scapegoating of the surviving spouse by other relatives also occur in some cases of suicides. Frequently, the marriages of suicides have been characterized as troubled prior to death, and this may heighten feelings of guilt and blame by others as well.

Institutionalized Elders: Overt and Indirect Self-Destruction

There are approximately 23,000 long-term care facilities serving over 2.5 million older adults. The average number of nursing home residents is expected to increase 76% between now and the year 2020 (Kramer, 1986). The institutionalized aged differ considerably from their counterparts living in the community. Compared to elderly living in the community, those living in institutions are much more likely to be female, unmarried and without family, old-old, white, poor, and physically and mentally impaired. Approximately one in five has a primary diagnosis of mental illness (Harper, 1986).

Residents of institutions experience many of the same losses and stresses experienced by those living in the community. They too are plagued by loneliness, depression, and alcoholism. However, nursing home residents also face a multitude of other losses, stresses, and problems associated with living in institutions. The person entering an institution is stripped of property, personal possessions, pets, and finally personal identity. Institutionalization represents a loss of freedom and physical separation from loved ones and home—possibly forever.

Among the negative consequences of living in nursing homes documented in the literature are the following: dehumanization, depersonalization, deprivation, and loss of personal autonomy and individual freedom (Johnson & Grant, 1985). These factors increase the vulnerability to death from overt suicide in this population.

However, overt suicidal behavior is only one form of self-destructive behavior to which older adults are especially vulnerable. The same factors listed above also increase the vulnerability of institutionalized elders to indirect life-threatening behavior (ILTB). ILTB is defined as repetitive acts by individuals directed toward themselves that result in physical harm or tissue damage that could bring about a premature end of life. Examples of ILTB include refusing to eat or drink, refusing medications, or refusing to follow specified medical regimens. These behaviors occur in the community resident elderly as well, in these and other forms, but little has been written about ILTB and noninstitutionalized older adults (McIntosh & Hubbard, 1989).

To date, limited research has been conducted on the nature and extent of overt suicide and ILTB in long-term care facilities. Studies that have been conducted reveal a fairly high incidence of such behavior. One early study conducted on the geriatric ward of a Veterans Administration medical center (Wolff, 1970) revealed that overt suicide does occur in such institutions. In another early study, Kastenbaum and Mishara (1971) found that 44% of the men and 22% of the women hospitalized in a state geriatric facility engaged in at least one form of ILTB during a one-week observation period. In a later study, Mishara and Kastenbaum (1973) found that what they termed self-injurious behavior (SIB) occurred with some frequency among elderly residents in mental hospitals. They also found that men were more vulnerable to such behaviors than were women. Examples of SIB documented in their study included refusal to eat, refusal of medications, eating foreign objects, and self-mutilations.

More recently, Nelson and Farberow (1980) explored the nature and extent of indirect self-destructive behavior (ISDB) in a sample of 99 male patients in nursing homes. They found that failure to eat and drink appropriately and noncompliance with medical regimens and advice were among the more popular methods of ISDB engaged in by residents. They concluded from their findings that "ISDB serves as an alternative form of suicide for many of these patients" (p. 964).

Osgood et al. (1988–89) recently completed the first national survey of suicide in long-term care facilities in the United States. A random sample of 1,080 institutions was chosen from the National Master Facility Inventory obtained from the Long-Term Care Statistics Branch of the National Center for Health Statistics. A written questionnaire containing items on facility characteristics, staff and residents, and number of overt suicides and deaths from ILTB was mailed to administrators of facilities. There were 463 (43%) questionnaires returned. A total of 294 residents (1%) engaged in some type of suicidal behavior. Suicidal incidents were experienced in 84 facilities in 1984 and 1985. Eleven facilities experienced nine or more instances of such behavior, and many facilities experienced four or five such incidents. Suicide rates per 100,000 were calculated for 1984 for individuals 60 years and over. The rate of death from suicidal behavior (overt and ILTB) was 94.9 per 100,000.

Studies of suicide and ILTB in nursing homes have revealed that certain individuals are more at risk of death from such behaviors than are others. Nelson and Farberow (1980) identified the following as high risks: diabetics and those suffering from Buergher's disease; those with low religious commitment; those who have experienced a fall or major accident in the nursing home, and those who lack psychological and social supports (cognitively impaired, little family contact). Mishara and Kastenbaum (1973) found that men were more vulnerable than women to death from ILTB. Osgood and colleagues (1988–89) found that males and Caucasians were more vulnerable to death from suicide than were females and non-Caucasians. The old-old (75 +) were more vulnerable to death from suicide than were the young-old (60 to 74) and those under 60.

Several factors have been identified as contributing to overt suicide and ILTB in the institutionalized population. Farberow and Moriwaki (1975), in a study of elderly hospitalized patients who had committed suicide, found that these individuals had experienced a lifelong history of isolation. Cautela (1972) identified social isolation, dependency, helplessness, and hopelessness as factors in suicide in this population. Kastenbaum (1964) identified feelings about the future as an important factor. Those who felt that time was running out and there is little time to live were the most vulnerable. Nelson and Farberow (1980) in their study of such behavior identified loss of ability to function as the major factor in suicide.

Based on in-depth qualitative study of four long-term care facilities, in which staff and residents were interviewed and medical records were examined, Osgood and Brant (in press) identified the following factors as contributing to overt suicide in ILTB in the institutionalized: loss (physical, cognitive, emotional, financial); depression; feelings of rejection, abandonment, and loss of love; and moving within the institution.

The depressed, alcoholics, the widowed, those who are socially isolated and lonely, the physically and terminally ill, suicide survivors, and elderly residents of long-term care institutions are the groups most vulnerable to suicidal behavior in late life.

SUICIDE PREVENTION AND SERVICE PROVISION

The prevention of suicide among the elderly is of major concern from an ethical, legal, and humanitarian perspective. The risk of suicide in this population can be greatly reduced in a number of ways.

Education

Among the caregivers and professionals who encounter the depressed suicidal elderly, few have accurate or comprehensive information about aging and the aged, depression, alcoholism, and suicide and ILTB. These areas are neglected components in the training of many professionals who work with the elderly (Lomax, 1986). Family members, relatives, and friends of depressed and suicidal older adults also have little accurate information about the signs and symptoms of alcoholism and depression and the warning signs and symptoms of suicide. Older people themselves also lack such information and may not recognize such behavior in themselves. Older adults may also have limited knowledge about diet and nutrition, exercise and physical fitness, stress reduction, coping with retirement and widowhood, and other essentials of achieving and maintaining high levels of wellness. They also may not know about various treatments and treatment facilities and other psychosocial services available to help them in their local area. Education and increasing awareness are major keys to suicide prevention in late life.

Service providers are in a unique position to identify the vulnerable suicidal older individual. Doctors, nurses, emergency room personnel, hospital discharge planners, administrators of long-term care and other living facilities, mental health professionals, aging professionals, clergy, law enforcement officers, and fire preventive specialists are among those who need to be educated about the aging process and the signs and symptoms of alcoholism, depression, and suicide in the elderly. In addition, these service providers need to be taught about specific suicide methods and specific techniques for interacting and intervening with suicidal individuals. They should be educated in how to interact with survivors of suicide and where to refer them for help (either therapy or support). Finally, they should receive education about the nature and location of existing services in their community that are available to alcoholic, depressed, or suicidal individuals. This type of education should also be a part of regular in-service training in long-term care facilities and other institutions in which older adults reside.

Family members of vulnerable older adults are also in a position to detect alcoholism, depression, and suicidal ideation in an older loved one. Like service providers, they need to be educated about the aging process; how to recognize the signs and symptoms of alcoholism, depression, and suicide in late life; and where to seek help in time of crisis.

In addition to general education concerned with the aging process and how to cope with loss, stress, retirement, and bereavement, older adults need wellness education. They need to learn how to achieve and maintain optimum physical and mental health through proper diet and nutrition, exercise and fitness activities, and techniques for relaxation and stress reduction. Older adults also need to be informed about alcoholism, depression, and suicide. They should not only be made aware of the symptoms of alcoholism and depression and of ways to recognize suicidal thoughts and impulses in themselves and others, but they should also be taught that alcoholism and depression are treatable and that suicide can be prevented. The vulnerable elderly in particular should be educated regarding the kind and variety of help available in their community: the psychological and mental health services; the support groups (for bereavement and other situations); and other church, community, and social services that can provide help and guidance.

Early Detection and Treatment

The alcoholic, depressed, and suicidal elderly are underserved by mental health professionals and services, as well as by suicide hot lines and crisis intervention services (McIntosh, 1987c; Redick & Taube, 1980). As a result, older alcoholics and the depressed and suicidal elderly often go unrecognized, undetected, and unhelped. Early detection and treatment of alcoholism, depression, and suicidal ideation is a key to suicide prevention. Education of service providers and family members increases the probability of early detection and treatment.

Aggressive case finding and active outreach are also needed to locate and reach the lonely, isolated, depressed, alcoholic, and suicide-prone older adult. Such persons must be actively sought, using tips from doctors, pharmacists, staff of adult day care centers, the clergy, the police, and others who come in contact with them. Health departments, welfare offices, Social Security offices, and geriatric screening programs can also provide relevant leads and information. McIntosh et al. (1981) suggest establishing separate hot lines for the elderly, setting up special centers to reach the troubled elderly, using other seniors in a sort of "buddy system" to reach those who are vulnerable, and establishing community-based outreach programs to find the suicide-prone elderly. In all these efforts, early case finding is a key to suicide prevention. Information sharing, coordination, and referral to appropriate community resources, agencies, and treatment programs increase the possibility of early treatment and decreases the risk of suicide in older adults.

Special groups, who are more vulnerable to suicide in late life, should be targeted. Whites; males; the divorced or widowed, especially those recently widowed and living along; and those with depression or physical illnesses are the most at-risk groups.

Service Development

To combat the isolation, loneliness, depression, pain, and losses of aging, and to provide new meaning in life and enhance self-esteem and self-worth, a variety of psychosocial, leisure, and geriatric mental health services and programs should be made available. Better health screening services and pain clinics and other services that provide relief from physical pain are necessary. More humane treatment of the dying and more hospices and other such environments should be made available to the terminally ill.

Geriatric mental health services of all types; geriatric alcoholism programs; bereavement counseling; support groups for the widowed, retired, and survivors of suicide; reminiscence and life review groups; and peer self-help groups would greatly benefit vulnerable older adults. Such services should be made much more widely available to older adults in need.

In addition to these medical and mental health services, various social programs and services are also important. Adult day care centers, senior centers, and other programs, based on a socialization mode, could help to reduce loneliness and social isolation. Creative arts programs (drama, dance, music, art), domestic animal programs, horticultural programs, trips and tours, intergenerational programs of all types, leisure activities of all types, and increased opportunities for volunteering in the Retired Senior Volunteer Program (RSVP) and other such programs should be greatly expanded to provide meaningful roles and activities, increase opportunities for friendship and socialization, and optimize wellness in late life.

Environmental Manipulation: Institutions

Suicide among the institutionalized elderly is a problem. Enhancing the institutional environment could help to reduce the risk of suicide and ILTB in this population. Mishara and Kastenbaum (1973) examined the impact of changed environment on intentional suicidal behavior of 40 residents in the medical unit of a large state hospital. They were interested in finding out whether or not enriching the environment would alter suicidal behavior. Subjects were divided into three groups: those living in a token economy, in which desirable behaviors were rewarded by tokens that could be exchanged for candy, permission to leave, and other privileges, and undesirable behaviors were punished by not rewarding with tokens or taking back tokens; those on an enrichment ward, which was cheerier and offered more activities and social stimulation, as well as more personal choice regarding food, personal grooming, and other activities; and those living in a traditional custodial care ward. After nine months on one of the three wards, residents' behavior was systematically observed and recorded by trained observers for seven days. Analysis of results confirmed that the nature and quality of the environment have a significant influence on level of suicidal behavior (ILTB) of residents. Residents on the token economy and enrichment wards engaged in significantly less suicidal behavior than did those living on traditional custodial wards. Mishara and Kastenbaum concluded that those who live in better environments engage in less suicidal behavior.

To reduce the risk of suicide and ILTB among their residents, administrators and staff of long-term care facilities and other living facilities should provide for the individual's needs for freedom of choice and personal autonomy, privacy, and personal space. Facilities should offer an enriched and supportive environment that includes appropriate and necessary architectural physical design and safety features; well-trained and caring staff members, who recognize the uniqueness and individuality of each older adult and treat him or her with dignity and respect as a human being, not as an object or a child; and a variety of recreational, social, and health-related services.

Method Restrictions: Firearms

The role of guns in suicide has been very well documented (Lester, 1988). Shooting represents the most lethal method of suicide. Lester (1988) has documented in his research that states with stricter handgun control laws experienced less of an increase in suicide. Guns are used to commit suicide by 65% of those 65 and over. In Virginia, 80% of older adults' suicides are by guns (Osgood et al., 1988). An important key to reducing the incidence of suicide is the restriction of the availability and use of firearms. In a similar fashion, restrictions with respect to medications that older adults may employ in suicide has also been suggested. "More careful prescribing practices could lead to a lower suicide rate" (Lindesay, 1986, p. 37) by self-poisoning among the elderly. Such restrictions and other related actions have proven useful with other readily available, commonly used, and lethal methods such as domestic gas in Britain.

Education of the general public and policymakers at all governmental levels about the role of guns in suicide is essential. In addition, advocacy for legislative changes to decrease the availability and use of firearms is necessary.

CONCLUSIONS

Suicide among the elderly, the most vulnerable age group, should be a high priority. Suicide is a recognizable, preventable, and unnecessary cause of death at all ages, including among the old. As at all ages, older adults communicate their suicidal intent and ideation verbally and behaviorally as well as by their membership in the high-risk situations and groups noted above (e.g., depressed, isolated and lonely, etc.). Education regarding the recognition of these signs and the mobilization of available support and professional resources can be effective in reducing individual vulnerability to suicidal actions. Education of older adults, family members, and service providers is an essential key to suicide prevention.

Prevention of the multidetermined action of suicide among the elderly will require attention to the diversity of concerns and problems that lead older adults to consider killing themselves. An eclectic therapeutic approach is essential to lessen individual vulnerablity to suicide. Recognition that there are often psychological, social, and biological factors (and interactions among them) in cases of suicide among older adults is important. Successful treatment may require attention to all three.

Prevention of suicide among the elderly is an important immediate social concern. This issue becomes even more crucial as we face continued and even more rapid expansion in the next century of our older adult population. Even if suicide rates in the future remain constant, the sheer number of cases will increase dramatically with the increased number of elderly. To lessen vulnerability to suicide for older adults generally and for specific high-risk subgroups of elderly, a number of steps are needed. Among these measures are (1) early detection and treatment of depression, alcoholism, suicidal ideation, and other forms of mental illness; (2) the development of specialized and appropriate psychosocial and mental health services and programs; (3) the implementation of environmental changes to improve and enhance institutions; and (4) firearm and other method restrictions such as drug monitoring. These and other efforts must be seriously considered if we as a society are to meet the needs of the vulnerable suicidal elderly in this country.

REFERENCES

Barter, J. T. (1969). Self-destructive behavior in adolescents and adults: Similarities and differences. In U.S. Department of Health, Education, and Welfare, *Suicide Among the American Indians: Two Workshops* (pp. 7–10). PHS Publication No. 1903. Washington D.C.: U.S. Government Printing Office.

Batchelor, I. R. C. (1957). Suicide in old age. In E. S. Shneidman & N. L. Farberow (Eds.), *Clues to suicide* (pp. 143–151). New York: McGraw-Hill.

Beck, A. T., Kovacs, M., & Weissman, A. (1975). Hopelessness and suicidal behavior: An overview. *Journal of the American Medical Association, 234,* 1146–1149.

Berardo, F. M. (1968). Widowhood status in the U.S.: Perspectives on a neglected aspect of the family life cycle. *Family Coordinator, 17,* 191–203.

Berardo, F. M. (1970) Survivorship and social isolation: The case of the aged widower. *Family Coordinator, 19,* 11–25.

Bienenfeld, D. (1987). Alcoholism in the elderly. *AFP, 36,* 163–169.

Blazer, D. (1982). *Depression in late life.* St. Louis: Mosby.

Bock, E. W. (1972). Aging and suicide: The significance of marital, kinship, and alternative relations. *Family Coordinator, 21,* 71–79.

Bock, E. W., & Webber, I. (1972). Suicide among the elderly: Isolating widowhood and mitigating alternatives. *Journal of Marriage and the Family, 34,* 24–31.

Bromberg, S., & Cassel, C. K. (1983). Suicide in the elderly: The limits of paternalism. *Journal of the American Geriatrics Society, 31,* 698–703.

Calhoun, L. G., Selby, J. W., & Selby, L. E. (1982). The psychological aftermath of suicide: An analysis of current evidence. *Clinical Psychology Review, 2,* 409–420.

Cattell, H. R. (1988). Elderly suicide in London: An analysis of coroner's inquests. *International Journal of Geriatric Psychiatry, 3,* 251–261.

Cautela, J. (1972). Manipulation of the psychological environment of the geriatric patient. In D. Kent, R. Kastenbaum, & S. Sherwood (Eds.), *Research planning and action for the elderly: The power and potential of social science* (pp. 61–69). New York: Behavioral Publications.

Dorpat, T. L., Anderson, W. F., & Ripley, H. S. (1968). The relationship of physical illness to suicide. In H. L. P. Resnik (Ed.), *Suicidal behaviors: Diagnosis and management* (pp. 209–219). Boston: Little, Brown.

Dunlop, J. D. (1986). Senior alcohol services revisited: Elderly alcoholism—Current state of the art. Paper presented at the National Nurses Society on Addictions Annual Education Conference, Chicago, IL.

Durkheim, E. (1951). *Suicide.* New York: Free Press. (Original work published 1897.)

Farberow, N. L., & Moriwaki, S. Y. (1975). Self-destructive crises in the older person. *Gerontologist, 15,* 333–337.

Frances, R. J., Franklin, J., & Flavin, D. K. (1987). Suicide and alcoholism. *American Journal of Drug and Alcohol Abuse, 13,* 327–341.

Gove, W. R., & Hughes, M. (1980). Reexamining the ecological fallacy: A study in which aggregate data are critical in investigating the pathological effects of living alone. *Social Forces, 58,* 1157–1177.

Harper, M. S. (1986). Introduction. In M. S. Harper & B. D. Lebowitz (Eds.), *Mental illness in nursing homes: Agenda for research* (pp. 1–6). DHHS Publication No. (ADM) 86–1459. Washington, D.C.: U.S. Government Printing Office.

Henry, A., & Short, J. F. (1954). *Suicide and homicide.* Glencoe, IL: Free Press.

Holmes, T. H., & Rahe, R. H. (1967). The social readjustment scale. *Journal of Psychosomatic Research, 11,* 213–218.

Johnson, C. L., & Grant, L. A. (1985). *The nursing home in American society.* Baltimore: Johns Hopkins University Press.

Kaprio, J., Koskenvuo, M., & Rita, H. (1987). Mortality after bereavement: A prospective study of 95,467 widowed persons. *American Journal of Public Health, 77,* 283–287.

Kasper, J. S. (1982). *Prescribed medicines: Use, expenditures, and source of payment.* DHHS Publication No. (PHS) 82-3320. Washington, D.C.: U.S. Government Printing Office.

Kastenbaum, R. (1964). The structure and function of time perspective. *Journal of Psychological Researchers, 8,* 1–11.

Kastenbaum, R. (1969). Death and bereavement in later life. In A. H. Kutscher (Ed.), *Death and bereavement* (pp. 28–54). Springfield, IL: Charles C. Thomas.

Kastenbaum, R., & Mishara, B. L. (1971). Premature death and self-injurious behavior in old age. *Geriatrics, 26,* 71–81.

Kiorboe, E. (1951). Suicide and attempted suicide among old people. *Journal of Gerontology, 6,* 233–236.

Kramer, M. (1986). Trends in institutionalization and prevalence of mental disorders in nursing homes. In M. S. Harper & B. D. Lebowitz (Eds.), *Mental illness in nursing homes: Agenda for research* (pp. 7–26). DHHS Publication No. (ADM) 86-1459. Washington, D.C.: U.S. Government Printing Office.

Lecso, P. A. (1989). Murder-suicide in Alzheimer's disease. *Journal of the American Geriatrics Society, 37,* 167–168.

Leibenluft, E., & Goldberg, R. L. (1988). The suicidal, terminally ill patient with depression. *Psychosomatics, 29,* 379–386.

Lester, D. (1988). Gun control, gun ownership, and suicide prevention. *Suicide and Life-Threatening Behavior, 18,* 176–180.

Lindesay, J. (1986). Trends in self-poisoning in the elderly 1974–1983. *International Journal of Geriatric Psychiatry, 1,* 37–43.

Lomax, J. (1986). A proposed curriculum on suicide care for psychiatry residency. *Suicide and Life-Threatening Behavior, 16,* 56–64.

MacMahon, B., & Pugh, T. (1965). Suicide in the widowed. *American Journal of Epidemiology, 81,* 23–31.

Massie, M. J., & Holland, J. C. (1988). Assessment and management of the cancer patient with depression. *Advances in Psychosomatic Medicine, 18,* 1–12.

Mayfield, D. G., & Montgomery, D. (1972). Alcoholism, alcohol intoxication, and suicide attempts. *Archives of General Psychiatry, 27,* 349–353.

McIntosh, J. L. (1984). Components of the decline in elderly suicide: Suicide among the young-old and old-old by race and sex. *Death Education,* 8(Suppl.), 113–124.

McIntosh, J. L. (1985). Suicide among the elderly: Levels and trends. *American Journal of Orthopsychiatry, 55,* 288–293.

McIntosh, J. L. (1987a). Hispanic suicide in ten U.S. states. Paper presented at the joint meeting of the American Association of Suicidology and the International Association for Suicide Prevention, San Francisco.

McIntosh, J. L. (1987b). Marital status and suicide: Recent U.S. data. Paper presented at the joint meeting of the American Association of Suicidology and the International Association for Suicide Prevention, San Francisco.

McIntosh, J. L. (1987c). Suicide: Training and education needs with an emphasis on the elderly. *Gerontology and Geriatrics Education, 7,* 125–139.

McIntosh, J. L. (1987d). Survivors family relationships: Literature review. In E. J. Dunne, J. L. McIntosh, & K. Dunne-Maxim (Eds.), *Suicide and its aftermath: Understanding and counseling the survivors* (pp. 73–84). New York: W.W. Norton.

McIntosh, J. L. (1988). Geographic changes in U.S. elderly suicide. Paper presented at the annual meeting of the American Association of Suicidology, Washington, D.C.

McIntosh, J. L. (in press). Trends in racial differences in United States suicide statistics. *Death Studies.*

McIntosh, J. L., & Hubbard, R. W. (1988). Indirect self-destructive behavior among the elderly: A review with case examples. *Journal of Gerontological Social Work, 13,* 37–48.

McIntosh, J. L., Hubbard, R. W., & Santos, J. F. (1981). Suicide among the elderly: A review of issues with case studies. *Journal of Gerontological Social Work, 4,* 63–74.

McIntosh, J. L., & Santos, J. F. (1985–86). Methods of suicide by age: Sex and race differences among the young and old. *International Journal of Aging and Human Development, 22,* 123–139.

Miles, C. P. (1977). Conditions predisposing to suicide: A review. *Journal of Nervous and Mental Disease, 164,* 231–246.

Miller, M. (1979). *Suicide after sixty: The final alternative.* New York: Springer.

Mishara, B. L., & Kastenbaum, R. (1973). Self-injurious behavior and environmental change in the institutionalized elderly. *International Journal of Aging and Human Development, 4,* 133–145.

National Center for Health Statistics (Annual volumes, 1937–1985). *Vital Statistics of the United States, Volume II—Mortality.* Washington, D.C.: U.S. Government Printing Office.

National Center for Health Statistics. (1988). Advance report of final mortality statistics, 1986. *NCHS Monthly Vital Statistics Report, 37*(6, Suppl.), 1–48.

Nelson, F. L., & Farberow, N. L. (1980). Indirect self-destructive behavior in the elderly nursing home patient. *Journal of Gerontology, 35,* 949–957.

Osgood, N. J. (1982). Suicide in the elderly: Are we heeding warnings? *Postgraduate Medicine, 72,* 123–130.

Osgood, N. J., & Brant, B. A. (in press). The suicidal patient in long-term care institutions. *Journal of Gerontological Nursing.*

Osgood, N. J., Brant, B. A., & Lipman, A. A. (1988–89). Patterns of suicidal behavior in long-term care facilities: A preliminary report on an ongoing study. *Omega, 19,* 69–77.

Osgood, N. J., & McIntosh, J. L. (1986). *Suicide and the elderly: An annotated bibliography and review.* Westport, CT: Greenwood Press.

Osgood, N. J., McIntosh, J. L., & Covey, N. R. (1988). *Final report on a study of suicide among the elderly in Virginia.* Submitted to the Virginia Department for the Aging.

Palola, E., Dorpat, T., & Larson, W. (1982). Alcoholism and suicidal behavior. In D. J. Pittman & C. R. Snyder (Eds.), *Society, culture and drinking patterns.* New York: Wiley.

Paykel, E. S., Prusoff, B. A., & Myers, J. K. (1975). Suicide attempts and recent life events. *Archives of General Psychiatry, 32,* 327–333.

Pierce, D. (1987). Deliberate self-harm in the elderly. *International Journal of Geriatric Psychiatry, 2,* 105–110.

Redick, R., & Taube, C. A. (1980). Demography of mental health care of the aged. In J. E. Birren & R. B. Sloane (Eds.), *Handbook of mental health and aging* (pp. 57–71). Englewood Cliffs, NJ: Prentice-Hall.

Roy, A., & Linnoila, M. (1986). Alcoholism and suicide. *Suicide and Life-Threatening Behavior, 16,* 244–273.

Saunders, J. M., & Valente, S. M. (1988). Cancer and suicide. *Oncology Nursing Forum, 15,* 575–581.

Seiden, R. H. (1984). Death in the West-A regional analysis of the youthful suicide rate. *Western Journal of Medicine, 140,* 969–973.

Sendbuehler, J. M., & Goldstein, S. (1977). Attempted suicide among the aged. *Journal of the American Geriatrics Society, 25,* 244–248.

Shneidman, E. S. (1985). *Definition of suicide.* New York: Wiley.

Siegal, K., & Tucker, P. (1984–85). Rational suicide and the terminally ill cancer patient. *Omega, 15,* 263–269.

Williams, M. (1984, Spring). Alcohol and the elderly: An overview. *Alcohol Health and Research World, 8*(3), 3–9.

Winokur, G. (1974). Lecture given at the Clark Institute of Psychiatry, Toronto, Canada.

Wolff, K. (1970). Observations of depression and suicide in the geriatric patient. In K. Wolff (Ed.), *Patterns of self-destruction: Depression and suicide* (pp. 86–95). Springfield, IL: Charles C. Thomas.

12
Family Caregivers: A Valuable but Vulnerable Resource

Linda S. Noelker

The chapter's title encapsulates the dominant theme in gerontological research on families caring for chronically ill older relatives. A decade of investigation suggests that while families are the preeminent and often the only source of community-based long-term care for impaired aged, the well-being of family caregivers is compromised in the process. This conclusion has created a dilemma for policymakers and service planners seeking to maintain the family's front-line position in the elderly's care, yet uncertain about how to prevent or attenuate caregiving's seemingly adverse effects. Although several intervention models with this goal have been translated into education, training, support, respite, and financial incentive programs, their effectiveness has generally not been empirically demonstrated or results have been inconsistent (Burdz et al., 1988; Middleton et al., 1987; Miller et al., 1986).

Currently, conclusions about family care's negative consequences are being called into question because many of the studies on which they are based have conceptual and methodological limitations (Matthews, 1988; Raveis et al., 1988; Stull, 1988). The most common limitation is the focus on caregiving's stressful effects rather than on potential benefits or positive consequences. This perspective is bolstered by the widespread use of purposive, volunteer, and clinical samples comprised of kin caregivers seeking support or treatment for care-related problems or care recipients in crisis (e.g., before entry into nursing home, after discharge from hospital). Families in which caregivers are less stressed or where care recipients are less impaired tend not to use formal services (Bass & Noelker, 1987) and, hence, are less likely to come to the attention of clinicians and researchers.

While most investigations have sought to determine caregiving's effects, they typically do not incorporate design features such as noncaregiving comparison groups, panel designs to detect change over the course of caregiving, and general well-being measures for which population norms are available. As a result, the specific effects that caregiving has on various family members have not been conclusively established. The weight of existing clinical and survey research, however, suggests that family caregivers are a vulnerable or at-risk population (Brody, 1985; George & Gwyther, 1986; Horowitz, 1985).

This chapter's first purpose is to review research that used a comparative or longitudinal approach to examine whether family caregivers exhibit poorer health and well-being, either over time or in relation to other populations. Second, findings from surveys of family caregivers conducted by the Margaret Blenkner Research Center of The Benjamin Rose Institute will be discussed, because these studies included both panel designs and matched comparison samples of noncaregiving family members. Together, the findings should help to clarify whether all family caregivers are equally at risk of stressful effects or whether certain types are more vulnerable. The forms or manner in which caregiving's stress is manifested by different types of kin caregivers will also be addressed. Third, an innovative model service program for caregiving families that was developed at The Benjamin Rose Institute will be discussed in terms of its relationship to the Research Center's findings on caregiver vulnerability.

FAMILY CAREGIVERS' HEALTH AND WELL-BEING

An early study of family caregivers that used a panel design involved interviews over a six-month period with 15 chronically disabled elderly men and their wife caregivers (Fengler & Goodrich, 1979). Because the respondents were recruited through the disabled husbands' referral to and participation in a newly established volunteer workshop, the well-being scores of husbands and wives before the onset of chronic disability could not be obtained. However, the use of life satisfaction measures to assess respondent well-being did allow comparisons with scores from a national sample. Results showed that the median life satisfaction score for the caregiving wives was lower than the scores for respondents 65 and over in the national sample, and even lower than the scores of the low-income and very aged (80+) respondents in the national sample. The conclusion often cited from this research is that caregiving wives are "hidden patients" in need of attention and support. Less often cited is the fact that approximately half the caregiving wives had scores in the range indicating relatively high life satisfaction.

A second early study using a panel design included a subsample of adult children from a larger survey that investigated social-psychological changes across the adult life course (Robinson & Thurnher, 1979). The study's advantages were that respondents were not selected because of their parents' impairment or their caregiving responsibilities, those who were helping their parent could be compared with those who were not, and the interviews were conducted over a five-year period so that changes in the quality of parent-child relationships could be assessed.

Findings showed that helping a parent was significantly related to lower morale scores and more negative appraisals of the parent-child relationship. The general direction of reported change in the parent-child relationship over the five years was negative for the total respondent group, and it was particularly negative when the adult children's parents had cognitive, sensory, or behavioral impairments. Gender differences were also noted, with sons appearing to experience less guilt and greater ability to distance themselves physically and emotionally from dependent parents than did daughters.

A third panel study of family caregivers minimized findings from the prior two, showing that there is variability among caregivers in reported strain and burden (Johnson & Catalano, 1983). In this study, interviews were conducted two to four weeks after hospital discharge and again eight months later with elderly patients and their family caregivers. Adult-child caregivers initially were rated as reporting higher levels of strain than spouse caregivers, but spouses were more likely to report personal health decline between the two measurement periods. Study data also indicated that the elderly patients' functional status showed slight improvement over time, yet low morale and loneliness increased, possibly because contacts with family members decreased as the patients became more functionally independent. Less than half the caregivers reported high strain at either time period, regardless of the level of dependency in the care recipient, and reports of strain significantly decreased over time.

Findings from five other investigations using longitudinal designs or comparison samples have been reported. However, the samples in these studies included only caregivers of elderly dementia patients (Anthony-Bergstone et al., 1988; George & Gwyther, 1986; Haley et al., 1987; Pagel et al., 1985; Zarit et al., 1986). Because of the dementia-specific nature of the samples and prior research showing that caregivers of mentally impaired individuals are especially stressed (Bass et al., 1988; Deimling & Bass, 1986), more extensive reports of health decline and poorer well-being would be expected. In fact, one study (George & Gwyther, 1986) concluded that caregivers of dementia patients are an at-risk population and especially vulnerable to emotional distress. The research showed that these caregivers used more psychotropic medications, averaged nearly three times as many stress symptoms, and had notably lower levels of affect balance and life satisfaction than did national comparison samples. In contrast to adult-child caregivers, the spouse caregivers exhibited poorer well-being on all four dimensions: physical health, emotional health, finances, and social activities. Sharing a household with the care recipient and perceiving that more social support is needed were also associated with poorer well-being.

Studies of spouse caregivers differ in their findings about the influence of gender on well-being. In one study of dementia patients, caregivers' wives had initially higher care-related burden scores than husband caregivers, but at follow-up, two years later, no differences were found (Zarit et al., 1986). In a subsequent investigation, a general measure of well-being (the Brief Symptom Inventory) was used, rather than one specific to the caregiving situation, to allow comparisons with normative samples of adults (Anthony-Bergstone et al., 1988). Findings showed that both age and gender were associated with caregiving stress. Older women caregivers of dementia patients had higher scores on the Obsessive-Compulsive, Depression, Anxiety, Hostility, and Psychotiocism subscales compared to the scores of older men and younger women caregivers. Caregivers, regardless of their age or gender, also had significantly higher scores on the Anger and Hostility subscales than did normative populations.

The investigators noted, however, that respondents were applicants for a caregiver training program and could have been particularly stressed. Also, they astutely questioned whether the use of comparison samples is appropriate, especially in the case of adult children who are more likely than spouse caregivers to self-select into the caregiving role. If this is the case, adult-child caregivers as a group could differ in specific ways, such as personality traits or the nature of their relationship with the parent. These differences would preclude legitimate comparisons with normative samples.

In summary, this review of research on family caregivers suggests that caregiving is not uniformly deleterious, but has variable effects on the well-being of family members. Some caregivers seem to withstand its rigors without reporting poorer health or functioning, while others may adapt to its demands over time. Moreover, a number of factors appear to influence caregiver well-being. Advanced age, being a woman, and being a spouse of the care recipient have been associated with poorer outcomes, along with caring for a relative with dementia, sharing a household with the care recipient, and perceiving that social support is inadequate. In the next section, data from the Margaret Blenkner Research Center's surveys will be reviewed to further explore caregiving's effects on the well-being of family members and the influence of various factors on caregiving's effects.

MARGARET BLENKNER RESEARCH CENTER'S SURVEYS OF KIN CAREGIVERS

In 1980, the Research Center began studying family members who were assisting chronically ill older relatives, to determine caregiving's effects on their health and well-being. Since then, three survey research projects have been carried out using cross-sectional and panel designs. The studies included a total of eight waves of interviews with over 1,600 spouse and adult-child caregivers, elderly care recipients, and comparison groups of noncaregiving spouses and adult children. The respondents were recruited from a wide variety of sources such as voluntary associations, service agencies, health care organizations, and media announcements.

In contrast to many other studies of caregiving families, the care recipients did not have a particular health condition; for example, Alzheimer's disease. Nor were their caregivers seeking services such as counseling or respite to alleviate their burdens. Instead, the studies' samples included families with different ethnic and cultural backgrounds; from urban, suburban and rural areas; with different income levels; and who lived with and apart from care recipients. By virtue of the samples' sizes and diverse compositions, the effect of different factors on the caregivers' general well-being and the care-related strains they reported could be examined.

Caregivers' General Well-Being

The well-being measures used in all the surveys included single-item ratings of physical and emotional health, a depression scale (Zung, 1965), and the Affect-Balance Scale (Bradburn, 1969). The latter two scales were used because data on population norms were available for comparison purposes and because depression had been widely reported among kin caregivers (Gurland, 1978).

In the one survey that included caregiving spouses and adult children and matched comparison groups of noncaregiving spouses and adult children, notable differences in well-being were found between the groups, especially for the spouses (Noelker et al., 1989). In contrast to their matches, caregiving spouses had significantly higher depression scores and lower ratings of physical health, emotional health, and positive affect. Significant differences were also found between the two groups of adult children, with the caregiving children rating their physical health, emotional health, and positive affect lower than did noncaregiving children. No significant differences appeared, however, between the caregiving and comparison children's depression scores, nor in the negative affect scores for any of the groups.

Although there were significant differences between the caregiving and comparison groups, the magnitude of caregiving's impact on well-being varied for spouse and adult-child caregivers. Among caregiving and non-caregiving spouses, caregiving status explained a relatively larger portion of variance in physical health ratings and positive affect than was found for adult children. Also, caregiving status explained significant amounts of variance in the spouses' emotional health ratings and depression scores, but not in the adult children's. Caregiver age and gender seemed to have little influence on well-being either for spouses or for adult children.

These findings suggest that the well-being of spouses and adult children is adversely affected by long-term caregiving. When compared to matched noncaregivers, spouse caregivers in particular seem to experience reduced well-being on more measures of physical and emotional health and a greater intensity than do adult-child caregivers.

It is possible, however, that the associations between caregiving status and well-being were less commonly found and weaker for adult children in this survey because the children generally were assisting less impaired older parents who lived in separate households. Consequently, other analyses were carried out that included adult-child caregivers who shared a household with their older parent (Noelker et al., 1989). The results suggested that adult-child and spouse caregivers in shared households with care recipients tend to have comparable levels of well-being. The most significant differences in well-being appeared between the spouse caregivers and the adult-child caregivers who lived apart from their impaired parents.

These findings indicate that family members who live with and care for a chronically impaired older relative may experience similar decrements in their reported physical health and emotional well-being, regardless of their relationship to the care recipient. In contrast, when older parents and caregiving adult children live apart, there seems to be less extensive and severe effects on the children's well-being. Possible reasons for these differences are that older parents who live independently are likely to be less impaired than those in shared households. Moreover, their impairments tend to be primarily physical rather than mental, and the latter may result in greater strain on caregivers (Deimling & Bass, 1986). In other words, the household context for caregiving may be linked to the nature and extent of the care recipients' impairments and, thus, to their care needs. These, in turn, negatively affect the caregiver's well-being.

An alternative explanation is that adult children who become involved in shared household care arrangements comprise a distinct group that differs from adult children in interhousehold care arrangements. If this is correct, then the factor(s) that incline these children to share a home with and care for an impaired parent may directly account for their lower well-being or may indirectly affect it via their role as coresident and kin caregiver.

In addition to the matched comparison groups, another strategy—panel analysis—has been used with the Research Center's survey data to determine how caregiving affects family members' well-being. One study using this technique tested the "wear and tear" hypothesis, which assumes that the stress of long-term caregiving eventually erodes family members' well-being (Townsend et al., 1989). The study included adult-child caregivers in separate households and focused on change over a 14-month period in their perceptions of how stressful caregiving was, how effectively they managed the care situation, their symptoms of depression, and their affect balance.

Findings showed that the amount of change in caregiver well-being was generally modest and varied across indicators and among respondents. For the respondent group as a whole, improvement was more common, as evidenced by reports of increased effectiveness at caregiving and fewer depressive symptoms. On the individual level, there was greater variability. For example, while 58% of the children reported a decrease in depressive symptoms, 34% showed an increase. Also, 36% indicated that the relative balance of affect became more positive, but 37% indicated that it became more negative. Thus, while some children seemed to experience a decline in well-being, most appeared to adapt to caregiving's demands.

Study findings also showed that duration of caregiving alone did not significantly affect change in caregivers' depression. However, when caregivers reported less effectiveness at caregiving and greater caregiving stress at the second measurement period, their depression scores were significantly higher than would be expected based on their initial depression scores. The study's conclusion was that duration of caregiving seemed less relevant to caregiver well-being than did the caregivers' perceptions of their immediate situation.

Care–Related Strain

Care-related strain measures generally refer to those negative effects that the caregiver attributes directly to the caregiving situation. They include deterioration in physical health, emotional health, social relationships, finances, job performance, leisure time, and social or recreational activities. Several arguments have been made against their use and for the use of general well-being measures when attempting to determine the nature and extent of vulnerability among family caregivers (George & Gwyther, 1986). It has been asserted that the use of care-related measures confounds the stressor (caregiving) with the outcome (care-related strain). In the Research Center's experience, however, both types of measures have had distinct advantages. The general well-being measures, for example, enabled comparisons between caregiving and noncaregiving, matching comparison family members so that the effect of caregiving status on well-being could be examined. On the other hand, care-related strain measures have had more utility for The Benjamin Rose Institute's clinical staff. Specifically, they have helped to identify and set priority areas for intervention, such as respite programs, because many family members perceive that their personal time and social activities have been restricted by caregiving. They are also useful for targeting caregivers with common complaints; for example, relatively prevalent reports of health decline among spouses due to caregiving suggest that health monitoring programs for these caregivers could be beneficial.

The multidimensional measures of caregiving strain developed at the Research Center include perceived activity restrictions, family relationship difficulties, and health decline (Bass & Noelker, 1987; Deimling & Bass, 1986; Deimling et al., 1989; Noelker, 1987). The use of multidimensional measures stands in contrast to other studies employing a single scale of caregiver strain that encompasses different dimensions of strain within it (Robinson, 1983; Zarit et al., 1980). Total scale scores, however, obscure the specific impact that caregiving has and, consequently, impede the practitioners' ability to designate the most appropriate area(s) for intervention (George & Gwyther, 1986).

Similarly, measures of the care recipients' impairment, developed at the Research Center, have also been multidimensional and include physical (activities of daily living—ADL), cognitive, social, and behavioral impairments. As a result of this approach, important relationships between the impairment and strain measures have been uncovered, and these findings have helped to specify the antecedents of caregiver strain and its relationship to general well-being.

One study, for example, found that when care recipients have cognitive impairments, other symptoms of mental impairment—namely, disruptive behaviors and poorer social functioning—seem to ensue (Deimling & Bass, 1986). In turn, behavioral and social impairments have the strongest direct negative effects on the caregivers' relationships with kin, although the care recipients' ADL impairments also have a smaller but significant effect. The strongest predictor of caregiver health decline and activity restrictions, in contrast, was ADL impairment in the care recipient, while behavioral and social impairments had much smaller direct effects. Lastly, these three types of impairments all had direct negative effects on caregiver depression. The study concluded that cognitive impairments per se are relatively less stressful for caregivers than are subsequent signs of mental deterioration, which include disruptive behaviors and impaired social functioning.

Other Research Center investigations have shown that the type of care-related strain varied by the relationship between caregiver and care recipient (spouse, child) and by household configuration. Among spouses, time and social activity limitations were more often reported by wife than by husband caregivers (Noelker & Wallace, 1985). Among the adult-child caregivers, negative family relationships due to caregiving were most common among married children in three-generation households. Care recipients' bladder and bowel incontinence also had a significant negative effect on family relationships, but not on the caregivers' reported health decline or activity limitations (Noelker, 1987).

A subsequent study that contrasted spouse and adult-child caregivers in shared and separate households found that caregivers in shared households, regardless of whether they were spouses or children, reported similar levels of care-related health deterioration, family relationship strain, and activity restrictions (Deimling et al., 1989). Moreover, these reports appeared to be linked to the nature and extent of impairment in the care recipient. Among adult-child caregivers, health decline was greater for those in shared households, and this was attributed to differences in the care recipients' impairments; namely, those in shared households were more impaired. Adult children in shared households also reported greater activity restrictions, but these restrictions seemed to be related to the shared household rather than to the care recipients' impairments. In contrast to the other two types of care-related strain, it was the adult children in separate households who reported more family relationship strain. However, relationship strain was generally not widely reported by caregivers, and the differences found were small, although significant.

In summary, findings from other research and the Research Center's surveys indicate that several factors are associated with lower levels of caregiver well-being and greater care-related strain in kin caregivers. Mental impairment in care recipients, manifested by "acting out" or disruptive behaviors and impaired social functioning, in contrast to confusion or memory loss, are especially problematic. Elderly care recipients with these impairments are more likely to share a household with a kin caregiver, whether a spouse or adult child, and to experience incontinence. All these factors adversely affect the caregivers' health and well-being and exacerbate their caregiving burdens.

Among all caregivers, the most prevalent complaint is the loss of personal time and diminished social activities due to caregiving's demands. It also appears that wife caregivers, compared to husbands, exhibit more diverse and severe deficits in well-being and strain. Adult-child caregivers, compared to spouse caregivers, report greater strain in family relationships, including their relationship with the impaired parent, as a result of caregiving.

These findings clearly indicate the need for respite programs that offer family caregivers, especially those caring for dementia patients, occasional or temporary relief from their responsibilities. Furthermore, they suggest that active outreach efforts should be undertaken in conjunction with respite programs to reach wife caregivers and those caring for older relatives with mental impairments. In view of the multidimensional nature of care-related strain, however, additional services may be required to address the caregivers' reports about family conflict and health decline. In the next section, The Benjamin Rose Institute's (BRI) model for a caregiver respite program is discussed in relation to how it was designed in accordance with research findings on family caregiving.

A RESPITE PROGRAM FOR CAREGIVERS OF DEMENTIA PATIENTS

In 1986, the legislature of the state of Ohio allocated funds to support pilot programs in respite and support services for persons with Alzheimer's disease (AD) and their informal helpers. The Ohio Department of Aging and the state's Alzheimer's Disease Advisory Committee were responsible for issuing the request for proposals, and currently they administer the program funds and monitor the 19 projects that were selected through a competitive review process.

In view of the extensive needs for respite in this special population, staff from the Institute's Community Services Division (CSD) and its Margaret Blenkner Research Center jointly prepared the Institute's application to reflect both their clinical and research experience with AD families. The respite program they designed contains five key components. The first is that the program offers an array of respite services from a central source. The array refers to the different services that can provide caregivers with respite, including in-home care from volunteers or home health aides, day care, and short-stay residential care.

The component's rationale is that a service array promotes continuity in the clients' care as needs change over the 5- to 15-year course of the illness. It thus enables the program to accommodate clients with diverse needs and also to meet the service preferences of caregivers. As either or both of their needs change, the service can be altered correspondingly. In addition, the service array maximizes the caregivers' choices about care arrangements while minimizing their need to shop around for services. The latter not only would impose another time-consuming burden on caregivers, but also might exacerbate feelings of helplessness as they try to negotiate the bureaucratic maze of different provider organizations. It is the Institute's standard practice, therefore, to enlarge the clients' service options whenever possible, thereby enhancing their feelings of control, which in turn can have a beneficial impact on their general well-being. This approach is facilitated by the organizational structure of BRI, which provides in-home, day program, and residential services and it can be duplicated through coalitions or consortia of single-service provider agencies.

The service model's second key component is to have the respite program's target area coterminous with the area served by the Community Services Division to ensure that clients with more complex needs have immediate access to professional social work and health care services. In view of the fact that caregiving families with mentally impaired relatives often report multiple sources of strain and poorer well-being, the availability of professional counseling and case management services through the CSD's neighborhood offices is deemed essential.

The model's third key component is to make respite services available during the evenings and on weekends. This component enhances the caregivers' choices about service delivery as well as service type and also recognizes that many social and recreational activities occur during these times. To optimize the caregivers' opportunities to socialize, respite services should be available beyond the usual workweek hours.

The model's fourth key component is to target respite services to low-income families. The reason is that respite service is not reimbursed by third-party payers and must be purchased by families. Even with a sliding fee scale, the out of pocket expenses for respite service may be more than many low-income families feel they can afford. This may help to explain why respite service users are typically middle- to upper-income families and why respite use by minority or ethnic families has not been extensively examined (Lawton et al., 1989; Rathbone-McCuan & Coward, 1985; Seltzer et al., 1988).

The model's fifth key component is to include ongoing research that would document the benefits of respite service use for caregivers. To implement this component, Research Center staff obtained support from a local foundation to conduct an evaluation of the respite program. As part of the evaluation, the Research Center staff and the respite program's nurse director jointly developed standardized inquiry, assessment, service monitoring, and follow-up forms useful for both clinical and research purposes. The comprehensive assessment and follow-up forms incorporate the Research Center's multidimensional measures of care-related strain and care recipient impairment, as well as sociodemographic, health, and social support items. The follow-up form also contains newly developed items on various dimensions of service satisfaction.

Preliminary findings from the program's first 18 months of operation showed that 296 service inquiries were made and two-thirds (192) were assessed for service (Deimling et al., 1988). Among families that were assessed, three out of four went on to use respite service. About half the families served over the study period were active at month 18 of the program. Program attrition was due primarily to the care recipient's death or nursing home placement (61%), which indicates the advanced stage of their illness. This is also evidenced by the fact that the majority of care recipients have multiple ADL, cognitive, and behavioral impairments.

Information on the characteristics of assessed families showed that the program was reaching the intended target group. Most were minority families (69%), and their average monthly income was about $1,500. More important, the caregivers reported, on average, severe activity restrictions due to caregiving (M = 7 with a top scale range of 10) and moderate health decline (M = 10.6 with a top scale range of 18). Reports of family relationship strain were less common.

In view of the care recipients' impairments, it was not surprising that in-home respite was the most frequently used service. Moreover, initial expectations of using volunteer companions for in-home respite proved unworkable, and home health aides had to be used exclusively because of the care recipients' extensive assistance needs. Study data also suggested that families using day care typically include less impaired care recipients and less stressed caregivers who can better withstand the rigors of getting the impaired relative up, dressed for, and transported to day care. Short-stay residential respite appeared to be used in preparation for long-term placement, since almost half of the users (43%) were institutionalized, compared to only 10% to 15% of the care recipients in the day program or receiving in-home respite service.

Although panel analysis as yet has not been conducted to ascertain respite service's effect on care-related strain or general well-being, preliminary data on caregiver satisfaction with the program suggest it is perceived as beneficial. The most common suggestion for improving the program is to offer greater amounts of service or more frequent service. This may reflect an effort on the part of some caregivers to convert the service from periodic respite care to on-going home health care.

In conjunction with the Global Deterioration Scale (GSD) (Reisberg et al., 1982), the respite program practice staff have found study data on the care recipients' impairments particularly useful for refining the respite service model in ways that improve both service plan design and the training of respite personnel (White & Ehrlich, 1988). Their observations of the care recipients' ADL, cognitive and behavioral impairment scores, and Mental Status Questionnaire (MSQ) scores (Pfeiffer, 1975) suggested that certain levels of functioning appeared to determine whether care recipients could benefit from the different forms of respite and what service interventions, apart from respite, caregivers were likely to require. For example, at the GSD's stage six (severe cognitive decline/middle dementia), the care recipient typically manifests several ADL limitations, often including the onset of incontinence, high cognitive impairment scores, one or more behavioral deficits, and 6 to 10 errors on the MSQ. Many of the Institute's respite program users were at this stage. For these care recipients, in-home respite is the preferred service option and should include personal care assistance, repetitive activities, and large muscle activities. Day care is a less viable option, unless it includes a special group for the highly impaired, and overnight respite use would require a protective unit.

In addition to respite service, caregivers assisting older relatives who are at this stage generally require education about behavior management. If behavioral problems are more acute, pharmacological management may be indicated. Caregivers who are not currently involved in support groups may find participation valuable at this time, especially if nursing home placement is being considered. Because of the care recipient's need for continuous supervision, the respite care provider may help out with homemaking activities, if or when the care recipient naps.

This brief description of one GSD stage should underscore the value of using standardized, multidimensional measures of care recipient impairment and caregiver strain and well-being, both for research and for practice staff. From the researcher's perspective, the relationship between care recipient impairment and caregiver strain and well-being can be clarified using different client populations and types of service users. From the clinician's perspective, study data provide an empirical basis for a refined service model that guides the delivery of different respite services and caregiver interventions.

SUMMARY

The review of prior research, using longitudinal or comparative designs to investigate the vulnerability of family caregivers, revealed that kin caregivers are not equally at risk of stressful effects, nor are the manifestations of care-related stress consistent across all types of caregivers. Findings from studies in which care recipients had a variety of disease conditions and functional impairments indicated that caregivers' reports of strain and well-being were more diverse than were those in which only care recipients with dementia were included. Greater care-related stress and poorer well-being were more consistently associated with the presence of cognitive and behavioral impairments in the care recipient, with spouse caregivers compared to adult-child caregivers, and with caregivers sharing a household with the impaired relative compared to living separately.

The Research Center's studies of family caregivers have furthered efforts to determine caregiving's effects on families by incorporating panel designs, matched comparison groups of noncaregivers, multidimensional measures of well-being and care-related strain, and more heterogeneous samples comprised of caregivers in shared and separate households and care recipients with different types of health conditions and impairments. These design features make it possible to examine the influence of different factors on well-being simultaneously. They also lend themselves to identifying the relationships between care-related strain and general well-being and the change in both over time.

Findings from these studies underscore the relatively important effect that mental impairment in the care recipient has on caregiver strain and well-being, particularly when the impairment is manifested in behavioral disturbances. Moreover, older individuals experiencing mental impairments are more likely to live with their caregivers due to their need for ongoing supervision, and the resulting constancy of caregiving responsibilities may contribute to greater caregiver strain and lower well-being. While reports of physical health deterioration were more prevalent among spouse caregivers, the most common complaint among caregivers was reduced personal time and social activities.

These results provided empirical support for the efficacy of developing a specialized BRI respite program for caregivers of older persons with mental impairments. Moreover, research findings that underscored the diversity in caregiver and care recipient characteristics and needs suggested that various forms of respite care should be incorporated into a respite program in order to accommodate differences in the care recipients' capacities and the caregivers' service preferences. These findings also indicated that additional professional and support services should be available to program participants who face other stressors that commonly confront caregiving families, such as strained relationships and caregiver health deterioration.

Research conducted in conjunction with BRI's respite program was useful to clinical staff because it enabled them to verify empirically that the care recipients' impairments were associated with the use of specific respite services. Thus, these data helped to refine the respite service model and guide the respite worker's design of subsequent care plans. From the research perspective, program data were valuable for investigating care-related strain and caregiver well-being in families assisting AD patients and in contrasting patterns of respite use and service outcomes in minority and white families.

REFERENCES

Anthony-Bergstone, C. R., Gatz, M., & Zarit, S. H. (1988). Symptoms of psychological distress among caregivers of dementia patients. *Psychology and Aging, 3*, 245–248.
Bass, D. M., & Noelker, L. S. (1987). The influence of family caregivers on elder's use of in-home services. *Journal of Health and Social Behavior, 28*, 184–196.

Bass, D. M., Tausig, M. B., & Noelker, L. S. (1988). Elder impairment, social support and caregiver strain: A framework for understanding support's effects. *Journal of Applied Social Sciences, 13*, 80–117.

Bradburn, N. M. (1969). *The structure of psychological well-being.* Chicago: Aldine.

Brody, E. M. (1985). Parent care as a normative family stress. *The Gerontologist, 25*, 19–29.

Burdz, M. P., Eaton, W. O., & Bond, J. B. (1988). Effect of respite care on dementia and nondementia patients and their caregivers. *Psychology and Aging, 3*, 38–42.

Deimling, G. T., & Bass, D. M. (1986). Symptoms of mental impairment among elderly adults and their effects on family caregivers. *Journal of Gerontology, 41*, 778–784.

Deimling, G. T., Bass, D. M., Townsend, A. L., & Noelker, L. S. (1989). Care-related stress: A comparison of spouse and adult-child caregivers in shared and separate households. *Journal of Aging and Health, 1*, 67–82.

Deimling, G. T., Noelker, L. S., & Chernin, J. L. (1988). Evaluation results from a comprehensive respite program for AD caregivers. Paper presented at the annual meeting of the Gerontological Society of America.

Fengler, A. P., & Goodrich, N. (1979). Wives of elderly disabled men: The hidden patients. *The Gerontologist, 19*, 175–183.

George, L., & Gwyther, L. (1986). Caregiver well-being: A multidimensional examination of family caregivers of demented adults. *The Gerontologist, 26*, 253–259.

Gurland, B. (1978). Personal time dependency in the elderly of New York City: Findings from the U.S.-U.K. cross-national geriatric community study. In *Dependency in the elderly of New York City: Policy and service implications of the U.S.-U.K. cross-national geriatric community study.* New York: Community Council of Greater New York.

Haley, W. E., Levine, E. G., Brown, S. L., Berry, J. W., & Hughes, G. H. (1987). Psychological, social, and health consequences of caring for a relative with senile dementia. *Journal of the American Geriatrics Society, 35*, 405–411.

Horowitz, A. (1985). Family caregiving to the frail elderly. In C. Eisdorfer, M. P. Lawton, & G. L. Maddox (Eds.), *Annual review of gerontology and geriatrics,* volume 5. New York: Springer.

Johnson, C. L., & Catalano, D. J. (1983). A longitudinal study of family supports to impaired elderly. *The Gerontologist, 23*, 612–618.

Lawton, M. P., Brody, E. M., & Saperstein, A. (1989). A controlled study of respite service for caregivers of Alzheimer's patients. *The Gerontologist, 29*, 8–16.

Matthews, S. (1988). Burdens of parent care: A critical evaluation of recent findings. *Journal of Aging, 2*, 157–165.

Middleton, L. Cairl, R., Miller, L., Keller, D., & Doblas, R. (1987). *The impact of Alzheimer's in-home respite care on patients and family caregivers.* Research report. Tampa, FL: University of South Florida Medical Center, Suncoast Gerontology Center.

Miller, D. B., Gulle, N., & McCue, F. (1986). The realities of respite for families, clients, and sponsors. *The Gerontologist, 26*, 467–470.

Noelker, L. S. (1987). Incontinence in elderly cared for by family. *The Gerontologist, 27*, 194–200.

Noelker, L. S., & Wallace, R. (1985) The organization of family care for impaired elderly. *Journal of Family Issues, 6*, 23–44.

Noelker, L. S., Townsend, A. L., & Deimling, G. T. (1989). A comparative analysis of family caregivers' health and well-being. Paper presented at the annual meeting of the North Central Sociological Association.

Pagel, M., Becker, J., & Coppel, D. (1985). Loss of control, self-blame, and depression: An investigation of spouse caregivers of Alzheimer's disease patients. *Journal of Abnormal Psychology, 94*, 169–182.

Pfeiffer, E. (1975). A short portable mental status questionnaire for the assessment of organic brain deficit in elderly patients. *Journal of the American Geriatric Society, 23*, 433–441.

Rathbone-McCuan, E., & Coward, R. T. (1985). Respite and adult day-care services. In A. Monk (Ed.), *Handbook of gerontological services*. New York: Van Nostrand Reinhold.

Raveis, V. H., Siegel, K., & Sudit, M. (1988). Psychological impact of caregiving on the care provider: A critical review of extant research. *Journal of Applied Social Sciences, 13*, 40–79.

Reisberg, B., Ferris, S., deLeon, M., & Cook, T. (1982). The global deterioration scale for assessment of primary degenerative dementia. *American Journal of Psychiatry, 139*, 1136–1139.

Robinson, B. (1983). Validation of a caregiver strain index. *Journal of Gerontology, 38*, 344–348.

Robinson, B., & Thurnher, M. (1979). Taking care of aged parents: A family cycle transition. *The Gerontologist, 19*, 586–593.

Seltzer, B., Rheaume, Y., Volicer, L., Fabiszewski, K. J., Lyon, P. C., Brown, J. E., & Volicer, B. (1988). The short-term effects of in-hospital respite on the patient with Alzheimer's disease. *The Gerontologist, 28*, 121–124.

Stull, D. (1988). Family caregiving for community elderly: Conceptual and measurement issues. Paper presented at the annual meeting of the North Central Sociological Association.

Townsend, A. L., Noelker, L. S., Deimling, G. T., & Bass, D. M. (1989). Longitudinal impact of interhousehold caregiving on adult children's mental health. *Psychology and Aging, 4*, 393–401.

White, J., & Ehrlich, P. (1988). Time off promotes strengths (TOPS): A model integrating practice and research in respite services. Paper presented at the annual meeting of the Gerontological Society of America.

Zarit, S. H., Reever, K. E., & Bach-Peterson, J. (1980). Relatives of the impaired elderly: Correlates of feelings of burden. *The Gerontologist, 20*, 649–655.

Zarit, S. H., Todd, P. A., & Zarit, J. M. (1986). Subjective burden of husbands and wives as caregivers: A longitudinal study. *The Gerontologist, 26*, 260–266.

Zung, W. W. K. (1965). A self-rating depression scale. *Archives of General Psychiatry, 12*, 63–70.

PART 3
Vulnerable Populations:
Policies, Programs, and Services

Introduction

Part 3 moves from the identification and definition of vulnerability in the elderly to the consideration of societal and systemic responses to the needs of vulnerable aged. The seven chapters in this section of the book consider vulnerability from a policy, programs, and services perspective, with an emphasis on historical, current, and future program and policy needs. The first three chapters (Chapters 13 through 15) focus on critical policy issues affecting the availability, funding, and structure of health and long term care services for the aged. Chapter 16 offers an overview of federal programs that provide benefits and funding of services for the aged. Chapters 17 and 18 offer a review and discussion of issues related to the organization and delivery of long-term care services for the vulnerable aged. The last chapter (Chapter 19) offers a discussion of issues related to the training of professional and paraprofessional staff serving vulnerable aged.

The seven chapters in this final section of the book address critical issues in policy formulation and policy development and provide the salient dimensions for the understanding and analysis of national policies. The chapters provide a critical review and analysis of programs, services, and workforce and offer directions for needed refinements and changes. This section of the book provides the basis for understanding the effects that policies and programs have on the quality and availability of benefits, services, and interventions. The chapters offer historical perspectives on the past, comparative perspectives on what is available at present, and suggestions for needed directions for a better and brighter future.

13

The Evolution of a Social Concern Base for Policy About Vulnerable Populations

Robert Morris

The usual discussion of the evolution of policy and programs deals with politics and recent history. Much has happened in the past few decades to enlarge public action about the condition of those, once called poor, helpless, or disadvantaged, who are now identified by the less stigmatizing term *vulnerable*. However, this brief survey uses a different, longer time span and seeks to link the evolution of specific programs to underlying social and economic forces. Rather than trying to explain the past, how we got from there to here, this chapter is a springboard from which to view the near-term future in the evolution of policy for vulnerable populations. There is reason to believe that the future may not be a simple straight-line projection from past to present to future; the patterns we have developed may have reached a plateau, and we now confront either stagnation or a change in direction.

The following observations concentrate on three questions: (1) What do we mean by the term *vulnerable* and how has it evolved, been expanded, or been inflated over a long history? (2) What is the relationship between our definition of the term, ambiguous as it continues to be, and the persisting tension between personal and collective responsibility? and (3) How and why did age become one of the criteria for identifying vulnerability? But first, a few words about how we got to today.

EARLY VIEWS ABOUT VULNERABILITY

For most of recorded history, people who were at risk were defined by conditions that were relatively easy to see in communities where daily face-to-face intimate personal contact between well and sick, rich and poor was the norm. Individuals and communities clearly and simply depended on each other. The family and clan were responsible for the helpless people they knew intimately, and individuals bore most of the responsibility for themselves as shaped by group mores. Collective action was aroused by the needs of those few whose needs and risks were obvious and tangible: widows without adult children; children orphaned by catastrophe such as war or epidemic disease; and those so disabled physically that they could not perform self-supporting work in a basically agricultural society. Helplessness was defined by gross lack of capacity, regardless of age.

Collective, as distinct from personal, responsibility for such individuals was accepted in biblical times—an early tenet of Judaism. In classical Greece and Rome, it was expressed in economic survival terms—the free provision of food. There were also social organizations created to look after such individuals by the ethical standards of the time. Most of the social institutions were religious in origin, but secular foundations existed before 100 A.D. and civic legislation was not uncommon (Hands, 1968; Morris, 1986).

These situations prevailed until the 16th century, when there were major changes in political and economic organization in western Europe and large displacements of population due to the aftermath of war and epidemic disease. These led to the poor laws of England, France, the lowlands, and Germany. These upheavals disrupted not only families but whole communities; the social disruptions aroused both public awareness and an increase in both public and private actions (Morris, 1986; Rimlinger, 1971; Loch, 1938; Vives, 1917).

Social instability plus human compassion led governments to expand their collective responsibility. But the vulnerable were still those clearly (to any layman) dependent or helpless; such as orphans, widows without other family, feeble aged, the grievously disabled whose begging was troubling, lepers, the tuberculous, and the mentally ill and retarded, who were grouped together as generally helpless or threatening or warranting charity. The defining characteristic of these vulnerable groups was helplessness, not caused by age or illness.

These increases in collective action still concentrated on people who could be seen, touched, and smelled daily as they begged or died in plain view in the small (by our standards) urban concentrations of the 16th and 17th centuries. The needs were clear and the beneficiaries visible, and human compassions were transformed from personal acts of charity to collective action, but always for unambiguous need and helplessness. But collective action also was seen as residual, after primary family responsibility failed. This long premodern history laid the foundations for public understanding about the helpless that still persists, along with belief in new technology and government funding.

THE MODERN ERA: THE GROWTH OF SPECIALIZATIONS

Beginning in the 19th century (at least in the United States), this long history began to change rapidly. The change was in the direction of specialization and the proliferation of specialized programs and approaches to subsets of the vulnerable population. The changes were propelled by several factors: the industrialization of American life, at first slow and then rapid, and the successive displacements of population as the continent was peopled: the land rush west, the gold rush, the absorption of millions of immigrants from many nations (Morris, 1986; Leiby, 1978).

In the modern era, family stability was upset and families were broken up. There was a corresponding shift in the way social problems were viewed by a people increasingly influenced by the rational, reductionist, and scientific thinking of the century, but now applied to the social and human as well as to the physical world. General problems were broken down successfully into their component parts so that smaller components could be more readily studied and managed; each part had a unity of its own and, if it later became necessary, the now better understood parts could be put back together into a coherent whole.

Health Services

First at local and state levels and later at the national level, there developed new and separate ways of dealing with and of studying mental illness, bizarre behavior, physical illness and disease, population displacement, and the human discards of an industrial world who were aggregating in larger and larger urban complexes. We saw the evolution not only of mental hospitals, and acute care and chronic disease (or contagious disease) specialized hospitals, but also homes only for the aged, or for orphans, foster care, and family services. Policies were not yet national, but a national precedent was set for veterans and merchant marine sailors, who suffered disablement in a succession of small wars and the massive destruction of the Civil War. For them, a base of national responsibility and, therefore, national policy began to evolve with commitment not only to treat and restore the wounded veteran, but also to maintain him in specialized institutions, for life if need be, though preferably with rehabilitation to restore him to civil life if possible.

The once charitable, simple, and generic approach of the poor house "home relief," where neighbors and families in stable communities provided social backup if needed, gave way to the asylum for the mentally ill, which in its inception was conceived as man's creation of a more ideal environment to heal sick minds bruised by a hostile outer world (Rothman, 1971). In turn, this led to specialized programs and policies to deal with the mentally ill separate from the retarded and, more recently, to special facilities for the cognitively impaired and for Alzheimer's patients. There has been a long train of theories about mental illness and how to treat it, but since defiitive conclusions still escape us, we have tried specialized facilities within which to try various approaches while we soldier on as best we can to provide at least relatively humane care and protection. Developmental disability, elder abuse, and child learning disabilities are only the latest in a long line of continuous subspecializing. All this has required specialized policies, institutions, financing, and—above all—specialized personnel in profusion.

The same spiraling cycle evolved in treatment of physical disease. At first, we had "pest houses" to isolate those with infectious diseases, once so dominant in health care. This was followed by specialized short-term care hospitals as we now know them, then chronic disease long-term hospitals, and rehabilitation hospitals. Where the vulnerable were not merely sick but poor as well, and most of the population was poor in the 19th and early 20th centuries, we built city and county hospitals. Special care centers for crippled children also followed.

Most recently, we have seen the emergence of geriatric medicine to improve attention to the sick elderly and several varieties of adult day care for physical or social ills. This came about either because there were some conditions found mainly among the aged and, therefore, believed to be diseases of age warranting specialized attention, or because the elderly with ills like those of younger people needed specialized attention since they were thought to heal more slowly or to respond to treatment differently because of lower levels of energy, and so on.

Economic Programs

Much the same specializing is found in our treatment of economic needs. The elderly are seen as a class of people who are discarded by the productive side of life and, since they may be economically vulnerable, require explicit social security or pensions. Similar specialization is provided for mothers without husbands and with small children (at least until the arrival of workfare) and for the totally and permanently disabled. Closely associated with these is the array of special housing programs for the elderly and handicapped.

Social–Psychological Services

The same tendency is seen in the evolution of policies, or perhaps attitude, toward those with psychological impairments and social or psychological limitations that prove to handicap some individuals as they confront a busy world moving rapidly and focused on work and personal freedom and independence. Varieties of counseling, family, and child care services have developed, although few of them have explicit national policy backing.

More subtly, these aspects related to services for the more helpless population begin to find their way into national policy through recognition that patients with long-term disablements need the help of case managers to help them negotiate the complexity of modern organization, and recent federal legislation provides for case managers, a form of social work. Congress also reintroduced a requirement that social workers be employed in nursing homes of a certain size. The Social Security Act Title XX is an instructive example of an attempt to apply a generic program to a mixed bag of specialized population needs.

Most recently, we have seen the rise of concern about abuse as a defining concept: abuse of children and of the aged and substance abuse by adults. These problems are treated separately in most jurisdictions, but the issues are similar for all. Abuse is hard to define and identify early, but is readily identifiable in its later stages. The causes are many and tangled, mixing alcoholism and drug use by adults, the ambiguities of breakdown in interpersonal relationships, and the frustrations and alienations of modern society.

While much of this abuse is approached within a medical/psychological model, a little-discussed dimension is what might be called *social abuse or neglect*. When significant numbers of adults are left stranded in our urban world without any family or children to turn to when physical or mental capacities fail, they are the potential victims who are not abused or neglected by families, but by the inadequate social arrangements we have made. They are found among the homeless, the lonely, the malnourished and the neglected, and those lost in large nursing homes or public hospitals. In recognizing these phenomena, we begin to confront a dark and selfish side of human nature found in most of us: reluctance to become involved with lonely, dependent ones.

SOME IMPLICATIONS OF THIS EVOLUTION

Without having gone into specific pieces of national legislation, I have tried to sketch out a long, but accelerating, evolution that has significance beyond legislation and institution. There has been a steady proliferation of specialized programs and actions, but these lack anything definable as a policy about the vulnerable. In a kind of organic growth, we have built up a great many cells for behavior and have left the relationship among them to somehow emerge from evolutionary trial and error. It is important to reevaluate the course of this proliferation for at least two reasons: (1) the efficient and effective use of resources can be adversely affected; and (2) it increases the need for a coherent and basic long-term care policy for the most vulnerable populations, replacing the ad hoc and chaotic evolution of the past.

Proliferation: Competing with Ourselves Versus a Shared Concept About Vulnerability

In this course of events, age has crept in as a defining factor. Whereas once the helpless aged, children, and youth shared a common vulnerability, now separate groups organize to educate the public, to raise money, and to administer age-specific programs; they break up into efforts for children, for the aged, for the spinal cord injured youth, for the mentally disturbed child, etc. The number of citizens activated has certainly increased, but this has the seeds of its own trouble. Each subspecialty competes with the others for resources of labor and dollars. Is the pool of resources infinite, or will these groups begin to compete with each other rather than combine their efforts against public indifference?

Second, the very variety retards, if it does not obstruct, the evolution of a general theory about vulnerability and collective responsibility in the modern world that can underpin policy. We may have to decide whether there exist separate theories, as well as policies, for each age group and also for the numerous other subsets of human beings constantly being defined as vulnerable: neurologically handicapped children, Alzheimer's patients, the feeble aged, the abandoned aged, learning disabled children, and parentally abused children, to name a few.

Third, greater specialization paradoxically can produce more unmet need. While more people may be served overall, specialty services, of necessity, must reject applicants who do not fall within the boundaries of the specialty, which are usually more and more narrow as specialization progresses. Thus, more and more people are at risk of falling between the cracks caused by self-limiting specialization. The most efficient use of a scarce service is to apply it to those who are best suited to benefit from it.

The rest are rejected or sent back to a system of vague "other agencies" that lacks coordination and even information about itself.

Although we lack a coherent set of conceptions with which to cope with this trend, a few principles can be identified, even though there is much disagreement about how each is to be operationalized. We believe, in a growing way, that human beings do have some basic obligation for whomever we define as vulnerable. But we are unclear about whether our obligations are personal (self-care), familial, or collective. We quarrel among ourselves about whether government or voluntary organizations are to be held responsible. Despite these differences, our unique political structure makes it possible for more and more groups to organize around specific types of human difficulty, to classify these groups as especially vulnerable or helpless, and to mobilize support for public or private dollars for each one, separately. The result is continuous increases in complexity and fragmentation.

We probably know that each subgroup among the helpless has pretty much the same basic social needs, even though each one may require different medical treatments. Still, each requires shelter, some form of psychological or physical support, some association with other human beings, some rationale for continued existence, nutrition, possible help with mobility or transportation, and so on. However, the bases for integrated provision or management of social care are usually lacking, since we have not put together a unifying concept about social care except in the most vague and general terms. General or universal provision for income, housing, or transportation seldom can incorporate efficiently (economically) the most helpless, and each of the more helpless groups we have identified struggles to secure its needs by emphasizing its distinctive condition, not its commonality with others.

Proliferation of Coordinating Agencies

As a result, our hopeful and open society proceeds on its course of proliferation. The complex of agencies, institutions, and programs that results from our specialized approaches compounds our organizational complexity, since we also create an added layer of coordinating mechanisms to help the professional, the citizen, the helpless, or the vulnerable to make use of the various specializations we have created. We have tried and still have social service exchanges, information and referral services, case committees, and coordinating and social planning councils; in addition, we now have case managers, hospital discharge planners, and even fee-for-service personal counselors. In Boston, there are some 200 information and referral services alone for 2,000 service agencies (Morris, 1986b). The ensuing complexity not only confounds the citizen, but also eludes the grasp of even professional staff in each field (Sarri, 1978). The latest remedy is that of management information systems, although we have not yet found a way to keep such systems up to date so that they are effectively helpful for the ultimate user in a timely fashion.

This evolution is likely to hamper our attempts to organize a more rational (in the production sense) use of basic social, medical, and financial resources for all vulnerable groups. But this becomes more necessary, and also more difficult, as labor and dollars available for our interests begin to have limits. We know the frustrations of no one having enough money, but there is also the trouble produced by specialty credentialing and standard setting, which can severely limit resource use. Numerous specialist caregivers can converge on a single patient, but in a poorly organized manner. We end up either with too many people clustering around one client with lots of downtime for workers, or with overqualified staff also giving simple care services. Current cost accounting cannot solve this. And we have no objective data, other than unit costing, that will tell us that specialization is more efficient for client and payer or whether a restructured set of delivery methods would be more effective. This dilemma is at the heart of our difficulty in improving coordination in any way that will make a difference either to the budget or to the client.

Growth and Influence of Institutional Self-Protection

Another little-remarked consequence of this history is the growth of institutional and bureaucratic interest in maintaining the complexity itself. There are certainly short-term advantages to many individual clients in the relative speed with which new vulnerabilities are identified and dealt with, at least in a time of economic abundance. But as each specialization has developed its own grouping of experts, aides, administrators, and fundraisers, the survival interest of each speciality must be noticed. But the survival thrust is as much to advance the specialization as it is to serve a larger societal need for effective care for all vulnerable populations within available resources. We are all familiar with the search for coordination and efficiency, the need for which all acknowledge, but each specialty believes that its particular arrangements are less violable than someone else's. This is not to argue against specialization, but to note that it effectively acts to divide the supporters of comprehensive policies (if such can be found at all) as each specialty struggles to maintain the primacy of its own turf. All goes well if economic growth permits a social surplus to satisfy all. But it is less and less clear that growth will continue indefinitely. Then, although as advocates we may agree that there should be a new set of priorities with which to redistribute the resources available (meaning redirection of resources away from the military or road construction or what have you), we are not noticeably eager to redistribute resources among ourselves.

The Self-Determined Individual Versus the Knowing Professional

There is another consequence of this specialization and its aftermath of professionalization. More and more, we are led to believe that every human need, including all those of the vulnerable, require higher degrees of professional skill for care, treatment, or management. Is all of it necessary or good? While the benefits of modern science—in medicine or the social sciences—are very real, there is an unexpected consequence: individuals become more and more dependent on professional decision-making, not only about medication and surgery, but about when to be admitted to a hospital, when to be discharged, where to live—in a nursing home or a mental hospital or one's own home—and how long one needs (or will get) any technical or socially supportive help.

The entire system is only partly based on user demand and provider supply. It is more and more like the medical system in which professional and expert judgment-based decisions are made in realms where the judgments are anything but objectively firm or scientifically validated. The variations in expert opinion, the trail of once certain and now abandoned treatments, testify to such a conclusion. In the growing arenas of human existence, the control has clearly tilted from the determining individual to the mostly knowing professional. For the most helpless, much of this is good and inevitable, but it has spread to areas of living where it is not so clearly inevitable: where an individual prefers to live versus where the current opinion requires that he or she live; how much of one's past life can be brought into an institution; how fast or slow the traffic allows us to walk if handicapped; what we will be fed and how fast we must eat in a nursing home. In turn, the beliefs about professionalization, and the need to rationalize demand for higher pay, push social and personal care and nursing along the path of medical specialization: helpers become attendants, who become aides, who become health workers, practical nurses, and then professional nurses.

A possible perverse outcome is reported in some studies. In one (Sager, 1983), professional staff in a long-term care institution generally thought that a patient's return to home life required more extensive and specialized care than did the patients or their families. If this is an example of experts overprescribing, it can be widespread, but not venal. It may be a case of professional pride as well as specialist myopic preoccupation with a part of a patient's life that ignores residual capacities, which, in turn, results in overcomplicated and even inflated patient care.

A central clash of concepts lies behind this matter. Specialization, at the heart of most professional development, has brought many benefits, but has also resulted in a loss of our ability to grasp the wholeness of human existence and life. It is not lack of recognition that wholeness in understanding is desired, but that not many experts have time both to be expert in their specialty and to integrate it with the rest of the human condition. The result is a resort to numerous less than perfect devices to bring many specialized outlooks together in the hope that a rounded picture will emerge. Slowly, through such means, professional insight is broadened, but most imperfectly, since each expert works in his or her specialized world, and this obtains in many of the comprehensive clinic settings. In the end, the patient is still the best integrator of life's experience and of technical services to meet his or her needs. But the partnership of physician or caregiver with patient or client has eroded as the expert has come to dominate the relationship. With increasingly busy professional lives, the opportunities for mutual understanding shrink and our tendency is to rely on expert means for reintegration rather than on patient/physician, client/social worker, or resident/homemaker interaction.

Expert Belief Versus Resource Reality

There are other consequences of this evolution, but one already mentioned merits another word. There is a well-known principle in political theory that wants always exceed resources. As advocates for the helpless, we are inclined to discount that reality by arguing that there are ample national means, but that they are misused for luxury goods, wars, etc. The misuses do exist in plenty, but they result from the tendency of different people to have different interests, each viewed through the narrow lens of that interest. Health and welfare advocates are not immune from this tendency, since we concentrate on the dilemmas that matter to us and can find ample arguments that our needs are more important, more valuable, or more moral than any other. Unfortunately, other interest groups feel the same way about the corner of the world in which they are interested.

There are widespread signs that the American cornucopia, while still full, is not ever-renewing; we may be entering a period when the demand of other parts of the world will begin to limit our boundless growth expectations just as much as will our own appetite for continous growth in all directions simultaneously. I suspect that this, if proven accurate, will alter the trends toward ever more specialization, proliferation, and growth in the service sector. Limited resources, especially labor, and major changes in the demographic profile (discussed elsewhere in this volume) can be expected to force a change, or many changes, in the way we craft future policies and programs.

THE WORK FORCE AND LONG-TERM CARE

One of the little-noted constraints on growth lies in the national labor picture. In the past, we have been justified in believing that there will always be workers to fill all the jobs we can dream about, drawing on natural population increase and a steady flow of immigrants, or that machines will take up many tasks. The human resources plus technology have been so ample that we have adopted policies to remove older people from the work force years before their physical and intellectual capacities justify it. But now a booming economy produces a tight labor market and affluence, and we find a grave shortage of people to staff our long-term agencies. If we raise wages a great deal, there will still be a shortage of labor. If the boom times recede, we can still expect a shortage of labor. When the present baby-boom generation begins to retire (in about 2015), we can look forward to a growing shortage, especially of both the less skilled aide and assistant workers and of professionals, due to reduced birth rates, lowered fertility pool, limits to immigration, and other related factors. The proportion of workers available between the ages of 20 and 65 in relation to the total population of minors plus seniors will decline, not catastrophically but seriously (Chen, 1988; Crown, 1988; Sandel, 1988). So labor resources as well as dollars become matters of concern, and it is doubtful that we can continue the kind of evolution we have had in the past.

Approaches to Labor

If, as can be expected, the supply of workers will decline relative to demand, two solutions need to be tested: (1) better use of presently underused labor pools, and (2) job restructuring, especially in institutions and home care.

Current labor policy in the human services has thus far been dominated by the need to train and upgrade younger workers. But the major underused labor pools are made up of the retired (or older) but able-bodied and active elders on one hand and minority youth on the other. Each presents unique challenges. Service agencies in general share industry's reluctance to hire older workers, and minority youth are all too often handicapped by poor education, by subtle racial prejudice, and by cultural difference, so that employing them in care for the disabled is seen as risky. Beyond such obvious problems, the past concentration on upgrading professional qualifications for staff has been accompanied by neglect of the vital role that low-skill and relatively untrained workers play in the structure of service delivery. Judgment and guidance by skilled professionals are understood, but less obvious is the extent to which carrying out expert judgments depends on the daily activities of the much larger number of unskilled workers involved in client and patient care and without whom professionals would be helpless.

Some on-the-job and in-service training for the unskilled has been offered widely, but has proven costly because of the high rate of labor turnover at the low skill end of employment and has been limited because of the constraint in service budgets for serious training. Conceptually, the training approach, used as the only method, is flawed, because it assumes, perhaps unconsciously, that early training should lead on to higher levels of education and work, with the result that the baseline caring staff (which is the largest labor component) is constantly being depleted as fast as it is employed by the natural desire for self-improvement. Either these workers move up a job ladder or move out to find better jobs.

This difficulty is compounded by the fact that the lower skilled jobs are not only very low paying, but the tasks as now organized are often and inevitably unattractive (especially in nursing homes and in home health care), and those who perform what are considered unspecialized menial tasks are not highly regarded by their peers, their supervisors, or society.

The customary solutions to this web of difficulty are to raise wages and to increase in-service training. These are useful but insufficient, and are likely to remain so, until this strategy is augmented by job restructuring. This recasting of the work structure has several interlocking components. If the underused labor pools are to be tapped, the jobs offered need to match the interests and capacities of individuals who make up the reserve. The able elderly are less likely to be interested in heavy-duty lifting and moving and may not want full-time work, but could be attracted to jobs that offer part-time work (or even divided shifts with their peers) and that recognize their basic capacities, including steadiness, some skills from a life of prior work, and perhaps the skills learned from rearing their families.

For minority youth, the prospect of learning skills that are seen as valued and that give them dignity, or that lead into an upward career path, will shape their readiness to accept jobs offered to them. For both youth and the elderly it is probably essential that they believe they enter a work situation in which they are valued by supervisors and professionals, valued as peer members of a team and not as "stoop" labor to carry out orders of superiors. Such a workplace may be idealized, but it has begun to emerge in industry—why not in the caring professions? What it requires is structuring a way for ideas, observations, and actions of such staff to be accepted and used by professionals as being worthwhile. It probably requires creating an environment in which staff, regardless of specialization, chip in on tasks outside their specialization; multifunction work unhappily violates both union and professional guidelines. Social work has paid lip service to this concept, but the pressures of most agency schedules and the attitudes of professional superiority make it difficult to translate an idea into a workplace.

Any such approach to the labor problem will necessitate not only higher wages, but, even more, a narrowing of the gap between low-skill staff pay and that of administrators and professionals, if all are to be seen as part of a professional team, regardless of credentialing level. Such increase in the cost of wages is unlikely to have public support unless the caring function is given a higher degree of public respect or regard. This can be earned not only through more professional credentialing, but also by an accompanying upgrading of the service structure itself so that all of an agency's activity and its worker tasks can be shown to be not only humane, but effective and professional as well.

The long-term labor problems thus require a multifaceted approach of higher pay, redesigning tasks to match available workers, job restructuring to tap unused labor pools, time for low-skill staff training, and bringing the low-skill staff into the professional team with respect for their function as observers, caregivers, and "therapists" on whose whole-hearted participation the therapeutic environment depends.

Such an approach raises the arguments of cost and quality. Cost will go up anyway, so the real issue is whether value is received for the increase. As to quality, there are uncertainties, but quality today depends as much or more on the activity of the low-skill caring staff in nursing homes and in home care as it does on the competence of professional staff who spend very little time in personal contact with each client or patient. In other words, quality will be protected or improved if *all* staff value quality and, in turn, are valued by others in a tangible way for delivering quality care.

REFLECTIONS ON THE FUTURE

I have no firm answers to the several questions raised, but I believe that they are worth serious thought and that the future will not be a straight-line projection of the trends of the past. A serious change lies ahead. To prepare, we would do well to search now for answers to such questions as these:

1. Are there as many disadvantages as advantages in a continuous proliferation of specialization and a continuous growth in services more rapid than either population or gross national product? The growth and specialization in social organization bear some comparison with biological growth. Each involves cell growth (the social unit in one case and a biological cell in the other). The biological organism has a normal, built-in mechanism to control cell growth and subdivision. But sometimes that normal control breaks down and fails. The result we sometimes call cancer. Can uncontrolled growth of social units have a comparable outcome?

2. Can we devise better methods for coordinating or integrating the current profusion? At least better than the current proliferation of coordinating mechanisms themselves? It may not be possible to design a better, more logical delivery system, so we'll continue to rely on trial-and-error evolution, but it's worth the effort to try to exercise more forethought.

3. How can patients retain, or reclaim, control over some part of the decision-making that affects their lives in the face of overwhelming technical and professional or expert authority? Is the imbalance between expert and consumer redressable? Is it worthwhile? Bills of patients' rights are a start, but they could end up being just words on paper.

4. How will we reorganize our services and how will we use available labor for long-term care? This is especially important for the lower skill staffs who outnumber the professional staffs in long-term care and on whom the experts rely if any of their expertness is to do any good. Is paying higher salaries a real solution or a temporary, self-defeating ploy when resources are in short supply? As the numbers of young and old combined increase, and the ratio to those of middle years rises, will technology answer our human, labor-intensive needs, or do we have to rethink how our essential tasks are to be divided and performed? Even if we have a depression, the long term demographic and financial outlook suggests that we can no longer assume an endless labor supply any more than we can assume an endless supply of dollars. Task restructuring will become inevitable; it may be carried out solely by budget criteria, or we can temper the natural tendency of organizations and their staff to protect themselves with a candid and critical checkup of how well our present operations produce the human benefits to which we are committed.

5. Can we rally the numerous interests behind a practical and achievable long-term care policy that spans all ages and conditions for the most disabled and vulnerable—a policy and set of programs within the framework of long-term needs that can guide the multiplicity of specialized interests into a path of understandable public responsibility?

REFERENCES

Chen, Young-Ping (1981). Making assets out of tomorrow's elderly. In R. Morris & S. Bass (Eds.), *Retirement reconsidered*. New York: Springer Publishing Company.

Crown, W. (1981). The prospective burden of an aging population. In R. Morris & S. Bass (Eds.), *Retirement reconsidered*. New York: Springer Publishing Company.

Hands, A. R. (1968). *Charities and social aid in Greece and Rome*. London: Thames and Hudson.

Leiby, J. (1978). *History of social work and social welfare in the United States.* New York: Columbia University Press.

Loch, C. F. (1938). *3000 years of social service.* London: Charity Organization Society.

Morris, R. (1986a). *Rethinking social welfare: Why care for the stranger.* White Plains, NY: Longman.

Morris, R. (1986b). *What lies ahead for information and referral services.* Boston MA: United Way of Massachusetts.

Rimlinger, G. (1971). *Welfare policy and industrialization in Europe, America and Russia.* New York: Wiley.

Rothman, D. (1971). *The discovery of asylum.* Boston: Little, Brown.

Sager, A. (1983). *Planning home care with the elderly.* Cambridge, MA: Ballinger.

Sandell, S. (1981). The labor force by the year 2000 and employment policy for older workers. In R. Morris & S. Bass (Eds.), *Retirement reconsidered.* New York: Springer Publishing Company.

Sarri, R. & Hasenfeld, Y. (1978). *The management of human services.* New York: Columbia University Press.

Vives, J. L. (1917). *Concerning the relief of the poor.* Translated by Margaret Sherwood. New York: New York School for Philanthropy (now Columbia University School of Social Work).

14
Critical Policy Issues in Health and Long-Term Care

Stanley J. Brody

Concern for health and long-term care services has evolved over the last several decades in response to a rapidly changing disabled population, many of whom are elderly. More recently, this interest has been reflected in legislative actions of elected officials and in administrative behavior of public officials designed to curtail rising costs and expenditures. At the same time, professionals continue to be committed to the quality and accessibility of adequate health and long-term care services.

This chapter reviews and discusses some critical issues related to health and long-term care policy, including defining the need for long-term care; the disabled elderly in long-term care; defining the need for a continuum of acute, transitional, and long-term care services; current policy issues concerning the cost and quality of long-term care services; other critical policy issues concerning the vulnerable aged; and finally, some reflections on what we should ascribe to in the development and refinement of long-term care services.

DEFINING THE NEED FOR LONG-TERM CARE

One of the apparent results of successful income maintenance benefits and accessible acute medical care has been the extension of life expectancy at 65 years of age. In this century, life expectancy has not only significantly increased at birth and in earlier years of life, but in the last 20 years there has also been a 15% increase in life expectancy at age 65 from 14.5 to 16.9 years, accounting for the whitening of an already graying society. But as Gruenberg (1977) has said, we are experiencing the "failures of success." Because of high-tech medical interventions, the developmentally disabled, those who suffered trauma in middle years, and those with chronic illnesses survive as disabled older people. Just as the 1910 Flexner report on medical education presaged the development of scientific medicine by 30 years, so the 1956 Commission on Chronic Illness report anticipated the need for a societal response to disability by a similar period.

While, at any given time, most of the elderly are free of significant disability, a large group, nevertheless, confronts adjustments associated with limitations in activities of daily living (ADL)—bathing, dressing, using the toilet, getting in or out of bed, mobility, eating, and continence. Katz et al. (1983) distinguished between life expectancy and active life expectancy, describing the last four and one-half years of life as characterized by disability for many aged, disability that is associated with death and not with age.

Fifteen years ago, a review of the estimates of the proportion of aged needing functional assistance suggested 30% as a reasonable midpoint between many estimates. Based on modified criteria, most recent National Health Interview Surveys (1984 and 1986) reported that six million, or 22.7% of the elderly, have at least one functional disability, either in ADL or in instrumental activities of daily living (IADL). IADLs include housekeeping, laundry, preparing meals, shopping, using public transportation, managing money, making telephone calls, and taking medications (Lawton & Brody, 1969). The per capita use of physicians, hospital care, and nursing beds has been static or decreasing. Furthermore, poor health is no longer the major reason cited by most people for leaving employment, and only 18% of recent retirees reported serious limitations of activities (Reno & Grad, 1985). All this presents a picture of an aging society that, although including a significant group of disabled elderly, cannot be described in the aggregate as "old, sick, and poor."

The heterogeneity of older adults is now accepted as a given, allowing us to differentiate among groups of aged. Just as a significant group of the elderly can be characterized as poor or as needing acute-care medicine, so, too, there is a group that can be described as disabled elderly needing assistance with the tasks of daily living. This group has been characterized as the long-term care segment of the continuity-of-care spectrum of services population.

THE DISABLED ELDERLY IN LONG-TERM CARE

Efforts to define the need for long-term care are well under way. Parallel initiatives in the fields of rehabilitation and gerontology have been proceeding for the last two decades. Contributors from both fields saw the need to measure function to determine the health status of the chronically ill. Katz's original identification (Katz et al., 1963) of ADL as the way to describe the level of function has been augmented by the Lawton and Brody (1969) IADL scale, the Barthel Index (Mahoney & Barthel, 1965), and other assessment instruments. The wide use of these methodologies by health care providers has allowed a description to develop of the need for long-term care services as part of the continuity of care.

The disabled elderly have now been measured in terms of the number and nature of ADL deficits. Although the level of the deficit provides a baseline from which to measure change, the number of ADL deficits is emerging in study after study as the key to overall need for services in a continuity-of-care services system. Most old people in nursing facilities have from five to six ADL deficits. In addition, 849,000 older persons living in the community also have five to six ADL deficiencies (NCHS, 1987a, 1987b). These groups used one-third of all informal and paid for assistance and spent more than half of the total out-of-pocket expenditures for services. Furthermore, hospital in-patients, dependent in five to six ADLs, were the ones most likely to exceed the average length of hospital stay for their Diagnosis-Related Group (DRG) classifications.

If the person's need for long-term care is defined as having deficits in five or six ADL functions, then the provision of continuity of care is not likely to become a bottomless pit, but one with clear dimensions.

The number of the elderly in nursing homes remained steady at one million residents for the five years between 1977 and 1982, as the result of more appropriate utilization of health services. That number has now risen to a population of 1.3 million because of the DRGs forcing more appropriate use of acute in-patient hospital beds and creating the need for short-term step-down services.

Admissions from hospitals to nursing homes rose to 40% of all entrants. Despite this increase, the 1975 congressional projection of three million skilled nursing facility (SNF) beds by 1985 was considerably off the mark (Brody, 1985). A significant part of the recent rise in the SNF population can be attributed to the one-half of SNF admissions who were admitted for less than a 90-day stay; their average stay was for a period of less than one month. Of these short-stay admissions (631,000), about one-fourth died, almost half returned home, and a large number went to acute-care hospitals.

The remaining 600,000 who are long-term residents (average stay two

and a half years) have multiple disabilities. Fifty-one percent required assistance in five to six ADLs; the mean number of dependencies was 3.9. It
is important to realize that, for this over-65 population, deteriorating cognitive functioning contributes more to dependency than do physical impairments. In 1985, 63% of elderly residents were disoriented or memory-
impaired. It should be noted that any advance in the control of senile
dementia, particularly of the Alzheimer's type, would have major implications for reduction in the number of those needing SNF placement (Brody,
1985).

A total of 1.5 million elderly disabled, or about 5% of the total population 65 years of age or over, living in the community or in institutions,
have more than five ADL deficits. This 5% may be objectively designated
as at risk of economic catastrophe for the long-term care sector of the
continuity-of-care services population. That figure is much lower than the
9% of Medicare beneficiaries who are at catastrophic risk for acute care
and who use 70% of all Medicare expenditures. As each successive cohort
of older people evidences an improved level of functioning, even in advanced old age, this 5% is a manageable societal risk.

Should the requirement of five deficits be deemed too harsh, Congress
has available adequate data to reduce eligibility for a long-term care program. Thus, decreasing the number of ADL deficits to four or more would
add 375,000 disabled living in the community and 175,000 living in SNFs,
for a total of two million elderly disabled or about 7% of the aged population. A decrease to three or more dependencies would add 500,000 disabled living in the community and 100,000 living in SNFs, for a total of
2.6 million, about 9% of the aged population. As the number of ADL
deficiencies drops, the rate of increase in the institutional population is
much lower than in the community population (viz., for two ADL deficits,
750,000 more community dwellers and 125,000 more institutionalized
residents would become eligible).

DEFINING THE NEED FOR A CONTINUUM OF
ACUTE, TRANSITIONAL, AND LONG-TERM CARE

As the older adults have aged, their needs can no longer be characterized
as either for acute care or for long-term care. As we have noted, 15 years
ago, the needs were described in terms of chronic care and as requiring
continuous health/social services. Six years later, it was pointed out that
society's response to the health needs of the elderly was a medical care
response with a ratio of 30 acute-care dollars being spent for each dollar
spent for health/social services. The goal for health care, as the 1978 Federal Long-term Care Committee (1978), chaired by Ethel Shanas, stated,

should be to achieve the maximum level of individual and family functioning. The credo of the masthead of the 1946 *Journal of the Gerontological Society*, "to add life to years, not just years to life," presaged that concept.

For the last 10 years, those working at Piersol at the hospital at the University of Pennsylvania, along with the leadership of the National Institute on Aging, have been advocating therapeutic optimism through rehabilitation for the disabled elderly. There has been a recognition that the goals of health care are changing from a focus only on curing to what Eisdofer (1986) has called "long-term caring." Binstock (1986) added that long-term care can no longer be separated from rehabilitation. In that sense, "custodial care" is an oxymoronic term, and there is a clear need for continuity of care.

Continuity of care moves through three stages: first, acute care, usually representing a hospital stay; second, transitional care, which is a relatively brief time period—usually less than 90 days—subsequent to a hospital stay and allowing for transition to community living; and third, long-term care, which may be intermittent, of varying intensity and locations, but continuous.

The movement of the disabled elderly through the health care system is continuous, as demonstrated by the fact that an elderly patient may see a succession of physicians or other health professionals, may be admitted to an acute-care hospital, and may either return home or go to a variety of other health care settings. These movements are now traceable. Take, for example, the interchange of the elderly between hospital and nursing home: within the period of a year, of every 100,000 over 65 years of age, there are 37,000 admissions to a hospital from the community. Of these in-patients, 2,365 are discharged to a nursing home and, in turn, 1,510 are discharged from the nursing home back to the hospital. This has been called the "ping-pong" effect. The movement of the aged disabled through the health care system is influenced by ADL and cognitive deficits and the availability of social supports. Thus, the aged entering the health care system should be able to anticipate continuity of care rather than segmented acute, transitional (subacute), or long-term care.

Repeatedly, the need for continuity of care has been called a catastrophic need based on both the individual's and family's involvement in long-term care. Multiple research studies, both by the federal government and by independent researchers, have repeatedly concluded that families provide 80% to 90% of long-term care in the community. Gerontologists describe the catastrophic need for assistance and the catastrophic quality of the family experience in providing care. Individual and family needs have been stated in broad terms, focused on personal and family strain. Multigenerational involvement is integral to continuity of care.

There is general agreement that the societal response to the needs of the individual and the family for continuity of care has been inappropriate and inadequate. The policy response, whether in the private or public sector, has been consistent with previous reactions to human catastrophe. The concern is with economic, not social, cost. As currently defined, the catastrophic need for continuity of care has been perceived, almost universally, as a bottomless economic pit. Long-term care is seen as endless, expensive nursing home and in-home care. The corollary to this perception is the view that the family will abdicate its responsibilities if formal services are provided. Researchers have disproven this last axiom, but the perception, however ill-founded, continues in some legislative corridors and administrative offices.

The need, then, is to recognize that the health care of the elderly disabled is based on chronic illness rather than only on acute disease. Secondly, chronic illness requires continuity of care that may be intermittent or constant and that includes a wide spectrum of acute, transitional, and long-term care services; in institutions, in the community, and in the home. Thirdly, the provision of continuity of care, and particularly transitional and long-term care, is dependent on an active social support system. Therefore, the goal of a system of health care for the disabled elderly is to provide for a full spectrum of continuity-of-care services. The objectives of continuity of care are to maximize the functioning of the disabled elderly and to support and strengthen families in their continuing and appropriate role in providing emotional and service support. Embracement of the idea of an "appropriate" family role acknowledges the legitimacy of institutional placement when the older person or the family becomes endangered. Formal service availability should be determined relative to the presence or absence of social supports.

Medicare has provided well for acute care. The prospective payment program provides evidence that incentives have been effective in restricting the inappropriate use of acute-care in-patient hospital beds. It has increased the need for and the utilization of home health care, short-term SNFs, and rehabilitation services. Thus, the need for a rational health care system that recognizes the interrelation of acute care with transitional care and with long-term care becomes apparent. The current Medicare definition of these three services is written in acute-care terms of disease, rather than in ADL terms of chronic illness.

Long-term care, too, has been developed as a medical service, and eligibility has been described in acute-care terms. Just as transitional services relate to acute care, so does long-term care. The population interchange among home health services, SNFs, acute-care hospitals, and other health services continuously reflects the needs of a chronically ill population, many of whom are disabled. Provision of long-term services to meet the needs of this population must be in the context of continuity of care.

ISSUES CONCERING THE COST AND QUALITY OF LONG-TERM CARE

Any discussion of quality, as used here, requires that the word be understood as the equivalent of excellence; and that good quality is the equivalent of best and poor quality is a modifier indicating worst. When we are addressing quality of care, we do so just as we do when we speak about the excellence of any other item. A discussion of quality, then, requires an agreement of what's good and, then, the development of a measuring device that will distinguish good from bad.

At stake are values—what is good care? It is reasonable to assume that, if we brought together 10 different health professionals, we would repeat the parable of the blind men and the elephant. And if we repeat the process with 100 senators and 435 representatives, the process could be bewildering. If we go to the electorate, particularly the target group of care providers, we may be overwhelmed with contradictions and confusion.

There is a need, therefore, to set the foundation for a knowledgeable, intelligent, and reasonable discussion of quality of care. And it is imperative to start with a common goal of excellence. This goal should be embodied in the mission statements of health and long-term care organizations. In enunciating the long-range process of accomplishing this goal, issues in strategic planning must be addressed.

Systems, and specifically health systems, provide the context for strategic planning. These systems organize a series of services whose meaning is in terms of specific goals. Commonly held goals provide the glue that holds together different facilities and services. When multiple organizations are in a system—in this case, the health care system—the missions of each organization must relate to the goal of the whole, to be effective and rational and to achieve quality.

On the other hand, there are short-term tactics for the achievement of more immediate objectives. Today, the "in" words for tactical planning are the development of "niches" and "windows of opportunity." These tactics have specific objectives such as gaining a competitive edge or producing capital and resources. To the extent that they are relevant to the mission of the organization and health system, they contribute to achieving the purpose of the whole; namely, quality of care.

Any discussion of health care requires, first, the identification of the goals of the health care system, or perhaps acknowledgment of the confusion about goals that now exists in public policy with respect to the health care system. Second, it is essential to describe the health care system, its parts and elements, and the role that nursing homes and other long-term care institutions play in carrying out the overall missions and commitments. And finally, there is a need for some discussion as to what our goals ought to be—what excellence ought to be, how quality of care should be measured, and whether these are likely to occur in the near future.

Decisions about goals are made in terms of basic values expressed in modern language: those of cost benefit and those of quality of life. Cost benefit defines excellence in terms of the cost of providing a safety net. Quality of life is expressed in terms of independence and enhanced level of functioning.

The reporting on these issues is clouded by seemingly contradictory descriptions and interpretations. The introduction of issues related to intergenerational conflict, reported on inaccurately, in terms of distributive justice, obscure the basic issue. Another red herring is the issue of greedy providers, busily playing the national game of monopoly. This is a distraction from the key issue of what the national goals should be for the health system. The basic picture gets confused by the diverse, often ambiguous, and sometimes overlapping agendas of the reporters.

THE VULNERABLE AGED: CRITICAL POLICY ISSUES

It is within this context that we need to examine the national policy perspectives with respect to the vulnerable aged. There is a general state of confusion among the reporters as well as among the social policy activists. One product of this state of confusion was the myth of family rejection of the aged. Now there is another concept emerging, labeled "generational equity," that involves an attempt to pit the generations against each other. The misguided assumption about the rejection of the aged where it does not exist and the malevolent invocation of intergenerational conflict have succeeded in distracting from the major issue of the need for public support for the entire family.

The invokers of the intergenerational conflict attribute the rise in the proportion of children living in poverty to the improved income position of the aged, although the facts show that the poverty of children is due largely to the economic consequences of marital disruption in young families (i.e., the increased number of unmarried mothers and the high divorce rate). The solution sought is unrelated to the cause. Rather, they recommend a reallocation of resources between children and the old and, in the process, none get help.

It is suggested that the Catastrophic Health Act of 1988—which the previous administration and Congress enacted—was the first effect of this crusade. For the first time, an age group was singled out to be taxed and deprived of earned benefits in the name of reallocation of resources. Never mind that no new resources were allocated to the younger members of the family.

Without any significant public debate, the elderly have been shorn of the benefits won at the bargaining tables from corporate employers over the last two decades. Congress itself, no later than in 1985, had established health support for the elderly based on a three-legged stool: the public, the beneficiary, and the corporation. Over 40% of the 65- to 70-year-olds had corporate guaranteed Medigap benefits. Two-thirds of all workers under the age of 65 had earned this benefit as part of their retirement package. In one fell swoop, the Catastrophic Act of 1988 was to relieve corporations of this responsibility—after a two-year hold-harmless provision.

Industry's share was to have been born by the beneficiary group and disproportionately by those with more than average income as determined by their tax returns. This latter share initially may amount to as much as $1,600 for an elderly household. To that extent, of course, these households would have been that much less able to anticipate the real catastrophe of chronic disability from a fixed income.

Social Security pensions were to have been cut. The Medicare Part B monthly premium deducted from monthly checks were to have gone up from $24 to $42.50 in four short years. This, in addition to the new tax bite.

The corporations involved anticipated breathing a sigh of relief. In 1989, the Financial Accounting Standards Board had planned to require all corporations to show on their books for the first time their potential obligation for their commitment to their retirees for health care benefits. The *Wall Street Journal* and others reported this to be at least $100 billion. Some net worths would be reduced by as much as 40%. One wonders whether this bill should be recast as the Corporation Relief Act of 1988.

In short, the Catastrophic Act was to have put the burden of health care financing of this bill entirely on the aged. As such, it was a temporary victory for the "intergenerational equity" lobby—the first time this country has used the taxing authority along these lines. To be consistent, children, or families with children, could be singled out to be taxed for health care for poor children or solely for their public education. In the context of what we know about intergenerational interdependence, about the common stake that generations have in each other (on the family level and the societal level), we could not afford to buy into such divisive and destructive notions.

Repeal of the Catastrophic Act of 1988 one year later reflected the outrage of elderly consumers in being used to balance the budget while being deprived of their negotiated Medigap protection. The avoidance by executive and legislative leadership of the real need mirrored the happenings of 25 years ago when Kerr-Mills was enacted in avoidance of confronting with the need for Medicare. From this experience we may well achieve a needed policy direction.

NEEDED POLICY DIRECTIONS: WHAT SHOULD BE ASCRIBED TO

I suggest that we are imprisoned by a 100-year-old idea that was valid then, given the state of knowledge and the historical circumstances. That idea was Pasteur's germ theory, and it focused our research, education, and practice on the control of diseases. It was reinforced by the 1910 Flexner Report, which shaped medical education for this century and, consequently, shaped our ideas for quality of care. Good things resulted from the idea that quality was equated with the absence or control of diseases caused by germs. One positive consequence was the elimination of childhood diseases, with the result that more of our population is living longer.

The down side is that we are left with halfway technology that doesn't kill, but certainly doesn't cure (Thomas, 1974). We are focused on medicine, but not on health. Our health system is really an acute medical care system. Our institutions are described and reimbursed based on medical standards, even when those criteria are irrelevant. For example, extended-care facilities and nursing homes are described in the 1965 and 1972 Medicare laws as medical facilities. The health planning legislation repeated that definition. As a result, elegibility for these services and their reimbursement is based on medical criteria, even though the need is for residential, social, and personal care and maintenance. The target population of chronically disabled is a round peg being fit into a square medical hole—the quality-of-care standard is irrelevant to the needs of the nursing home resident. The real needs of the elderly person include assistance with functioning. The health problem of the aging that we are facing is disability. Providing quality of care requires understanding the trajectory of chronic disability—the need for continuity of care.

If we agree that quality of care for today's vulnerable population is based on the need for a continuum of care—with a health system that supports a spectrum of home-, community-, and institution-based services—we can then look to answering the question: *Will we pay for quality health care?*

If we look to the recent past, as evidenced by the Catastrophic Act of 1988, the answer is a resounding negative. If we look to the future with an evolutional perspective, the answer may be affirmative. In sequence, we have met the needs of older people systematically. Initially, we met the basic needs for income maintenance and, incrementally, improved the social response to that issue through Supplemental Security Income and cost of living adjustments. In a cyclical development, Medicare was enacted to meet the needs of an aging society for acute care. The Catastrophic Act may not have been a barrier to continuity of care. Rather, if administered broadly, it may have provided for transitional care from the hospital to step-down services. The need, however, for continuity of care, which includes acute, transitional, and long-term care, remains.

There are indications that Congress is beginning to appreciate the need for continuity of care. The 100th Congress had on its agenda major proposals that underlined need for services in functional terms rather than in the language of acute care. Furthermore, case management was an agreed-upon mechanism for the administration of continuity-of-care services, which included homemaker, respite, and day care as well as nursing home care.

The late Wilbur Cohen, in one of his last conversations, predicted another 30-year legislative cycle. In 1935, the Social Security Act was passed. Thirty years later we saw the passage of Medicare. Perhaps 1995—or even sooner—will be the year for continuity of care.

REFERENCES

Binstock, R. H. (1986). Aging and rehabilitation: The birth of a social movement. In S. J. Brody and G. E. Ruff (Eds.), *Aging and Rehabilitation: Advances in the State of the Art* (pp. 357–364). New York: Springer.

Brody, S. J. (1985). The future of nursing home. *Rehabilitation Psychology, 30* (2), 109–120.

Eisdorfer, C. (1986). Aging and rehabilitation: Summary of meeting. In S. J. Brody and G. E. Ruff (Eds.), *Aging and Rehabilitation: Advances in the State of the Art* (pp. 357–364). New York: Springer.

Gruenberg, E. M. (1977). The failures of success. *Milbank Memorial Fund Quarterly, 55* (7), 3–24.

Katz, S., Branch, L. G., Branson, M. H., Papsidero, J. A., Beck, J. C., & Greer, D. S. (1983). Active life expectancy. *The New England Journal of Medicine, 309* (20), 1218–1224.

Katz, S., Ford, A. B., Moskowitz, R. W., Jackson, B. A., & Jaffee, M. W. (1963). Studies of illness in the aged. The index of ADL: A standardized measure of biological and psychosocial function. *Journal of the American Medical Association, 185*, 914–919.

Lawton, M. P., & Brody, E. M. (1969). Assessment of older people: Self-maintaining and instrumental activities of daily living. *The Gerontologist, 9*, 179–186.

Mahoney, F. I., & Barthel, D. W. (1965). Functional evaluation: The Barthel index. *Maryland State Medical Journal, 14*, 61–65.

National Center for Health Statistics. (1987a—June 10). Aging in the eighties. *133.*

National Center for Health Statistics. (1987b—May 14). Use of nursing homes by the elderly. *135.*

Reno, V. P., & Grad, S. (1985). Economic security, 1935–85. *Social Security Bulletin, 48* (12), 18.

Thomas, L. (1974). *The Living Cell.* New York: Bantam Books.

U.S. National Committee on Vital and Health Statistics. (September 1978). *Long-Term Health Care: Minimum Data Set.* Preliminary Report of the Technical Consultant Panel on the Long-Term Health Care Data Set. Washington, D.C.: U.S. Public Health Service.

15

National Policies and the Vulnerable Aged: Present, Emerging, and Proposed

Robert H. Binstock

An observer of contemporary popular culture in the United States would be unlikely to conclude that many older persons are especially vulnerable. Indeed, some of the media—particularly national magazines—would have us believe that today's older persons are invulnerable to problems of income, health, housing, employment, and other aspects of well-being. Typical of such depictions was a cover story in *Time* entitled "Grays on the Go" (Gibbs, 1988). It was filled with pictures of senior surfers, senior swingers, and senior softball players. Older persons were portrayed as America's new elite—healthy, wealthy, powerful, and "staging history's biggest retirement party."

Although such stories present grossly distorted images of the wealth, health, and selfishness of an artificially homogenized group labeled "the aged," it is certainly true that the aggregate situation of older Americans has improved dramatically over the past several decades. A great deal of this improved protection for the elderly has been achieved through policies of our national government, through which 26% of the annual federal budget is expended on benefits to the aging (U.S. Senate Special Committee on Aging, 1988).

Social Security has been remarkable in helping to reduce the proportion of elderly persons in poverty from about 35% three decades ago (Clark, 1990) to 12.8% today (U.S. Senate Special Committee on Aging, 1988). For over two decades, Medicare and Medicaid have provided all older persons with public insurance coverage for a great many health care services to which they might not otherwise have had access. The Age Discrimination in Employment Act, through its 1978 and 1986 Amendments, has eliminated mandatory retirement in most sectors of American society. The Older Americans Act of 1965 has provided needed services to countless older persons. The Employee Retirement Income Security Act of 1974 now protects pension benefits for workers who have earned them through years of employment. One could go on and on with respect to how national policies—such as federal housing, low-income home energy assistance, legal services, and transportation—have reduced vulnerability among older Americans.

Despite these ameliorative national policies, however, we know that many older persons remain highly vulnerable with respect to income, ill-health and functional status, and other dimensions of fundamental well-being. And this vulnerability will persist, and probably increase, unless national policies are reformed. Moreover, some of the policy proposals that are current in American political discourse threaten to exacerbate vulnerability for the elderly, particularly those who are in the oldest age brackets, by withholding life-sustaining medical care from them, categorically.

PRESENT VULNERABILITY: POVERTY AS AN ILLUSTRATION

Despite the $300 billion our national government expends annually in benefits to the aging, some 3.6 million older persons have an annual income that is below the government's official poverty line; an additional 4.4 million persons aged 65 and over are in families that have annual incomes that are between the poverty level and 150% of that level—in other words, within a few hundred to a few thousand dollars of poverty. The subgroups of older persons most heavily represented in these vulnerable income categories are blacks and females. For instance, among older persons living as "unrelated individuals," the percentage of black females in poverty is 60% compared with 24% of white females and 17% of white males (U.S. Senate Committee on Aging, 1988, pp. 6–7).

Unless national policies are changed substantially in the years immediately ahead, such clusters of older persons who are extremely vulnerable with respect to income will not disappear. The eligibility and benefit structures of the Old Age Insurance (OAI) program of Social Security are based upon the labor force record of potential recipients. Persons who do not have a long and stable history of employment, or who work in jobs not included in the Social Security taxation system, receive very low OAI benefits or do not qualify for them at all. Still others receive benefits that are not sufficient for adequate living in retirement (Schulz, 1988). Consequently, although Social Security has saved tens of millions of older Americans from poverty, and will continue to do so in the years ahead, its program structure is such that millions more older persons will remain vulnerable to poverty because of their limited work histories within the Social Security system.

While the federal Supplemental Security Income (SSI) program provides a minimum guaranteed income payment averaging $187 per month to older persons who qualify through means tests (Social Security in Review, 1988), most estimates are that only 40% to 60% of those who are eligible for it apply. Reasons for this lack of participation are not precisely clear, but researchers have suggested a variety of possible factors. These include ignorance of the program; distaste for the stigmatization of being a welfare recipient; the severity of the asset and income tests that are applied to determine eligibility; and the small marginal value of the income to be obtained through SSI payments (Commonwealth Fund Commission on Elderly People Living Alone, 1987; Schulz & Leavitt, 1988; U.S. Senate Special Committee on Aging, 1988; Zedlewski & Meyer, 1987). For most of those who do receive SSI payments, the amount is not sufficient to bring their incomes up to the poverty line even in communities where the state government supplements the federal payment.

These are but a few illustrations of how older persons can remain vulnerable within the context of national policies designed to provide income in old age. Reforming such policies to achieve an adequate income for all older persons is not a difficult technical problem. Practical proposals for changing OAI and SSI so as to target income maintenance policies to the most economically vulnerable elderly have been put forward for years (Cohen & Friedman, 1972; Commonwealth Fund Commission on Elderly People Living Alone, 1987; Munnell, 1977; Pechman et al., 1968). But they have not been strongly supported politically, either by Congress or by the organizations in the field of aging. The Villers Foundation, a small organization without a mass membership constituency, is the only so-called aging advocacy group that has a primary mission to focus on the plight of the poor and vulnerable elderly (Villers Foundation, 1983).

EMERGING VULNERABILITY: ILL HEALTH AND DISABILITY AMONG THE VERY OLD

For an older person, the very process of aging still further tends to sharply increase the probability of ill health and disability. Despite substantial improvements in life expectancy in this century, older persons become more vulnerable to acute and long-term disabilities as they advance in years, particularly as they reach their late 70s and their 80s. Health care may delay such vulnerabilities, but apparently cannot reduce the high prevalence of them in late life.

The differences in hospital utilization rates among age groupings within the older population, for example, are substantial. Persons aged 85 and older use hospitals at a rate that is 91% higher than for those aged 65 to 74 (U.S. Senate Special Committee on Aging, 1988).

As an old age cohort becomes older, the prevalence of functional limitations within it also rises. An increasing proportion of cohort members have difficulty carrying out their personal care or home management activities—that is, activities of daily living (ADLs)—such as bathing, dressing, eating, transferring, walking, getting outside, and using the toilet. More than three times as many persons aged 85 and over have difficulties in independently performing two or more ADLs than do persons aged 65 to 69 (Dawson et al., 1987).

A reflection of the comparatively high prevalence of many long-term chronic diseases and other disabling conditions among populations aged in their late 70s and in their 80s (Gruenberg, 1977; Schneider & Brody, 1983) is the relative rates of institutionalization among age categories within the older age grouping. About 2% of persons aged 65 to 74 years in the United States are in nursing homes; this compares with 7% of persons 75 to 84 years of age, and 16% of persons aged 85 and older (U.S. Senate Special Committee on Aging, 1986).

The rapidly changing age structure within our older population indicates that the aggregate vulnerability of older Americans to ill health and functional disability is likely to rise substantially in the decades immediately ahead. In 1980, for example, persons aged 85 and over constituted only 8.8% of the American older population; by 1990, they will be 10.5%, and in the year 2000, they will be 14%. Similarly, in 1980, persons aged 75 and older constituted 39% of the older population; in 1990, they will be 43%; and at the turn of the century, they will be 50% (U.S. Senate Special Committee on Aging, 1987–88).

The greater numbers of persons who soon will be in the older old-age categories is a major factor in projections that the current nursing home population of 1.5 million persons will increase to 2.1 million by the year 2000 and reach 4.4 million some 40 years later (U.S. Senate Special Committee on Aging, 1986). Parallel projections suggest that there will be even greater numbers of noninstitutionalized older persons who will be as severely disabled as those who are in nursing homes (Committee on an Aging Society, 1985).

While substantial attention has been given to national policies for improving the financial coverage of care for older persons through private insurance and Medicare and Medicaid reform (Blumenthal et al., 1986;

Kane & Kane, 1987; Rivlin & Wiener, 1988), little attention has been given to policies for developing effectiveness in prevention, treatment, and maintenance of functional capacity. Yet, much can be done through national policy to deal with the current and growing vulnerability of our older population to long-term conditions of ill health and disability.

To be sure, there is no scientific evidence as yet to support the optimistic paradigm that the prevalence and duration of morbidity can be compressed to a short period at the end of the life span (Binstock, 1987a; Fries, 1987; Schneider & Guralnik, 1987). But research could well yield advances in preventing and treating such conditions as urinary incontinence, osteoporosis, stroke, and organic brain syndromes, and could have substantial impact in delaying the onset of chronic illness and disability to older ages than at present, thereby reducing both the prevalence and duration of morbidity near the end of life.

In addition, we could focus health promotion and disease prevention among older persons in a different fashion than we do for their younger counterparts. The traditional targets of prevention—cancer, heart disease, accidents, and stroke—should be broadened to include what have been termed "geriatric syndromes"—common disorders such as urinary incontinence, falling, dementia, nutritional imbalances, and acute confusional state—each of which renders older persons extremely vulnerable.

Perhaps the most important consideration for reducing the vulnerability of older persons to ill health and disability is a focus on functional capability. In addition to those older persons who are in nursing homes, a substantial proportion of older persons who are not institutionalized have major limitations in their ADLs, such as bathing, dressing, toileting, and eating. Such functional impairments are clearly age-related among the elderly, increasing from about 5% within the 65-to-74-year-old group to nearly 40% by age 85 (National Center for Health Statistics, 1983).

Consequently, a major national policy goal for an aging society should be the maintenance of functional capabilities, regardless of chronic illness, as nearly as possible to the end of the life span. The goal requires far greater demonstration efforts and research on rehabilitation among the elderly than we have had to date. Very little is known about the efficacy of rehabilitative efforts with older patients; indeed, such efforts are often not even undertaken with respect to very old patients. Yet, rigorously designed and implemented studies may be able to show us that such efforts are cost-effective, particulary if they reveal that rehabilitation can restore daily functional capacities in some older patients sufficiently to eliminate their need for long-term care (Binstock, 1987b).

PROPOSED VULNERABILITY:
SCAPEGOATING THE AGED

In 1982, I presented a lecture to the Gerontological Society of America entitled "The Aged as Scapegoat." In it, I suggested that older persons were taking the blame for a variety of anxieties in American life and might, therefore, become vulnerable in economic, social, and political dimensions previously unknown to us (Binstock, 1983).

At that time, the phenomenon was only beginning. A handful of economists were suggesting that Social Security benefits were too high (e.g., Feldstein & Feldstein, 1982). A few magazines and newspapers were running feature stories about the wealthy and healthy elderly, who were "feasting" off their old-age entitlements (e.g., Flint, 1980).

Now, scapegoating the aged is in full fashion. A dominant theme in contemporary discussions of older persons is that their selfishness is ruining the nation. The *New Republic* highlighted this selfishness theme early in 1988 with a cover depicting "Greedy Geezers." The table-of-contents "teaser" for the story that followed (Fairlie, 1988) announced that "The real me generation isn't the yuppies, it's America's growing ranks of prosperous elderly."

An impressive list of American problems has been attributed (or at least linked) to the prosperity and selfishness of the elderly. Former Secretary of Commerce Peter Peterson (1987) has proposed that a prerequisite for the United States regaining its stature as a first-class power in the world economy is a sharp reduction in benefits for older Americans. Demographers (Preston, 1984) and advocates for children have blamed the political power of the elderly for the plight of youngsters who have inadequate nutrition, health care, education, and supportive family environments. From the late 1970s until the late 1980s there were many complaints that the Old Age and Survivors Insurance trust fund would be continually on the verge of "going broke," thereby posing an intolerable burden to American workers and their employers. Now that projections show substantial trust fund surpluses for the decades ahead, economists have begun analyzing and debating whether such surpluses will adversely affect the performance of the American economy (Kilborn, 1988; Munnell & Blais, 1988).

Perhaps the most serious scapegoating of the aged—in terms of vulnerability for older persons and, indeed, vulnerability for all persons in our society—has been with respect to health care. A widespread concern about high rates of inflation in health care costs has somehow been refocused from the health care providers, suppliers, administrators, and insurers who are responsible for those costs to the elderly patients that they charge for care.

Older persons account for one-third of our annual health care expenditures (U.S. Senate Special Committee on Aging, 1988, p. 12). Because the elderly population is growing, health care costs for older persons have been depicted as an unsustainable burden or, as some have put it, "a great fiscal black hole" (Callahan, 1987, p. 16) that will absorb an unlimited amount of our national resources.

To date, this particular theme of scapegoating the aged may be the most pernicious. It has developed to the point that specific proposals have been put forward to deny health care to older persons. Moreover, such proposals have received substantial attention in serious public forums.

Age–Based Health Care Rationing

Health care in the United States has always been rationed informally on the basis of availability of resources and the conditions and characteristics of individual patients. But proposals for official policies that would deny care on the basis of membership in a demographically identified group are a substantial departure from existing practices.

The suggestion that health care be rationed on the basis of old age began to develop, through implication, in 1983. In a speech to the Health Insurance Association of America, economist Alan Greenspan, now Chairman of the Federal Reserve Board, noted that 30% of Medicare is annually expended on 5% to 6% of Medicare eligibles who die within the year. He pointedly asked "Whether it is worth it" (Schulte, 1983).

In 1984, the governor of Colorado was widely quoted as stating that older persons "have a duty to die and get out of the way" (Slater, 1984). Although he denied making this specific statement, he has been traveling throughout the nation since leaving office, delivering the same message in somewhat more delicately worded fashion (Lamm, 1987).

During the past few years, this issue has spread to a number of forums. Philosophers have been generating principles of equity to undergird "justice between age groups" in the provision of health care (Daniels, 1988). Conferences and books have explicitly addressed the issue of "Should Health Care Be Rationed By Age?" (Smeeding et al., 1987).

Late in 1987, this theme reached new heights of legitimacy with the publication of a widely reviewed book by Daniel Callahan, a well-known bio-medical ethicist. The book, entitled *Setting Limits: Medical Goals in an Aging Society*, is a proposal that older persons should be denied life-extending health care if they are in their "late 70s or early 80s" and/or have "achieved a natural life span."

The significance of this book lies in the extraordinary attention it received. It was reviewed in national magazines: the *New York Times*, the *Washington Post*, the *Wall Street Journal*, and just about every relevant professional and scholarly journal and newsletter. It now seems legitimate in American society to consider old-age-based rationing of health care as a national policy.

Callahan (1987) views older Americans as "a new social threat" and a "demographic, economic, and medical avalanche . . . that could ultimately (and perhaps already) do great harm" (p. 20). His remedy for this threat is to use "age as a specific criterion for the allocation and limitation of health care" (p. 23). He justifies his proposal by emphasizing the burdensome costs of health care for older persons and by arguing that "the meaning and significance of life for the elderly themselves is best founded on a sense of limits to health care" (p. 116).

Older persons, in addition to being numerous and requiring large amounts of health care, are regarded by Callahan as selfish. He blames their selfishness on "mainline" advocates for the aged who have stressed for over two decades the rights and entitlements of the elderly and brainwashed older persons to believe that the process of aging is utterly diverse, the aged are varied (like any other age group), and old age is a time of renewed vigor, growth, self-discovery, and contributions to the community.

Although Callahan presents his case for rationing in a judicious style, with a veneer of scholarly balance, his arguments are seriously flawed because they are often incomplete, imbalanced, illogical, and internally contradictory (Binstock & Kahana, 1988). Two flaws, in particular, should be highlighted because of their very serious moral implications.

One flaw is that Callahan does not even attempt to convey how much money would be saved if his proposal were implemented. If the costs of health care for older persons are an unsustainable burden for our society, to what extent would that burden be relieved by old-age-based rationing? Previous calculations have suggested that even if all the funds that are spent on very high-cost Medicare patients who die within a year were not expended, the savings would be negligible (Rowe & Binstock, 1987).

In 1987, we spent $511 billion on health care in the United States, and $170 billion of that was on persons aged 65 and older. If Callahan's proposal had been implemented, would the aggregate savings have been $1 billion, $5 billion, $25 billion? Assuming that any amount of money could justify his proposal, shouldn't he provide some basis for judging whether it is worth it? Otherwise, we are left with what amounts to a naked attack on older persons.

The other major flaw is Callahan's total neglect of the moral implications of singling out any group of Americans as not worthy of life-extending care. What impact would such a policy have on the moral fabric of American society? What group might be singled out next as undesirable, burdensome, and costly? If the aged can become vulnerable through scapegoating, who among us is next in line? Are the economic burdens of health care costs greater than the moral burdens of officially denying health care to a demographically defined category of citizens?

Despite such flaws, the very fact that a proposal such as Callahan's might be put forward and treated seriously in the mainstream of American public discourse is an indicator of a new vulnerability for the aged in American public opinion. This proposal and the attention it has received many not represent the climax of the process through which the aged have become a scapegoat. A new organization established to propound issues of "intergenerational equity," Americans for Generational Equity (AGE), appears to have solid political and financial backing (Quadagno, 1989). And, as exemplified by the title of one of its recent conferences—"Children at Risk: Who Will Support Our Society?"—AGE will likely persist in pitting the young and the middle-aged against the old.

COMBATTING VULNERABILITY

These few illustrations of the different ways in which older persons are vulnerable have been offered to suggest that a substantial challenge lies ahead. Regardless of the image that the elderly are now well off, and even though reductions in vulnerability have been achieved over the past several decades, advocates for the well-being of older persons have much with which to be concerned.

What indications are there in national policy of efforts to reduce the current vulnerabilities of older Americans or to prevent the development of new vulnerabilities? In what ways, if any, has the status of the elderly as a political constituency changed in Washington? The principal trend in the 1980s seems to be an acknowledgement that "the elderly" are a diverse group economically and socially, and that old age is not necessarily a good marker of economic status. The Social Security Reform Act of 1983 began this trend by taxing Social Security benefits for recipients in higher income brackets. The Tax Reform Act of 1986 eliminated the extra personal exemption available to all persons 65 years and older when filing their federal income tax, while providing tax credits to very low-income older persons on a sliding scale. The Medicare Catastrophic Coverage Act of 1988, although repealed in 1989, was to be financed in part by payments from older persons in accordance with their income levels. And the Older Americans Act has been evolving toward sliding-fee scales in a number of its programs.

The artificiality of treating older persons through policy as if they were all the same seems to have been abandoned. Our national government seems more sensitive to the different circumstances among older persons.

Yet, at the same time, scapegoating the aged seems to have diverted attention from helping those among the elderly who remain highly vulnerable with respect to income, health, and many other dimensions of fundamental well-being. Other than the quickly-repealed Catastrophic Coverage Act, there have been no major expansions of benefits to the aged since 1972 when Social Security benefits were markedly elevated. No major new initiatives appear under way to help those categories of vulnerable older persons who are not substantially helped by the structure of our current public policies and have not been helped for decades. There are many current proposals for public long-term care insurance legislation, but they appear to arise primarily from a middle-class concern about "spending down" in the process of becoming eligible for Medicaid. Little attention is being paid to those who have nothing to spend down. And health policies toward aging, generally, are more focused on financing issues than on goals for prevention, treatment, and maintenance of independent functioning in activities of daily living.

The main contemporary challenges to those of us in the field who would be advocates, it seems to me, are twofold. First, we must confront the broad campaign of scapegoating that is inaccurately blaming greedy older persons for the economy's troubles, the welfare of children, the strains that the payroll tax puts on business, and the high costs of health care. We have seen that this type of process, portraying the aging as a social threat in American society, can lead to proposals such as Callahan's that call for older persons to be denied life-saving care, and to suggestions that the aged need to understand that their appropriate social role is to die. If this vitriolic campaign is not countered effectively, it may someday lead to a proposal that all older persons be rounded up in a government-run "life care community" to be served with programs there, through economies of scale, that take the place of Social Security, Medicare, Medicaid, and other expensive entitlement programs.

The other challenge is to advocate for policies that may finally bring adequate assistance to the vulnerable elderly. Building upon the contemporary recognition by Congress of the diversity among older persons, it is time to focus on targeting resources to those most in need. We should not focus on saving Social Security to the exclusion of those persons who are not saved by the Social Security program under its current structure. We should focus on having federal SSI payments increased to the poverty line. We should advocate for housing policies that will at least provide adequate shelter to everyone.

In short, while a scapegoating campaign has made the aging vulnerable in a new and important sense, we must not allow our attention to be distracted from the plight of the worst cases—those who are still highly vulnerable, and have been all along.

In fact, it may be time to drop age from the picture altogether and focus on vulnerability, per se. For the ultimate issue is whether our governments will provide effective help to those who are not in a position to help themselves, regardless of age. If they are vulnerable children—and they are not helped—they will end up being vulnerable aged, if they live that long.

About a quarter of century ago, I directed a White House Task Force on Older Americans to which President Lyndon B. Johnson presented a highly open-ended charge: "What are the most important things that can be done for the well-being of the most older Americans?" The Task Force members well understood that vulnerability in old age is the product of a life course of experiences, binding us all together. Their priority statement to the President was that "economic and social opportunities for current generations of the young and middle-aged are the most effective measures for ensuring opportunities for future generations of older Americans" (President's Task Force on Older Americans, 1968, p. 1). That kind of understanding of our common human vulnerability is what we need more of today.

REFERENCES

Binstock, R. H. (1983). The aged as scapegoat. *The Gerontologist, 23*, 136–143.

Binstock, R. H. (1987a). Exhortatory and scholarly approaches to the compression of morbidity. *Gerontologica Perspecta, 1*, 16–19.

Binstock, R. H. (1987b). Rehabilitation and the elderly: Economic and political issues. In R. E. Dunkle & J. W. Schmidley (Eds.), *Stroke in the elderly* (pp. 186–200). New York: Springer.

Binstock, R. H., & Kahana, J. (1988). An essay on *Setting limits: Medical goals in an aging society*, by Daniel Callahan. *The Gerontologist, 28* (3), 424–426.

Blumenthal, D., Schlesinger, M., Druimheller, P. B., & the Harvard Medicare Project (1986). The future of Medicare. *New England Journal of Medicine, 314*, (11) 722–728.

Callahan, D. (1987). *Setting limits: Medical goals for an aging society*. New York: Simon and Schuster.

Clark, R. L. (1990). Old age income maintenance policies in the United States. In R. H. Binstock & L. K. George (Eds). *Handbook of aging and the social sciences* (3rd ed., pp. 382–397) San Diego: Academic Press.

Cohen, W. J., & Friedman, M. (1972). *Social security: Universal or selective?* Washington, D.C.: American Enterprise Institute.

Committee on an Aging Society/Institute of Medicine and National Research Council (1985). *Health in an Older Society*. Washington, D.C.: National Academy Press.

Commonwealth Fund Commission on Elderly People Living Alone (1987). *Old, alone and poor: A plan for reducing poverty among elderly people living alone*. Baltimore: Commonwealth Fund Commission on Elderly People Living Alone.

Dawson, D., Hendershot, G., & Fulton, J. (1987). Aging in the eighties: Functional limitations of individuals age 65 years and over. *Advance Data*, No. 133, June 10. National Center for Health Statistics, U.S. Department of Health and Human Services.

Daniels, N. (1988). *Am I my parents' keeper? An essay on justice between the young and the old*. New York: Oxford University Press.

Fairlie, H. (1988). Talkin' 'bout my generation. *The New Republic, 198* (13) 19–22.

Feldstein, M., & Feldstein, K. (1982). It's time to do something about Social Security costs. *The Boston Globe*, February 2, p. 46.

Flint, J. (1980). The old folks. *Forbes*, February 18, pp. 51–56.

Fries, J. F. (1987). An introduction to the compression of morbidity, *Gerontologica Perspecta, 1*, 5–8.

Gibbs, N. R. (1988). Grays on the go. *Time, 131*, (8), 66–75.

Gruenberg, E. N. (1977). The failures of success. *Milbank Memorial Fund Quarterly/Health and Society, 55*, 3–24.

Kane, R. A., & Kane, R. L. (1987). *Long-Term care: Principles, programs, and policies*. New York: Springer.

Kilborn, P. T. (1988). New issues on budget horizon: What to do about surpluses. *The New York Times*, April 2, p. 1.

Lamm, R. D. (1987). A Debate: Medicare in 2020. In *Medicare reform and the baby boom generation*, edited proceedings of the second annual conference of Americans for Generational Equity, Vol. 1, pp. 77–88. Washington, D.C.: Americans for Generational Equity.

Munnell, A. H. (1977). *The future of social security*. Washington, D.C.: The Brookings Institute.

Munnell, A. H., & Blais, L. E. (1988). Do we want large Social Security surpluses? *The Generational Journal, 1*, (1), 21–36.

National Center for Health Statistics (1983). *Americans needing help to function at home*. Hyattsville, MD: U.S. Public Health Service.

Pechman, J. A., Aaron, H. J., & Taussig, M. K. (1968). *Social Security: Perspectives for reform*. Washington, D.C.: The Brookings Institution.

Peterson, P. (1987). The morning after. *The Atlantic, 260*(4), 43–69.

President's Task Force on Older Americans. (1968). *Report of the President's task force on older Americans*. Washington, D.C.: Executive Office of the President of the United States.

Preston, S. H. (1984). Children and the elderly in the U.S. *Scientific American, 251* (6), 44–49.

Quadagno, J. (1988). Generational Equity and the politics of the welfare state. *Politics and Society, 17* (3), 353–376.

Rivlin, A. M., & Wiener, J. M. (1988) *Caring for the disabled elderly: Who will pay?*: Washington, D.C.: The Brookings Institution.

Rowe, J. W., & Binstock, R. H. (1987). Aging reconsidered: Emerging research and policy issues. In E. Ginzbery (Ed.), *Medicine and society: Clinical decisions and societal values* (pp. 96–113). Boulder, CO: Westview Press.

Schneider, E. L., Brody, J. A. (1983). Aging, natural death, and the compression of morbidity. *New England Journal of Medicine, 309*, 854–856.

Schneider, E. L., & Guralnik, J. M. (1987). The compression of morbidity: A dream which may come true, someday! *Gerontologica Perspecta*, *1*, 8–14.

Schulte J. (1983). Terminal patients deplete Medicare, Greenspan says. *Dallas Morning News*. April 26, p. 1.

Schulz, J. H. (1988). *Economics of aging*, 4th edition. Dover, MA: Auburn Publishing House Company.

Schulz, J. H., & Leavitt, T. D. (1988). *Time to reform that SSI asset test?* Washington, D.C.: American Association of Retired Persons.

Slater, W. (1984). Latest Lamm remark angers the elderly. *Arizona Daily Star*, March 29, p. 1.

Smeeding, T. M., Battin, M. P., Francis, L. P., & Landesman, B. M. (Eds). (1987). *Should medical care be rationed by age?* Totowa, NJ: Rowman & Litterfield.

Social Security in Review (1988). *Social Security Bulletin*, *51*, (7), 3.

U.S. Senate Special Committee on Aging (1986). *Aging America: Trends and projections—1985–86 edition*. Washington, D.C.: American Association of Retired Persons.

U.S. Senate Special Committee on Aging (1987–88). *Aging America: Trends and projections—1987–88 edition*. Washington, D.C.: American Association of Retired Persons.

U.S. Senate Special Committee on Aging (1988). *Developments in aging: 1987—volume I.* Washington, D.C.: U.S. Government Printing Office.

Villers Foundation (1983). *Mission and guidelines. Nurturing a movement of empowerment among elders*. Washington, D.C.: The Villers Foundations.

Zedlewski, S. R., & Meyer, J. A. (1987). *Toward ending poverty among the elderly and disabled: Policy and financing options*. Washington, D.C.: The Urban Institute.

16

Federal Programs for the Vulnerable Aged

John H. Skinner

The topics of vulnerability and aging are often thought of as being synonymous. This chapter will address the distinctions between being elderly and being vulnerable. It will also clarify the differences in vulnerability and long-term care. Attention is given to separating the conditions of the elderly from the kinds of services that are rendered to help them.

Federal programs are the public policy expressions of the government. These programs, with the aid of intermediaries at the state and local levels, provide direction and funding for an array of services and activities (Wholey et al., 1973). This chapter provides information about the public policy context in which federal programs operate. Part of the backdrop for understanding public programs is the puritan ethic and the Elizabethan poor laws. It is this mind-set that leads to programs that focus on the most needy and only those services necessary to maintain survival.

In considering the kinds of federal programs that address the needs of the vulnerable aged, three types of programs are identified. This typology of programs—consisting of client assistance, system optimizing, and service enhancement—is described and specific programs are categorized under the three groupings. This review then considers federal programs within the concept of the continuum of care. The existence of the continuum is examined against the reality of existing federal programs. The chapter ends with a discussion of future directions in federal programs for the vulnerable elderly.

PLACING VULNERABILITY IN A PUBLIC POLICY CONTEXT

Early in the Reagan administration, we were reminded that the bulk of the elderly are reasonably healthy and physically fit. This was used to argue in favor of cutbacks in social programs and services to the elderly. The administration wanted to ensure that those not worthy of public support would be purged from the public rolls and that funds would be retargeted on the truly needy. However, with program funding cuts and increasing deductible and copayments, benefits for the most needy, when adjusted for inflation, did not increase (Palmer & Sawhill, 1984). Among the groups that have been considered the deserving poor are the aged, yet the Reagan administration sought to cut, abolish, or contain these programs during its time in office. To a great extent, what remains of federal programs and benefits for the aged is the result of efforts by proponents for the aged to defeat the proposals of the Reagan administration.

The elderly in the United States have been identified as a special subgroup of the population and, to some degree, singled out for special attention (Lowy, 1980). Estes (1979) has argued that this separation legitimizes the aged as a special group and leads to public policies that perpetuate that condition. The by-product of the separation of the aged is the creation of a network of service providers in whose interest it is to continue existing local power relationships (Estes, 1979). Another side effect of emphasizing the marginal status of the aged has been the rising concern that the elderly, at the expense of other age groups, may be receiving a disproportionate amount of public benefits. More recently, there has been some effort to minimize criticisms about intergenerational tensions by emphasizing the interdependence of the generations (Kingston et al., 1986).

Defining Vulnerability

The subject of vulnerability in aged persons has been discussed at considerable length. However, it is important to briefly review vulnerability as a concept before moving into an examination of how programs for the elderly address this special population. One reason for dwelling on the concept of vulnerability is that it is a little like the term *pornography*: it is hard to define, but we know it when we see it. Literally, being vulnerable is being capable of being wounded, being open to attack. Clearly, this connotation is limited, although very real for some segments of the aged population, particularly those living in high crime areas. We may extend this rather narrow definition to include persons who are frail, disabled, living alone, ill, and at risk of fundamental changes in their ability to live independently. This broader definition more fully encompasses elderly persons that need societal concern and public support.

The vulnerable elderly represent a special subset of the aged population. In some respects, it is this group that fosters the negative images of frailty and illness in the elderly. As a subset of the total aged population, the vulnerable elderly are those persons who are frail, ill, disabled, or isolated in the community. The 1987 Amendments to the Older Americans Act (PL 100–175) define the frail aged as "those having a physical or mental disability, including Alzheimer's disease or a related disorder with neurological or organic brain dysfunction, that restricts their ability to perform daily tasks or threatens their capacity to live independently" (Special Committee on Aging, 1987). The test of frailty in the aged population would require an assessment of each elderly person. Short of this difficult task, population estimates are often made by identifying those groups in which the incidence of frailty is high. These target groups provide a convenient method of estimating the size of the problem, although these estimates are subject to gross errors (Skinner, 1990).

The literature on the aged has documented the increasing incidence of frailty with age, particularly at the extreme age levels above 75 years old. Other studies have shown that frailty in old age is also differential by sex, with females tending to be more frail than men. Race has also been identified as being highly related to frailty, with blacks and minorities being more frail than whites. Therefore, persons over 75, women, and minorities are the primary targets for service planning and delivery.

Vulnerability and Long-Term Care

The term "services for the vulnerable elderly" is not synonymous with "long-term care services for the elderly," but it is very closely related. While all persons receiving long-term care are vulnerable, by definition, not all vulnerable persons require long-term care. The difference is that vulnerability describes a condition or state of being, while long-term care describes a complex of services designed to address specific conditions. Programs providing support for the vulnerable elderly and long-term care services cover income assistance, service financing, housing and shelter, access services, health care, and social service programs. While long-term care is considered an important area of service, no federal programs exist for the provision of comprehensive long-term care services. Most federal long-term care activities are best described as specialized efforts that provide part of the patchwork for the quilt of comprehensive long-term care. The ability to address future program planning and development may rest on how well we facilitate the interrelationship between vulnerability and long-term care.

SOCIETAL APPROACH TO PUBLICLY FUNDED PROGRAMS

Traditionally, this society has been very reticent to acknowledge a public role in the provision of programs and services to its citizens. The position has generally been that it is the role of families, private organizations, or voluntary and charitable organizations to engage in health and welfare programs. Traditionally, when government has become involved, it has been to address problems of the most needy. Those most in need are seen as those who have slipped through the existing nongovernmental mechanisms and remain unserved, or who might be better served through government intervention. As a society, the United States has been reluctant to have its federal government engage in the operation of health and welfare programs, with notable exceptions during the periods of the New Deal and the Great Society. These two periods of our history brought about fundamental changes in the way federal and state governments functioned with regard to the general health and welfare of their citizens. Besides these two landmark periods in the domestic policy of the United States, cyclical shifts in social policy have been between a stronger or weaker role for government in the care of those less fortunate members of the population.

During the current cycle of political climate, the pendulum has swung away from a strong role for government in health and welfare programs to a greater emphasis on the family and private resources, with government support reserved as the last resort. Directing publicly supported programs toward the truly needy has led to an overemphasis of programs and services that address only basic survival needs. This results in a focus on health, shelter, and nutrition services.

With the increasing concern over rising health care costs, the public and the government have placed increased emphasis on alternatives to institutionalization. While these increased concerns may have humanitarian seeds, the policies are basically cost-avoidance strategies. They have as their main goal the diversion of costs from institutions and government to the family, the private sector, and voluntary organizations. The latest emphasis on services to families caring for long-term care patients is a case in point. For the most part, national efforts have been primarily to reduce the cost of services, be they health or social services. While cost-containment strategies have resulted in minor efficiencies, they have merely shifted some of the cost of services from one source of service funding to others.

Visibility of Federal Programs

If we look at federal programs for the aged, we find that these programs are often amorphous and vaguely identifed entities in the minds of most people. As such, a national program is generally a complex of services and activities that have a common theme that is funded and administered through one federal agency. The specific mix of services or activities may vary from state to state and by community within states.

Often, the only knowledge that the general public and clients have of federal programs is through their limited contact with selected services funded by the program. Even when clients have contact with federally funded programs, they seldom know that the services are funded with federal dollars. This filtering of the identity of federal programs at the local level has had a negative effect on constituency-building in support of these programs. Because most users of services do not know that they are receiving federally supported services, they are not aware of how they are affected by federal decisions about these programs and services. A better understanding of this symbiotic relationship between federal programs and the availability of local services is essential if we are to ensure that those who are vulnerable get the services they need.

A TYPOLOGY OF FEDERAL PROGRAMS

What are the goals of programs that serve the vulnerable aged? The objectives of each program are highly specific, yet there are some general goals that can be summarized here. Federal programs serving the vulnerable elderly can be generally categorized as client assisting, service enhancing, or system optimizing.

Client assistance programs have as a general goal the provision of income assistance that provides the minimum support to maintain one's basic needs (Lowy, 1980). This is true even of Social Security, which is designed to provide a floor below which older retired people will not fall (Schulz, 1988). Client assistance programs have been thought of as "welfare benefits" or "earned benefits" programs. Social Security is seen as an earned-benefit program because of employee contributions made prior to retirement. In the case of "welfare benefits," which are generally means tested, the intent has been to provide substance income that will serve as a deterrent for those not receiving support and as an incentive for those receiving this support to get off the public rolls. This policy is supposed to discourage freeloading and loafing. The provision of minimum financial support, by itself, may reduce vulnerability. For many elderly, low income is often associated with frailty, illness, disability, and living alone, factors that exacerbate vulnerability in the aged. These benefits are received directly by older persons.

System optimizing programs aim primarily to ensure effective and efficient services that fulfill their mandated mission and maintain quality. The

Prospective Payment System through the use of Diagnosis-Related Groups (DRGs) attempts to contain the cost of acute care by regulating the amount of reimbursement to hospitals serving Medicare eligible patients. The Long-Term Care Ombudsman Program, operated under the Administration on Aging, serves as an advocate of the vulnerable elderly residing in long-term care facilities. These programs monitor direct service programs to protect the rights and privileges of program receipients. Programs for vulnerable elderly often require systematic oversight because many beneficiaries are unable to represent or protect themselves.

Service enhancement programs directly fund service providers to render services to those in need. Since the funds go to the providers and not to the clients, these programs enhance the availability and accessibility of provider organizations and agencies to provide those services deemed necessary and appropriate to address the need.

The unique aspect of the service enhancement program is that no money need ever touch the hand of the service recipient. In essence, the recipient is "taken care of" without much opportunity for input or choice. If the service is needed and asked for, it is provided. The recipient needs only to make himself or herself available to receive the service. This approach to service enhancement, may in some ways, be rather demeaning and parochial. However, it is the predominant method of supporting services to the aged in this country.

Table 16.1 presents federal programs that address the needs of the vulnerable aged. In the chart, departments and/or agencies responsible for program administration are identified.

Client Assistance Programs

Programs that provide direct client assistance are the Social Security Old Age Survivors Disability Insurance (OASDI), Supplemental Security Income (SSI), Food Stamps, and Social Security health insurance (Title XVII, Medicare).

Old Age Survivors Disability Insurance (OASDI) includes three income maintenance programs: Old Age Insurance, Survivors Benefit program, and Disability Insurance. Old Age Insurance is a retirement program based, at present, on earning a minimum of 40 working quarters to become insured. The Survivors Insurance part of the OASDI provides cash payments to surviving spouses and dependent children if the deceased worker met the requirements for full or partial retirement coverage. The Disability Insurance provides cash benefits to workers under 65 who are unable to perform "substantial gainful work."

The *Supplemental Security Income (SSI)* program, authorized under the Social Security Act, pays a national minimum income to poor persons who

TABLE 16.1 Federal Programs Serving the Vulnerable Aged

Program	SSA	HCFA	VA	NIMH	HUD	AoA	USDA
Social Security, OASDI	C						
Supplemental Security, SSI	C						
Food stamps							C
Medicare		C					
Medicaid		S					
Prospective payment system		O					
Peer review organizations		O					
Section 8 housing					C		
Section 202 housing					S		
Congregate housing					S		
LTC ombudsman						O	
Legal assistance						O	
Access services						O	
Nutrition services						S	
In-home services						S	
Community mental health				S			
Veterans programs			S				
Research/demonstration	S	S	S	S	S	S	S

C = Client Assistance, O = System Optimization, S = Service Enhancement

are aged, blind, or disabled. Persons eligible for this benefit are vulnerable, and states are given the option to target special groups to receive additional supplements.

The *Food Stamps* program provides direct assistance to clients in the purchase of food stuffs. Foods stamps must be purchased by the beneficiary, and the face value of the food stamps is more than the price of purchase. Elderly persons who are homebound due to disability or frailty can use food stamps to purchase home-delivered or congregate meals.

The *Medicare* program is an acute-care health insurance program divided into two parts: hospital insurance and medical insurance. Eligibility for Medicare benefits is determined by age or disability. This program thereby encompasses the vulnerable elderly.

Housing programs offer rental subsidies for low-income families unable to afford decent and sanitary places to live. Section 8 housing, one of these programs, is initiated by local communities applying for funding to the Department of Housing and Urban Development (HUD). After approval for section 8 housing, low-income families receive in benefits the difference between fair-market rent payments and 15% to 25% of the tenant's adjusted income.

All of the client assistance programs have one feature in common: they provide benefits directly to individual clients who may, in some cases, have some discretion over how to use them. Poor and low-income older people receive valuable relief through these programs. The next group of programs focuses more on the providers of services.

System Optimizing Programs

The *Long-Term Care Ombudsman* program, operated by the Administration on Aging (AoA), is one program serving the vulnerable elderly by ensuring that they receive needed services. Most long-term care ombudsman programs operate at the state level. The program also is responsible for advocating for the rights, health, and well-being of older persons in long-term care facilities.

The *Legal Services* program is operated by the AoA and provides assistance to elderly persons with taxes, benefits, health and life insurance, and legal matters.

The AoA also requires states to offer access services with the general purpose of helping the elderly to obtain access to the services they need. *Access Service* emphasizes the connecting of people with the services they need. Services offered under this program include transportation, outreach, information and referral, client assessment, and case management. These access services provide the linkages to other services that are often needed by the vulnerable aged.

The Medicare program operates two system optimizing service programs. One program is the *Prospective Payment System (PPS)* which, through the use of *Diagnosis-Related Groups (DRGs)*, attempts to control the cost of acute hospital care while maintaining the quality of that care. The other program is the *Peer Review Organizations (PROs)*, whose mission is to ensure that hospitalization is medically necessary and that the care rendered during hospital stays meets acceptable medical care standards.

These programs aim to ensure that the vulnerable elderly get the services to which they are entitled. The next group of programs provide funding for service providers to meet the needs of vulnerable elderly persons.

Service Enhancement Programs

Service enhancement programs provide funding directly to provider agencies that act as agents for the federal and state governments. The federal programs usually stipulate the kinds of services and activities that will be supported. Most federal programs require that states go through some form of planning process that is intended to elicit consumer input, but this is often very limited. The resulting programs represent, to a great extent, the judgments of public officials and service professionals.

The *Medicaid* program is a service enhancement program, because bills for services are submitted by the provider to the state agency or designated insurance carrier. The program has two basic categories of beneficiaries: (1) the categorically needy, and (2) the medically needy. Eligibility for this program may vary from state to state. Medicaid is an important source of support for vulnerable aged.

Section 202 Housing is a HUD program that is designed to promote construction of housing specifically for the elderly. This program provides for low-interest interim construction loans for sponsors who can secure long-term financing for the project. Another HUD program that is directly related to the vulnerable elderly is that of congregate housing. This program gives HUD the authority to enter into contracts with public housing and section 202 sponsors to provide congregate services to their residents.

The *Older Americans Act (OAA)*, which is administered by the Administration on Aging, operates a number of programs that serve the needs of vulnerable aged. The OAA programs, addressing the needs of the vulnerable aged, are supportive services, senior centers, congregate meals, and home-delivered meals. The congregate meals and home-delivered meals programs provide for the nutritional needs of older persons, while the other programs provide for other service needs of this population, including those of the vulnerable aged.

The *Community Services Block Grant* program supports states and their grantees in the provision of services and activities designed to have a major impact on poverty in communities. This program is supposed to assist low-income people, including the elderly poor. The kinds of services that are supported by this program are such things as employment, education, and housing. Emergency assistance to address urgent and family needs through loans or grants is also provided.

The *Social Services Block Grant, Title XX*, aims to eliminate dependency and support economic self-sufficiency. The program is also concerned with neglect and abuse of children and adults who are unable to protect themselves. This includes the prevention or avoidance of inappropriate institutionalization and the promotion of community-based service alternatives. This program provides funds to grantee agencies that, in turn, offer services to the target population. The law specifically prohibits direct payments to clients for subsistence and room and board, except where it is an integral part of a social service or protective service.

The Alcohol, Drug Abuse, and Mental Health Administration sponsors the *Community Mental Health Center* program. The services offered by this program are all funded directly to the centers. This service enhancement program provides for the delivery of specialized services to the elderly; however, the responsiveness of these centers to the needs of the elderly has been less than enthusiastic (Skinner, 1986). The elderly with mental health problems are clearly a vulnerable group.

The *Veterans Administration (VA)* offers a full array of service enhancement programs for vulnerable elderly veterans. These programs mirror those services offered to the civilian population. The VA sponsors domiciliary care, nursing home care, and home care services.

Research and Demonstration Programs

The programs that have been presented above are related to agency-specific service enhancement programs for the vulnerable elderly. However, there is one program that is available to most federal agencies that offers additional opportunities for service provision to specialized groups like the vulnerable elderly. This program is the research and demonstrations (R&D) program. Demonstrations become an avenue for service delivery to special populations who are not being adequately served by the existing service system.

Research and demonstration programs are often the only truly discretionary areas in the budgets of national agencies. It is through these mechanisms that many innovative and avant garde programmatic efforts can be advanced and tested. Research and demonstration programs can provide a logical developmental process for the exploration of new ideas and the refinement of existing systems. This program provides a method of testing new ideas and approaches and offers the potential of documenting successful program alternatives.

CONTINUUM OF CARE

A popular notion in public social policy and service planning for the elderly is *the continuum of care*. This term is rather vague and escapes any clear definition; however, it is often used to describe an array of services that vary in degree from rather simple services like information to very complex services like personal care. The impression is given that a comprehensive service delivery system offers this array of services to meet the differing needs of the aged population. How real is the continuum of care? Does it exist and, if so, where? At what level? These questions will continue to remain rhetorical.

This chapter identified 18 different programs operated by 7 different federal agencies that have either a direct or an indirect impact on the vulnerable elderly. No doubt there are other programs that might be classified as serving the vulnerable elderly, directly or indirectly. It is often stated that little or no coordination occurs among those responsible for the administration of these programs. If coordination is difficult at the federal program level, it is nearly impossible at the state and local levels. States tend to create agencies that mirror organizations at the federal level. This approach may be administratively appropriate, but it perpetuates the already disparate relationships between programs at the federal level. To add to the confusion, only AoA has been given the explicit directive to coordinate services for the aged that are provided by other agencies, a mandate that has no authority to enforce compliance. The combination of categorical laws with restrictive target groups and eligibility requirements, separate funding authorizations, and distinct regulatory agencies makes any attempts at true coordination nothing more than superficial tinkering and public relations agreements.

The lack of a comprehensive social service and long-term care strategy at the federal level creates an environment that is more inclined to support parochial interests than to seek efficiencies and effectiveness. At present, there is no federal long-term care program that supports comprehensive services extending from community living to institutional care. The continuum of care concept is much more an idealistic goal for services to the vulnerable aged than it is a reality. While it is possible to find elements of what might be considered a continuum of care in most states and some large cities, the continuum does not exist in any real sense for most clients in search of services.

Part of the solution to the disarray of programs for the vulnerable elderly is the case management approach to service brokering. Case management offers the possibility of protecting the client and his or her family from the idiosyncrasies of disparate and fragmented health and social service programs. The case management process places a template over the disparate array of services and filters out the dissonance. It gives the client a window of continuity in a sea of confusion. Professional case managers are able to serve as a buffer between the client and the morass of programs and regulations to ensure that the best package of services is made available to the client. Case management may offer the closest thing to a continuum of care that we can reasonably hope for in the near future.

PROGRAMS FOR VULNERABLE ELDERLY:
FUTURE DIRECTIONS

All population projections into the 21st century reveal that we can expect the population of persons over 64 years of age to continue to grow. Of particular interest to those concerned with program development for the vulnerable elderly is the even greater growth of the older age groups of the elderly; namely, those over 75 and 85 years of age. These age groups are of special interest because those in the most advanced age groups are most likely to suffer frailties and disabilities. We can expect the public concern for long-term care and programs for the vulnerable elderly to continue, even though some of this concern may be expressed as negative reactions of younger populations to their belief that they may be carrying an unfair burden in support of these programs.

The numbers and proportion of vulnerable elderly in the United States may be affected as much by life-style trends as by population changes in the 21st century. Adults who are in their 30s and 40s in 1988 will be in their 60s and 70s in 2018. These elderly persons will be affected by the social mores of their age cohorts.

What trends today will affect the vulnerability of the aged tomorrow? More women are working; this will ensure that more women will have access to retirement income. Women are choosing to have children later in life; this may result in more stress on children as caregivers to their parents because they may have younger children of their own to care for. There is a trend toward more single-parent families; this may result in no spouses and less informal support resources. U.S. society is becoming more mobile; this may result in fewer children and siblings living nearby to provide informal supports. More women working and smoking may change death rates as they become more exposed to the same hazards as men; this may mean that the gap in death rates by sex may narrow and reduce the years that many women spend in widowhood. The high cost of owning a living is causing many young people to rent or to buy homes that are smaller than they once were; this trend could result in children not having the room to accommodate the care of a parent in their homes. These and many other trends in the current society will have tremendous ramifications for the elderly in the future.

The evolution of health and social programs has led to a proliferation of programs created under different laws, administered by different federal agencies, and supported by different constituencies. The existence of programs is as much a part of the problem as it is a part of the solution. As long as the problems of the elderly in general, and the vulnerable elderly specifically, are addressed in a piecemeal fashion, we can expect the continued disarray of services that exists today. One possible solution in the long-range future is the movement toward a national health and social services program. Such a program would pull together the financing, delivery, and control functions into one comprehensive program.

Into the early 1990s, we can expect to see the major federal program efforts devoted to containing costs and finding more effective and efficient ways to work with limited resources. More attention will be directed toward new financing schemes and cost-avoidance strategies. In this environment, proposals that threaten to increase the public expenditure will be discouraged.

In conclusion, the near future, not unlike the present, appears to be moving in the direction of selectively tinkering with the collection of health and social service programs serving the vulnerable elderly. Without any fundamental reform of these programs, we cannot expect minor modifications of categorical programs to perform as a comprehensive whole. Until we, as a society, are ready to reexamine our individual health and social services programs as one complex program of support for all of our citizenry, we will continue to be faced with piecemeal, fragmented, inefficient, and ineffective solutions.

REFERENCES

Department of Health and Human Services. (1986). *Catastrophic illness expenses.* Washington, D.C.: Department of Health and Human Services.

Estes. C. L. (1979). *The aging experience.* San Francisco: Jossey-Bass.

Kingston, E. R., Hirshorn, B. A., & Cornman, J. M. (1986). *Ties that bind: The interdependence of generations.* Cabin John, MD: Seven Locks Press.

Lowy, L. (1980). *Social policies and programs on aging.* Lexington, MA: Lexington Books.

Palmer, J. L., & Sawhill, I. V. (Eds.) (1984). *The Reagan record: An assessment of America's changing domestic priorities.* Cambridge, MA: Ballinger.

Schulz, J. H. (1988). *Economics of aging,* 4th edition. Dover, MA: Auburn.

Skinner, J. H. (1986). Mental health: The response to community needs of special populations. In E. Aronowitz & E. Bromberg (Eds.), *Mental health and aging.* Canton, MA: Prodist.

Skinner, J. H. (1990). Targeting benefits for the black elderly: The Older Americans Act. In Z. Harel, E. McKinney, & M. Williams (Eds.), *Black aged: Understanding diversity and service needs.* Washington, D.C.: National Council on Aging.

U.S. Senate Special Committee on Aging (1987). *Developments in aging: 1986— volume I.* Washington: U.S. Government Printing Office.

Wholey, J. S., & Vogt, L. M. (1973). *Federal evaluation policy: Analyzing the effects of public programs.* Washington, D.C.: The Urban Institute.

17
Issues in Long–Term Care Services

Sheldon S. Tobin

In the development and implementation of all human-service systems, including long-term care systems, three kinds of issues must be considered: those who are to be served, the services provided to them, and how the services are to be delivered (Tobin et al., 1976; Tobin & Toseland, 1985). These issues are certainly germane to long-term care services for vulnerable elderly persons.

Who is to be served by long-term care services is the issue discussed in the first section of this chapter. The conventional wisdom is that the target population is those who have lost capacities to function in everyday life and, thus, whose capacities can be restored or preserved despite chronic illnesses. This targeting, however, may be too simplistic; ignored, for example, are those who can benefit from the prevention of illnesses. This chapter also gives attention to what should be provided. There are many diverse kinds of services, but they can be systematized by, for example, considering the location of services; that is, in-home services, congregate organized programs, and congregate living arrangements. For each geographical location, services can be identified for those with minimal, those with moderate, and those with severe impairments. The chapter next will consider how services should be provided, focusing particularly on issues in the organization and implementation of services. This section will cover case management, reimbursement systems for ensuring long-term care, and the pros and cons of the provision of services by a single agency versus the purchase of services. In the section that follows, selective issues regarding community planning will be discussed, including how the achievement of a comprehensive service delivery system necessitates a loss of autonomy for participating agencies. How the availability of funding often encourages agencies to expand into providing services that can detract from achieving their primary mission is also discussed. Next, some persistent issues will be addressed: the barriers to promoting wellness programs that can limit chronic illness; the too-prevalent disregard for cultural differences in service provision; the inability to ensure a work force capable of providing hands-on care to the most debilitated elderly individuals; ethical issues related to terminal care and allocation of resources; and the role of the elderly in modern societies. Finally, some suggestions will be presented for an ideal system of long-term care.

WHO SHALL BE SERVED?

Discussing the continuum of services in long-term care, Evashwich and Branch (1987) targeted a population "composed of individuals who have complex problems, functional disabilities, are not able to care for themselves, and cannot depend entirely on their informal support system. The goal is to help get the support they need to achieve the highest level of health and functional independence" (p. 45). Thus, the vulnerable population targeted is those who can benefit from tertiary prevention through formal services.

Tertiary prevention refers to the limiting of the consequences of diseases or chronic disabilities. For example, prosthetic devices such as eyeglasses and hearing aids permit elderly persons to function better despite chronic diseases. Respite care to family caregivers of victims of Alzheimer's disease can help to enhance the functioning of these patients by providing relief from caregiving. Tertiary prevention is decidedly different from primary prevention, where the aim is to reduce the incidence of disease itself. Ways to eliminate age-associated diseases such as presbyopia, presbyacousis, and Alzheimer's disease are primary preventions. Secondary prevention is the early detection and treatment of disease. Early detection and treatment of presbyopia may limit the rate of decline of vision, but early treatment of cataracts clearly can assist in maintaining vision.

Thus, whereas tertiary prevention refers to facilitating functioning and reducing adverse consequences for those who have a chronic disease, secondary prevention refers to early detection and treatment, and primary prevention refers to eliminating the occurrence of disease. When the focus of long-term care services is only on restoring and preserving the functioning of those already diseased (only on tertiary prevention), then those who can benefit from early detection and treatment (secondary prevention) and from elimination of disease (primary prevention) are ignored.

Unfortunately, those who are likely to benefit from primary interventions early in life that can reduce later life disability are not now perceived to be the target for long-term care, nor are those who can benefit from primary prevention. The best primary prevention, the elimination of poverty, would obviously permit many children now growing up in impoverished conditions and who lack, among other necessities, adequate nutrition and adequate health care, to not only live longer but also to enjoy lives free of debilitating chronic diseases. Moreover, primary prevention should certainly encompass midlife programs, such as promoting physical activity and calcium intake among women before menopause, so that they have heavier bone mass after menopause with consequently less likelihood of fractures. A concern with earlier secondary prevention, detection, and treatment would lead to targeting all aging persons as the vulnerable population. Health screening followed by treatment is essential for cure as well as for enhancing prognosis when cure is not possible.

Thus, a first issue is whether the vulnerable population for long-term care has been too narrowly defined. To be sure, tertiary prevention through adequate long-term care is essential, but not at the expense of primary and secondary prevention. Is it necessary to neglect primary and secondary prevention because of the great need for tertiary prevention among those with limitations from chronic disease? The answer must be a resounding no! Targeting only those with current functional impairments reveals a lack of foresight, because without eliminating some chronic diseases and treating others early, the amount of chronic disease will increase in the future. Unfortunately, our here-and-now approach to health care indeed lacks foresight, dooming us to a future of a probably accelerating accumulation of chronic impairment among the oldest-old.

Parodoxically, however, additional early life preventions may only increase the vulnerable chronically ill elderly population. With medical advances, the mortality curve has been squared, with more people living to advanced old age. Unfortunately, however, this may reflect what Isaacs et al. (1972) have called "the survival of the unfittest." As people have lived closer to their genetic endowment of 110 years or so, the preterminal period of disability has increased. Indeed, if the three leading causes of death (cardiovascular disease, cancer, and stroke) were to be conquered, the average life expectancy could increase 10 to 15 years—but, apparently, not without musculoskeletal degeneration, incontinence, and Alzheimer's disease. The current estimate is that beyond 80 years of age, one of three persons will have Alzheimer's disease.

When targeting tertiary prevention, the variables used most often to sort out people are age, sex, and socioeconomic status. Thus, it is not at all surprising that the oldest-old, who are now referred to as the extreme aged (Rosenwaite & Dolinsky, 1987; Suzman & Riley, 1985), those 85 years of age and over, are receiving attention. Simply stated, health statistics reveal an accelerating accumulation of diseases and impairments among the extreme aged. The corresponding accelerating health costs for those 85 and over has been cause for alarm. Women in the extreme aged group deserve attention because of their impoverishment from widowhood and also because of widowhood itself, a lack of a spouse to provide home care. Branch et al. (1988) found that women who entered nursing homes after living alone became impoverished, spent down to Medicaid, within 13 weeks. Using only age, gender, and economic resources as criteria is obviously too restrictive, but within the targeting of tertiary care for those whose funtioning is to be restored or preserved, special efforts must be made for the most vulnerable among the vulnerable.

Demographic characteristics are not the only way of targeting. Those discharged from hospitals "quicker and sicker" because of Diagnosis-Related Group (DRGs) guidelines warrant adequate discharge planning (see, for example, Coulton et al., 1988), as well as intensive services following discharge. In turn, those most able to benefit from programs and services can be targeted. Through triage, for example, those who can be restored to higher levels of activities of daily living (ADL) can be separated from those who can only be maintained and those who are terminal. Combining approaches leads to assessing patients upon hospital discharge to determine who can benefit from intensive follow-up services, and then limiting access to services for others. In essence, this is a strategy for rationing costly health services.

However, if rationing is not intended—but rather identifying vulnerable groups who can most benefit from programs and services—it is not difficult to do so. Moreover, these groups would encompass more than the small percentage of elderly persons who live in the community and who can benefit from restorative programs and services. Why not, for example, focus on patients in acute-care hospitals who are likely to be afflicted with iatrogenic diseases and dysfunctions from diagnostic procedures and therapies? The accumulation of medications from diverse medical specialists can easily result in adverse drug interactions. Also, assessing the hospitalized patient who has pseudodementia because of depression as a victim of Alzheimer's disease can indeed have dire consequences. Misdiagnosis of Senile Dementia of the Alzheimer's Type (SDAT) is common not only in hospitals; thus, it is sensible to target those likely to be misdiagnosed who reside in the community. Additionally, among those elderly persons who are homebound, the terminally ill can readily benefit from in-home hospice care that includes counseling for them and their families. Indeed, the heterogeneity among the elderly population permits the identification of innumerable target groups that can be considered vulnerable; that is, likely to deteriorate unless circumstances change. For many, if not most, of these groups, circumstances can be changed through our interventions.

WHAT SHOULD BE PROVIDED?

What is to be provided follows from the needs of those who are targeted. More than 12% of persons 65 and over who live in the community have physical and mental status comparable to the 5% or so who live in nursing homes. Weissert (1985) has provided an estimate of 12.7%. At any one time, 7% to 8% of those 65 and over are likely to be homebound (3% to 4% are likely to be bedridden), and another 4% or so can leave their homes only with surveillance. Most, however, are in stable states, and only about 2.5% at any one time need intensive services for recovery and restoration to ADL (see, for example, Leutz et al., 1988). What do these 2.5% need?

Obviously, in-home personal care services that encompass diverse forms of home health and homemaker services are essential. Also, out-of-home services are necessary, particularly medical day care and geropsychiatric day care programs that provide therapy to elderly infirm individuals, as well as respite for family caregivers. Also needed is a variety of structured living arrangements, including congregate housing with supportive services and adult homes. The combination of in-home services, congregate services for community dwelling elderly individuals and congregate living arrangements reflects a locational, or geographical, approach to identifying dissociated services needed by the chronically impaired. For each of the three geographical locations of service delivery, discrete services can be identified for individuals of diverse levels of impairment; for example, for the well elderly or minimally impaired, the moderately impaired, and the extremely impaired. Congregate living arrangements include senior citizens housing for the well elderly, enriched housing and adult homes for the moderately impaired, and nursing homes for the most impaired. Congregate programs for those living at home include senior centers, psychosocial day care, and medical and geropsychiatric day care. In-home programs and services include volunteer opportunities and home repair for the well elderly who live independently, homemaker services, and home health care. Thus, for elderly persons with varying levels of impairments, programs and services can be provided that can be classified as in-home programs, congregate day programs, and congregate living arrangements.

Returning to community care for the 2.5%, it is essential to recognize that these most vulnerable persons are likely to also need acute medical services. People with chronic impairments are those who are most likely to have acute flare-ups requiring hospitalization. But they also need short-term in-patient evaluation, stabilization, and treatment that can be provided in a geriatric evaluation unit (GEU) and, of course, rehabilitation programs (Brody, 1987).

HOW SERVICES ARE TO BE PROVIDED

How can all the warranted and essential programs and services be provided? At least three perspectives must be considered. First is the integration of services for individuals. Case management, the integration of discrete services for clients by a case manager, will be discussed. Second is systems for the integration of services. Briefly discussed will be the three emerging kinds of systems: long-term care insurance (LTI), continuing care retirement communities (CCRCs), and social health maintenance organizations (SHMOs). A third perspective pertains to organizational issues that confront all systems of long-term care, here discussed as provision versus purchase of services. A completely comprehensive provision system would own and deliver all necessary services, whereas a totally purchase-of-services system would permit complete shopping around for services. Each approach has its pros and cons, and within the discussion of pros and cons reside vexing questions, such as: How comprehensive can a system of long-term care be? Is it best that consumers have first choice to purchase whatever they deem necessary for restoration and preservation of functioning?

Case Management

The common language of long-term care service delivery has become case management (see, for example, Steinberg, 1985; Steinberg & Carter, 1983). And rightly so! The purpose of case management is to implement the provision of services simultaneously and sequentially over time; that is, to integrate the delivery of the more discrete services identified by an approach such as the geographical arrangement of services. In case management, as in all delivery of services, the initial step is assessment (see, for example, Kane, 1985), not only of the client's disabilities and service needs, but also of resources including the capacity of informal supports, particularly family members. A service plan is then implemented and modified as the situation changes.

Service plans must be developed with, and implemented by, family caregivers. Formal providers of service and informal, family caregivers each have their function and together, with shared functions, can work together most successfully. Whether labeled "a balanced system," as by Litwak and Meyer (1966) or "an auxiliary model," as by Silverstone and Burack-Weiss (1983), the task is to mesh formal and informal care to create maximum benefit for the maintenance and restoration of functioning.

Reimbursement Systems

Organizing a case management system in which services are ensured obviously requires reimbursement for the services. Three forms of insurance are emerging: LTIs, CCRCs, and SHMOs. LTIs may provide reimbursement for discrete services, but are unlikely to result in provider organizations using case managers to provide services and to prevent unnecessary and premature institutionalization (Rivlin & Wiener, 1988). CCRCs, which are available to the more affluent (Ruchlin, 1988), and SHMOs are likely, however, to use case management because of capitation funding. That is, the pool of money from clients to the organization must be cautiously spent to avoid heavy hospital and institutional costs. SHMOs, now in the experimental stage, when under the auspices of established HMOs rely heavily not only on case management, but also on innovative geriatric evaluation units and rehabilitative services to maintain and restore ADL functioning. Even efficient use of personnel and facilities, however, cannot eliminate hospital stays, which may be covered by Medicare and catastrophic health insurance. Nor can efficiency limits in the form of extended stays in nursing homes, which now can quickly overtax revenues but may be covered in the future by a federal reimbursement plan. Thus, SHMOs must limit reimbursement of nursing home days, requiring that their members spend down to Medicaid eligibility.

Case management focuses on integration of services at the client level, whereas SHMOs and CCRCs also do so at the systems level. LTI, in turn, resolves the issue by letting consumers purchase their services, for which they are then reimbursed. In either instance, the agency providing services must decide on the comprehensiveness of its service provision. To what extent can any service provider own all the specialized services necessary for long-term community care? Some, such as Kaiser-Permanente's SHMO (Leutz et al., 1988), can be quite comprehensive, owning hospitals and rehabilitation centers. Most, however, must develop purchase agreements with specialized agencies. The pros and cons of each, comprehensiveness and purchase agreements, are illustrative for understanding systems of service integration.

Provision Versus Purchase of Services

The arguments for a provision-of-services arrangement are greater accountability and control, ease and economy of administration, and easily identifiable programs and clients. When an agency furnishes the services, its control over the actual provision, including the selection of clients and the nature and quality of the services themselves, is more direct than it would be under a purchase agreement. The agency is able to hire the service staff, set the rules and policies regarding selection of clientele, and establish standards. It is also able to enforce those policies and standards, given managerial control. Direct control is not possible under purchase-of-service strategies, although indirect means of control, such as making or withholding referrals, can also be very effective. In addition to having more direct control, the agency that provides services itself benefits from an administratively simpler and less expensive arrangement, because it avoids the costs of regularizing agreements and special reporting and accounting procedures. A third benefit of direct provision arises out of the unitary administrative control. Data for planning purposes are easier to obtain because the agency has direct access to client service records. Information about the characteristics of clients, the nature of the services provided, costs, and the effects of services are more accessible than if the agency must obtain data from others who may be reluctant to have outsiders look over their shoulders. Moreover, performance data kept by others may be more limited than needed for planning. Complete records are important because they permit the identification of trends in demand for services and the evaluation of interventions.

The three major arguments in favor of a purchase-of-services arrangement are the ability to meet diverse client needs, to respond rapidly to new needs, and to act as an advocate for the aging. An agency might consider purchasing services when demand is insufficient or too varied to support a number of highly trained, full-time specialists. In such instances, it may be simpler and cheaper to purchase services from another agency that already has the capability in a desired area. By purchasing services from another agency, an agency effectively increases the range of client needs it can meet. It might also be advisable to purchase services when a new service is to be offered (for example, when required by new legislation) for which the demand is likely to be very large. If the responsible agency were to provide the service directly, it would probably need to expand its staff dramatically in a short period. Purchase-of-services agreements enable an agency to gear up quickly for a new service. Relying on existing services is a way to respond both rapidly and effectively. Purchase-of-services arrangements also promote advocacy for the aging.

Which is the preferred mechanism, provision or purchase of services, given client considerations? To answer this question, it is necessary to consider the assumptions behind each social service strategy. A provision system assumes that the client is not able to select the optimal service and must be protected. A purchase system, on the other hand, assumes the competence of the client and emphasizes freedom of choice. Despite the advantages to the client of a purchase-of-services arrangement, many of the elderly, particularly among the vulnerable, are not equipped to determine which service provider best meets their needs. Physical and mental impairments or simple inexperience with social services make a provision-of-services model appropriate, with its emphasis on professionalism and client protection. For this population, a provision system appears more effective.

COMMUNITY PLANNING

A critical issue confronting communities is how best to achieve a mix of comprehensive provision systems and specialized agencies. Given the extent and diversity of specialized voluntary, not-for-profit and proprietary, for-profit agencies in communities, the focus now tends to be on stimulating coordination among agencies. Yet comprehensive provision systems require more than coordination and even more than efficient collaboration. A confederation in which several agencies are joined under a single sponsorship is what is needed. However, because of reluctance to relinquish automony, rather than confederating, one agency expands at the expense of other agencies, absorbing the functions of autonomous specialized agencies. This obviously occurs when CCRCs or SHMOs are developed, as well as when hospitals develop extensive hospital based community care systems. On Lok Senior Center, the Chinese Center in San Francisco, is being promulgated as a model for all communities. On Lok has now developed a Medicare Waiver Program providing a full range of services to chronically impaired homebound elderly.

If the movement toward comprehensive provision systems under a single umbrella is good, and also inevitable, roles for autonomous agencies of limited focus must be renegotiated. One example is the current situation of many senior centers. Having perceived a service gap, as well as the availability of funds, many senior centers have expanded to provide care to the more physically and mentally impaired elderly, not only congregate nutrition programs and day care, but also case management services. In doing so, these centers not only have a problem maintaining a normalizing environment for the more vigorous and educated young-old but also find themselves expanding into services that may not be reimbursed in the near future because funding is not through capitation systems. Recently, the newly appointed executive director of a voluntary agency that has several senior centers became alarmed that so much of the budget was from the kind of public funding that ebbs and flows and often dries up quickly. The previous executive director has been lauded for the great expansion of services by the agency, but the newly arrived executive director was rightly alarmed.

When services gaps are readily apparent and funding is available, even if it is short term and unstable, it is indeed difficult to resist the opportunity for expansion. Unfortunately, competition among agencies for the new funding leads away from rational community planning. Because of how uncoordinated nonsystems develop from competition for limited resources, funding increasingly goes to collaborating agencies. Autonomous agencies are then forced to collaborate to obtain public or foundation support.

Yet, as noted earlier, autonomous, limited-purpose agencies have their place. Senior housing for the well elderly, for example, can and should take many forms. When, however, the resident population becomes infirm, they must be maintained in the housing to the greatest extent possible without destroying the fabric and ambience of independent living. One solution, the New York State solution, is an Enriched Housing Program in which a social service agency is reimbursed for delivering supportive services to the more impaired residents and the management of the apartment complex is left to its sponsoring agency. This appears to be a workable solution that facilitates the development of housing options under independent management, while ensuring supportive services to those who are becoming frail. Yet, it can be argued that if the senior housing was part of a CCRC, the next level of care—most likely intermediate nursing home care—would be readily available if deterioration necessitated discharge from the complex. Currently, when discharge is necessary, housing managers who have no responsibility for placement leave the onerous task of relocation to a nursing home to the resident and, if available, to her or his family.

Thus, it can be argued again that autonomous single-purpose agencies should be absorbed by more comprehensive umbrella agencies. There are, however, compelling examples of where it is inefficient, or even irrational, for absorption to occur. Because churches and synagogues are important in the lives of the elderly (Tobin et al., 1986), home visitation by clergy or laity can be especially meaningful to homebound elderly. No one would argue, however, that churches and synagogues should be under the auspices of a homemaker or family service agency. Similarly, would SHMOs that recognized the importance of participation in senior centers perceive a need to own centers? I doubt it.

Compounding issues of autonomous agencies is the diversity of sponsorship in the United States, where we have parallel public, voluntary, and for-profit service provision. Unfortunately, encouragement of a free market in service provision can lead to a skimming of clients, leaving those who can least afford services—and who therefore are the most vulnerable—to the voluntary and public sector. In turn, voluntary agencies must decide their roles—particularly sectarian agencies, which must understand what secularization means to people not only in this era, but also in the future when cohorts of elderly persons will be less religious. Still, it is from voluntary agencies that many, if not most, innovations in human services come. Ehrlich and Frank's (1988) Family Life Line program is certainly one such example. This program provides coordination of services when families live at a distance from their impaired elderly member. The flexibility to initiate this kind of program has been assumed to be characteristic of voluntary agencies.

SOME OTHER PERSISTENT ISSUES

Among the many persistent issues, five warrant comment.

The first issue is how best to promote primary and secondary prevention. Some kinds of prevention are more feasible and cost effective than others. Not very feasible, for example, is urging women not to marry men older than they are and thereby suffer an average of seven years of widowhood. By marrying men who average 4-1/2 years older and having a statistical probability of 2-1/2 years more of life, with current marital patterns, elderly women are less likely than men to have spouses to care for them when they become ill. Nor is it feasible in today's political climate to eradicate poverty, the best kind of primary prevention. Yet it is possible and cost effective to expand efforts to enhance family caregiving. Industries, for example, are becoming aware that their middle-aged female workers who are caregivers lose an average of 12 days of work per year. Thus, many companies are increasingly providing lunchtime opportunities for caregiver support groups. For the young-old, Canada has developed the Seniors Independence Program, in which priorities are given to community groups composed mainly of seniors, or that actively involve seniors, and to those projects that address the needs of special target groups such as older women and those in rural and remote areas.

Related to targeting is a second issue, that of special initiatives for atypical elderly persons and communities. Unacculturated groups are generally unaware of benefits from, and entitlements to, programs and services. Harel (1986) has noted, for example, that for many Euro-American groups, efforts to enhance knowledge of and access to programs and services must include initiatives at the neighborhood level. Similarly, reaching elderly black individuals and their families may necessitate working with local churches in their neighborhoods. Indeed, Blazer (1985) observed that receiving home health care is largely serendipitous because of the lack of knowledge of availability of services.

A third, and different kind, of issue relates to the work force. Who will provide care to the most debilitated among the elderly, such as those who are incontinent? Throughout the world, there is an increasing unwillingness to work at these arduous menial jobs. At the other end of the spectrum, it is necessary to train and educate sophisticated specialists to work with the elderly.

A fourth issue is the ethics of care. This includes not only terminal care such as active and passive euthanasia, living wills, and helping people to have the best death possible, but also the ethics of the distribution of services. As Neugarten (1982) has asked, for example, why should we target the elderly rather than those in need regardless of age? Should special programs be developed for the disabled elderly when there is likely to be an equivalent number of younger persons with chronic disabilities? Answers to these kinds of policy questions will have an increasing impact on community services for older persons.

Related to distribution of resources among the old and the young is a fifth issue: the role of older people in an aging society. A self-serving push for benefits can lead (or has led) to the development of a backlash against older people. Different consequences would occur if the traditional role of elder was assumed in which elderly persons acted for the common good. Should we assist the future elderly to become a 20th century version of the elders in earlier times who, as the voice of experience, took leadership in deciding what was the common good? Gutmann (1987) has called for "reclaimed powers" in which elders reclaim the initiative in acting for the good of all citizens.

TOWARD AN IDEAL SYSTEM

Who must be served? Obviously, a long-term care system must target those vulnerable elderly persons whose functioning can be restored and preserved. But tertiary prevention is insufficient. Secondary prevention, the early detection and treatment of disease, is also essential, as is primary prevention, the elimination of chronic disease. The definition of the vulnerable population must be expanded to include everyone. All people age and, if they live long enough, will suffer from chronic diseases that limit their capacities to function. All but those who die suddenly when young are vulnerable to becoming functionally impaired from chronic diseases. Yet, within the targeting of tertiary preventive care for those whose functioning can be restored or preserved are particularly vulnerable groups. Among them are elderly widows who become impoverished and lack spouses to provide home care. Also among the most vulnerable, because long-term care tertiary preventive services are insufficiently attentive to their needs, are diverse cultural groups and those victimized by current practices and policies, such as elderly persons likely to be misdiagnosed as having Alzheimer's disease.

What should be provided? The list of warranted and necessary services in tertiary prevention is indeed long. Discrete services can be identified by a locational or geographical approach in which services are divided into in-home, congregate organized, and congregate residential services. For the three kinds of locations, services can be tailored for the well elderly or minimally impaired, for the moderately impaired, and for the extremely impaired. Because, for example, the extremely impaired are so heterogeneous, many can benefit from each kind of service organization. Some are best served only with in-home services, some with a combination of in-home and congregate organized day programs, and still others in congregate residences including nursing homes. Therefore, the division does not suggest alternative ways to organize services, but parallel ways to organize services for different target groups among the vulnerable elderly population whose activities of daily living can be restored or preserved.

How should services be delivered? Professional case management ensures the integration of services for each client. Case management, as the essential individualizing element in an SHMO, permits these organizations to ensure cost-effective care, as well as to generate innovative rehabilitative and other forms of care that minimize costs and maximize restoration and preservation of functioning. SHMOs should be as comprehensive as possible. In becoming comprehensive, specialized agencies must either become absorbed or relinquish autonomy through purchase-of-services agreements.

Still, a role exists for specialized agencies, not only because of expertise in their specialization, but also because of their potential to identify and provide new forms of service. Innovations are indeed essential as long-term care is broadened to encompass primary and secondary prevention. But in doing so, the idiosyncracies of local communities must not be ignored. Communities with unacculturated groups of elderly people are decidedly different from typical middle-American communities. It may be possible to have ideal targeting, the proliferation of warranted and essential parallel services, the integration of services for individuals, the creation of viable comprehensive service delivery organizations, the development of innovative forms of service and sensitivity to communities by making services available and modifying their delivery—but still, long-term care cannot be ensured without an adequate work force to do the tasks of caring for extremely impaired elderly individuals. Nor can services be provided without considering the ethics of care, encompassing issues both in terminal care and in the distribution of health resources. Finally, we cannot ignore the role of the future elderly who can, and hopefully will, become a force for a rational allocation of health resources based on the needs of individuals rather than on entitlements to care by age.

REFERENCES

Blazer, D. (1988). Home health care: House calls revisited. *American Journal of Public Health,* 78, 238–239.

Branch, L. G., Friedman, D. J., Cohen, M. A., Smith, N., & Socholitzky, E. (in press). Impoverishing the elderly: A case study of the financial risk of spend-down among Massachusetts elderly. *The Gerontologist.*

Brody, S. J. (1987). Strategic Planning: The catastrophic approach. *The Gerontologist,* 27, 131–138.

Coulton, C. J., Dunkle, R. E., Chow, J. C-C., Haug, M., & Vielhaber, D. (1988). Dimensions of post-hospital care decision-making: A factor analytic study. *The Gerontologist,* 28, 108–111.

Ehrlich, P., & Frank, T. (1988). Family lifeline: Bridging the miles. *The Gerontologist,* 28, 108–111.

Evashwick, C. J., & Branch, L. G. (1987). Clients of the continuum of care. In C. J. Evashwick & L. J. Weiss (Eds.), *Managing the continuum of care.* Rockville, MD: Aspen.

Gutmann, D. (1987). *Reclaimed powers: Toward a new psychology of men and women in later life.* New York: Basic Books.

Harel, Z. (1986). Ethnicity and aging: Implications for service organizations. In C. L. Hayes, R. A. Kalish, & D. Gutmann (Eds.), *European-American elderly: A guide to practice.* New York: Springer.

Isaacs, B., Livingstone, M. & Neville, Y. (1972). *Survival of the unfittest.* Boston: Routledge and Kegan Paul.

Kane, R. A. (1985). Assessing the elderly client. In A. Monk (Ed.), *Handbook of gerontological social work.* New York: Van Nostrand Reinhold.

Leutz, W., Abrahams, R., Greenlick, M., Kane, R. & Prottas, J. (1988). Targeting expanded care to the aged: Early SHMO experience. *The Gerontologist,* 28, 4–17.

Litwak, E., & Meyer, H. J. (1966). A balance theory of coordination between bureaucratic organizations and community primary groups. *Administrative Science Quarterly,* 11, 31–58.

Neugarten, B. L. (Ed.) (1982). *Age or need?* Beverly Hills, CA: Sage.

Rivlin, A. M., & Wiener, J. M. (1988). *Caring for the disabled elderly.* Washington, D.C.: The Brookings Institution.

Rosenwaite, I., & Dolinsky, A. (1987). The changing demographic growth of the extreme aged. *The Gerontologist,* 27, 275–280.

Ruchlin, H. S. (1988). Continuing care retirement communities: An analysis of financed viability and care coverage. *The Gerontologist,* 28, 156–162.

Silverstone, B., & Burack-Weiss, A. (1983). *Social work practice with the frail elderly and their families: The auxiliary function model.* Springfield, IL: Thomas.

Steinberg, R. M. (1985). Access assistance and case management. In A. Monk (Ed.), *Handbook of gerontological social work.* New York: Van Nostrand Reinhold.

Steinberg, R. M., & Carter, G. W. (1983). *Case management and the elderly.* Lexington, MA: Lexington Books.

Suzman, R., & Riley, M. W. (Eds.). (1985). The oldest old. *Milbank Memorial Fund Quarterly, 63,* 1–149.

Tobin, S. S., Davidson, S. M., & Sack, A. (1976). *Effective social service for older Americans.* Ann Arbor, MI: Institute of Gerontology.

Tobin, S. S., Ellor, J. W., & Anderson-Ray, S. (1986). *Enabling the elderly: Religious institutions within the service system.* Albany, NY: State University of New York Press.

Tobin, S. S. & Toseland, R. (1985). Models of service for the elderly. In A. Monk (Ed.), *Handbook of gerontological services.* New York: Van Nostrand Reinhold.

Weissert, W. G. (1985). Estimating the long-term care population: Prevalence rates and needs. *Health Care Finance Review, 6,* 1373–1379.

18

Benjamin Rose Institute: A Model Community Long-Term Care System

Alice Kethley and Phyllis Ehrlich

Issues surrounding the vulnerable elderly have been addressed from the perspectives of social and psychological theories, environmental considerations, policy issues, and special populations such as the homeless, caregivers, and others needing protective services. The goal of this chapter is to address and integrate these theoretical and professional concerns into a rational, organized service model.

The Benjamin Rose Institute (BRI) will be presented as a case study of an agency whose history parallels the development of services to the vulnerable elderly. The chapter is organized into four sections: (1) BRI's history and service philosophy, (2) highlights of other service models, (3) the BRI community services model, and (4) issues challenging the service system.

BRI'S HISTORY AND SERVICE PHILOSOPHY: ALMOST A CENTURY OF EXPERIENCE

Since 1908, the Benjamin Rose Institute has wrestled with the problem of how best to allocate its resources in fulfilling its mission to serve the elderly. That mission was set forth in the will of Benjamin Rose, in which he stated, "There is nothing more sad than to observe the plight of elderly individuals who have worked hard all of their lives, but live out their final days in poverty." After a great deal of deliberation, the first board of trustees decided that the greatest need among the elderly of that time (1908) was financial; therefore, BRI clients in those days received money. Early records of the agency reveal that in order to receive "relief and assistance" from BRI, clients—or beneficiaries, as they were called—documented need through financial disclosure and letters from clergy and friends attesting to good character and worthiness. Staff and trustees weighed the evidence to determine the amount of assistance an applicant should receive, keeping in mind the limitations of the endowment as well as the needs of other applicants. Being a Benjamin Rose beneficiary carried with it a provision of lifetime benefits that increased as one aged and one's needs became greater. Hence, the concept of meeting the changing need associated with aging and the responsibility of the service system to respond to those changes has appropriately been a tradition. Today, there are still a limited number of beneficiaries who are receiving support from the Institute, including for the payment of nursing home care.

Terms such as vulnerability, at-risk, and frailty were not part of the language used in determining need in the earlier years of the agency. Such terms grew out of decades of the agency's experience in serving elderly clients and wrestling with how the board of trustees and staff could most effectively use the resources available to alleviate the problems of the aged. Old reports and records document very well that eligibility for service was based on physical, social, economic, and psychological functioning, just as it is today, but without the availability of sophisticated, computerized assessment instruments. The presence of a caregiver or social support weighed heavily in determining need. The goal of the deliberation (care planning) that went into determining those early beneficiaries is the same today: to provide the appropriate mix of services to elderly clients to promote individual dignity and quality of life. While there is now a great deal more knowledge available in the areas of gerontology and service delivery, the individual client is still central to the service plans of both the agency's on-site residential clients and in-home clients. The agency has changed in response to the diversity in today's elderly population, advances in the field of gerontology and service delivery, and the economic climate. The Institute prides itself on being a leader in the field, meshing clinical practice with research to stay abreast of the changing needs of its clients in both community homes and the nursing home setting. The lessons learned through the experience of BRI have been integrated into the gerontological literature and closely parallel that of other agencies. This makes it a good model for describing services to the vulnerable elderly. The agency provides a study in how services to the aged have been developed and changed during the past eight decades.

The focus on the elderly as a population group, to be studied and treated specially, was given its real thrust in 1965 with the passage of two landmark pieces of federal legislation: Medicare (Title XVIII of the Social Security Act) and the Older Americans Act (OAA). From a historical perspective, these two pieces of legislation set into motion the concept of entitlement for the elderly regardless of income. While Medicare was restricted to acute medical care, the OAA fostered the early development of community-based services or alternatives to institutional care. The impact was felt by all agencies serving the elderly, including private nonprofit organizations such as BRI and agencies in the public sector. Community-based services for the elderly, as well as the development of the aging network as a national movement, evolved as a consequence of the OAA. Throughout the 1960s and 1970s, the field of gerontology and gerontological services grew and developed constituencies among not only the elderly, but also those professionals who chose to work with the elderly. The trend seemed to be toward entitlement programs for all persons 65 and over, with references to "early retirement" and the "golden years."

Out of that period of time (the 1960s and the 1970s), when the focus was less on the alarming consequence of having large numbers of elderly living longer with a greater need for services, came a number of lessons that BRI has integrated into its program philosophy. First of all, most elderly clients prefer to remain in their own homes regardless of income level, gender, cultural background, disabilities, or condition of the home. Home is the place of choice. In recognition of that preference, the agency has responded by developing an array of social, health, personal care, and supportive services, coupled with case management to work with the client and available family and/or other supports to honor that goal.

The trustees and staff recognized, however, that the need for nursing home care was inevitable for some BRI clients, and in 1961, the Institute opened the doors of its residential care facility, the Margaret Wagner House. Every effort was made to design a facility that would mirror a homelike atmosphere. The focus was on rehabilitation to maintain the highest level of functioning possible among the residents. Home, however, continues to be the place of choice for the elderly, and honoring this preference is a challenge BRI and other agencies must meet as we develop community service systems.

Second, single answers to meeting the needs of the elderly do not exist. The interaction among medical, social, environmental, and economic factors is compounded by the delicate balance that operates within each of those domains. This becomes painfully clear to our case-management staff as they attempt to support an older client in the home and are forced to deal with the domino effect of problems—one problem seems to set off a series of other problems. Nutritious meals, adequate housing, convenient transportation, appropriate medical care, counseling, and so on, are all part of a package of services that may have to be activated before an older individual's life situation can be stabilized. How sensitively and effectively the case manager orchestrates the services to meet individual needs determines whether or not the client is rehabilitated sufficiently to remain at home, as well as sets the appropriate degree of ongoing services necessary. BRI prefers to work closely with other community agencies, depending upon their cooperation to ensure that the client's needs are met. It is assumed that case management and agencies working together can form an effective system for dealing with the multifaceted problems of the elderly.

Third, losses in elderly individuals do not necessarily occur in a unidirectional, logical, predictable sequence. This rather perplexing aspect of the elderly client's situation can lead to quite rewarding results when the unexpected turn of events is a more speedy recovery and return to a higher level of functioning than the service plan indicated. It can be distressing to all— the elderly client, the family and supports, and our staff—when the unexpected turn is in a negative direction, resulting in permanent loss of functioning. This tendency to fluctuate in and out of need for services calls for a flexible service system that can respond to a client load that moves in and out, up and down. Sometimes a client will need highly skilled and intensive care, while at other times he or she requires nothing more than occasional telephone monitoring. To BRI, this has meant that the term *continuum of care*, as an agency concept, denotes a striving toward a system that can accommodate any client, on any given day, regardless of the level of need. The clients move in and out of the system as their problems dictate; hence, BRI has clients who have been in and out of the system for a period of up to 17 years.

Fourth, the elderly are as heterogenous in their values and beliefs as they are in their physical and psychological functioning. At BRI, this factor influences hiring practices as well as the way in which services are delivered. Cleveland not only has a large number of minorities such as blacks and Hispanics, but also has concentrated pockets of ethnic groups from eastern Europe. It is not uncommon for agency workers to find themselves attempting to explain the U.S. system to an aging Ukrainian who never mastered English or to a newly arrived Puerto Rican grandmother who is overwhelmed by both language and culture. Despite the earlier federal efforts to provide educational grants to make university education accessible to minorities and special ethnic groups, it is very difficult to find social workers, nurses, and other licensed professionals representative of minority and ethnic groups. While it may not be absolutely necessary to match worker and client by race, creed, and ethnicity, it has been BRI's experience that workers representative of the neighborhood population facilitate a better understanding and working relationship with the informal networks (families and churches). It is difficult enough to grow old in a rapidly changing society without having to cope with human service workers who are foreign in terms of both history and generational values. BRI attempts to integrate this knowledge into its hiring practices as well as into the training of staff to be culturally sensitive. In the following section, critical components of service delivery models are reviewed and discussed.

SERVICE MODELS: PLANNING AND SERVICE DELIVERY ISSUES

Austin (1988) defines community-based long-term care (CLTC) as a "range of preventative and supportive health and social services including case management as a core component. Services, delivered in the community, home or institutional settings, are provided in the least restrictive environment and based on individually assessed client needs" (p. 6). The initial steps in the development of a CLTC service model include indentification of both the target group to be served and the service needs to be met.

Client Identification

> We must reconceptualize the roles of older people in our society. No longer should they be perceived as people with chronic, organic, and, therefore untreatable problems but individuals who are functioning well in society albeit with an increased risk for display of a list of difficulties. (Eisdorfer, 1984, p. 226)

This description of the elderly person suggests the need for a fluid service model that responds differentially to individual needs and social concerns. For the current BRI community service model, risk and vulnerability, as descriptive client and service terms, provide an excellent rationale for a service system as determined during the planning stage. An informal review of tables of contents of both gerontological clinical and practice textbooks, published during the last 10 years, however, indicates that social and health services have not been developed in this manner. The terms *risk* or *vulnerable* were absent as descriptive characteristics of individuals or of service systems' principles. The terms were found, however, in the psychological and sociological theoretical literature dealing with the interactions of personal coping skills and social stresses (AARP, 1988). A gap exists between social/psychological research data in these areas and program implementation.

Webster (1981) defines *risk* as "exposure to the chance of injury, damage or loss." This could be perceived as the presence of potential environmental stressors to which both the individual and the system must react. Intervention to bring about change and reduce risk is consistent with the overall social goal of the helping professions.

The same dictionary defines *vulnerability* as "capable or susceptible of being wounded, physically injured or hurt." Vulnerability, then, may be perceived as personal factors that impact on or are affected by risk or stress. Frailness is a term used to describe "persons over 60 who suffer from impairments or enervating conditions that can temporarily or permanently interfere with autonomous function" (Silverstone & Burack-Weiss, 1983). It identifies the person at the extreme end of the vulnerability continuum. Interventions to enable, actualize, and support the vulnerable individual are consistent with the clinical goals of the helping professions.

The following case example portrays risk factors impacting on client vulnerability.

> Mrs. C is a 75-year-old childless widow of six months living in an apartment. She has a modest income and the intellectual ability to learn the tasks formerly handled by her husband. Of late, however, she has begun to cry in the presence of neighbors and/or to isolate herself for no apparent reason. It can be suggested that the long-term social and managerial stressors related to widowhood for an elder without a family have placed Mrs. C at risk of both mental and physical ill-health outcomes. A brief supportive and educational intervention may be all that Mrs. C needs to lower her risk threshold by reestablishing her sense of self. Mrs. C. would become less emotionally vulnerable and would be able to remain outside the formal system for long-term care.

Anthony (1974), in an analysis of issues for child development, described risk as a function of the physical, social, and psychological environments and vulnerability as states of mind determined by stressors or risks. Though this differentiation appears clear, the Catch 22 of the risk/vulnerability relationship is the difficulty of empirically determining the causative, mediating, and outcome factors. Nevertheless, a service model design that builds upon the risk/vulnerability differentiation, as defined, can facilitate diagnosis, individual treatment, and social interventions. As suggested by Rose and Killien (1983), "Either one or both of the factors (risk/vulnerability) can be modified to improve the state of health or to prevent illness" (p. 8).

Determinants of Need: Stressors in Aging

Some common life crises in old age that may place even the seemingly invulnerable aged person at risk include death of significant others, lowered income and/or social status, sensory decrements, chronic pain, widow(er)hood, retirement, decreased mobility, isolation, caregiving, hospitalization, involuntary relocation, and institutionalization. Rosow

(1967), in his study of community-residing elderly, hypothesized a downward trajectory of responses to late life stressors based on diminishing resources and abilities. Though it is well known that most elderly persons do adapt and cope well with late life changes, there are those, as described by Rosow, for whom the increasing level of vulnerability requires intervention by the formal system.

Ehrlich (1988) identified and categorized the psychosocial environmental stressors or risk factors that affect the interaction between individual adaptation of aged persons and systems' responses:

1. Societal stereotypes: One sees today an ever-increasing, active young-old population. However, the increasing old-old, the group potentially at high risk, continues to reinforce the negative stereotypes of aged persons, though the chronological age for this stereotyping may have been raised. Gerontophobia (Bunzel, 1969), the fear of personal aging as demonstrated through unwillingness to be with aged people, remains a prevailing negative social attitude reinforced by the elderly themselves through ageism turned inward.

2. Societal change: The speed of technological, environmental, and social changes today increases the difficulty for the aged person to personally adapt his or her own life and to contribute to family and society. The exchange theory of positive aging (Dowd, 1975) posits that power for the elderly person rests on intergenerational exchange or contribution. Since past life experiences provide less opportunities for present intergenerational exchange, the areas for independent and innovative contribution become narrower and the value of an older person in society is thus limited.

Losses: Adaptation to losses is a life-long task, not something superimposed on the aging process. The ability of a great many elderly to deal appropriately with the grief resolution of loss and change is determined by the coping capacities refined over the years. Nevertheless, late life vulnerability should be considered in terms of the problems of adaptation to increased intrinsic and extrinsic losses, compounded by negative social stereotypes and technological changes.

4. Environmental dependency: Lawton (1980) postulated the inverse relationship between elderly competence and environmental demand as a determining factor in vulnerability. Coping and adaptation depend on the fit of person and environment—thus, too demanding an environment can be as damaging as one that has too little stimulation.

Response to environmental dependency, as to losses, is a life-long learned experience. Younger people with greater physiological competence frequently find it easier to either adapt to or rise above negative environmental press. For the elderly, these demands may lead to considerations of relocation or institutionalization—issues of great concern to the individual, the family, and the service system.

5. Intergenerational relationship: Today, the intergenerational service focus primarily emphasizes the relationship of caregiver role to needs, based on elderly frailty. Concern over caregiver burden is seen in the plethora of research studies and calls for in-home and day care respite services. Intergenerational interventions, however, need a broader preventive focus, preparing each generation for dependency by teaching "responsible dependency" to the elderly (Butler & Lewis, 1982) and "filial maturity" to the children (Blenkner, 1965). The preventive approach to service with the well elderly and their families may minimize caregiver stress in the support of the most vulnerable.

The components of this five-part typology of stressors or risk factors are not mutually exclusive, but rather interdependent and interactive, having a cumulative impact on individual vulnerability. CLTC organizational and clinical models, then, must be designed to address the interrelationship of risk factors and vulnerability.

Alternative Models

Historically, in a less complex society with a smaller and generally younger elderly population, traditional systems (e.g., social agencies, churches, and hospitals) met specific needs of the elderly through development of categorical programs providing direct services from the formal provider to the client. In this linear, unidirectional pattern of traditional service delivery, the service systems were the caregivers and the aged were the care recipients. Too frequently, this traditional formal system focused on the categorical need or pathological condition, giving far less credence to the role of the elderly person in planning, making decisions, and engaging in self-help, as well as to the contribution of the informal network (Ehrlich, 1979).

Today, both social gerontologists and geriatric health care providers are charged with the responsibility of enabling a larger and more diverse elderly population to remain in the community at the highest possible functional level. They must accept the challenge of designing more complex models that respond holistically to the person within his or her suprapersonal environment (Lawton, 1980), as well as to the pathological condition or specific social need.

Functional capacities and limitations of the elderly individual predominate as the prevalent model in CLTC services. The World Health Organization (1959) established the appropriateness of this concept when it supported the belief that health in the elderly is best measured in terms of function with the degree of fitness rather than extent of pathology used as a measure of the amount of service the aged will require from the community. Functional status or health can be defined as the total ability of the person to carry out the activities necessary for daily living.

Becker & Cohen (1984) suggest a functional taxonomy composed of various biological, psychological, and social capabilities that are integrated in order to perform activities necessary to ensure an individual's well-being. This model, which is based on a definition of aging as a biopsychosocial process, suggests (1) a multidimensional functional status, and (2) the need for complex interventions that integrate the biological, psychological, and social spheres impacting upon the elderly individual, his or her network, and the community system itself.

The Gerontological Society of America (GSA) (1978) suggested a second approach to model design. They identified a taxonomy based on target groups: the unimpaired, the minimally impaired, the moderately impaired, and the severely impaired elderly. Comprehensive assessment is recommended that goes beyond evaluation of functional ability to perform independent activities of daily living (IADL) and activities of daily living (ADL) to include a multidimensional assessment of the individual's psychosocial needs in relation to the support network and the environment. This model suggests that needs for health care, social services, personal enrichment, and so on, vary considerably across degrees of impairment.

A third approach to building a service model is that of Lowy (1979). His model is a goal-related circular continuum in which programs are designed to "cure, prevent and enhance" at each point along a continuum of need. The model integrates both the individual and the organizational contexts. Curing services are those that ameliorate debilitating, disabling, or crisis conditions. Enhancement develops strength and capacities for the maximum potential self-actualization. Both curing and enhancing interventions impact both on prevention of individual conditions and on personal/societal issues that, in turn, create yet another opportunity or level for individual and societal change.

Each of the taxonomies presented here suggest a differing organizational principle for the development of a CLTC system's functional capabilities, target groups, and programs. At the same time, it should be noted that all three build upon the multidimensions of functional levels, human conditions, personal support systems, and societal response. Each, then, provides an organizational framework in which to respond programmatically to social stressors and clinically to levels of individual vulnerability.

There is a long road, however, between the theoretical design and its implementation. Factors influencing implementation are varied, including funding source requirements; market forces; communal and agency history; and federal, state, and local social policies. Specific policy changes in the major funding sources for services for the aged and the market response to these changes represent the primary barriers today impeding the

building of a CLTC service system capable of responding along a continuum that includes the biopsychosocial, functional, and environmental
needs of elderly persons and their support networks. These policy developments include the following:

1. Targeted changes in OAA funds: The original intent for services
funded by the OAA was to reach all elderly equally—a federal entitlement
program for the elderly. Today, this program has become more highly
targeted toward a narrower population of low-income and "frail" elderly
(Federal Register, 8/31/88). There are less funds to serve both the at-risk
and the vulnerable.

2. Limitations of third-party reimbursements: Medicare and third-party
insurers target the "frail" for single-condition acute health care service,
only with health care needs defined very narrowly. Only Medicaid can
provide some limited services in a chronic care situation and this varies
from state to state. "Medically necessary," rather than prevention, is the
criterion for authorization of service and reimbursement.

3. Competitiveness of the proprietary health care system: The growth
of the proprietary health care system, providing only third party-reimburs-
able services, limits the ability of the sectarian and nonsectarian not-for-
profit agency to obtain these funds while increasing the pressure on these
agencies to provide the needed nonreimbursable services for preventive
and chronic care.

The above barriers, then, have been responsible for the growth of a
"medicalized" service system, far removed from the models discussed in
this chapter as appropriate to the global needs of the population. Instead,
we have primarily a CLTC system that operates for clients at one point in
time, providing neither early intervention for primary prevention nor long-
term planning and care. Vulnerability, narrowly defined by present funding policies and under the control of only one category of service providers, leads to a broader scope of vulnerability and need in the future.
The danger has been aptly described by Binney et al. (1988, p. 204):

> In many ways our nation's demographic and policy trends appear to be work-
> ing at cross-purposes. Demographers warn that, as we approach the turn of
> the century, there will be more older persons and more of the oldest-old in
> our population than ever before. This means there will be more people with
> problems of chronic illness than ever before. But, also, it means that there will
> be more individuals attempting to deal with all aspects of old age than at any
> time in our history—well people, ill people, people in need of housing, ade-
> quate income, social support and services and various other kinds of care of
> which medical care is only one. In many ways we will be needlessly un-

prepared to address the issues that confront our aging society. In supporting the unchecked "medicalization" of old age, we become important contributors to—if not producers of—the problems of aging

The BRI community service model, to be discussed in the next section, represents one specific application integrating the general issues of model development while responding to the barriers discussed above. This model may be replicable in its totality by some service agencies or community planning bodies. For others, one component part (i.e., conceptual framework, intake procedures, staff roles, service paramaters, etc.) can be integrated into already existing service systems.

BRI COMMUNITY SERVICES MODEL: LONG-TERM SOCIAL/HEALTH SERVICES FOR THE AT-RISK AND VULNERABLE ELDERLY

The Community Service Division (CSD) of BRI has expanded from only one discipline of social work to today's multidisciplinary teams of social workers (MSW, BSW), nurses (RN, BSN, MPH), therapists (OT, PT, ST), homemaker/home health aides, senior companions, and case manager assistants. BRI has periodically modified its services to respond to changing times, demographic needs, and resources. The flexibility enjoyed by a voluntary trust-supported agency led to BRI's decision in 1979 to use its resources to serve primarily the "frail" or most vulnerable elderly, as defined by the health care system. By 1986, it was apparent that the CSD was facing the crisis or challenge of community-based long-term care—how to meet the increasing and diverse needs of our community's elderly and of the families and friends whose lives impact upon their well-being.

The challenge agreed to by both trustees and staff was to reexamine service strategies and develop a new organizational model. The trustees reviewed and revised the agency mission statement to again endorse services within a global definition of aged, rather than the more narrow one of frailty. The staff addressed the issue of social responsibility to serve low-income elderly as efficiently and effectively as possible through systems reorganization. Involvement in the planning and implementation process included all staff levels from the executive director to direct service staff.

The strategic planning had as its goals:

- To resolve the Catch 22 dilemma wherein smaller numbers of clients were using larger amounts of the agency's available resources
- To facilitate the equitable allocation of resources to meet nonreimbursable chronic care needs

- To address the difficulty of being both an acute and chronic care provider
- To allow for the expansion of our services to previously unserved communities and to a more diverse client population

Model Framework

The BRI CLTC model (Table 18.1) integrates the three approaches to service design discussed earlier in this chapter: (1) Becker and Cohen's (1984) biopsychosocial functional approach; (2) GSA's (1978) psychosocial needs in relation to the support network/environment approach; and (3) Lowy's (1979) goal-related circular continuum, integrating both individual and organizational contexts approaches. The CLTC model defines and takes into consideration the continuum of functional abilities, diverse client groups, and cyclical program goals of cure, enhancement, and prevention. Being at risk of vulnerability receives equal clinical/supportive attention with resolving the care needs of the highly vulnerable. Thus, CLTC (an expanded long-term care service system) services are available for planning, advocacy, and support long before the elderly person or his or her family is in crisis, needing acute mental or physical care. The service parameters to accomplish this include the following:

1. The BRI model is an ongoing rather than a crisis-oriented response system.
2. Chronic as well as acute needs are addressed at intake for all clients whether they are referred, uncompensated, or beneficiaries of third-party-reimbursable services.
3. Multidisciplinary professional and paraprofessional staff contribute equally to a team effort—which frequently requires compromises in modifications of opinions concerning risk level, prevention, client autonomy, and care—on a clinical, case-by-case basis.
4. Services are provided from neighborhood-based offices that maintain close ties to all related formal and informal service units in their catchment area.
5. BRI provides health/social and supportive services to clients, ranging from those in need of uncompensated services to those able to pay full fees.
6. BRI provided leadership to develop joint ventures with both for-private and not-for-profit systems to meet unmet needs.

The Organizational Model at Work

The model illustrated in Table 18.1 depicts the way in which newly defined client categories and services are integrated into an operational sys-

TABLE 18.1 Community Long-Term Care Service Model

	Target groups		
	CATEGORY I CLIENTS ambulatory/ functional	CATEGORY II CLIENTS Lives alone, functional in ADLs, needs some IADL help and/or emotional support or lives with significant other who needs help with caregiving.	CATEGORY III CLIENTS Lives alone, needs help with ADLs and IADLs, needs emotional support or lives with significant other who needs help with caregiving and/or respite.
Services			
Advocacy		Entitlements Environmental issues	Entitlements Environmental issues
Case management	Dispersed family case management	Social service/RN consultation	Nursing service/ social worker assigned as needed
Consultation	Individual or family service	Individual, family	Individual, family
Counseling	Individual or family service	Individual, family	Individual, family
Daily living tasks		IADL assistance	ADL and IADL assistance
Education		Individual and family clients	Individual and/or family clients
Groups		Family therapy with clients Elderly client groups	Caregiver groups from caseload and community
Health services		RN as consultant	In-home nursing care, HHA personal care, therapies, day care

TABLE 18.1 (*continued*)

	Target groups		
(*continued*)	CATEGORY I CLIENTS	CATEGORY II CLIENTS	CATEGORY III CLIENTS
Information and referral	Informational service at congregates sites BRI inquiry calls Corporate contracts	Intake/case coordination	Intake/case coordination
In-person assessment		Social service assessment	Nursing assessment
Protective services			Social service case manager/RN assigned as needed
Research		Evaluation component of each new service, studies of outcomes, etc.	Evaluation component of each new service
Respite		In-home, day care, overnight	In-home, day care, overnight

Benjamin Rose Institute, 1988.

tem. The structure clarifies intake decisions, ensuring appropriate staff assignments for case management and other interventions. The staffing pattern for service provision takes into consideration disciplinary expertise and preferences and adherence to federal and state regulations. The chart is organized into two components:

1. Target groups: The BRI client population was first defined and then categorized into the three target groups for operational purposes (Category I, II, and III, defined below).
2. Services: The 13 areas of service may be provided by BRI staff alone or in collaboration with other agencies.

Aging concerns and needs, not chronological age, are the distinguishing characteristics of the BRI clients. However, only those 60 years of age or older may receive the in-home direct services, such as homemaking and personal care. Clients include persons 60 years and older who are experiencing functional declines, acute traumatic events, declining sense of well-being, loss of social support, changes in environment and/or progressive loss of coping skills; individuals of all ages who are concerned about or responsible for elders; and individuals of all ages who are concerned about issues of aging.

Client target groups are differentiated on the basis of functional level, living arrangement, and/or caregiver needs. Varying levels of risk can be identified within each target group, depending on the combination of affective and physical needs.

In Category I, clients of all ages who are ambulatory and functional need professional services of information, referral, counseling, consultation, and—for dispersed families—case management.

In Category II, the elderly person is ADL-independent (i.e., able to carry on activities, such as bathing, getting around on one's own), but needs emotional support and/or assistance with IADL tasks (i.e., housekeeping, food preparation). He or she may be alone or with a caregiver who needs assistance with IADL tasks. Since personal care services for ADLs are not needed, Category II clients are assigned social work case managers who also supervise homemaker services. CSD nurses provide health care consultation to the social workers as well as limited home visits for health assessment or health care instruction.

In Category III, the elderly person is IADL- and ADL-dependent, lives alone, or has a caregiver in need of respite and assistance with ADL and/or IADL tasks. Clients in this category have nurses as case managers who also supervise the in-home personal care services of the home health aides. Due to the complexity of these cases and the demands placed on a small nursing staff to provide as much direct nursing care as possible to clients with chronic, nonreimbursable conditions, social workers are assigned to collaborate with the nurse case managers as needed and to case-manage Category III protective cases.

Operational Model at Work

An organizational model is incomplete without an operational strategy. The strategies developed by a multidisciplinary planning team include the following:

1. Definition of case management: BRI maintains an expanded case management service in terms of worker roles and management models.

Case manager roles for both social workers and nurses integrate assessment, service coordination, monitoring, and advocacy for client needs and social policy change, along with the clinical functions of counseling and direct nursing care. This model is akin to that of traditional social work (Austin, 1987) and public health nursing (Freeman & Heinrich, 1981).

Its management model is an amalgamation of two of the three suggested models: *brokerage* and *consolidated* (Quinn & Burton, 1988). Workers have the option of using the CSD support staff of homemaker-home health aides, case manager assistants, and senior companions to provide assistance with IADL and ADL tasks or may broker for other formal or informal assistance. The CSD encourages staff to maintain a strong community profile to reinforce the cooperation essential for its brokerage role.

2. Team roles: The CLTC model, with its long-term care emphasis on both preventive and chronic care, recognizes the importance of a multidisciplinary professional and paraprofessional staff, contributing equally to the team effort. Disciplinary tokenism is considered counterproductive; attempts are consistently made to recognize the distinct contribution and service expertise of each discipline. Operating procedures maximize consultation, peer review, and support, while minimizing the collective decision making process that frequently impedes the timely of service.

3. Service parameters: Operational expectations have been designed to guide clinical staff and supervisors in management of caseloads. These include (a) visit expectations of 15 to 20 in-person contacts per week for professionals and 10 to 15 contacts for aides and case manager assistants; (b) nursing and aide contacts of no more than two per week (except for Medicare); and (c) case-type categorization into inquiry cases (expanded telephone information, referral, and follow-up), short-term cases (five contacts or less to resolve a specific identified problem), and ongoing cases (to expedite intake and minimize paperwork).

The above plan is BRI's response to the challenge of the two service alternatives: remain the same and serve an increasingly smaller, sicker caseload with more hours of service per capita; or reexamine the service strategy and develop more stringent guidelines for service to a larger number of those in need. The success of internal reorganization, however, is highly dependent on the continued commitment of all service providers to the vulnerable elderly, in meeting the social policy challenges facing us.

ISSUES CHALLENGING THE SERVICE SYSTEM: TOMORROW WILL BE DIFFERENT

Tobin, in Chapter 17 of this book, outlined issues facing policymakers and service providers concerned about long-term care today: client targeting, service categories, operational models, reimbursement criteria, and community planning. Though the BRI community services model attempts to respond to each of these items for its own service system, its success and potential for replicability depends on continued efforts to resolve the policy and service issues as outlined by Tobin and as categorized by the authors below:

1. Lack of definition of community long-term care: What long-term means in terms of service provision is still an unanswered question. How long is long? How much is care? These questions lead to the greater dilemma of the priority of client need versus the service system capability. Thus, when brought down to the level of service reality, it may be considered that the issue of definition must deal with systems survival as well as client survival.

2. Lack of comprehensive reimbursement systems: Can there be comprehensive services in a medical model reimbursement system? The funding mechanisms provide little assistance in meeting needs other than those defined as acute health care. Though legislation with a broader perspective may be submitted in the next Congress, its chances for passage are limited at best.

How we serve the many whose needs (particularly, affective needs) are not met by the present reimbursable mechanisms is only one part of the funding issue. There must be a response as well to the challenge of serving the many who are at 125% of the poverty level. This minimal income puts them at risk of impoverishment due to long-term care needs as they fall between the cracks of support from public funds for which they are ineligible and their ability to meet full payments on their own. Whose responsibility is it to help this group?

3. Need for social planning leadership at the local level: What constitutes leadership in each community is the overriding issue at this time of diminishing federal resources. Even if each individual agency determined its service maximums based on redefinitions and response to reimbursement mechanisms and then restructured to increase caseloads, the outcome would not be adequate. At the local level, the challenge remains within the potential of linking resources along the continuum of cure, enhancement, and prevention for the at-risk to the highly vulnerable.

In summary, while a spirit of cooperation in service delivery is admirable at any time, today it is imperative. With the cutback of federal dollars and the limited availability of charitable dollars, two things need to happen if nonprofit service agencies are to survive: (1) the services must be needed, affordable, and attractive to clients who can pay; and (2) nonprofit agencies with compatible missions, serving the same populations and deriving support from the same sources (both public and private), must begin working together more closely to form a system or network of services that will effectively meet the needs of both those who can pay and those who cannot.

The key to the second issue is working together. It requires more cooperation in planning, funding, and risk-sharing. It may involve partnerships and joint ventures. The objective should be the attainment of a network of high-quality health and social services for all elderly, regardless of need or financial resources.

With a focus on collaboration rather than a duplication of efforts, the Benjamin Rose Institute is committed to a new era. As a nonprofit, charitable organization, BRI is committed to the provision of social and health services to the vulnerable elderly as they have been described in this and other chapters of this book. BRI is also committed to strengthening the long-term care services system. It is not possible to predict the exact characteristics of the client population of the next decade, but it is reasonable to project that agencies need to think in terms of community systems that can maximize financial resources while continuing to provide sensitive and appropriate care, care that will enable the elderly and their support system. The goal of the community long term care system must always be that of preserving the dignity and the quality of life of those it serves.

REFERENCES

American Association of Retired Persons. (1988). *Ageline data base on middle age and aging*. Washington, D.C.: American Association of Retired Persons.

Anthony, E. J. (1974). The syndrome of the psychologically invulnerable child. In E. J. Anthony & C. Koupernik (Eds.), *The child in his family: Children at psychiatric risk* (pp. 529–544). New York: Wiley.

Austin, C. (1987). Case management: Refining social work. Paper presented at the NASW Professional Symposium, New Orleans.

Austin, C. (1988). Testimony before the Ohio House Health & Retirement Committee.

Becker, P., & Cohen, H. (1984). The functional approach to the care of the elderly: A conceptual framework. *Journal of the American Geriatrics Society, 32*, 923–929.

Binney, E., Estes, C., & Ingman, S. (1988). Medicalization, public policy and the elderly: Social services in jeopardy? In Final Report. Vol. II, *Organizational and community response to Medicare policy: Consequences for health and social services for the elderly*. San Francisco: Institute for Health & Aging, University of California.

Blenkner, M. (1965). Social work & family relationships in later life with some thoughts on filial maturity. In E. Shanas & G. Streib (Eds.), *Social structure &*

the family: Generational relations (pp. 46–59). Englewood Cliffs, N.J.: Prentice-Hall.

Bunzel, J. (1969, July/August). Gerontophobia—some remarks on a social policy for the elderly. *The Humanist*, 17–18.

Butler, R., & Lewis, M. (1982). *Aging & mental health: Positive psychosocial & biomedical approaches*. Columbus, OH: Charles E. Merrill.

Dowd, S. (1975). Aging as exchange: A preface to theory. *Journal of Gerontology*, 30, 584–594.

Ehrlich, P. (1979). *Mutual help for community elderly: Final report, volume 1*, Carbondale, IL: Southern Illinois University.

Ehrlich, P. (1988). Treatment issues in the psychotherapy of holocaust survivors. In J. Wilson, Z. Harel, & B. Kahana (Eds.), *Human adaptation to extreme stress: From the Holocaust to Vietnam* (pp. 285–304). New York: Plenum Press.

Eisdorfer, C. (1984). Models of mental health care for the elderly. In J. Abrahams & V. Crooks (Eds.), *Geriatric mental health* (pp. 217–229). Orlando, FL: Grune & Stratton.

Federal Register (8/31/88). *Rules and regulations, 53*, (169), 33758–33759.

Freeman, R., & Heinrich, J. (1981). *Community health nursing practice*. Philadelphia, PA: Saunders.

Gerontological Society of America. (1978). *Working with older people: A guide to practice. Vol. II: Human services*. Contract #HRA 230-76-0291. Rockville, MD: U.S. Department of Health, Education and Welfare.

Lawton, M. P. (1980). *Environment and aging*. Monterey, CA: Brooks/Cole.

Lowy, L. (1979). *Social Work with the aging*. New York: Harper & Row.

Quinn, J., & Burton, J. (1988). Case management: A way to improve quality in long term care. In K. Fisher & E. Weisman (Eds.), *Case management: Guiding patients through the health care maze* (pp. 8–14). Chicago: Joint Commission on Accreditation of Healthcare Organizations.

Rose, H., & Killien, M. (1983, April). Risk and vulnerability: A case for differentiation. *Advances in Nursing Science*, 60–73.

Rosow, I. (1967). *Social integration of the aged*. New York: The Free Press.

Silverstone, B., & Burack-Weiss, A. (1983). *Social work practice with the frail elderly and their families*. Springfield, IL: Charles C. Thomas.

Webster's Third New International Dictionary (Unabridged). (1981). Philip Babcock Gove (Ed.). Springfield, IL: Merriam-Webster, Inc.

World Health Organization. (1959). The public health aspects of the aging of the population. Copenhagen, Denmark.

19
Training Needs for Work with the Vulnerable Elderly

John F. Santos and Richard W. Hubbard

Making a positive impact on an individual's developing attitudes, knowledge, and skills is the ultimate goal of education. Geriatric training in general and lessons related to the vulnerable elderly in particular share these objectives; but, to achieve them, several fundamental questions about the vulnerable aged need to be asked and responded to. Who are the vulnerable elderly? How can they be found and how can services be provided to them? What are their special needs? It is also important to recognize attitudinal barriers in serving the vulnerable elderly; particularly, women and minorities who are largely representative of the vulnerable elderly population (Butler & Lewis, 1982). A set of skills, ranging from advocacy to crisis intervention, is needed in approaching the vulnerable elderly, and typically these services will be applied in a multidisciplinary framework.

Recent increases in gerontological and geriatric professional training have been apparent in core health and mental health disciplines. Faculty development in these disciplines has also been on the rise. Fellowships in geriatric medicine are increasing, and cooperative efforts among the human-service professions in research, training, and service are also improving (Hubbard & Kowal, 1988). Overall, this suggests that the time may be appropriate for the development of more specialized geriatric/gerontologic training programs. Despite these trends, significant barriers remain that still must be overcome.

Recent efforts have identified why vulnerability is an important topic and have dealt with the conceptual complexities involved in establishing what vulnerability means and what health care professionals ought to be doing about it. From an educational perspective, it would appear that the complexities, combined with the urgency of the problems themselves, are magnified when inadequately prepared or unprepared professionals are confronted by clients who meet some or all of the criteria for vulnerability.

An important perspective on what vulnerability is and who the vulnerable elderly are can be gained by first considering where they are most likely to be found. Homeless elderly, suffering from malnutrition and inadequate shelter, victimized by street crime and social isolation, represent the extreme case. Clients of Adult Protective Services, who by definition meet certain criteria of "endangerment," represent a second group for special attention. Clearly, these two groups are composed of individuals living in the state of vulnerability. Other groups such as the homebound, institutionalized, or demented elderly, by reason of disease states and loss of function, may be composed of a variety of individuals; some of whom are vulnerable, others of whom are at risk of becoming vulnerable, and still others of whom are well protected and cared for. Variables influencing whether a member of this group is or becomes vulnerable would include economics, the presence of informal and formal support systems, physical health, and a host of other physical and psychosocial factors. For purposes of this discussion, training needs will be approached from the perspectives of clients in a state of vulnerability or at a high risk of becoming vulnerable.

The question of what causes or contributes to vulnerability in old age has obvious importance to training decisions. Again, the answers will vary as will the research support for them. In many, though certainly not all cases, vulnerability may result from a synergism of physical, social, and psychological factors. This seems to stress the need for multidisciplinary training. Vulnerability may be an acute or chronic condition, requiring training programs to consider both types of care. It may be partially a result of personal choice (such as refusal of service, indirect self-destructive behavior, etc.), victimization (such as adult abuse), physical disease, mental decline, emotional illness, social status, or any possible combination of these factors. This lends emphasis to training approaches that include content on interdisciplinary assessment, treatment plans, and interventions.

Finally, educators need to consider what vulnerability in old age is and, relatedly, what elderly individuals are vulnerable to. At one extreme, vulnerability relates to an enhanced likelihood of death; yet, at a statistical level, vulnerability along this dimension increases for everyone on a daily basis. It seems clear that this type of vulnerability, produced by a natural consequence of living, is not what causes concern. Similarly, increased morbidity in some cases appears to be a statistically normal consequence of aging; hence, the increase in chronic health problems of those over age

75. The type of vulnerability considered in this chapter may be characterized by the following factors:

1. It is composed of conditions and behaviors that the individual and informal or formal support systems can reduce, treat, or modify.
2. If left untreated, the conditions and/or behaviors may *unnecessarily* increase the likelihood of death, disease, abuse, decline in function, or loss of independence.
3. The conditions and behaviors may be lifelong (e.g., the older chronic alcoholic) or have an onset in old age (e.g., dementia), and they may be either acute (e.g., postsurgical trauma in an elderly patient) or chronic (e.g., cognitive decline).
4. The conditions or behaviors are not normal consequences of the aging process; they represent problems in the physical, social, or psychological spheres and, as such, they are abnormal.

Thus, educators developing training programs in this area need to be concerned with the nature of vulnerability, the settings and individuals in which it is most likely to occur, and the factors associated with it. This chapter will deal with several training questions related to work with the vulnerable elderly. It will begin with a consideration of the types of professionals that should be trained; followed by a delineation of attitudinal, knowledge-based, and skill-oriented topic areas that a core curriculum should include; and, finally, a discussion of how training should be provided.

BARRIERS TO TRAINING

Progress in developing training programs for those working with the elderly in general, and the frail and vulnerable elderly in particular, has been uneven, at best. A modest surge of interest in the preparation of outreach workers to serve the frail and vulnerable elderly was shown by the Administration on Aging and the National Institute of Mental Health in the early 1970s. Since that time, of course, there has been increasing attention to and awareness of the type and extent of problems that the elderly face in this country. Recent emphasis on the understanding and care of the old-old will hopefully also help to emphasize the importance of identifying and serving frail and vulnerable older persons.

To be sure, a number of barriers have contributed to the failure to fully recognize and emphasize the vulnerable elderly in training programs. The varied and complex nature of vulnerability requires multidisciplinary insights, knowledge, and training in academic institutions. Unfortunately, many of these institutions have demonstrated little experience or interest in developing such training and programs.

It is also apparent that the vulnerable elderly represent a small but significant segment of the older population. Not every student in gerontology or geriatrics will be interested in learning about or working with this group. Obviously, this will have an impact on class size and, potentially, on institutional support. Another significant barrier is the fact that vulnerability often involves poor advocacy and self-empowerment skills on the part of clients, so that they are not in a strong position to demand increased and improved services or better training for professionals working to meet their needs.

WHO SHOULD BE TRAINED?

One of the paradoxes of service delivery to the vulnerable elderly is that this group of individuals, who often have the most severe problems, are typically served by those with the least amount of training. Nursing assistants in long-term care facilities, for example, spend far more time with depressed, vulnerable elderly than do clinical psychologists or social workers; and paraprofessional outreach workers spend more time with the homeless elderly than do trained geriatricians. The labor shortages that currently exist (Department of Health and Human Services, 1987), along with the priorities of and access to currently funded programs, strongly suggest that improving and increasing contacts between vulnerable clients and health care professionals is unlikely. Ironically, the results of some peer counseling, outreach, and paraprofessional programs suggest that direct professional involvement beyond the levels of training and field supervision may be less necessary than might be expected (Smyer & Gatz, 1983).

Thus, from the perspective of educational planning, it is important that any training initiatives not neglect those professionals and others who are already serving the vulnerable elderly. This should apply particularly to nursing assistants, volunteers, paraprofessionals, outreach workers, hospital emergency room staff, police officers, low-income housing personnel, and a variety of individuals frequently referred to as "gatekeepers."

It is interesting to note that vulnerable old people have long been referred to as the "hidden elderly," but certainly those in the health and mental health professions should know where they are and make every effort to meet their needs. It may be that professionals are hiding from the vulnerable elderly more often than the vulnerable elderly are hiding from the professionals.

A central issue in any consideration of vulnerability should include the multiple and interactive nature of the problems facing the aged individual. This theme should be reflected in educational programs that include diverse topics and disciplines such as medicine, nursing, social work, psychology, and the allied health professions. It is important that the combination of the extent and complexity of vulnerability and the reality of the marked lack of contact between clients and professionals should play a prominent role in educational planning and implementation. This simple and straightforward solution, in fact, goes to the very heart of the problem.

Certainly, it may be asked whether the failure of some professions to reach out to the vulnerable elderly contributes to their at-risk status. If this is so, shouldn't some training efforts and resources be directed toward these professionals? While it may be hard to argue with this position, the limitations of funding, the shortage of available trainers, and the immediacy of the problem probably require that modest and realistic training goals be set that might begin with more specialized training of professionals and others already working with the vulnerable elderly population.

An educational model involving a three-tiered approach to training mental health workers to serve the frail and vulnerable elderly has previously been proposed (Santos et al., 1983). The model grew out of many years of providing mental health outreach training for paraprofessionals and poor counselors. The basic cadre in the proposed system was made up of well-trained and well-supervised outreach workers who were prepared to work closely with an intermediate group of middle-level geriatric specialists. These specialists, in turn, operated under the supervision of a small number of specially trained geriatric professionals in disciplines such as psychology, psychiatry, nursing, and social work. While this approach, in fact, represents a stopgap measure, it also faces up to the reality that it is unlikely that enough professionally trained geriatric health care professionals will be available in the foreseeable future to meet the needs of the growing numbers of frail and vulnerable older people in this country.

Since working with the vulnerable elderly can be particularly demanding, difficult, and frustrating, it follows that the highest quality of training in supervision of this type of work is essential for success. Supervisors must be properly trained with respect to knowledge and skills that are relevant and useful in helping the vulnerable elderly. The supervisory aspects of training, unfortunately, have been largely neglected and ignored. However, without proper support and supervision, geriatric workers may easily develop the same sense of isolation and frustration that they encounter in many of their elderly clients (Hubbard, 1984). This is particularly true when vulnerability involves chronic and severe physical and/or mental health problems that are resistant to treatment and require persistent efforts to even manage the problems, let alone eliminate them. Professionals who choose or are assigned to supervisory positions in geriatrics must be knowledgeable about a variety of health, psychological, and social areas, as well as have the available knowledge relevant to problems of the vulnerable elderly.

WHAT SHOULD BE INCLUDED IN TRAINING?

Training topics may be divided into the areas of content, process, and professional issues. These areas reflect the need for an integrated approach that incorporates attitudes, knowledge level, and skills as they relate to work with the vulnerable elderly. It has already been pointed out that working with the vulnerable elderly is very demanding. Simply informing workers and trainees about the problems that their clients may face is not enough. Training should include theoretical frameworks that may facilitate understanding and analysis, case examples with problems and solutions, and empirical data that provide support for clinical decisions and interventions. At present, the ability to offer this type of framework is definitely limited by a lack of research in the area.

This poses another important educational challenge for consideration. Are there enough trained social scientists, health care personnel, and others with appropriate knowledge, experience, and skills to be able to prepare researchers in the study of vulnerability? The vulnerable elderly rarely appear in volunteer subject pools, and their functional limitations may preclude the use of many research procedures and measures. In fact, many of the criteria and screening methods currently employed in gerontological research projects are likely to exclude the vulnerable elderly from those subjects who may be studied. Obviously, success in training may be directly linked to the quality and quantity of research on the vulnerable aged that educators can rely on in constructing presentations and courses.

The proposed content areas and components in Table 19.1 are already in place in some training programs. However, they are not often organized into an integrated curriculum oriented toward the problems of the vulnerable elderly. This, of course, is not surprising, given the early developmental stage of geriatric education in general and the academic and financial resources available at this time. Certainly, the dramatic reductions in training funds in recent years has made the labor situation increasingly critical, even in more established fields and specialty areas. Emerging problem areas such as homelessness, the minority elderly, and geriatric mental health, have had little or no chance to develop or expand training, research, and service programs. It is not sufficient to deplore and call attention to these problems in political campaigns and scholarly publications. There is a clear need to fund and implement new and difficult programmatic initiatives in these topical areas.

TABLE 19.1 Training Topics Relevant to Work with the Vulnerable
Elderly

Content	Process	Professional issues
Sociodemographics • Age/sex/race • Living arrangements (e.g., homeless, SRO's, low-income housing, long-term care facilities, neigborhoods, etc.)	Case management	Advocacy
Physical health	Assessment	Functioning in an interdisciplinary framework
Mental health/illness	Crisis intervention	Ethical issues
Public policy	Inter-agency collaboration techniques	Burnout
Programs and resources		Counseling

Given the current combination of low priorities of both geriatric and gerontological training initiatives, severe budget limitations, the relatively recent emergence of awareness related to the vulnerable elderly, and the confusion inherent in defining and identifying this group, it is not surprising that professionals are faced with a difficult task in program development. There is an urgent need to recognize and agree on the serious and growing nature of these problems and an equally urgent need to initiate educational, research, and service program developments in this area.

In considering the training of persons for work with the vulnerable elderly, much of the confusion and many of the process-related issues again arise. How to decide whether or not an individual should be regarded as vulnerable is a difficult, practical, and clinical challenge that is crucial in effective service delivery. The experience of Adult Protective Service programs, in identifying their cases, is instructive and useful in the present context (see e.g., Quinn & Tomita, 1986). Other important issues are the type and frequency needed for the assessment of vulnerability, and the type of training needed to best perform such assessments. As educators begin to deal with these questions in the context of curriculum development, it may become clear that there is an inadequate knowledge base that renders the organization of quality training particularly difficult at this time.

The preferred procedure for assessment of frail and vulnerable older persons should involve multidisciplinary input. Not only are the problems likely to be multiple, but they are also likely to interact in presenting a unique configuration that produces the vulnerable state. Vulnerability may reflect a synergism of conditions and problems, like a web that will be difficult to unweave. However, it may be that eliminating or moderating one condition will weaken or break the chain of vulnerability or, perhaps, significantly reduce the overall severity or risks. Unfortunately, there are few multidisciplinary curricula or programs currently in place within the educational system. Recommendations for establishing or improving such training have been made on a number of occasions (Santos, 1985; Stearns & Hubbard, 1988).

The timing of assessment poses another important question. Are there critical periods or events that appear to be correlated with vulnerability (e.g., widowhood, hospitalization, relocation, etc.), or is the condition and concept too vague to be tied down to specific events and factors? Clearly, there is a need to know more about risk factors that might target an individual for assessment, and there is also a need to know when and how to conduct the most accurate assessment and prediction of changes in vulnerability. If vulnerability involves a process or interaction of processes, then a one-time assessment without follow-up or monitoring would not likely be of much predictive value in terms of intervention and therapy. In training personnel for such work, there is a need to prepare them, not only to identify vulnerability and know when they have found it, but also, and more importantly, to know what can be done to deal with the problems that are related to or precipitate the condition and process.

Consideration of professional issues in training requires emphasis on some of the unique aspects of working with this population. This will certainly include identifying and accessing a variety of services; therefore, advocacy will be an important element in the case management process. While some existing training programs and courses may recognize the importance of preparing professionals to serve an effective advocacy role and facilitate delivery of needed services and assistance, few disciplines, other than social work, seem to assign this task sufficient emphasis.

The development of multidisciplinary health care teams in geriatrics has been stimulated by the needs of the service settings, such as ambulatory care programs in hospitals, and by the nature of the problems that older adults encounter. The structure and procedures involved in the operation of such teams vary widely, as do the techniques employed in evaluation and assessment. Trainees must be adequately prepared for their roles in multidisciplinary care systems—roles that can be formidable and confusing without proper preparation, training, and experience.

Ethical issues involved in working with the vulnerable elderly are certainly related to the job frustration that geriatric personnel must face. Decisions regarding competency, institutionalization, the right to refuse treatment, and the controversial obligation of agencies to usurp personal rights in the face of self-endangering behavior are numerous. In spite of these well-recognized quandaries, it is rare to encounter training content related to such issues as part of academic, agency, or professional in-service education.

HOW SHOULD TRAINING PROGRAMS BE IMPLEMENTED?

Educational programs in this area will require the employment of a variety of short-term, stopgap, and long-term strategies. Stopgap programs will be needed to allow the academic institutions time to catch up with the labor and service needs in this area. In-service and continuing education programs for professionals will have to be expanded to provide one type of temporary solution. Often, however, these programs tend to focus too strongly on consciousness-raising rather than skill enhancement. They call attention to problems of which many current professionals are painfully aware, rather than offering useful skills to help them deal with these problems. Training options that include minicourses and workshops (of 10 to 16 hours' duration) and more extensive programs of formal training for personnel in frequent contact with the frail and vulnerable elderly are needed in addition to short and superficial sessions.

Also, close supervision of work with the more complicated cases must be employed to provide badly needed one-on-one training. Specially prepared manuals that carefully spell out relevant casework procedures could also offer additional and useful help. Obviously, there are various training methods that could be employed, but if the problems of the vulnerable elderly are to be adequately addressed in training, the importance of this approach must be recognized.

From a long-term perspective, training programs and possibilities for work with the frail and vulnerable elderly can be expected to vary and increase relative to a number of factors. Not the least of these will be the availability of funds from private and federal funding agencies, as well as the degree to which these agencies identify and encourage the development of educational, research, and service initiatives for this population. However, such initiatives alone, while necessary, are not enough. It will also be important to have the interest and support of professionals in the field who are already involved in geriatric activities in order to attract, encourage, direct, and train students and current workers who wish to enter this area of work. Without a doubt, there must also be more attractive positions available in the field and a persistent and concerted effort on the part of the trainers to place their trainees in appropriate jobs.

Unfortunately, harsh reality and experience indicate that important problems and issues do not necessarily become or remain popular topics solely on their merit. There are many notable examples of this in gerontology/geriatrics, such as various needs related to improved nursing homes and home health care. Even after many published reports and recommendations based on years of research and hearings, those problems persist.

The development of training for work with the frail and vulnerable elderly will very likely also depend to a considerable extent on the general development of gerontology/geriatrics within higher education. Thus far, this development has been steady, even though to many in the field it may have seemed slow and frustrating because of budget cuts and other setbacks over the past few years.

Peterson (1986, 1989), who has followed the growth of gerontology programs over a number of years, has considered various indicators that best reflect academic progress in the field. Among those that have been employed is the number of courses within various curricula. However, without knowing the level (e.g., nondegree, undergraduate, graduate, postgraduate) and frequency of offerings and the availability of these organized course sequences, the level and content of these courses remain unclear.

The development of undergraduate and graduate courses, degrees, and certificate programs has been traced as a way to chart the growth of the field. This approach is likely to be a more accurate gauge in identifying curriculum as opposed to single or unintegrated course offerings. Certificate programs, however, vary widely in their requirements; but more importantly, they often stand alone rather than as part of a single or multidisciplinary program. The growth in the numbers of dissertations in the field has also been an encouraging indicator. However, it is important to keep in mind that an increase in the studies that may use old age as a variable does not in itself ensure or reflect solid curricular development.

At a more specific level, it is unclear how vulnerability is included as a single topic or issue within a variety of courses, as an integral part of, or as the central theme in, current courses and curricula in the field. It is unclear if special problems such as those related to minority and vulnerable elderly are covered and, if so, what type of coverage is given to these topics. Factual coverage of problems related to vulnerability would appear to deserve full and adequate attention in the basic content of all gerontological and geriatric training. The complexity of these problems also requires specialized emphasis in appropriate field placements and supervised clinical experience.

SUMMARY AND CONCLUSIONS

Application of the traditional educational triad of knowledge, attitudes, and skills to training professionals for work with the vulnerable elderly reveals a number of important issues. The topic of vulnerability in old age poses a special challenge to the educational system; it requires multi-disciplinary teaching and closely supervised clinical experience, while attracting a rather small percentage of students. Similar problems are encountered in professional and continuing education programs where training time is limited and the need to move beyond consciousness-raising is strong.

Clearly, an accurate picture of gerontological and geriatric program development is still lacking at this time. Even at universities that appear to have fully developed programs, there is limited information about the type and number of students attending and completing the training. It is possible that more students are introduced to the area generally than are likely to serve as professionals for the field.

While vulnerability may not be a significant problem for the majority of older Americans, it is an important experience for many of the elderly who come in contact with a variety of health, mental health, and other geriatric service personnel. Therefore, in training of professionals and paraprofessionals, vulnerability problems must be given adequate attention in course content and practicum experience

Gerontology and geriatric education are relatively new arrivals in academic institutions, so that while their future is improving, it is still uncertain how they will fare in the competition with established departments and programs for funds and resources. The needs and challenges of frail and vulnerable older persons, along with those of the poor, minority, and homeless elderly, are problem areas that are certainly relevant issues within the realm of these emerging fields of education, research, and services. It is to be hoped that the growing knowledge and expertise will allow professionals to more effectively treat, intervene, and, above all, minimize such problems in the future. To do this, there will certainly be a need for more effective planning and program development in the future. There is a clear need for improvement over the haphazard approaches of the past, approaches too easily characterized as "Ready, fire, aim!"

REFERENCES

Butler, R. N., & Lewis, M. I. (1982). *Aging and Mental Health*. St. Louis, MO: C. V. Mosby.

Hubbard, R. W. (1984). Clinical themes in the supervision of gerontological practice. *Educational Gerontology, 10*, (4–5), 317–324.

Hubbard, R. W., & Kowal, J. (1988). Guest editors, special issue on geriatric education centers. *Gerontology and Geriatrics Education, 8*(3), 1–3.

Peterson, D. A. (1986). Extent of gerontology instruction in American institutions of higher education. *Educational Gerontology, 4*, 519–529.

Peterson, D. A. (1989). Organizational structure of gerontologic instructional programs. *Gerontology and Geriatrics Education, 10*, (1), 37–51.

Quinn, M. F., & Tomita, S. K. (1986). *Elder Abuse and Neglect.* New York: Springer.

Santos, J. F. (1985). Gerontology and geriatric education: Retrospect and prospect. *Gerontology and Geriatrics Education, 5*, (3), 1–6.

Santos, J. F., Hubbard, R. W., Burdick, D. C., & Santos, M. A. (1983). Mental health outreach and the elderly. In M. Smyer & M. Gatz (Eds.), *Mental Health Programs for Older Adults.* Beverly Hills, CA, Sage.

Smyer, M. A., & Gatz, M. (1983). *Mental Health and Aging—Programs and Evaluations.* Beverly Hills, CA: Sage Publications.

Sterns, H., & Hubbard, R. W. (1988). The challenge of caregiver education. *Gerontology and Geriatrics Association for Gerontology in High Education Newsletter*, March 1988, pp. 1–2.

U.S. Department of Health and Human Services (1987). *Personnel for Health Needs of the Elderly Through Year 2020.* Bethesda, MD: National Institute on Aging.

Epilogue

In concluding this book on vulnerability and the vulnerable aged, we think that several points need to be emphasized to more effectively ensure the safety, security, and well-being of the vulnerable aged.

First, vulnerable aged persons constitute a heterogeneous population. Recognition and consideration of this diversity is essential for any serious attempt to develop more effective policies, programs, interventions, and preventive measures on their behalf. Recognition and understanding of the needs and preferences of service consumers, coupled with effective communications with the elderly and members of their informal support system, are essential in work with the vulnerable aged.

Second, attention must be given to the need for a national health care policy and a national long-term care policy designed to ensure the survival, security, and well-being of all Americans, including the vulnerable aged.

Third, it is important to underscore the importance of adequate funding for health and social services required for effective planning, organization, delivery of services, and education needed to meet the needs of all aged, including vulnerable aged.

Fourth, the informal support system is of central importance in the lives of all the elderly, including the vulnerable aged. While informal caregivers play an important role, they cannot shoulder all the responsibility and meet all the service needs of their elderly family members. National policies need to enhance the potential and actual involvement of the informal support system in the care of the vulnerable aged.

Fifth and finally, it is important to underscore the fluctuations in the public commitment and the fragmented nature of the health and social service system in the United States. The availability of the need-based benefits and services in the United States varies across and within different states and changes from year to year. The extent to which benefits and services may be available for vulnerable aged may, therefore, vary considerably in different locations. It is essential that public officials and the professional community strive to develop a more effective and more equitable system of public benefits and services that more adequately meet the needs of all members of our society, including the vulnerable aged.

Index

Abuse and neglect, 7, 139, 140–146,
    212
  caregiving and, 144–145
  individual characteristics and, 140
  policy implications, 146
  system characteristics and, 143
Access Service, 255
Activities of daily living (ADL),
    limitations in, 22–24, 38, 106,
    200, 224–226, 238, 264, 284,
    290
Acute care, 226–228, 265, 207
Administration on Aging, 253, 255
Adult day care, 53, 200, 211, 269
Adult protective services, 7, 145, 296
Adversity, finding meaning in, 73
Advocacy, 16, 237, 295, 298
Affective/emotional coping, 78–80
Affective support, 76
Age, 263–264
  caregiver stress and, 192
  gender and, 54–59
  health vulnerability and, 42
  social resources and, 94, 95
  suicide rates and, 168–169
Age discrimination, 21, 236
Age Discrimination in Employment
    Act, 236
Ageism, 108
Aggressive/violent behavior, suicide
    and, 171
Ahlbrandt, Roger, 120, 126, 127
Alcohol, Drug Abuse, and Mental
    Health Administration, 256
Alcohol abuse, 42, 150, 172, 178,
    181
Altruism, 73

Alzheimer's disease, 37, 211, 226
  competent behavior and, 113
  coping strategies and, 77
  gender and, 44
  misdiagnosis of, 264
  prevalence of, 263
  respite programs and, 198–201,
    262
  suicide and, 171–172
Anxiety, 36, 68, 173
Area Agencies on Aging, 258
Assessment, 11, 37, 144, 276, 304
Asylums, 211

Bag ladies, 150
Barter, J. T., 167
Bed, restriction to, 35, 55–56
Behavior management, dementia and,
    201
Benjamin Rose Institute, 198–201,
    276–293
Bereavement, 11, 45, 67, 174–175,
    177
Biegel, D., 126, 127
Binney, E., 285
Biopsychosocial functional approach,
    287
Black elderly, 43, 122–125, 129,
    236. See also Ethnicity
Board and care homes, unlicensed, 29
Brody, Elaine, 113
Buergher's disease, suicide and, 179
Burghardt, S., 164

Calcium intake, 263
Callahan, Daniel, 241–242
Cancer, 34, 176–177

Care
  continuum of, 226–228, 232, 257–
    258, 262, 279
  ethics of, 272
  quality of, 232
Caregiving, 139, 144–145. *See also*
  Family caregivers
Case management, 212, 214, 233,
    258, 266–267, 269, 273, 278,
    290–291
Cash assistance, 277
Catastrophic Health Act of 1988,
    230–231, 232–233
Categorical vulnerability, 8–9
Chatters, L., 124
Children, poverty of, 230. *See also*
  Family
Chronic illness, 19, 54–58, 296–297
  continuity of care and, 228
  coping strategies and, 80
  gender and, 43–44
  incidence of, 34
  old-old and, 238
  race and, 43
  suicide and, 176
  tertiary prevention and, 262–263
Chronic pain, 281
Church
  ethnic elderly and, 123, 126, 128,
    131, 132, 279
  home visitation and, 270
Cigarette smoking, 42
Client assistance programs, 252,
    253–255
Client identification, 280–281
Cognitive function, 7, 10, 37
  age and, 42
  behavioral impairments and, 195
  IADL and, 41
  long-term care and, 226
Cognitive skill, coping and, 71–73,
    79–80
Cohen, C., 158
Cohen, Wilbur, 233
Collective responsibility, 209–210,
    213
Communication disorders, 10

Community housing, 110–112
Community-based services, 12, 160,
    280, 286–291
Community leaders, 126
Community Mental Health Center
  program, 256
Community planning, long-term care
  and, 269–271
Community Services Block Grant
  program, 256
Congregate housing, 256, 265
Congregate services, 112
Continuing care retirement
  communities, 267
Coordinating agencies, 214
Coping, 64–82, 280, 282
Coping resources, 68–76
Coping strategies, 70–71, 73–76
Cost benefit, 230
Credentials, 215
Crime, inner city and, 123, 130
Crisis intervention, 295
Crying, coping and, 79
Cultural characteristics, abuse and,
    142
Cultural pluralism, 117

Day care, 52, 200, 211, 269
Death, homelessness and, 161
Decision-making capabilities, 8
Defense mechanisms, homelessness
  and, 156
Dementia, 37, 42, 191–192, 226,
    296
Dependency, 12, 74–75
  abuse and, 141, 144
  environmental, 282
  intergenerational, 124, 283
  suicide and, 179
Depression, 11, 40, 68
  age and, 42
  alcohol use and, 173
  bereavement and, 175
  early detection of, 181
  family caregivers and, 193, 195
  gender and, 44

institutionalization and, 178
prevalence rates, 36
stress and, 96
suicide and, 171
Diabetes, suicide and, 179
Disability, 34–35, 224
Disaster control, 13–15
Discrimination
age, 21, 236
black elderly and, 122
Douglass, R., 158
Drop-in centers, 156, 161–162
Drug interactions, 264
Drug use, 42, 150
Durkheim, E., 173–174

Economic programs, 211
Economic resources, 70, 89, 92, 94,
95. *See also* Income
Education, suicide prevention and,
180–181
Education level, health status and,
44
Ehrlich, P., 282
Emotional support, neighbors and,
121
Employee Retirement Income Security
Act of 1974, 236
Environment
abuse and, 142
assessment of, 11
cognitive function and, 11
coping strategies and, 74
defined, 116
functional limitations and, 38
neighborhood, 116–132
psychosocial, 282–283
residential, 110–114
suprapersonal, 105–108
vulnerability and, 104–114
Environmental docility hypothesis,
68, 117
Environmental press, 117, 282
Environmental proactivity, 111–112
Environmental resources, 67, 70
Erikson, E., 157, 158, 160, 165
Ethical issues, 302–303

Ethnicity, 116–132
age-leveling hypothesis and, 129
churches and, 123, 126, 128, 131,
132, 279
double-jeopardy hypothesis and,
129
environment and, 116–132
health status and, 42–43
neighborhoods and, 120–132, 271
poverty and, 129
service delivery and, 218
suicide and, 169
vulnerability and, 42–43, 61–62
Ethnic youth, 218–219
Exchange theory, 282
Exercise, 42, 263
Extended family, 128, 129

Fabricant, M., 164
Family, 11–12, 120
continuity of care and, 227–228
extended, 128, 129
illness and, 67
long-term care and, 24–25, 227
proximity to, 122–123, 128, 131
service plans and, 266
suicide prevention and, 181
white ethnic elderly and, 127–128
Family caregivers
depression and, 193, 195
health and well-being of, 190–198
vulnerability and, 189–202
support groups and, 271
Family history, health conditions and,
41
Family service agency, 270
Farberow, N. L., 167
Federal budget, aging expenditures in,
235
Federal programs, 248–260
future directions, 258–260
homelessness and, 160
societal approach to, 251–252
typology of, 252–257
visibility of, 251–252
See also National policies; *specific
programs*

Financial vulnerability, 25–28, 67.
   See also Economic resources;
   Income
Firearms, suicide and, 183–184
Food Stamps program, 254
Frail elderly, 7, 11, 12–13, 18, 23,
   30, 250
Friends, social support and, 120,
   122–123, 127–128, 155
Functional impairments, 38–40, 43,
   44, 224, 238
Functional networks, 125
Functional status, 239, 283–284

Gatekeepers, 298
Gender, 263–264
   age and, 54–59
   caregiver stress and, 192
   health vulnerability and, 43–44, 46
   suicide and, 169, 174, 175
Gender inequalities, 21
Generational equity, 107, 230, 241,
   243
Genetics, health conditions and, 41
Geriatric evaluation unit, 265
Geriatric medicine, 211, 295
Geriatric syndromes, 239
Gerontology, 7, 278
Gerontophobia, 282
Geropsychiatric day care, 265
Global health vulnerability, 37–38
Goal-related circular continuum, 287
Government programs, *see* Federal
   programs; *specific programs*
Greenspan, Alan, 241
Guttmann, D., 126, 127

Health care
   costs of, 47, 240–243, 263–264
   evolution of, 210–211
   homeless and, 151, 163
   policy issues in, 223, 230–233,
     236
   proprietary systems, 285
   quality of, 229
   rationing, 241–243, 264
   scapegoating and, 240
   suicide prevention and, 182

Health Care for the Homeless
   projects, 151
Health status
   blacks and, 129
   caregivers and, 196
   coping strategies and, 80
   homelessness and, 156–157, 159–
     160
   national policies and, 238–239
   socioeconomic status and, 44, 46
   suicide and, 176–177, 179
Health vulnerability, 32–48, 237–
   239
   defining, 33
   family history and, 41
   genetic factors, 41
   global, 37–38
   life-style and, 41–42
   physical, 34
   service need and, 47–48
   social resources and, 45
   sociodemographic factors, 42–44
   stress and, 45
Hearing impairment, 35
Heart disease, 34
Hebrew Rehabilitation Center for
   Aged (HRCA) Vulnerability
   Scale, 7
Helplessness, 167, 170, 179, 209
Help-seeking behaviors, 124–125,
   127–128
Hispanics, health vulnerability and,
   43
Holocaust, survivors of, 73
Homebound, 106, 139, 296
Home equity, 25
Home health aides, 200, 291
Home health care, 10, 53, 219, 265,
   271
Homelessness, 29, 67, 149–165, 296
   adaptation to, 156–168
   causes of, 155–156
   interventions, 158–163
   overview of, 150–152
Homemaker services, 265, 290
Home management activities, 55
Hopelessness, suicide and, 167, 170,
   171, 179

Hot lines, suicide, 181
Housing, 270
    planned, 112–113
    shared, 28
    substandard, 155
    unplanned community, 110–112
    vulnerability and, 28–29
Housing programs, 212, 254
Human services, labor policies and, 218

Identity, institutionalization and, 178
Illness, incidence of, 34
Impairment, abuse and, 141
Income, 21, 281
    coping strategies and, 79
    health status and, 44
    life satisfaction and, 97
    loss of, 70, 74
    See also Economic resources
Incompetence, 7, 8
Incontinence, 35, 197
Independent living, 64
Indirect self-destructive behavior, 178
Indirect life-threatening behavior, 178
Information, problem solving and, 13
Information and referral services, 214
In-home respite, 200–201
Injury, vulnerability to, 8
In-service training, 219
Institutionalization, 113, 278, 281, 296
    admission from hospitals and, 225
    coping strategies and, 73–75, 78–80
    incontinence and, 35
    lower-skilled jobs and, 219
    Medicaid and, 24, 25
    old-old and, 106
    projected use, 238
    self-destructive behavior and, 177–180
    social workers and, 212
    suicide and, 177–180, 182–183
    See also Long-term care
Institutions, self-protective behavior of, 215

Instrumental activities of daily living (IADL), 22–24, 38, 39, 41, 224, 284, 290
Instrumental/behavioral coping, 79–80
Insurance industry, risk calculation and, 7
Interdependence, 124, 165, 283
Intergenerational exchange, 282
Invulnerability, 89–91, 99–101
Isolation
    abuse and, 141
    alcohol use and, 173
    poverty and, 155
    risk and, 11, 67, 70, 281
    suicide and, 170, 175–176, 179

Job restructuring, 219

Labor force
    long term care and, 218–220
    service quality and, 14–15
    shortages in, 218, 298
Legal Services program, 255
Life choices, right to make, 144
Life cycle, coping efforts and, 81
Life expectancy, 42, 43, 117, 129, 223–224, 263
Life satisfaction, income and, 97
Life-span perspective, 107
Life-style, health conditions and, 42
Living alone, health status and, 46
Living arrangements, coping strategies and, 79
Locus of control, 71–73, 75, 76
Loneliness, 11, 170, 175–176, 178
Long-term care
    catastrophic risk for, 226
    community planning and, 269–271
    cost of, 230
    defining need for, 223–224, 225–228
    families and, 227
    federal programs and, 250
    ideal system, 272–273
    issues in, 261–273
    model community, 276–293
    policy issues, 223, 230–233

Long-term care (*Cont'd*)
　quality of, 229–230
　vulnerability and, 53–54, 139
　work force and, 218–220
　See also Institutionalization
Long-term care insurance, 267
Long-Term Care Ombudsman
　　Program, 253
Loss, 11, 67, 279
　adaptation to, 282
　homeless and, 161
　of resources, 67–73, 93–94
　of social resources, 93–94
　status and, 45
　suicide and, 167, 170, 174–175
Low income families, respite services
　　for, 199

Management information systems,
　　215
Margaret Blenkner Research Center,
　　193–198
Marital dissolution, 94
Marital status, suicide and, 169. *See
　　also* Widowhood
Mastery, 72–73, 80
Medicaid, 24, 235, 238, 244, 256,
　　264, 267
Medical care, *see* Health care
Medical day care, 265
Medical specialization, 216
Medicare, 228, 235, 238, 241, 254,
　　278
　Diagnosis-Related Groups, 225,
　　　253, 255, 264
　Peer Review Organizations, 255
　Prospective Payment System, 253,
　　　255
Medicare Catastrophic Coverage Act
　　of 1988, 243
Memory problems, gender and, 44
Men, widowed, 19. *See also* Gender
Mental health, 10, 35–37, 211
　age and, 42
　ethnicity and, 43, 129
　gender and, 44
　homelessness and, 150, 160, 163

institutionalization and, 177
　neighborhood attachment and, 126
　physical illness and, 40–41
Mental health outreach training, 299
Mental health services
　homeless and, 163
　suicide prevention and, 182
Mentally retarded, 37
Minnesota law, 8–10
Minorities, *see* Ethnicity
Mobility, 38, 281
Moriwaki, S. Y., 167
Mortality rates, 91
Motor impairment, 35

National policies, 235–245
　health status and, 238–239
　poverty and, 236–237
　See also Federal programs; Policy
　　making
National responsibility, veterans and,
　　210–211
Negative outcomes, risk of, 87, 88–
　　89, 90, 98–101
Neglect, *see* Abuse and neglect
Neighborhoods
　attachment to, 121–122, 125–127
　ethnicity and, 120–132, 271
　networks and, 112
　urban, 118–132
　vulnerability and, 116–132
Neighbors, social support from, 120,
　　123, 125, 131
Nurses, case management and, 290–
　　291
Nursing assistants, 298
Nursing homes, *see*
　　Institutionalization; Long-term
　　care
Nutritional status, 44
Nutrition programs, 269

Older Americans Act of 1965, 236,
　　243, 250, 256, 278, 285
Old-old
　ADL impairments, 22
　coping strategies and, 80

health costs and, 263–264
hospital utilization and, 238
institutionalization of, 106
invisibility of, 106, 107–108
stereotypes of, 282
suicide and, 168–169, 179
On Lok Senior Center, 269
Organic brain syndrome, suicide and,
    171–172
Orthopedic impairments, 35
Outreach services, 160–161, 298,
    299

Pain, suicide and, 176–177
Paranoia, 36
Paraprofessional programs, 298
Personal characteristics, abuse and,
    141
Personal control, institutionalization
    and, 113–114
Personal freedom, 11
Personality characteristics, coping
    and, 71–73, 74
Personal resources, 64, 71
Peterson, Peter, 240
Physical illness, mental problems and,
    40–41
Physical vulnerability, 21–25, 34–35
    See also Health status
Policy making
    abuse and neglect and, 146
    federal programs and, 248–260
    funding and, 284–285
    long-term care and, 223–233
    resource availability and, 217
    social concern base for, 208–221
    See also National policies
Poverty, 11, 25, 91, 263
    abuse and, 141
    of children, 230
    client assistance programs and,
        254–255
    ethnicity and, 117–118, 122, 129
    health status and, 44, 46
    homelessness and, 155–156
    inner city and, 130
    isolation and, 155

national policies and, 236–237
Social Security and, 235–237
vulnerability and, 89, 236–237
women and, 264
Prevention, 89, 239, 284
    primary, 262–263, 271
    secondary, 262–263, 271
    tertiary, 262–263, 273
Proactive behavior, 111–112
Professionalization, specialties and,
    216–217
Professional training, 295–305
Protective services, *see* Adult
    protective services
Pseudodementia, 264
Psychological resources, 5, 68, 70–73
Psychological well-being, 65, 68
Psychosocial needs, 287
Psychosocial resources, 77–81
Public housing, 29
Public policy, *see* Policy making

Quality control, mechanisms for, 14–
    15
Quality of life, 230

Race, *see* Ethnicity
Reagan administration, 249
Rehabilitation, 162, 211, 227, 265,
    278
Reimbursement systems, 267, 285,
    292
Religion, suicide and, 179. *See also*
    Church
Relocation, 67, 281, 282
Rent-subsidized housing, 29
Research and demonstration
    programs, 257
Residential respite, 200
Resources, 19
    availability of, 217
    coping, 68–76
    economic, 70, 89, 92, 94, 95
    external deficits, 70
    loss of, 67–73, 93–94
    psychological, 5, 68, 70–73

Resources (*Cont'd*)
  psychosocial, 77–81
  See also Social resources
Respite programs, 197–201, 283
Retired Senior Volunteer Program,
  182
Retirement, 281
  mandatory, 236
  role loss and, 175
  transition to, 94
  women and, 259
Risk, vulnerability and, 7, 15–16, 18,
  87, 88–89, 90, 98–101, 280–
  281
Risk factors, 282–283
Role loss, 94, 175
Rose, Benjamin, 276

Safety net, 164
Scale of Vulnerability, 7
Scapegoating, 240–243
Schizophrenia, 36
Section 8 housing, 254
Section 202 Housing, 256
Self-actualization, 284
Self-concept, alcohol use and, 173
Self-destructive behavior,
  institutionalization and, 177–180
Self-disclosure, 73
Self-efficacy, 72–73
Self-esteem, 71–72, 75, 156, 161
Self-injurious behavior, 178
Self-neglect, 145
Senior centers, 265, 269
Sensory impairment, 35, 281
Service enhancement programs, 253,
  255–257
Service models, 280–286
Services
  coordination of, 257–258
  funding sources for, 284–285
  provision versus purchase of, 267–
  269
  range of, 14
Shared households, caregiver strain
  and, 197
Shelters, homeless in, 156

Sherman, W., 126, 127
Shopping facilities, inner city and,
  123
Siblings, loss of, 68
Single-parent families, 259
Single room occupancy dwellings, 29,
  153, 154
Situational characteristics, abuse and,
  141–142
Social abuse, 212
Social factors
  stress inoculation and, 97–98
  vulnerability and, 86–101
  well-being and, 92–101
Social health maintenance
  organizations, 267, 273
Social interaction
  black elderly and, 122–124
  planned housing and, 112
  white ethnic elderly and, 125–126,
  127
Socialization, 94
  neighborhoods and, 119
  to old age, 104–106
Social planning leadership, 292
Social-psychological services,
  evolution of, 212
Social relationships
  alcohol use and, 173, 174–175
  neighborhoods and, 119
  white ethnic elderly and, 125–126
Social resources, 64
  as compensatory factors, 95
  health vulnerability and, 45–46
  loss of, 67, 93–94
  as moderating variables, 95–97
  quality of, 100
  social factors and, 92
  vulnerability and, 98–101
  See also Social support
Social Security, 21, 31, 235–237,
  240, 244, 252, 253
Social Security Act, Title XX, 212
Social Security Reform Act of 1983,
  243
Social Services Block Grant, Title
  XX, 256

Social status, 281
Social support, 70, 92
  caregiver stress and, 191, 192
  continuity of care and, 228
  coping strategies and, 76
  loss of, 67
  neighborhoods and, 120–121
  suicide and, 179
  See also Social resources
Social values, suprapersonal
    environment and, 107–108
Social welfare, homelessness and,
    160
Social workers, 212, 290–291
Societal change, 282
Society, structural inequality of, 21
Sociodemographic factors,
    vulnerability and, 53–63
Socioeconomic status, 263–264
Socioenvironmental factors,
    vulnerability and, 104–114
Specialization, professional services
    and, 210–217
Status, gender and, 46
Stereotypes, 106–108, 282
Stigmatization, 106–108, 120
Strain, care-related, 195–198
Stress, 45, 67, 70, 280
  alcohol use and, 173
  caregiving and, 144
  compensatory factors, 95
  coping and, 64–82
  extreme, 45, 67
  inoculation against, 97–98
  moderating variables, 95–97
  paradigm of, 65
  resources and, 68–73
  social factors and, 87, 92, 93–94
  suicide and, 167, 170
  well-being outcomes and, 68
Stressors, 64, 67, 93–94, 96, 109–
    110, 281–284
Stroke, 34
Stewart B. McKinney Homeless
    Assistance Act of 1987, 159
Suburbs, white ethnic elderly in,
    128

Suicidal elderly, 139, 167–184
  alcohol abuse and, 172–173
  demographic factors, 168–170
  depression and, 171
  health problems and, 176–177
  institutionalization and, 177–180,
    182–183
  isolation and, 175–176
  loneliness and, 175–176
  organic brain syndrome and, 171–
    172
  service provisions and, 180–184
  survivors and, 177
  widowhood and, 173–175
Supervision, training and, 303
Supplemental Security Income (SSI),
    30–31, 233, 237, 253–254
Support systems, neighborhood-
    based, 120–122. *See also* Social
    support
System optimizing programs, 252–
    253, 255

Tax Reform Act of 1986, 243
Team effort, 291
Terminal illness, suicide and, 176–
    177
Therapeutic optimism, 227
Tobin, Sheldon, 292
Training needs, 295–305
Transitional care, 226–228
Transitional shelters, homeless and,
    162–163
Transitions, stressful, 94
Transportation vulnerability, 29, 123,
    132

Unemployment, 90, 150
Urban ethnic elderly, 117–132
Urban sample, 59

Veterans, national responsibility for,
    210–211
Veterans Administration, 256
Visual impairments, 35
Volunteer programs, 162

Vulnerability, 3
  abuse and neglect and, 140–146
  assessment of, 11
  categorical, 8–9
  causes of, 19
  concepts of, 18–19
  coping and, 64–82
  defining, 7–10, 87–92, 249–250,
    281
  early views about, 209–210
  environment and, 104–114
  exemplars of, 5
  extent of, 4, 139
  family caregivers and, 189–202
  federal programs and, 248–260
  financial, 25–28
  functional, 38–40
  health, 32–48, 237–239
  homelessness and, 149
  housing, 28–29
  impairment and, 9–10
  long-term care and, 53–54, 250
  mental/cognitive, 35–37
  national policies and, 235–245
  neighborhoods and, 116–132
  physical, 21–25
  poverty and, 236–237
  predicting, 12
  race and, 61–62
  social concern base and, 208–221
  social factors and, 86–101
  sociodemographic factors and, 53–
    63
  socioenvironmental factors and,
    104–114
  types of, 21–31
Vulnerable Adults Protection Act
  (Minnesota), 8–10

Warren, Donald, 125
Well-being, 68, 92–101
Wellness education, suicide
  prevention and, 181
White ethnic elderly, 117, 125–128
Widowhood, 19, 67, 271, 281
  age of, 96–97
  coping strategies and, 79
  poverty and, 264
  suicide and, 173–175
Women
  incomes of, 21
  poverty and, 236, 264
  retirement and, 259
  See also Gender; Widowhood
Work force, *see* Labor force